The
TYRANNY
of the
MAJORITY

MARTIN KESSLER BOOKS

THE FREE PRESS
A Division of Macmillan, Inc.
NEW YORK

Maxwell Macmillan Canada
TORONTO

Maxwell Macmillan International
NEW YORK   OXFORD   SINGAPORE   SYDNEY

The
TYRANNY
of the
MAJORITY

Fundamental Fairness in
Representative Democracy

LANI GUINIER

The Free Press
A Division of Macmillan, Inc.
866 Third Avenue, New York, N.Y. 10022

Maxwell Macmillan Canada, Inc.
1200 Eglinton Avenue East
Suite 200
Don Mills, Ontario M3C 3N1

Macmillan, Inc. is part of the Maxwell Communication Group of Companies.

Printed in the United States of America

printing number

1   2   3   4   5   6   7   8   9   10

Library of Congress Cataloging-in-Publication Data

Guinier, Lani.
    The tyranny of the majority : fundamental fairness and
representative democracy / Lani Guinier.
        p.   cm.
    ISBN 0-02-913172-3
    1. Proportional representation—United States.   2. Representative
government and representation—United States.   3. Afro-Americans—
Suffrage.   4. Minorities—Suffrage—United States.   5. Voting—
United states.   I. Title.
JF1075.U6G85   1994
328.73'07347'08996073—dc20   93-50556
                                                                CIP

Chapters 2 through 6 originally appeared in the following sources:
    "Keeping the Faith: Black Voters In The Post Reagan Era," 24 Harvard Civil Rights Civil Liberties Law Review 393 (1989).
    "The Triumph of Tokenism: The Voting Rights Act and the Theory of Black Electoral Success," 89 U. Mich. L. Rev. 1077 (1991).
    "No Two Seats: The Elusive Quest for Political Equality," 77 U. Va. L. Rev. 1413 (Nov. 1991).
    "Groups, Representation, & Race Conscious Districting: A Case of the Emperor's Clothes," 71 Texas Law Review 1589 (June 1993).
    "Lines in the Sand," 72 Texas Law Review 315 (Dec. 1993).

This book is dedicated to
Nolan and Nikolas Bowie
two poets in their own right

Contents

Foreword

Late in the eighteenth century, political opponents of George Washington's nominee for Chief Justice, John Rutledge, hit on a strategy that has characterized confirmation battles ever since: Unable to whip up sufficient senatorial anger by pointing to their disagreements with his political views, they decided to call him crazy instead. The charges stuck, and when the Senate eventually rejected the nomination, one publicly stated ground was that poor Rutledge had taken leave of his senses. Nobody took any political risks, and Rutledge was smeared with a label that persists in some popular histories to this day.

No opponents of Lani Guinier's nomination to be Assistant Attorney General in charge of the Civil Rights Division actually called her crazy (although some came close), but they called her so many other things that the casual follower of the news might be pardoned for not realizing that the dispute was not about high moral principles, still less about Lani Guinier's qualifications, but about the proper interpretation of a few snippets of writing from her many scholarly articles—which made it, sad to say, much like other grueling confirmation battles in our history.

Lani Guinier, as just about everybody knows by now, was nominated by President Bill Clinton early in 1993 to be the administration's civil rights enforcement chief. Her nomination was withdrawn a few months later in the wake of an opposition campaign that evidently took a rookie White House staff by surprise. According to her critics, Guinier was an obsessive advocate of a "racial spoils system," arguing that virtually all government

Stephen L. Carter is the William Nelson Cromwell Professor of Law at Yale University. His most recent book is *The Confirmation Mess*, to be published in the spring of 1994 by Basic Books. He is also the author of *The Culture of Disbelief: How American Law and Politics Trivialize Religious Devotion* (Basic Books, 1993) and *Reflections of an Affirmative Action Baby* (Basic Books, 1991). Heidi Durrow, of the class of 1995 at Yale Law School, contributed invaluable research to this essay.

benefits—including the fruits of elections—must be assigned along racial lines. She believed, opponents charged, that white Americans remain implacably hostile to black progress. She was said, moreover, to have described black Republicans as only "descriptively" and not "authentically" black.

This is the way we conduct confirmation discussions in the late twentieth century: We hurl accusations. Moreover, in the need to package the accusations in bites that the mass media will be able to translate—in the need, in short, to simplify—we distort, whether we mean to or not. It is vital that the accusations *sound bad.* And when the competing sounds are aired, the side that wins is the side whose sounds are better able to rouse the public's ire. That, in turn, will usually be the side whose sounds are less complex, especially if the responses by the nominee's defenders are complex.

The attacks on Guinier ignited a firestorm that the White House was unable to quell. Although furious Guinier supporters insisted that she was being railroaded, the President who had nominated her finally made the hard choice to withdraw her name. This decision, though perhaps inevitable, denied her even the opportunity for a hearing on her views (a privilege, her friends pointed out, granted even to such doomed nominees as Zoe Baird and Robert Bork, and, for that matter, to Clarence Thomas, whom Washington insiders mistakenly believed was doomed). On the other hand, it spared Senators the apparently unwelcome task of standing up to be counted on one side or the other of the controversy.

And it was all a terrible shame, for this time, finally, as we as a nation were once more caught up in what sometimes seems our semimonthly confirmation angst, there was actually something to be accomplished by holding hearings. Had Lani Guinier had her hearing, her chance to defend herself and explain her views, no one can tell whether she would have been confirmed. Certainly the deck was stacked against her, and, more often than not, political reality will out. Nevertheless, had her accusers been forced to raise their charges in a forum in which Guinier herself was entitled to equal time—the hearing room—we might have had the televised "national seminar" that some have said we got in the Bork hearings, this time on the fundamental dilemma that has shaped our nation's history: the dilemma of race.

Instead of conversation about the Guinier nomination, we have so far had essentially useless and sickening noise, for which this book should provide a healthy antidote.

The Partisan Noises

The noise began when conservative activist Clint Bolick fired a shot across the nomination's bow in an article in the *Wall Street Journal* on April 30, 1993, criticizing Guinier as an exponent of a racial quota system for voting: "[S]he demands equal legislative outcomes, requiring abandonment not only of the 'one person, one vote' principle, but majority rule itself." The *Journal,* in its wisdom, chose as the headline "Clinton's Quota Queen." And the fight was on.

Or at least one side of it was. At first, Guinier's critics seemed to dominate. A week after the Bolick piece, *Journal* columnist Paul Gigot warned that Guinier was the reincarnation of John C. Calhoun—"better qualified for the Bosnian desk at State than civil rights at Justice." Bolick himself continued his campaign over the airwaves. "Lani Guinier's writings are profoundly anti-democratic," he announced on the National Public Radio program "Morning Edition." "In my view, they amount to a racial apartheid system." Other conservative critics echoed these themes. Said Senate Minority Leader Robert Dole: "If nothing else, Ms. Guinier has been consistent in her writings—consistently hostile to the principle of one person, one vote; consistently hostile to the majority rule; and a consistent supporter, not only of quotas, but of vote-rigging schemes that make quotas look mild." Senator Alan Simpson accused Guinier of "reverse racism." George Will wrote that Guinier "favors federal imposition on state and local governments of rules that would generate results pleasing to groups she prefers."

Uneasiness was hardly confined to conservatives. Many moderates and some liberals wondered openly whether Guinier's views were consistent with Clinton's own racial rhetoric. Chuck Alston of the Progressive Policy Institute issued a stark warning: "Politically speaking, an awful lot of work has been done to put together a biracial Democratic Party in the South. This raises the potential of splitting it up and Balkanizing the party." Thomas Mann of the Brookings Institution summed up this point of view: "The president talked about racial accommodation, about bringing us together, saying there is no us and them. . . . And yet Lani Guinier's writings assume a degree of polarization that would make such integration virtually impossible."

Indeed, even some traditional allies of the civil rights community seemed reluctant to embrace Guinier. The *New York Times* stated its uneasiness for the record. Said a spokeswoman for Senator Edward M. Kennedy, "He will make his final decision after the committee's hearings." (One might say that all Senators should take this position on all nominations, but we live in a world with different rules.) And Senator Carol Mosely Braun, the only African American on the Judiciary Committee, refused to meet with Guinier or to make a public comment.

The media, for the most part, repeated the charges as though they were facts. For example, an Associated Press story at the beginning of June stated blithely that Guinier had called for a "minority veto" in legislatures and that she did not consider black elected officials with heavily white constituencies to be "authentic" representatives. The AP, like many other media outlets, seemed unaware that it was slanting its stories toward one side of the argument. Indeed, many news organizations seemed unaware that there was an argument at all. The stories were written as though the question was how her supporters would defend what she said rather than whether she had actually said what opponents charged.

The point is not to suggest that the media lack competence to cover scholarship. It is not actually that hard, but one must be willing to do the work. This is why it is a little bit scary to learn from Laurel Leff's excellent article in the *Columbia Journalism Review* that many of the reporters who covered the Guinier story did not bother to read the scholarship about which they were writing, offering such excuses as the claim that they were covering the controversy, not the articles. Indeed, the failure of many in the media to bother to read the work meant that those who had done the reading—initially, her detractors—became quite influential in crafting the general journalistic response. Thus, although Clint Bolick received the most coverage, Guinier's most influential media detractor was probably Stuart Taylor, the respected columnist for the *American Lawyer*, whose detailed knowledge of her work ultimately formed the basis for articles by other journalists, too lazy or incompetent to read her essays for themselves. But Taylor, although a fine reporter, was against Guinier and should therefore have been considered by his colleagues a biased source.

Guinier's defenders argued that her critics had taken her words out of context, reducing complicated legal arguments to a brief phrase or sentence. She was well within the mainstream, her defenders argued, pointing out that the critics seemed to have no idea just where the mainstream flowed. One Guinier supporter, law professor Patricia Williams, noted in the *Village Voice*, tongue slightly in cheek, that while she, Williams, might have been a great believer in quotas (and, thus, a "quota queen"), Guinier was . . . well . . . to her right. Moreover, Guinier's defenders pointed out (correctly) that most of her controversial proposals were well known in the literature. They argued (correctly once more) that her references to "authentic" and "inauthentic" representatives, although perhaps inelegant, were not meant in the judgmental fashion that her opponents suggested. (More on this shortly.) And, more interesting still, they noted that the proposed remedies that her opponents described as so radical in her work had actually been fashioned in civil rights litigation led by the two previous administrations, both the domain of conservative Republicans. Former Justice Department lawyers confirmed this analysis, although the media, and the critics, treated it as a non sequitur. Bolick himself ultimately conceded that most of what he objected to in Guinier's work had been enforced by the Civil Rights Division under President Bush and, to some extent, under President Reagan, but he seemed oddly reluctant to indict the Assistant Attorneys General from those administrations as the dangerous radicals that they surely were, if his analysis of Guinier was correct.

The Reverend Ben Chavis, head of the NAACP, called some of the criticisms by politicians "reactionary," and doubtless some of them were. Some were doubtless principled as well, even if the principles were applied to snippets of Guinier's work rather than to Guinier herself. Most of the skepticism by politicians, however, might better be described by other words: *panicky* comes to mind. So does *thoughtless*. These, however, are the attitudes that our relentless media focus on the sound bite and the latest polling data encourage in our politicians, which is surely what Senator Patrick Leahy had in mind when he complained that the law professor "was tried in the press." (He said it on the radio.)

Even some who were not Guinier supporters recognized that she was mistreated. Former Education Secretary and conservative activist William Bennett, an opponent of the nomination, remarked, "I think she was given a very raw deal." Political commentator Mark Shields put the matter more precisely, pointing out that Clarence Thomas in 1991 "had a staunch, unflinching champion in Senator Jack Danforth and a supportive White House," whereas Guinier "had nobody on Capitol Hill for her, and the White House was distracted, disorganized, and in disarray."

That disarray was reflected in the sad fact that nobody in the media seemed ultimately to care whether she was in the mainstream or not, which means that her opponents won the battle for spin control; which means that the nomination was thereafter doomed. And the adoption of this particular spin suggests that Guinier was successfully borked. Borking is a common part of our politics and a familiar part of our parlance. You could almost put it in the dictionary:

bork \bo( )rk\ *vt* **1** to vilify by spreading false or grossly misleading information, especially in an effort to prevent confirmation to high federal office **2** to injure the reputation by attempting to show personal venality: *smear.*

And although liberals seem to believe that only conservatives bork and conservatives seem to believe that only liberals bork, the unhappy truth is that everybody borks, because nobody has any choice: The alternative in a confirmation fight is to focus on the issues, and issues are terribly boring. In an era when no side can be guaranteed more than ninety seconds on the evening news, being boring is deadly to the cause.

Suppose, for example, that Lani Guinier's foes had tried to say this on the evening news: "Well, it is true that her views are well within the civil rights mainstream, and it is true that most of her concrete proposals for improving voting rights enforcement are already in the literature or already part of the current law, but we think it is time for a real debate in this country on whether the Voting Rights Act as it stands and as it has recently been interpreted is consistent with the principle of color-blindness, which we happen to think most Americans support. Consequently, we are opposing Lani Guinier not because she is a dangerous radical or because she will overturn any precedents, but because her nomination provides us the chance to raise issues that need to be discussed."

How dull! (Would the newscasts even carry it?) And how hypocritical it would sound! (A debate on an issue instead of on a personality?) Besides, there is nothing terribly compelling about opposing a nominee on the ground that you are afraid she will enforce the law, even if another part of your message is a suspicion that most Americans do not understand what the law is and wouldn't like it if they did. Better, surely, to fit snugly into our nation's odious confirmation tradition: When in doubt, demonize. If challenged, why, demonize some more! The demand is for evidence of personal mendacity. Perhaps we think there is no other way to get the mass media to sit up and take notice. Perhaps we think there is no other way to rouse an apathetic public to anger. But there is another possibility as well: We are willing to be mean and nasty because we are willing to do anything to win.

As it happens, I agree that Guinier's words were, in almost every case, taken out of context, her meaning often mangled, which seems to be the fate of scholars when they enter the domain of public life. That does not mean that I agree with her every idea, but differences of opinion make horse races; they do not, except at confirmation time, make thoughtful and creative people into dangerous radicals. Having read Guinier's corpus, I am quite certain that she is neither radical nor dangerous—except, perhaps, to voting systems that freeeze out minority voters. With some exceptions, to which I will shortly turn, I will not burden the reader now with my reasons: Lani Guinier, after all, is her own best defender, and, with the publication of this book, the reader has her words in full context and with her own full explanations.

Instead, I would like to come at the opposition from a different direction, trying to understand not the reasons for the disagreements but the reasons for the vehemence. The answer, I think, is that most of her critics used Guinier as a symbol to fight a quite different battle: a battle to preserve a vision of America that almost nobody really believes in but almost everybody desperately wants to. In this vision, we are united in a common enterprise and governed by common consent. Although the nation has problems, some of them caused by racism, we are people of good will, aiming at a fairer, more integrated society, which we will achieve through the actions of our essentially fair institutions. And the key to this enterprise—the focus, too, of Lani Guinier's work—is voting.

What the Noise Was All About

The argument about Lani Guinier was only in part about the *substance* of her views. It was also, in perhaps equal part, about the *subject* of her views.

Although often disdained by cynics, the right to vote is the most important and dramatic emblem of democratic citizenship. The social history of America could be written as the saga of a slowly expanding franchise: to the nonpropertied, to the freed slaves, to women, to those old enough to fight. When we vote, wrote the late Judith Shklar, "[w]e are taking part in a serious and personally significant ritual." Whether or not our side wins, the ritual affirms our membership in America: "The simple act of voting is the ground upon which the edifice of elective government rests ultimately."

So when a scholar chooses to spend her career testing the fairness of voting procedures, she embarks upon a project that inevitably calls for judgments on what it means to be a part of America, how to tell when people are left out, and what to do about their exclusion. This is Lani Guinier's project. Her scholarship assesses voting systems and asks a question of first importance: Are there permanent, locked-in winners and losers? She believes that there are and that race is too often the divide along which victories and defeats can be measured. She tosses out ideas—lots of them—for fixing what is wrong. One may quibble here and there with her arguments or her conclusions, but one can scarcely deny the necessity of her effort, for in this democracy, no right is more fundamental than the right to vote.

Many of her critics misunderstand her work because they fail to meet her at her starting point: Votes, Guinier believes, should *matter*. She does not quarrel with the symbolic import of the voting act, but she also has no patience with the notion that symbols alone are sufficient. Black Americans were denied the vote, in vast areas of the country, until 1965, and the right to vote was bought with blood. That right signals, as Shklar would say, full formal membership in the American polity, but it also means, as Guinier is quick to note, the chance to force the nation to change. In other words, although the mere ability to vote counts for a great deal, the power that voting brings matters as much or more—at least to people who have long been denied their chance at self-governance.

Thus, the first point to understand about Lani Guinier's scholarship is that she is unconvinced that the act of voting alone signals the fairness of the process. This does not mean, in the extravagant claims of her critics, that she believes that black voters should win in the legislature in proportion to their numbers or that minority groups should have a veto over any measures that affect their interests. It does mean, however, that Guinier believes a group interest exists and that voting procedures cannot be called fair when that interest always loses.

The second point to understand about her scholarship—and here, too, the critics generally missed the boat—is that her arguments are complicated. Her articles are not, as a number of commentators proclaimed in self-important dismissal, poorly written, and Guinier, contrary to some reports, never said so. What she actually said, in an appearance on "Nightline," was, like most of her words, carefully nuanced:

> I perhaps have not been as clear as I should have, but I was writing to an academic audience and in the context of the expectations of academic scholars. One has to appreciate the various nuances and complexities and you write in a way that's dense and ponderous and often misunderstood, particularly when it's reduced to a sound bite.

In other words, Guinier noted, scholarly articles are written for specialists, not for a lay audience. It is scarcely surprising that news reporters, impatient with detail and hoping for a sound bite, lost their way in the complexities.

Although I have promised to let her work speak for itself, a single example will suffice. Many of Guinier's critics argued that she exalted the group vote over the individual vote, which would lead, some said, to the balkanization of America. Guinier's critics are doubtless correct that when a majority behaves as a singular group—voting its common interest on one issue after another—there is a divisive threat to democracy. But the problem was not invented in the Voting Rights Act, and the insight is as old as America. Asked Tocqueville: "What is a majority, in its collective capacity, if not an individual with opinions, and usually with interests, contrary to those of another individual, called the minority?" Nor did he imagine that a group was wiser than its parts: "Have men, by joining together, changed their character? By becoming stronger, have they become more patient of obstacles?" In any democracy, the answers to Tocqueville's last two questions are too often negative, which means that majorities do clobber minorities, and they do it all the time. The fact that a majority supports a policy is no evidence of its wisdom; might and right, the American idea insists, are not synonymous.

Yet the American democracy, especially in the glorious hyperbole of its political leaders, implies precisely the opposite. When groups identify collective interests and vote them, elections become winner-take-all. Minorities—whether defined by race or geography or income or what have you—wind up losers. This is not Lani Guinier's discovery, nor is it what she advocates. But she recognizes the problem and wants to do something about it. The obsession of her scholarship therefore turns out to be precisely the reverse of what her critics ascribe to her: She believes in democracy and opposes the democratic spoils system.

Race, although central to her work, is therefore cast as a kind of metaphor; it is simply one of the many lines along which electoral majorities and minorities may divide. Although the phenomenon of racism is obviously unlike other cultural symbols, Guinier's analysis pivots less on this fulcrum than is commonly supposed. Were one to take her Voting Rights Act scholarship and substitute "geographic locale" for "race," much of her argument would be precisely the same. In other words, far from resting on the presumption that race is special and different, Guinier's work rests on the presumption that every division is special and different. Whenever there are consistent winners and losers, her analysis applies. Thus, her concern for fair voting procedures, although articulated through analyses of racial discrimination, becomes universal; her many proposals for reform become ways for any groups with identifiable interests to maximize their chances for representation.

One might object, of course, that groups (all groups) should not be encouraged to vote their self-interests; they should vote the national interest instead. The notion that voters might be trained to so behave is a pleasant fantasy, and it would make for a finer nation. Sadly, it has nothing to do with today's America.

The Noise of Majority Rule

Consider now just what it means to say, as Guinier certainly has, that majority rule is not a reliable instrument of democracy in a racially divided society. Despite the media's reduction of this line to a series of meaningless but ominous sound bites, there are actually three very difficult concepts embedded in it, any one of which could occupy far more time than the evening news is prepared to give. What is majority rule? What is democracy? And is our society racially divided?

Majority rule, loosely put, is the proposition that 51 percent of the people should be able to get whatever they want. Some consider this the same as democracy, but it is not; at least, it is not the same as American democracy. There is not a single place in the United States (and, I would bet, in the world) in which 51 percent of the people are in fact entitled to whatever they want. Instead, majorities face often considerable obstacles in transforming their preferences into policy. The most obvious obstacles are the state and federal constitutions, which limit what majorities can do and are not easy for those same majorities to change. Why place these limitations on what the majority can do? The reason can only be that majorities are not fully trusted, or, rather, that the larger, more thoughtful, and harder-to-assemble majority that is needed to construct a constitutional clause is more to be trusted than the smaller, more passionate, easier-to-arouse majority that quickly assembles around almost any issue.

Just as important to understanding the interaction between democracy and majority rule is the fact that the great majority of the people never has the opportunity to vote directly on the great majority of the issues. The divisive issues—abortion, school prayer, taxes—are never on the ballot. (Some states do allow initiative and referendum, but with substantial procedural difficulties.) Instead, we all vote for representatives who will then cast votes in our name. Not only does this system dilute direct democracy—sometimes the system openly frustrates it.

Consider the many issues on which 51 percent of the people are unable to get their way, despite the lack of constitutional obstacles. Conservatives like to point to strong majorities who support school choice plans and term limits but are unable to get even a vote in the Congress. Liberals counter with citations to the equally strong majorities who support gun control and federal funding for abortion. And in both cases, advocates are correct that only the vicissitudes of the legislative process stand between the people and the legislation the people want. What the advocates doubtless know but are reluctant to acknowledge is that those vicissitudes are precisely what give representative democracies their advantages. Sometimes, unless one is a simplistic majoritarian tyrant, the 51 percent must lose.

Very well, pure majority rule is un-American. This far, Guinier is very much in the mainstream. But what about the larger charge, that she is being divisive in her insistence on the implacable racial hostility of white Americans?

The first and easy answer is that this is not quite what she says. She does, however, attribute many of the legislative difficulties of African Americans to racism. One might answer that most white Americans are not racist. Probably they are not. But—at the risk of being labeled a dangerous radical—there is a sense in which Guinier is obviously right. When she writes of racial hostility, she is, unfortunately, telling a simple truth. I do not mean the truth as determined in our strange postmodern academic world, in which each of our stories is as valid as any other. I mean the truth as ascertained the old-fashioned way, by studying data and counting votes.

As bad as our confirmation process has become, being forced to think about race only makes it worse. To be sure, most nominees who are people of color, like most nominees who are white, pass Senate muster with scarcely a murmur of dissent. But when a black nominee suddenly grows controversial, the battles seem far more bitter than when the controversial candidate happens to be white. No one has ever faced quite so vicious an onslaught as Thurgood Marshall, the first nonwhite Supreme Court nominee and the first (and last) Supreme Court nominee forced to sit, in effect, through a demeaning constitutional law and history trivia quiz in order to demonstrate his intellectual acumen and gain Senate approval. The tragic hearings on Anita Hill's charges of sexual harassment against Clarence Thomas split the black community down the middle; today, when the polls show Americans almost evenly divided on who was telling the truth and who was lying, everyone agrees that *somebody* was smeared beyond all decency and reason. And although Zoe Baird was President Bill Clinton's first nominee to run into the rather unpredictable buzzsaw of public opposition, the media's unforgivably reckless assaults on her seem, in retrospect, almost gentle when compared with the distorting vituperation of the attacks on Lani Guinier.

Race, more than any other organizing category—with the possible exception of sexual orientation—continues to drive our nation into frenzies that lead to unparalleled viciousness. It is not simply a matter of pointing to a particular incident of racial violence, whether by an angry mob, strutting neo-Nazis, or a few thugs in police uniforms. It is more a matter of considering our national attitudes on race—attitudes that are far more frightening than any acontextual snippet from Lani Guinier's substantial opus. Some critics excoriated Guinier for her insistence that our society faces a future of implacable racial division, but rather than asserting her wrong, they should have examined the data.

For example, they might have asked by what majority white Americans are in favor of open housing laws. The answer is that fewer than half of white Americans generally favor open housing laws; in other words, if you are a citizen of color and you see on the street an unknown fellow citizen who happens to be white, the chances are excellent that your fellow citizen would prefer not to live next to you, for no other reason than race. Indeed, very careful studies (using testers, not subjective impressions) have determined that an absolute majority of black Americans probably face racial discrimination in seeking housing.

Data on housing are no more than the tip of the proverbial iceberg; what lies beneath the surface is far more dangerous. The most recent (1990) General Social Survey (GSS) from the University of Chicago's National Opinion Research Center revealed much scarier information. Among white Americans, the GSS found, some 78 percent believe that black Americans prefer living on welfare, 56 percent think them more violence prone than whites, and 53 percent consider them on average less intelligent. Nor do black Americans suffer this bigotry alone. In the same survey, 74 percent of white Americans thought Hispanic Americans prefer to live on welfare, 50 percent believed them violence prone, and 55 percent considered them less intelligent.

Indeed, so stark and revealing are the actual data—as against our national aspirations—that it ultimately becomes silly to pretend that it is possible to talk about what happened to Lani Guinier without talking about race. This is not to say what is obviously untrue—that only a racist could possibly find fault with her. Anybody can find fault with anybody, especially in the confirmation context, and it has been so ever thus. The point, rather, is to recognize that we yet live in a nation in which every black nominee comes before the Senate and the public with a particular cross to bear: the need to dispel a set of assumptions about work ethic, rationality, and intelligence. The strident and relentless polemics that form the staple of the opposition's case in any confirmation fight carry the serious risk of playing into these stereotypes, as the *Wall Street Journal's* "Quota Queen" headline doubtless did.

Perhaps a white woman would have been awarded the same crown, but it is easy to harbor doubts. The term *quota queen* resonates mellifluously with *welfare queen,* a phrase never, in my experience, applied to recipients of public assistance who are white—as it happens, a majority. (Bolick says he had nothing to do with the headline, and having written for the *Journal* myself, and thus having run into its rule about not telling writers what title will run above their pieces, I believe him.) The headline writer may not have chosen the term in a deliberate effort to draw the connection, but the connection itself is so difficult to resist that one must wonder what subconscious forces were at work. Or perhaps there was no subconscious connection either; but in that case, the headline writer evidenced a tragic historical blindness in an effort to be clever. In other words, whether the person who chose "Quota Queen" saw the connection, the imagery is so stark that one would prefer not to think the headline writer just missed it. For what kind of a world would such a person live in, to realize neither that many people of color would be offended, nor that many white people would see the connection and laugh?*

To be sure, there are points in her scholarship with which one might forcefully disagree. For example, I am less certain than Guinier sometimes seems to be that members of racial minority groups share points of view and electoral interests; it may be that I see our communities as more internally diverse than she does.† On the other hand, as Guinier herself points out in one of her most recent essays, the assumption that citizens who happen to share the same race also share the same opinions is no more peculiar than the assumption that citizens who happen to live in the same geographical area also share the same opinions—but the second of these, when used as a basis for shaping electoral districts, is almost conclusively presumed to be fair.

Besides, the fact that it is possible to dispute either her premises or her

---

* Does this description seem ad hominem and unfair? Might it be that the headline writer was only looking for a catchy phrase? Yes, of course—but my unfairness is intentional, if only to give the critics a very small taste of their own medicine. In other words, I am intentionally borking the headline writer, for no other reason than to make my point with greater force.

† It is only in this context that Guinier refers to some black elected officials as "inauthentic," and all that she means is that if most of their constituents are white, black officials, as good politicians, will respond to those majority interests that have elected them. So although she might have picked a better set of terms, I do not believe she actually meant, as some implied, to question anybody's blackness. As one who has occasionally suffered the criticism of lack of authenticity from people who really mean it, I am confident that Guinier has only electoral *realpolitik* in mind.

analysis can hardly by itself be taken as a reason for opposition. It is difficult to discern, within the bounds of reasonable disagreement, the basis
for the conclusion that Guinier is a dangerous radical. Certainly there are
legal scholars who do believe in a racial spoils system, who are certain that
the right quota will solve almost any problem, who insist that those who
disagree with their views are betraying the race, and these are dangerous
views, but to place among them Lani Guinier, who has often been their
critic, is something of a cruel joke.

Lani Guinier, in short, was badly treated, and the decision to withdraw
her nomination was, as President Clinton himself has acknowledged, the
low moment of his first year in office. She is a tough, experienced civil
rights litigator, with a deep firsthand knowledge of both the theory and
practice of her art. She might have been the finest head the Civil Rights
Division has ever had. But because of our national fascination with sound
bites and demonization and our national discomfort with the brute facts of
racial injustice, America has been denied her services.

Of course, your reading of her work might be different from mine,
which is why it is well that this book is available. Even if, as some conservatives insisted, the assault on Guinier was "payback" for the liberal attacks (some said smears) on Clarence Thomas, Robert Bork, or even
William Bradford Reynolds, there was an important distinction: Each one
of them had a hearing. Not having received that courtesy, Lani Guinier
has produced this book.

Failed nominees have a history of shooting themselves in the proverbial foot. After the Senate rejected John Rutledge's 1795 nomination as
Chief Justice, he attempted suicide, thus helping out those who had tried
to ruin him with rumors of insanity. And many a defeated aspirant to ap-
pointive office has turned bitter and partisan, as though the post in question was an entitlement, cruelly snatched at the last minute.

In offering a collection of her essays, Lani Guinier has chosen a wiser
path. The debate, after all, was about her written record. It is high time,
then, for the record to be available for all to view. Let readers make up
their own minds, without the intercession of media experts and electronic
sound bites. After all, in the words of the Sanza Player in Aimé Cesaire's
play, *A Season in the Congo,* "Even when a man has good eyes, you have
to show him some things."

STEPHEN L. CARTER

1

The Tyranny of the Majority

I have always wanted to be a civil rights lawyer. This lifelong ambition is based on a deep-seated commitment to democratic fair play—to playing by the rules as long as the rules are fair. When the rules seem unfair, I have worked to change them, not subvert them. When I was eight years old, I was a Brownie. I was especially proud of my uniform, which represented a commitment to good citizenship and good deeds. But one day, when my Brownie group staged a hatmaking contest, I realized that uniforms are only as honorable as the people who wear them. The contest was rigged. The winner was assisted by her milliner mother, who actually made the winning entry in full view of all the participants. At the time, I was too young to be able to change the rules, but I was old enough to resign, which I promptly did.

To me, fair play means that the rules encourage everyone to play. They should reward those who win, but they must be acceptable to those who lose. The central theme of my academic writing is that not all rules lead to elemental fair play. Some even commonplace rules work against it.

The professional milliner competing with amateur Brownies stands as an example of rules that are patently rigged or patently subverted. Yet, sometimes, even when rules are perfectly fair in form, they serve in practice to exclude particular groups from meaningful participation. When they do not encourage everyone to play, or when, over the long haul, they do not make the losers feel as good about the outcomes as the winners, they can seem as unfair as the milliner who makes the winning hat for her daughter.

Sometimes, too, we construct rules that force us to be divided into winners and losers when we might have otherwise joined together. This idea was cogently expressed by my son, Nikolas, when he was four years old, far exceeding the thoughtfulness of his mother when she was an eight-year-old Brownie. While I was writing one of my law journal articles, Nikolas and I had a conversation about voting prompted by a *Sesame Street Magazine* exercise. The magazine pictured six children: four children had raised their hands because they wanted to play tag; two had their hands down because they wanted to play hide-and-seek. The magazine asked its readers to count the number of children whose hands were raised and then decide what game the children would play.

Nikolas quite realistically replied, "They will play both. First they will play tag. Then they will play hide-and-seek." Despite the magazine's "rules," he was right. To children, it is natural to take turns. The winner may get to play first or more often, but even the "loser" gets something. His was a positive-sum solution that many adult rule-makers ignore.

The traditional answer to the magazine's problem would have been a zero-sum solution: "The children—all the children—will play tag, and only tag." As a zero-sum solution, everything is seen in terms of "I win; you lose." The conventional answer relies on winner-take-all majority rule, in which the tag players, as the majority, win the right to decide for all the children what game to play. The hide-and-seek preference becomes irrelevant. The numerically more powerful majority choice simply subsumes minority preferences.

In the conventional case, the majority that rules gains all the power and the minority that loses gets none. For example, two years ago Brother Rice High School in Chicago held two senior proms. It was not planned that way. The prom committee at Brother Rice, a boys' Catholic high school, expected just one prom when it hired a disc jockey, picked a rock band, and selected music for the prom by consulting student preferences. Each senior was asked to list his three favorite songs, and the band would play the songs that appeared most frequently on the lists.

Seems attractively democratic. But Brother Rice is predominantly white, and the prom committee was all white. That's how they got two proms. The black seniors at Brother Rice felt so shut out by the "democratic process" that they organized their own prom. As one black student put it: "For every vote we had, there were eight votes for what they wanted. . . . [W]ith us being in the minority we're always outvoted. It's as if we don't count."

Some embittered white seniors saw things differently. They complained that the black students should have gone along with the majority: "The majority makes a decision. That's the way it works."

In a way, both groups were right. From the white students' perspective, this was ordinary decisionmaking. To the black students, majority rule sent the message: "we don't count" is the "way it works" for minorities. In a racially divided society, majority rule may be perceived as majority tyranny.

That is a large claim, and I do not rest my case for it solely on the actions of the prom committee in one Chicago high school. To expand the range of the argument, I first consider the ideal of majority rule itself, particularly as reflected in the writings of James Madison and other founding members of our Republic. These early democrats explored the relationship between majority rule and democracy. James Madison warned, "If a majority be united by a common interest, the rights of the minority will be insecure." The tyranny of the majority, according to Madison, requires safeguards to protect "one part of the society against the injustice of the other part."

For Madison, majority tyranny represented the great danger to our early constitutional democracy. Although the American revolution was fought against the tyranny of the British monarch, it soon became clear that there was another tyranny to be avoided. The accumulations of all powers in the same hands, Madison warned, "whether of one, a few, or many, and whether hereditary, self-appointed, or elective, may justly be pronounced the very definition of tyranny."

As another colonist suggested in papers published in Philadelphia, "We have been so long habituated to a jealousy of tyranny from monarchy and aristocracy, that we have yet to learn the dangers of it from democracy." Despotism had to be opposed "whether it came from Kings, Lords or the people."

The debate about majority tyranny reflected Madison's concern that the majority may not represent the whole. In a homogeneous society, the interest of the majority would likely be that of the minority also. But in a heterogeneous community, the majority may not represent all competing interests. The majority is likely to be self-interested and ignorant or indifferent to the concerns of the minority. In such case, Madison observed, the assumption that the majority represents the minority is "altogether fictitious."

Yet even a self-interested majority can govern fairly if it cooperates with the minority. One reason for such cooperation is that the self-interested majority values the principle of reciprocity. The self-interested majority worries that the minority may attract defectors from the majority and become the next governing majority. The Golden Rule principle of reciprocity functions to check the tendency of a self-interested majority to act tyrannically.

So the argument for the majority principle connects it with the value of reciprocity: You cooperate when you lose in part because members of the current majority will cooperate when they lose. The conventional case for the fairness of majority rule is that it is not really the rule of a fixed group— The Majority—on all issues; instead it is the rule of shifting majorities, as the losers at one time or on one issue join with others and become part of the governing coalition at another time or on another issue. The result will be a fair system of mutually beneficial cooperation. I call a majority that rules but does not dominate a Madisonian Majority.

The problem of majority tyranny arises, however, when the self-interested majority does not need to worry about defectors. When the majority is fixed and permanent, there are no checks on its ability to be overbearing. A majority that does not worry about defectors is a majority with total power.

In such a case, Madison's concern about majority tyranny arises. In a heterogeneous community, any faction with total power might subject "the minority to the caprice and arbitrary decisions of the majority, who instead of consulting the interest of the whole community collectively, attend sometimes to partial and local advantages."

"What remedy can be found in a republican Government, where the majority must ultimately decide," argued Madison, but to ensure "that no one common interest or passion will be likely to unite a majority of the whole number in an unjust pursuit." The answer was to disaggregate the majority to ensure checks and balances or fluid, rotating interests. The minority needed protection against an overbearing majority, so that "a common sentiment is less likely to be felt, and the requisite concert less likely to be formed, by a majority of the whole."

Political struggles would not be simply a contest between rulers and people; the political struggles would be among the people themselves. The work of government was not to transcend different interests but to reconcile them. In an ideal democracy, the people would rule, but the minorities would also be protected against the power of majorities. Again, where the rules of decisionmaking protect the minority, the Madisonian Majority rules without dominating.

But if a group is unfairly treated, for example, when it forms a racial minority, *and* if the problems of unfairness are not cured by conventional assumptions about majority rule, then what is to be done? The answer is that we may need an *alternative* to winner-take-all majoritarianism. In this book, a collection of my law review articles, I describe the alternative, which, with Nikolas's help, I now call the "principle of taking turns." In a racially divided society, this principle does better than simple majority rule if it accommodates the values of self-government, fairness, deliberation, compromise, and consensus that lie at the heart of the democratic ideal.

In my legal writing, I follow the caveat of James Madison and other early American democrats. I explore decisionmaking rules that might work in a multi-racial society to ensure that majority rule does not become majority tyranny. I pursue voting systems that might disaggregate The Majority so that it does not exercise power unfairly or tyrannically. I aspire to a more cooperative political style of decisionmaking to enable all of the students at Brother Rice to feel comfortable attending the same prom. In looking to create Madisonian Majorities, I pursue a positive-sum, taking-turns solution.

Structuring decisionmaking to allow the minority "a turn" may be necessary to restore the reciprocity ideal when a fixed majority refuses to cooperate with the minority. If the fixed majority loses its incentive to follow the Golden Rule principle of shifting majorities, the minority never gets to take a turn. Giving the minority a turn does not mean the minority gets to rule; what it does mean is that the minority gets to influence decisionmaking and the majority rules more legitimately.

Instead of automatically rewarding the preferences of the monolithic majority, a taking-turns approach anticipates that the majority rules, but is not overbearing. Because those with 51 percent of the votes are not assured 100 percent of the power, the majority cooperates with, or at least does not tyrannize, the minority.

The sports analogy of "I win; you lose" competition within a political hierarchy makes sense when only one team can win; Nikolas's intuition that it is often possible to take turns suggests an alternative approach. Take family decisionmaking, for example. It utilizes a taking-turns approach. When parents sit around the kitchen table deciding on a vacation destination or activities for a rainy day, often they do not simply rely on a show of hands, especially if that means that the older children always prevail or if affinity groups among the children (those who prefer movies to video games, or those who prefer baseball to playing cards) never get to play their activity of choice. Instead of allowing the majority simply to rule, the parents may propose that everyone take turns, going to the movies one night and playing video games the next. Or as Nikolas proposes, they might do both on a given night.

Taking turns attempts to build consensus while recognizing political or social differences, and it encourages everyone to play. The taking-turns approach gives those with the most support more turns, but it also legitimates the outcome from each individual's perspective, including those whose views are shared only by a minority.

In the end, I do not believe that democracy should encourage rule by the powerful—even a powerful majority. Instead, the ideal of democracy promises a fair discussion among self-defined equals about how to achieve our common aspirations. To redeem that promise, we need to put the idea of taking turns and disaggregating the majority at the center of our conception of representation. Particularly as we move into the twenty-first century as a more highly diversified citizenry, it is essential that we consider the ways in which voting and representational systems succeed or fail at encouraging Madisonian Majorities.

To use Nikolas's terminology, "it is no fair" if a fixed, tyrannical majority excludes or alienates the minority. It is no fair if a fixed, tyrannical majority monopolizes all the power all the time. It is no fair if we engage in the periodic ritual of elections, but only the permanent majority gets to choose who is elected. Where we have tyranny by The Majority, we do not have genuine democracy.

My life's work, with the essential assistance of people like Nikolas, has been to try to find the rules that can best bring us together as a democratic society. Some of my ideas about democratic fair play were grossly mischaracterized in the controversy over my nomination to be Assistant Attorney General for Civil Rights. Trying to find rules to encourage fundamental fairness inevitably raises the question posed by Harvard Professor Randall Kennedy in a summary of this controversy: "What is required to create political institutions that address the needs and aspirations of all Americans, not simply whites, who have long enjoyed racial privilege, but people of color who have long suffered racial exclusion from policymaking forums?" My answer, as Professor Kennedy suggests, varies by situation. But I have a predisposition, reflected in my son's yearning for a positive-sum solution, to seek an integrated body politic in which all perspectives are represented and in which all people work together to find common ground. I advocate empowering voters and their representatives in ways that give even minority voters a chance to influence legislative outcomes.

But those in the majority do not lose; they simply learn to take turns. This is a positive-sum solution that allows all voters to feel that they participate meaningfully in the decisionmaking process. This is a positive-sum solution that makes legislative outcomes more legitimate.

My work did not arise in a vacuum. Lost in the controversy over my nomination was the long history of those before me who have sought to change the rules in order to improve the system. There have been three generations of attempts to curb tyrannical majorities. The first generation focused directly on access to the ballot on the assumption that the right to vote by itself is "preservative of all other rights." During the civil rights movement, aggrieved citizens asserted that "tyrannical majorities" in various locales were ganging up to deny black voters access to the voting booth.

The 1965 Voting Rights Act and its amendments forcefully addressed this problem. The act outlawed literacy tests, brought federal registrars to troubled districts to ensure safe access to polls, and targeted for federal administrative review many local registration procedures. Success under the act was immediate and impressive. The number of blacks registered to vote rose dramatically within five years after passage.

The second generation of voting rights litigation and legislation focused on the Southern response to increased black registration. Southern states and local subdivisions responded to blacks in the electorate by switching the way elections were conducted to ensure that newly voting blacks could not wield any influence. By changing, for example, from neighborhood-based districts to jurisdiction-wide at-large representatives, those in power ensured that although blacks could vote, and even run for office, they could not win. At-large elections allowed a unified white bloc to control all the elected positions. As little as 51 percent of the population could decide 100 percent of the elections, and the black minority was permanently excluded from meaningful participation.

In response, the second generation of civil rights activism focused on "qualitative vote dilution." Although everyone had a vote, it was apparent that some people's votes were qualitatively less important than others. The concerns raised by the second generation of civil rights activists led Congress to amend the Voting Rights Act. In 1982, congressional concern openly shifted from simply getting blacks the ability to register and vote to providing blacks a realistic opportunity to elect candidates of their choice. Thus, the new focus was on electing more black officials, primarily through the elimination of at-large districts, and their replacement by majority-black single-member districts. Even if whites continued to refuse to vote for blacks, there would be a few districts in which whites were in the minority and powerless to veto black candidates. The distinctive group interests of the black community, which Congress found had been ignored in the at-large, racially polarized elections, were thus given a voice within decisionmaking councils.

The second generation sought to integrate physically the body politic. It was assumed that disaggregating the winner-take-all at-large majority would create political access for black voters, who would use that access to elect black representatives.

In many places, second-generation fights continue today. A number of redistricting schemes have been challenged in court, and not all courts agree on the outcomes, let alone the enterprise itself. Nevertheless, few disagree that blacks continue to be underrepresented in federal, state, and local government.

Even in governments in which minority legislators have increased, the marginalization of minority group interests has often stubbornly remained. Third-generation cases have now begun to respond. Third-generation cases recognize that it is sometimes not enough simply to ensure that minorities have a fair opportunity to elect someone to a legislative body. Under some unusual circumstances, it may be necessary to police the legislative voting rules whereby a majority consistently rigs the process to exclude a minority.

The Supreme Court's recent decision in *Presley v. Etowah County* heralds the arrival of this concern. Although black representatives for the first time since Reconstruction enjoyed a seat on the local county commission in Etowah and Russell counties in Alabama, they did not enjoy much else. Because of second-generation redistricting, black county commissioners were elected to county governing bodies in the two counties. Immediately upon their election, however, the white incumbents changed the rules for allocating decisionmaking authority. Just like the grandfather clauses, the literacy tests, the white primary, and other ingenious strategies devised to enforce white supremacy in the past, rules were changed to evade the reach of the earlier federal court decree.

In one county the newly integrated commission's duties were shifted to an appointed administrator. In the other county, its duties were shifted from individual commissioners to the entire commission voting by majority rule. Because voting on the commission, like voting in the county electorate, followed racial lines, "majority rule" meant that whites controlled the outcome of every legislative decision. The incumbents defended this power grab as simply the decision of a bona-fide majority.

This happened as well in Texas when the first Latina was elected to a local school board. The white majority suddenly decided that two votes were henceforth necessary to get an item on the agenda. In Louisiana, the legislature enacted a districting plan drawn up by a group of whites in a secret meeting in the subbasement of the state capitol, a meeting from which all black legislators were excluded.

Through these three generations of problems and remedies, a long trail of activists has preceded me. In 1964, ballot access was defended eloquently by Dr. Martin Luther King, Jr., and Fannie Lou Hamer. In 1982, redistricting was the consensus solution to electoral exclusion championed by the NAACP, the League of Women Voters, the Mexican-American Legal Defense Fund, and many others.

My ideas follow in this tradition. They are not undemocratic or out of the mainstream. Between 1969 and 1993, the Justice Department under both Democratic and Republican presidents disapproved as discriminatory over one hundred sets of voting rules involving changes to majority voting. None of these rules was unfair in the abstract, but all were exclusionary in practice. President Bush's chief civil rights enforcer declared some of them to be "electoral steroids for white candidates" because they manipulated the election system to ensure that only white candidates won.

This history of struggle against tyrannical majorities enlightens us to the dangers of winner-take-all collective decisionmaking. Majority rule, which presents an efficient opportunity for determining the public good, suffers when it is not constrained by the need to bargain with minority interests. When majorities are fixed, the minority lacks any mechanism for holding the majority to account or even to listen. Nor does such majority rule promote deliberation or consensus. The permanent majority simply has its way, without reaching out to or convincing anyone else.

Any form of less-than-unanimous voting introduces the danger that some group will be in the minority and the larger group will exploit the numerically smaller group. This is especially problematic to defeated groups that do not possess a veto over proposals and acts that directly affect them or implicate concerns they value intensely. Thus, the potential for instability exists when any significant group of people ends up as permanent losers.

The fundamentally important question of political stability is how to induce losers to continue to play the game. Political stability depends on the perception that the system is fair to induce losers to continue to work within the system rather than to try to overthrow it. When the minority experiences the alienation of complete and consistent defeat, they lack incentive to respect laws passed by the majority over their opposition.

As Tocqueville recognized, "[T]he power to do everything, which I should refuse to one of my equals, I will never grant to any number of them." Or as Hamilton put it, when the many are given all the power, "they will oppress the few." The problem is that majoritarian systems do not necessarily create winners who share in power. Politics becomes a battle for total victory rather than a method of governing open to all significant groups.

This is what happened in Phillips County, Arkansas, where a majority-vote runoff requirement unfairly rewarded the preferences of a white bloc-voting majority and, for more than half a century, excluded a permanent voting minority. Predominantly rural and poor, Phillips County has a history of extremely polarized voting: Whites vote exclusively for white candidates and blacks vote for black candidates whenever they can. In many elections, no white person ever publicly supports or endorses a black candidate. Although qualified, highly regarded black candidates compete, local election rules and the manipulation of those rules by a white bloc have meant that no black person in over a century had been elected to any countywide office when I brought a lawsuit in 1987. Yet blacks were just less than half of the voting-age population.

Reverend Julious McGruder, a black political candidate and a former school board member, testified on the basis of fifteen years of working in elections that "no white candidate or white person has come out and supported [a] black." Black attorney Sam Whitfield won a primary and requested support in the runoff from Kenneth Stoner, a white candidate he had defeated in the first round. In a private conversation, Stoner told Whitfield that he personally thought Whitfield was the better remaining candidate but that he could not support him. As Whitfield recounted the conversation at trial, Stoner said, "He could not support a black man. He lives in this town. He is a farmer. His wife teaches school here and that there is just no way that he could support a black candidate."

Racially polarized voting is only one of the political disadvantages for blacks in Phillips County. Blacks, whose median income is less than three thousand dollars annually, also suffer disproportionately from poverty, which works to impede their effective participation in the political process. For example, 42 percent of blacks have no car or truck, while only 9 percent of the white population are similarly encumbered; and 30 percent of blacks, compared to 11 percent of whites, have no telephone. Thus isolated by poverty, black voters are less able to maneuver around such obstacles as frequent, last-minute changes in polling places. County officials have moved polling places ten times in as many elections, often without prior notice and sometimes to locations up to twelve to fifteen miles away, over dirt and gravel roads. Moreover, because of the relative scarcity of cars, the lack of public transportation in the county, and the expense of taxis, the election campaigns of black candidates must include a get-out-and-vote kind of funding effort that a poor black community simply cannot afford.

Black candidates who win the first round come up against one particular local election rule—the majority vote runoff law—that doubles the access problem, by requiring people to get to the polls two times within a two-week period. Because this rule combines with local racism, almost half the voters for over a century never enjoyed any opportunity to choose who represents them. As a numerical, stigmatized, and racially isolated minority, blacks regarded the majority vote requirement as simply a tool to "steal the election"—a tool that had the effect of demobilizing black political participation, enhancing polarization rather than fostering debate, and in general excluding black interests from the political process. As Rev. McGruder testified, running twice to win once *"just kill[s] all the momentum, all of the hope, all of the faith, the belief in the system."* Many voters "really can't understand the situation where you say 'You know, Brother Whitfield won last night' and then come up to a grandma or my uncle, auntie and say 'Hey, you know, we're going to have to run again in the next 10 days and—because we've got a runoff.' "

In fact, between the first and second elections, turnout drops precipitously, so that the so-called majority winner in the runoff may receive fewer votes than the plurality winner in the first primary. In fact, in all three black-white runoff contests in 1986, the white runoff victor's majority occurred only because the number of people who came out to vote in the second primary went down.

Indeed, the district court that heard the challenge in 1988 to the Arkansas law did not dispute the facts: that no black candidate had ever been elected to countywide or state legislative office from Phillips County and that "race has frequently dominated over qualifications and issues" in elections. The court, nonetheless, preferred to stick with this obviously unfair electoral scheme, reasoning that The Majority should prevail even when The Majority is the product of a completely artificial and racially exclusionary runoff system. It is decisions like this one that continue to inspire me to work for a better way.

The court failed to see that the unfairness wrought by winner-take-all majority rule was inconsistent with democratic fair play in this county. At first blush, the unfairness of 51 percent of the people winning 100 percent of the power may not seem obvious. It certainly seems to be much less than the unfairness of a professional hatmaker's competing against kids. But in some ways it is worse. For example, when voters are drawn into participation by seemingly fair rules, only to discover that the rules systematically work against their interests, they are likely to feel seduced and abandoned. Moreover, those Brownies who made their own hats could at least be assured that others would sympathize with their having been taken advantage of. People who have been systematically victimized by winner-take-all majority rules usually get little sympathy from a society that wrongfully equates majority tyranny with democracy.

As the plaintiffs' evidence demonstrated, this was precisely the situation in Phillips County, where the fairness of the majority requirement was destroyed by extreme racial polarization, the absence of reciprocity, and the artificial majorities created in the runoffs. Judge Richard Arnold put it simply in a related case: Implementation of the majority vote requirement in eastern Arkansas represented a pattern of actions in which "a systematic and deliberate attempt" was made to "close off" avenues of opportunity to blacks in the affected jurisdictions.

In other words, my project has been to return the inquiry to its most authoritative source—the voters themselves. For example, Milagros Robledo, a Latino voter in Philadelphia, is one of many voters who say they are angry, confused and more cynical than ever about the political process. After a recent scandal involving the solicitation of absentee ballots in a hotly contested local election, Mr. Robledo lamented, "After going through this whole thing, I now really know the value of my vote. It means nothing to me, and it means a lot to the politicians." For Mr. Robledo, his community has continuously been shortchanged by elected officials who are more interested in getting elected than in representing the people.

I take my cue from people like Milagros Robledo. I seek to keep their faith that votes should not count more than voters. I struggle to conceptualize the representatives' relationship with voters to make that relationship more dynamic and interactive.

It is in the course of this struggle that I made my much maligned references to "the authenticity assumption." Authenticity is a concept I describe within my general criticism of conventional empowerment strategies. The Voting Rights Act expressly provides that black and Latino voters must be afforded an equal opportunity "to participate in the political process and to elect representatives of their choice." The question is:

which candidates are the representatives of choice of black or Latino voters?

Authenticity subsumes two related but competing views to answer that question. The first version of authenticity seeks information from election results to learn how the voters perceive elected officials. In this view, voting behavior is key. Authentic representatives are simply those truly chosen by the people. The second authenticity assumption is that voters trust elected officials who "look like" or act like the voters themselves. In this view, authenticity refers to a candidate who shares common physical or cultural traits with constituents. In this aspect of authenticity, the nominally cultural becomes political.

Despite the importance of voter choice in assessing minority preferred or minority sponsored candidates, those who support the second authenticity assumption substitute the concept of presumptive or descriptive representativeness in which candidates who look like their constituents are on that basis alone presumed to be representative. In the name of authenticity, these observers have argued that the current voting rights litigation model is effective because it provides blacks or Latinos an opportunity to elect physically black or culturally Latino representatives. This is an understandable position, and I present it as such, but it is not *my* position. Indeed, I term it "a limited empowerment concept."

My preference is for the first view of authenticity, the one that focuses on the voter, not the candidate. In *Thornburg v. Gingles,* a 1986 Supreme Court opinion, Justice William Brennan stressed that it is the "status of the candidate as the chosen representative of a particular racial group, not the race of the candidate, that is important."

This leads to two complementary conclusions that are firmly embedded in the caselaw and the literature. First, white candidates can legitimately represent nonwhite voters if those voters elected them. I state this explicitly in my Michigan Law Review article, reproduced here in chapter 3. And second, the election of a black or Latino candidate or two will not defeat a voting rights lawsuit, especially if those black or Latino elected officials did not receive electoral support from their community. Just because a candidate is black does not mean that he or she is the candidate of choice of the black community.

Borrowing from the language of the statute, I say voters, not politicians, should count. And voters count most when voters can exercise a real choice based on what the candidates think and do rather than what the candidates look like.

As I wrote these law review articles, my thinking evolved. New ideas emerged and old ones were rejected as I struggled to understand the tyranny of different majorities. But one idea remained constant: I am a democratic idealist, committed to making American politics open to genuine participation by all voters. It is as part of this life-long commitment to democratic fair play that I explore the many dimensions of majority tyranny.

Concern over majority tyranny has typically focused on the need to monitor and constrain the substantive policy outputs of the decisionmaking process. In my articles, however, I look at the *procedural* rules by which preferences are identified and counted. Procedural rules govern the process by which outcomes are decided. They are the rules by which the game is played.

I have been roundly, and falsely, criticized for focusing on outcomes. Outcomes are indeed relevant, but *not* because I seek to advance particular ends, such as whether the children play tag or hide-and-seek, or whether the band at Brother Rice plays rock music or rap. Rather, I look to outcomes as *evidence* of whether all the children—or all the high school seniors—feel that their choice is represented and considered. The purpose is not to guarantee "equal legislative outcomes"; equal opportunity to *influence* legislative outcomes regardless of race is more like it.

For these reasons, I sometimes explore alternatives to simple, winner-take-all majority rule. I do not advocate any one procedural rule as a universal panacea for unfairness. Nor do I propose these remedies primarily as judicial solutions. They can be adopted only in the context of litigation after the court first finds a legal violation.

Outside of litigation, I propose these approaches as political solutions if, depending on the local context, they better approximate the goals of democratic fair play. One such decisionmaking alternative is called cumulative voting, which could give all the students at Brother Rice multiple votes and allow them to distribute their votes in any combination of their choice. If each student could vote for ten songs, the students could plump or aggregate their votes to reflect the intensity of their preferences. They could put ten votes on one song; they could put five votes on two songs. If a tenth of the students opted to "cumulate" or plump all their votes for one song, they would be able to select one of every ten or so songs played at the prom. The black seniors could have done this if they chose to, but so could any other cohesive group of sufficient size. In this way, the songs preferred by a majority would be played most often, but the songs the minority enjoyed would also show up on the play list.

Under cumulative voting, voters get the same number of votes as there are seats or options to vote for, and they can then distribute their votes in any combination to reflect their preferences. Like-minded voters can vote as a solid bloc or, instead, form strategic, cross-racial coalitions to gain mutual benefits. This system is emphatically not racially based; it allows voters to organize themselves on whatever basis they wish.

Corporations use this system to ensure representation of minority shareholders on corporate boards of directors. Similarly, some local municipal and county governments have adopted cumulative voting to ensure representation of minority voters. Instead of awarding political power to geographic units called districts, cumulative voting allows voters to cast ballots based on what they think rather than where they live.

Cumulative voting is based on the principle of one person–one vote because each voter gets the same total number of votes. Everyone's preferences are counted equally. It is not a particularly radical idea; thirty states either require or permit corporations to use this election system. Cumulative voting is certainly not antidemocratic because it emphasizes the importance of voter choice in selecting public or social policy. And it is neither liberal nor conservative. Both the Reagan and Bush administrations approved cumulative voting schemes pursuant to the Voting Rights Act to protect the rights of racial- and language-minority voters.

But, as in Chilton County, Alabama, which now uses cumulative voting to elect both the school board and the county commission, any politically cohesive group can vote strategically to win representation. Groups of voters win representation depending on the exclusion threshold, meaning the percentage of votes needed to win one seat or have the band play one song. That threshold can be set case by case, jurisdiction by jurisdiction, based on the size of minority groups that make compelling claims for representation.

Normally the exclusion threshold in a head-to-head contest is 50 percent, which means that only groups that can organize a majority can get elected. But if multiple seats (or multiple songs) are considered simultaneously, the exclusion threshold is considerably reduced. For example, in Chilton County, with seven seats elected simultaneously on each governing body, the threshold of exclusion is now one-eighth. Any group with the solid support of one-eighth the voting population cannot be denied representation. This is because any self-identified minority can plump or cumulate all its votes for one candidate. Again, minorities are not defined solely in racial terms.

As it turned out in Chilton County, both blacks and Republicans benefited from this new system. The school board and commission now each have three white Democrats, three white Republicans, and one black Democrat. Previously, when each seat was decided in a head-to-head contest, the majority not only ruled but monopolized. Only white Democrats were elected at every prior election during this century.

Similarly, if the black and white students at Brother Rice have very different musical taste, cumulative voting permits a positive-sum solution to enable both groups to enjoy one prom. The majority's preferences would be respected in that their songs would be played most often, but the black students could express the intensity of their preferences too. If the black students chose to plump all their votes on a few songs, their minority preferences would be recognized and played. Essentially, cumulative voting structures the band's repertoire to enable the students to take turns.

As a solution that permits voters to self-select their identities, cumulative voting also encourages cross-racial coalition building. No one is locked into a minority identity. Nor is anyone necessarily isolated by the identity they choose. Voters can strengthen their influence by forming coalitions to elect more than one representative or to select a range of music more compatible with the entire student body's preferences.

Women too can use cumulative voting to gain greater representation. Indeed, in other countries with similar, alternative voting systems, women are more likely to be represented in the national legislature. For example, in some Western European democracies, the national legislatures have as many as 37 percent female members compared to a little more than 5 percent in our Congress.

There is a final benefit from cumulative voting. It eliminates gerrymandering. By denying protected incumbents safe seats in gerrymandered districts, cumulative voting might encourage more voter participation. With greater interest-based electoral competition, cumulative voting could promote the political turnover sought by advocates of term limits. In this way, cumulative voting serves many of the same ends as periodic elections or rotation in office, a solution that Madison and others advocated as a means of protecting against permanent majority factions.

A different remedial voting tool, one that I have explored more cautiously, is supermajority voting. It modifies winner-take-all majority rule to require that something more than a bare majority of voters must approve or concur before action is taken. As a uniform decisional rule, a supermajority empowers any numerically small but cohesive group of voters. Like cumulative voting, it is race-neutral. Depending on the issue, different members of the voting body can "veto" impending action.

Supermajority remedies give bargaining power to all numerically inferior or less powerful groups, be they black, female, or Republican. Supermajority rules empower the minority Republicans in the Senate who used the Senate filibuster procedure in the spring of 1993 to "veto" the President's proposed economic stimulus package. The same concept of a minority veto yielded the Great Compromise in which small-population states are equally represented in the Senate.

I have never advocated (or imagined) giving an individual member of a legislative body a personal veto. Moreover, I have discussed these kinds of exceptional remedies as the subject of court-imposed solutions only when there has been a violation of the statute and only when they make sense in the context of a particular case. I discuss supermajority rules as a judicial remedy only in cases where the court finds proof of consistent and deeply engrained polarization. It was never my intent that supermajority requirements should be the norm for all legislative bodies, or that simple majority voting would ever in itself constitute a statutory or constitutional violation.

Both the Reagan and Bush administrations took a similar remedial approach to enforcement of the Voting Rights Act. In fact, it was the Reagan administration that *approved* the use of supermajority rules as a remedial measure in places like Mobile, Alabama, where the special five-out-of-seven supermajority threshold is still in place today and is credited with increasing racial harmony in that community.

But—and here I come directly to the claims of my critics—some apparently fear that remedies for extreme voting abuses, remedies like cumulative voting or the Mobile supermajority, constitute "quotas"—racial preferences to ensure minority rule. While cumulative voting, or a supermajority, is quite conventional in many cases and race neutral, to order it as a remedy apparently opens up possibilities of nonmajoritarianism that many seem to find quite threatening.

Indeed, while my nomination was pending, I was called "antidemocratic" for suggesting that majority voting rules may not fairly resolve conflict when the majority and minority are permanently divided. But alternatives to majority voting rules in a racially polarized environment are too easily dismissed by this label. As Chief Justice Burger wrote for the Supreme Court, "There is nothing in the language of the Constitution, our history, or our cases that requires that a majority always prevail on every issue." In other words, there is *nothing inherent in democracy that requires majority rule.* It is simply a custom that works efficiently when the majority and minority are fluid, are not monolithic, and are not permanent.

Other democracies frequently employ alternatives to winner-take-all majority voting. Indeed, only five Western democracies, including Britain and the United States, still use single-member-district, winner-take-all systems of representation. Germany, Spain, the Netherlands, and Sweden, among other countries, elect their legislatures under some alternative to winner-take-all majority voting. As the *New Yorker,* in a comment on my nomination, observed, President Clinton was right in calling some of my ideas "difficult to defend," but only because "Americans, by and large, are ignorant of the existence, let alone the details, of electoral systems other than their own."

No one who had done their homework seriously questioned the fundamentally democratic nature of my ideas. Indeed, columnists who attacked my ideas during my nomination ordeal have praised ideas, in a different context, that are remarkably similar to my own. Lally Weymouth wrote, "There can't be democracy in South Africa without a measure of formal protection for minorities." George Will has opined, "The Framers also understood that stable, tyrannical majorities can best be prevented by the multiplication of minority interests, so the majority at any moment will be just a transitory coalition of minorities." In my law journal articles, I expressed exactly the same reservations about unfettered majority rule and about the need sometimes to disaggregate the majority to ensure fair and effective representation for all substantial interests.

The difference is that the minority I used to illustrate my academic point was not, as it was for Lally Weymouth, the white minority in South Africa. Nor, did I write, as George Will did, about the minority of well-to-do landlords in New York City. I wrote instead about the political exclusion of the black minority in many local county and municipal governing bodies in America.

Yet these same two journalists and many others condemned me as antidemocratic. Apparently, it is not controversial to provide special protections for affluent landlords or minorities in South Africa but it is "divisive," "radical," and "out of the mainstream" to provide similar remedies to black Americans who, after centuries of racial oppression, are still excluded.

Talking about racial bias at home has, for many, become synonymous with advocating revolution. Talking about racial divisions, in itself, has become a violation of the rules of polite society.

We seem to have forgotten that dialogue and intergroup communication are critical to forging consensus. In my case, genuine debate was shut down by techniques of stereotyping and silencing. As Professor Randall Kennedy observes, I was "punished" as the messenger reporting the bad news about our racial situation. I dared to speak when I should have been silent.

My nomination became an unfortunate metaphor for the state of race relations in America. My nomination suggested that as a country, we are in a state of denial about issues of race and racism. The censorship imposed against me points to a denial of serious public debate or discussion about racial fairness and justice in a true democracy. For many politicians and policymakers, the remedy for racism is simply to stop talking about race.

Sentences, words, even phrases separated by paragraphs in my law review articles were served up to demonstrate that I was violating the rules. Because I talked openly about existing racial divisions, I was branded "race obsessed." Because I explored innovative ways to remedy racism, I was branded "antidemocratic." It did not matter that I had suggested race-neutral election rules, such as cumulative voting, as an alternative to remedy racial discrimination. It did not matter that I never advocated quotas. I became the Quota Queen.

The vision behind my by-now-notorious law review articles and my less-well-known professional commitments has always been that of a fair and just society, a society in which even adversely affected parties believe in the system because they believe the process is fair and the process is inclusive. My vision of fairness and justice imagines a full and effective voice for all citizens. I may have failed to locate some of my ideas in the specific factual contexts from which they are derived. But always I have tried to show that democracy in a heterogeneous society is incompatible with rule by a racial monopoly of any color.

By publishing these law journal articles as a collection, I hope to spark the debate that was denied in the context of my nomination. We will have lost more than any one individual's opportunity for public service if we fail to pursue the public thirst for information about, and positive-sum solutions to, the issues at the heart of this controversy. The twentieth-century problem—the problem of the color line, according to W. E. B. Du Bois—will soon become a twenty-first-century problem if we allow opposing viewpoints to be silenced on issues of race and racism.

I hope that we can learn three positive lessons from my experience. The first lesson is that those who stand for principles may lose in the short run, but they cannot be suppressed in the long run. The second lesson is that public dialogue is critical to represent all perspectives; no one viewpoint should be permitted to monopolize, distort, caricature, or shape public debate. The tyranny of The Majority is just as much a problem of silencing minority viewpoints as it is of excluding minority representatives or preferences. We cannot all talk at once, but that does not mean only one group should get to speak. We can take turns. Third, we need consensus and positive-sum solutions. We need a broad public conversation about issues of racial justice in which we seek win-win solutions to real-life problems. If we include blacks and whites, and women and men, and Republicans and Democrats, and even people with new ideas, we will all be better off.

New ideas about how to resolve old problems are critical to shaping consensus solutions. To reach consensus we must do more than simply maneuver to avoid controversy. Consensus must be built, not just located. We have become so polarized that we have difficulty speaking to each other, as demonstrated by the controversy over recent judicial opinions condemning race-conscious districting. I believe we may forge a genuine consensus if we consider anew some of the ideas discussed in this collection of essays—the very same ideas previously dismissed as "out of the mainstream."

I am grateful for the opportunity provided by the publication of my law journal articles to participate in a national, public conversation about race, justice, and fundamental fairness. I would like to lower the decibel level but increase the information level on public discussion that surrounds race. I hope that those who actually read what I wrote will challenge decisionmakers—from politicians to pundits—to represent fairly and more carefully the broad spectrum of public opinion about race.

Most of all, I hope we begin to consider the principle of taking turns as a means to bring us closer to the ideal of democratic fair play. Justice Potter Stewart wrote in 1964 that our form of representative self-government reflects "the strongly felt American tradition that the public interest is composed of many diverse interests, [which] . . . in the long run . . . can better be expressed by a medley of component voices than by the majority's monolithic command." In that "strongly felt American tradition," I hope more of us aspire to govern like Madisonian Majorities through "a medley of component voices." In that "strongly felt American tradition," I hope more of us come to reject the "monolithic command" of The fixed Majority.

After all, government is a public experiment. Let us not forget Justice Louis Brandeis's advice at the beginning of this century: "If we guide by the light of reason, we must let our minds be bold." At the close of the same century, I hope we rediscover the bold solution to the tyranny of The Majority, which has always been more democracy, not less.

2

Keeping the Faith
Black Voters in the Post-Reagan Era

This essay, written in 1988 and 1989, begins with a retrospective on the Reagan Civil Rights Division, which I criticize as too confrontational, ideological, and politically partisan. I argue that the political system must be rejuvenated to offer an inclusionary vision of the future in which candidates mobilize the electorate and give voters a reason to participate throughout the political process. In drawing from my experience as a litigating attorney with the NAACP Legal Defense Fund (LDF), I use examples of the illegal exclusion of black voters from local politics and the perception of insensitivity to the interests of blacks in the 1984 and 1988 presidential campaigns. I argue for creating electoral constituencies from which blacks can elect candidates responsive to their interests and electorally accountable to them. I contend that a lifeline to equitable access in legislative decisionmaking for blacks will help to legitimate the constitutional system for everyone, and will promote reciprocity in bargaining. I also point to the importance of coalition building among black, labor, environmental and feminist groups.

This exposition of my ideas is based on my advocacy experience as an LDF attorney, and is not necessarily representative of my current thinking. As is true of all the articles in this collection, I have updated factual references to reflect contemporary developments. I have also authorized the editors to drop the more technical footnotes and to delete unnecessary passages that are simply redundant of ideas developed further in subsequent chapters.

Introduction

When President Ronald Reagan left office in January 1989, many of us within the black community collectively sighed with relief.[1] For eight years the Reagan Administration had sowed conflict and division between itself and civil rights groups, and had contributed to an increasing sense of isolation among African-Americans.[2]

The Reagan legacy has directly affected the role of blacks in the political process. On the one hand, black registration and turnout has increased in response to Reagan's perceived anti–civil rights agenda. As blacks begin to vote at levels approximating their numerical strength in the community, they see the ballot as an important tool for preserving a traditional civil rights agenda.[3] Electing Democrats, or moderate Republicans, is the most obvious way for blacks to assure their community of some voice in the public debate, especially since Ronald Reagan gave blacks no public forum and made no effort to seek out or appoint traditional civil rights leaders.

On the other hand, many blacks have felt particularly stifled by the traditional two-party approach to black political participation. One party has taken blacks for granted; the other, at best, ignored them. Mainstream Democrats do not accept black Democrats, such as Jesse Jackson, as legitimate party spokespersons, and too often only whites are allowed to run for office on the Democratic ticket. On the other hand, Republicans have refused to court the black vote at all. Blacks may vote, but it is whites who will govern. It is this dilemma, exacerbated by the Reagan success in polarizing the electorate, which presently challenges black voters. Can we keep the faith?

This chapter attempts to spotlight the Reagan civil rights legacy by examining, through the prism of black political participation, both the Reagan Administration's record in voting rights enforcement and its success in polarizing the electorate. It then examines the importance of vigorous voting rights enforcement to the empowerment of the black community, and offers recommendations . . . on inclusionary ways to address the racial divisions of the body politic. The chapter suggests that we should reclaim the Voting Rights Act for those it was intended to benefit, along with eliminating all barriers to universal voter registration. Finally, it stresses that we should make a concerted effort to promote black political clout through actual, and not simply virtual, representation.

I. The Reagan Legacy

Under the leadership of its Department of Justice, the Reagan Administration identified race-conscious civil rights policies which it considered inherently suspect. Reagan proposed the repeal of affirmative action,[4] the end to many effective class-based remedies, and the abandonment of most racial discrimination cases except those filed on behalf of "identifiable" victims of racism. Propelled in part by the philosophic engines of New Right cost-benefit analysis, the Administration attempted to drive civil rights laws out of the marketplace for being more costly than they are worth.

The message became clear in the first days of the Administration when it abruptly changed sides in several cases, most notoriously the *Bob Jones University* case, involving the revocation of tax-exempt status for segregated private schools. This pattern continued throughout Reagan's term as president: the Department of Justice filed briefs in employment and voting cases opposing women and minority plaintiffs, took the position that only intent to discriminate should be covered by the Voting Rights Act of 1982, and generally demonstrated greater sympathy for white males, who were perceived as the victims of "reverse discrimination" rather than for those "actual, identifiable" black victims of state-supported legal segregation.[5] The President also fired members of the United States Civil Rights Commission for doing their jobs[6] and vetoed the Civil Rights Restoration Act.[7] Some suggest that President Reagan's popularity was helped by these blatant appeals to the perception that federal civil rights policy unfairly benefitted blacks and other minorities.[8]

Progressives congratulated themselves because the neoconservative philosophy of civil rights failed to triumph in two well-reported contests over the eight years of the Reagan Revolution. The Administration tried to put Robert Bork on the Supreme Court, but the largest Senate majority in history voted against his confirmation. The President also cast the first veto in 121 years on a civil rights bill, but Congress overrode his veto by enacting the Civil Rights Restoration Act. This congressional override in particular seemed a rejection of Reagan's efforts to take civil rights in America back to the days of President Andrew Johnson.

Despite these congressional victories for civil rights, Reagan has left an enduring mark on national civil rights policies. Before offering prospective nominees appointments to the federal bench, his advisers tested them by using ideological litmus tests on civil rights issues such as school desegregation, affirmative action, and other race-conscious remedies. The 366

Reagan appointments made to the bench now represent over half the federal judiciary, yet only seven were black, proportionately fewer than were appointed by Richard Nixon from a pool of available minority talent one-seventh its present size. This predominantly white, male, Reagan judicial legacy, constitutionally vested with life tenure, will continue to shape judicial policy well into the twenty-first century.

The Reagan legacy also survives in the framing of civil rights issues in general. The Reagan Administration successfully recast civil rights as "special interest" politics. It also refocused attention on deficit reduction and big government, thereby diverting attention in both parties from new federal programs in employment, job training, education, health care or housing for the poor. While Reagan appointees admitted that blacks might in fact be worse off than whites, they blamed this on individual failings rather than entrapment by the awful legacy of discrimination. Relying on the extension of formal equality, conservative civil rights theorists applied a market analysis to civil rights policymaking. Aggressive, affirmative government efforts to end discrimination were deemed unnecessary because individual blacks held within themselves the key to their own advancement: hard work and the Protestant ethic in a robust, free-market economy.

While the Administration failed to undermine completely the bipartisan consensus which forged our present anti-discrimination and equal opportunity laws, it gave free rein to the radical right to recast, refocus and polarize the debate.[9] In as turbulent a policy area as race relations, the assistant attorney general for civil rights proposed in a 1988 memorandum that the Administration should seek not consensus but confrontation. Of course, his extraordinary exhortation to polarize the debate exacerbated tensions between blacks and other Americans and cast doubt upon the role of the public sector in advancing the status of historically disadvantaged groups. Recently, the Administration's campaign against affirmative action has met with notable success.[10] Now, even progressive political, social and economic analysts have begun discounting or ignoring pervasive vestiges of America's racist heritage.

II. Voting Rights Enforcement Under Reagan

The Voting Rights Act of 1965 (the "Act") was enacted as a complex statutory web for federal monitoring of local elections to ensure that protected racial and, since 1975, language minorities enjoy the right to vote on an equal basis with other members of the population. The initial legislation focused on forestalling innovative disfranchisement techniques that historically accompanied litigation victories. By requiring administrative preclearance of all election law changes in targeted areas, the Act barred southern jurisdictions from implementing new schemes that would evade the reach of case-by-case adjudication. Hailed as "the most successful" civil rights measure ever passed, the Act ultimately convinced even its early opponents that minority voting rights required the exercise of congressional authority for protection. Although it has been attacked recently as promoting "affirmative action" for racial minorities, no one prior to the Reagan Administration had seriously contended that the Act's intended beneficiaries were other than racial and language minority victims of entrenched, official and continuing discrimination.[11] In other words, there was no question that, at a minimum, the Act was passed and renewed to protect full exercise of the franchise by black and other minority voters.[12] Despite this clear background, the Reagan Administration's Department of Justice took every opportunity through its enforcement authority under the Act to protect incumbent white elected officials. This was done without regard for the effect such policies would have upon black voters, although their interests were the primary concern of the initial legislation and all succeeding amendments.

Specifically, the Civil Rights Division of the Department of Justice had, and continues to have, primary enforcement responsibility for the Voting Rights Act of 1965. The Division began in 1939 as a section to enforce the right to vote within the Criminal Division. As a full-fledged Division within the Department since 1957, it had traditionally followed a "shared enforcement" strategy, relying as much as possible on voluntary compliance for statutory voting rights enforcement. Even during the Carter Administration, the Division was never a "hotbed of radicalism or of overreaching in government." Deeply committed to the goals of civil rights enforcement, career attorneys within the Division adhered to its traditions of "caution, moderation, respect for precedent, patience in the face of protracted litigation, commitment to the system as is and painstaking attention to detail." These career professionals considered themselves apolitical guardians of the middle ground. Yet, all of this changed during the Reagan Administration. While the career attorneys attempted to preserve the Division's standards of professionalism, moderation and a "sense of obligation to the law," the newly appointed leadership of Attorneys General Smith and Meese and Assistant Attorney General William Bradford Reynolds encouraged conservative policymakers of the Reagan Justice Department to launch a profound assault on Division policies and goals, and upon those whom the Act was intended to protect.[13]

In particular, a 1982 report on the Justice Department by the Leadership Conference on Civil Rights (LCCR)[14] recited a litany of examples in which Republican politicians were able to alter normal decisionmaking channels to hamper voting rights enforcement.[15] The report concluded that in several voting cases, partisan politics or reactionary civil rights ideology had been allowed "to corrupt the fair administration of the law" to the detriment of minority voters. While the LCCR Report reviewed the Administration's very early record of voting rights enforcement, the hearings on Mr. Reynolds' 1985 nomination to the position of Associate Attorney General provided examples of a continued pattern of unabashed ideological mongering and lackluster enforcement of even routine voting matters.

Most prominent was the Department's rearguard action on the statutory standard for discerning discriminatory voting results under Section 2 of the Act. Section 2 raised the question whether plaintiffs in litigation challenging longstanding discriminatory practices would have to prove that the jurisdiction and the legislature intended to discriminate when they originally devised the practice, even if it was a hundred years ago. The Supreme Court interpreted Section 2 in *City of Mobile v. Bolden*[16] to require direct proof of discriminatory purpose. A broad coalition of civil rights and "good government" groups urged Congress to amend the statute to specify that discriminatory results alone would establish a violation. From the beginning, the Department opposed strengthening statutory protections for minority voting rights. Its official explanation was that, after sixteen years of enforcement, more time was needed to "study it."

The Administration took credit, nevertheless, for the "results language" in the 1982 amendments to the Act, claiming that the Justice Department had "worked closely with Congress in devising a compromise amendment on Section 2 of the Voting Rights Act."[17] Contrary to claims made in speeches and briefs after the passage of the 1982 amendments, Mr. Reynolds had testified against the "results" test and any modifications to the extremely difficult intent test of Section 2 which had been promulgated in *Bolden*. In fact, the Administration reluctantly joined the supporters of the 1982 legislation only after the House of Representatives ratified the results test, and it became clear that the Senate would reach a similar compromise.

For the next year and a half, despite its alleged support of the amendment, the Administration failed to file any new lawsuits to enforce Section

2.[18] Moreover, having failed to persuade Congress to retain an intent test, the Administration seized the first opportunity to limit the meaning and application of the results test. The Department of Justice filed a brief opposing black plaintiffs in the first Supreme Court case to interpret the 1982 Act's statutory standard. The Administration argued that the Court should not enforce the 1982 results test on behalf of black voters in North Carolina, a state covered by the Voting Rights Act, because some—though concededly not equal—electoral opportunity existed. In a dramatic departure from its traditional stance of protecting minority voters, the Department asked the United States Supreme Court to reverse the three-judge court's findings of racial vote dilution.[19] Its position did not prevail.

In an earlier Supreme Court case, the Administration declined to file a brief supporting black voters, where both the district court and the court of appeals had found evidence of discrimination based on proof of discriminatory intent.[20] In fact, a January 4, 1982, memorandum from Mr. Reynolds to Solicitor General Rex Lee revealed that for Mr. Reynolds "the preferred course of action," but for a timeliness problem, would have been to support the white commissioners.[21]

In addition to this litigation strategy, which in effect promoted the incumbency of white politicians, the Division failed to protect vigorously the intended beneficiaries of the Voting Rights Act in its most important mission: administration of the Section 5 preclearance provision.[22] In the Section 5 preclearance process, Mr. Reynolds had the responsibility of acting both as judge and as prosecutor. When a jurisdiction submitted a proposed election change, the assistant attorney general for civil rights had the statutory duty to investigate the factual basis for the change and to conduct a non-adversarial proceeding. In this proceeding, the Department determined whether the jurisdiction had discharged its burden of proving that the change did not discriminate against minority voters.

In several instances, the Reagan Justice Department used its administrative discretion to modify the statutory enforcement scheme by reallocating the statutory burdens of proof to the disadvantage of minority voters.[23] Between 1981 and 1985, there were at least thirty instances in which Mr. Reynolds overruled staff attorneys who urged him to object to a voting law change which they considered discriminatory. The assistant attorney general unilaterally shifted "the advantage of time and inertia"[24] away from racial minorities to benefit instead white elected officials.

In one particularly disturbing case, *Major v. Treen*,[25] black voters challenged the Division's preclearance of a New Orleans congressional gerrymander, more commonly known as the "Donald Duck" plan because this congressional reapportionment plan carved the New Orleans black community into a district which looked very similar to the cartoon character.[26] Again over the objections of staff attorneys, Mr. Reynolds approved the plan despite persuasive evidence that it was adopted as part of a discriminatory effort to assure the re-election of a white Republican incumbent to the United States Congress. As the following discussion reveals, Mr. Reynolds failed as a prosecutor to investigate fully the facts of the *Treen* submission; he also failed in his statutory role as a judge to listen to both sides. Furthermore, as the primary federal enforcer of the 1965 Voting Rights Act, Reynolds refused to challenge this discriminatory redistricting change, although the submitting jurisdiction did not sustain its burden of proof.

In *Treen,* pursuant to its responsibilities under Section 5 of the Voting Rights Act, the Division staff had investigated the Louisiana redistricting proposal. Besides the usual review, the Division also received over 100 letters and comments from blacks in Louisiana, all opposing the plan. The staff eventually recommended an official objection to the plan as intentionally discriminatory. During the time that the matter was under submission to the Department of Justice, Mr. Reynolds personally met at least twice with Republican Governor David Treen, whose involvement was pivotal in getting the Louisiana legislature to pass the "Donald Duck" plan.[27] In addition to these meetings, Mr. Reynolds spoke with Treen at least nine times on the telephone while the plan was being reviewed by the Division staff, while he had neither telephone conversations nor meetings with local black leaders about the plan.

When his staff sent out a routine request for more information about the redistricting plan, specifically inquiring about several statements the Governor allegedly made during the reapportionment process, Mr. Reynolds recalled the letter. The Governor had publicly threatened to veto an earlier New Orleans–based plan that seemed to meet Voting Rights Act requirements: it had a fifty-four percent black population district, met criteria of geographic compactness, and respected natural boundaries and parish lines. Nonetheless, Mr. Reynolds declined to inquire about the Governor's role or his public statements in opposition to *any* majority black district. The lawmakers thereafter sought to meet the Governor's black population ceiling by whatever means necessary; they excluded all black legislators from a secret meeting on the redistricting proposal which was held in the basement of the Senate chambers. As one legislative staff member testified at the subsequent trial, "The textbook stuff went out the window."[28]

Despite his staff's findings and recommendation, Reynolds approved the "Donald Duck" plan, finding no evidence of racial intent on the part of the Governor or the legislature. His decision to overrule a staff recommendation was clearly influenced by the personal lobbying effort of the Governor of Louisiana on behalf of a plan which was "perceived as aiding the retention and election of Republican representatives."[29]

Speaking for President Reagan and his administration, Reynolds had often condemned civil rights policies based on affirmative action and other race-conscious remedies. He criticized such remedies in a speech at Amherst College for creating a "racial spoils system" in America.[30] Yet, in the face of a race-conscious effort to assure the re-election of a white Republican incumbent, he declined to act.[31] His decision to overrule the staff voting rights experts was directly contrary to Department of Justice regulations on allocating the burden of proof. Section 55.39(e) of the Department's regulations implementing the Act provides that if the evidence regarding racial purpose was conflicting, or if the assistant attorney general had any doubt, such doubt should have been resolved by objecting to the redistricting proposal. The burden of proof in this situation was upon the submitting jurisdiction to demonstrate, with clear and convincing evidence, that the plan lacked any racial purpose or racial effect.

The Department's failure to enforce the Voting Rights Act had serious implications. The Act itself allocates primary responsibility for its enforcement to the Department of Justice and the attorney general. When the attorney general or his assistant fails to enforce the Act he causes a greater harm than simply ignoring a statutory duty. Reynolds undermined the foundation of an entire enforcement scheme. Moreover, by attempting to nullify federal statutes and Departmental regulations and replacing them with ad hoc judgments, the Reagan Justice Department abandoned the minority victims of discrimination to fend for themselves.

The Division's Reagan-era record in the area of voting rights is not completely blemished. In some routine enforcement matters, the Division has remained relatively active.[32] Most of the credit for holding the line in such instances belongs to the tenacious career attorneys in the Voting Section of the Division, who have persuaded "Mr. Reynolds to take positive actions, frequently only after extensive argument."[33]

Not withstanding the vigilant efforts of the Department's bureaucracy, the Division should renew its efforts to promote the interests of black voters to assure their ability to participate as equals in the political process.

For example, the Division should make plans to monitor the 1990 re-apportionments under Section 5 and to activate the Section 2 litigation unit. The Act, as amended by Congress in 1982, should be viewed not as a shield for local "democratic" arrangements, but affirmatively as a sword to impale discriminatory election systems such as at-large elections, majority vote run-off requirements, and gerrymandered districts. As the Act's intended beneficiaries, blacks deserve and, as continuing victims of disempowering policies, need a full opportunity to enjoy actual representation. To address generations of inequality and to eradicate racial discrimination, the Division must impose the full panoply of existing remedies, including majority black electoral districts which give black voters the opportunity to elect representatives of their choice. Moreover, a lifeline to equitable distribution of legislative decisionmaking for blacks will help to legitimate the constitutional system for everyone.[34]

III. Keeping the Faith

The polarizing philosophy of the Reagan years affected more than the Administration's enforcement activities. Its legacy, engrafted upon Reconstruction era stereotypes about black elected officials, has perpetuated and accentuated a racially skewed reality in which blacks vote but do not govern, at least not in majority white jurisdictions.

In the effective pursuit of political empowerment, black voters have begun to relinquish the presumption that a Democratic White House is necessarily the ticket to a better future. Management by good people with excellent credentials will not alone lead America into the twenty-first century.

Political euphoria about the possibility of a Democratic presidential victory in 1988 was neither justified nor shared by the black community. In 1986, Democrats gained a majority in the United States Senate on the strength of four predominantly southern victories; these triumphs were built on the solid base of black Democratic support[35] Black political activity also figured decisively in the Democrats' greatest symbolic success in recent years—the defeat of Robert Bork.[36] Even Governor Dukakis' early lead in the 1988 presidential race was provided largely by African-Americans. On election day, Dukakis received almost 90% of the black vote while Bush polled nearly 60% of the white vote nationwide, and more than 70% in the deep South.[37] Yet, the vision Democrats offered in 1988 hardly mentioned, even indirectly, problems of race, and it deliberately ignored connections between racism and poverty. Similarly, Jesse Jackson's second place showing in the primaries did not secure blacks a place at the bargaining table.

Snubbing its loyal black constituency, the Democratic Party has responded to racial polarization by distancing itself from black interests. Thus, many white Democratic Party candidates have not actively sought black allies, nor have they aggressively supported black leaders who are Democrats. While the Democratic Party . . . elected Ronald H. Brown as its first black national chair, Mr. Brown's ties to the Jackson wing of the party were generally perceived as a disadvantage. Indeed, the events surrounding Ron Brown's election may signal recognition of the Jackson "problem," not the Jackson "program."

Some Democrats asserted that Mr. Jackson's high profile in the party contributed to the November 1988 election defeat. Thus, despite their consistent loyalty to the Democrats, African-Americans have not been able to protect themselves with a "voice and a vote." Democrats, who control both houses of Congress, seem unaware that reciprocity in bargaining requires the active promotion of black interests, not just the occasional subvention and authorization of civil rights enforcement. In other words, black legislative issues can be ghettoized from the Left as well as the Right.

The Democrats' policy of benign neglect toward African-Americans has not gone unnoticed. Where racial concerns should properly be a campaign issue, to mask controversial stands in euphemism easily offends if white decisionmakers have demonstrated in the past that they do not take into account minority interests. Consequently, when Governor Dukakis "snubbed" Jesse Jackson, who learned from a reporter of his being passed over for the vice-presidency, blacks took affront. It reemphasized that white politicians have not demonstrated fairness, and that blacks have reason to feel abandoned and unprotected without someone in a leadership role with whom they can identify and who identifies with their interests.

Although black voters are frustrated with the Democratic Party's response to their interests, they are hardly convinced of the sincerity of the Republican Party's nascent and token outreach. Republican Party leaders, including President Bush, now claim that they want to attract black voters to the party ranks. Despite the racially offensive tactical choices which they have made in recent campaigns, these same leaders now repudiate the racial views of white supremacists who also proclaim themselves to be GOP leaders. While the condemnation of racism is minimally appropriate, the Bush Administration has rejected important opportunities to enforce its rhetorical approach to public policy with substantive evidence of the "Republican outreach."

The evolution in black priorities from a civil rights protest agenda to electoral politics carries with it the continued need for opportunities for mass mobilization, in which the governed systematically give their consent to their government. However, blacks cannot mobilize to participate in the political process unless candidates offer an inclusionary vision of the future. This is essentially an instrumental formulation of the causes of political activity. People participate "where, when and how" they think it matters. If the political system is unresponsive, people "tend to withdraw or seek nonsystemic means of pursuing their demands."[38]

How then are blacks to mobilize to participate in the political process without a vision of the future that reaches out to include them broadly and not just euphemistically? Certainly, part of the answer for African-Americans is to push for the removal of existing barriers to voter participation, to make voting and registration a one-step process. The United States still permits a variety of state-erected barriers to simple and convenient registration. Most voter registration requirements in the United States were enacted in the late 1800's to exclude blacks in the South and new immigrants in the North from voting. Although such requirements have been rationalized by the need to prevent voter fraud, most election fraud actually occurs in voting, not in registration, and is typically committed by election officials. Whatever the arguable justification, these requirements primarily serve to reduce voter participation among all citizens, especially minorities.

First, registration rules require that the citizen make an affirmative effort to enter the voting rolls rather than allowing automatic inclusion; enrolling citizens by social security number, for example. Believing individual initiative to register is a legitimate voting requirement, many local officials treat the franchise as a privilege which the voter must earn. Whereas other democratic governments assume the responsibility, both financial and administrative, of canvassing eligible voters to enroll them on the registration list, in the United States, only volunteers and private individuals perform this task.

Second, rules which require the initiative of individual voters make it difficult for blacks who are more likely to be without cars or telephones, or who may hold a notion of political participation which pre-dates the passage of the Act, to register. Restrictive local registration practices still exist that are both burdensome and discriminatory. They are burdensome because they make voting a two-step process that must occur during working hours. They discriminate because private resources such as cars and telephones, which are critical to functioning in this two-step process, are unavailable to poor people, especially racial and language minorities. This is especially true in the South where most registration occurs at the county courthouse and where there is no public transportation. In rural Arkansas, for example, according to the 1980 census, 42% of blacks (compared with 9% of whites) have no access to a car, truck or van; 30% of blacks (compared with 10% of whites) have no telephone. Without these politically relevant private resources, poor blacks are effectively excluded from both registering and voting.

Many rural counties in the South have only one place to register and that location is typically closed weekends, evenings and at lunchtime. Some county officials refuse to appoint blacks as volunteer deputy registrars who could go door to door to register blacks. By relying on blacks' unequal access to private resources, incumbent politicians effectively exclude eligible black voters from the electorate. As a result, large numbers of blacks remain unregistered and thus are outside the political process. For example, in *Operation PUSH v. Allain,* a federal district court found that census survey figures routinely over-estimate the number of registered blacks because they are based solely on reports of a respondent's unverified past activity. Unlike questions of present fact that do not require much thought, such as the number of vehicles available, or indoor plumbing, census questions that call for specific past information are often answered inaccurately, due to the self-image that the respondent wishes to project. This leads, for blacks more than whites, to over-reporting. The court found a twenty-five percent gap between white and black registration rates, a clear sign that even rudimentary statistical parity had not been realized. . . .

The election of more black representatives proves a second important opportunity for substantive rather than rhetorical outreach. At present the electoral process is permeated by a subtle, yet pervasive, racial atmosphere that deters black candidates from running, that dismissed *prematurely* Jesse Jackson's presidential aspirations (on the basis of his race) and that permits jurisdictions not to recognize members of a sizable minority as part of the governing coalition. Indeed, a recent survey indicated that the higher the office in question, the less whites are inclined to vote for a qualified black candidate.[39]

Predictably, black voters seek more candidates, with more responsive programs, from which to choose. They seek both to overcome the deep-seated prejudice many whites harbor against black office-holders and to share political power through their ability to choose their own representatives. Blacks cannot enjoy equal dignity and political status until black representatives join the council of government.

Of course, not all minority-sponsored candidates are selfless public servants, but at least through "actual" representation, the mechanism exists for improving accountability. The black community can demonstrate its displeasure at the next election if black voters have a right to elect representatives of their choice, a right enforced through the drawing of district lines or alternative remedies which lower the threshold of exclusion to permit minority group representation. The enforcement of this representational right does not require legislative set-asides, color coded ballots, electoral quotas, or "one black, two votes" remedies which some might argue are also justified. Thus, many of the worries implicit in opposition to affirmative action in employment are inapposite. Moreover, black electoral success does not mean the displacement of "innocent whites" who are being forced to bear society's burdens at the ballot box unless whites have a right to be represented only by whites. Indeed, the whites being displaced are not voters but incumbent politicians who may not get re-elected in a reconfigured, racially fair, single member district plan. These incumbents, however, are usually direct beneficiaries of prior discrimination, who have no particular right to their position. The rights at stake are those of the voter, not the candidate.

Blacks have thus been attempting, through federal litigation under Section 2 of the Voting Rights Act, to exercise real legislative and executive power, not merely imagined electoral influence. They want the option of nominating, and being represented by, other black representatives. They are no longer satisfied with automatically choosing the Democratic candidate or with the ephemeral role of "the swing vote," in elections between two moderate-to-conservative white candidates.[40] Black voters want, and need, aggressive advocates, not momentarily concerned opportunists.[41]

For a group that has been excluded as long as blacks, aggressive advocacy is essential to ensure that black interests are taken seriously. Technical, formal access to the political process may not be enough to guarantee even good faith representation. This is a particular problem where black voters are less likely to engage in the "extended political process" of post-election day accountability with white representatives.

The obvious role that black lawmakers perform within a legislative body was expressly endorsed by Congress when it amended Section 2 of the

1965 Voting Rights Act in 1982. In recent interviews, members of the House of Representatives acknowledged that regarding questions concerning blacks, black representatives "exert special influence on their colleagues," providing "internal leadership" to which people defer. Scholars and experienced observers of the political process have found that minority candidates "enhance minority turnout, especially where they have a realistic chance of winning." For blacks, black representation is a "crucial lever for obtaining the benefits—patronage, contracts, public services—that must be bargained for in the public arena."[42] Moreover, diversity of representation that promotes political activity is in itself a collective good. Minority officeholding increases political consciousness and signals to constituents that the system is legitimate and ought to be supported. Thus, it promotes values of "civic inclusion," meaning a "sense of connectedness to the community and of equal political dignity, greater readiness to acquiesce in governmental decisions and hence broader consent and legitimacy, and more informed, equitable and intelligent governmental decisionmaking."[43]

The question for the immediate future is whether blacks will have the opportunity to elect other blacks to advocate their interests and aggressively articulate their muted voices in the legislative hall.[44]

The courts have recognized the importance for blacks of the opportunity to "elect candidates of their choice, . . . to have their ideas on political matters afforded the recognition to which they are entitled on their merits and by virtue of their individual citizenship and their numerical strength in the community."[45] The importance of this opportunity derives from fundamental assumptions about representative democracy: that the government's authority depends on the consent of the governed and that the interests of those who are bound by governmental actions cannot be arbitrarily ignored in the legislative process. But, this notion of "opportunity" has been transformed into one of "right" to empower a historically disenfranchised and politically despised group. The most notable example of institutional vindication of this right is the enactment of the Voting Rights Act.

The courts have recognized that creating a minority group "right to representation" may be appropriate in the political arena for several reasons. First, the fundamental nature of the right to vote stems from its role in preserving all other rights. Other rights, even the most basic, are illusory if the right to vote is undermined. The franchise gives status to the individual voter but derives its vitality from its exercise by a "politically cohesive" group of citizens who elect representatives to promote consideration of group interests in public policy.[46] A voice in the process of self-government is heard only through the medium of elected representatives; the opportunity to vote is the vital means of affecting representation. Unlike other government benefits, the right to vote is therefore a *meaningful* entitlement. For the minority, the meaningful right to vote must include the correlative opportunity to elect a representative of that group's choice. Even if, as Reaganism posits, blacks are merely another "special interest," it is important that they be represented. In a racially polarized situation, this means creating districts or electoral opportunities in which such a representative can be elected.

Second, equal status as participants within the political sphere is possible only if members of the group are allowed to participate at all stages of the process. . . . A meaningful right to vote contemplates minority participation in post-election legislative policymaking as well as pre-election coalition building and deliberation.[47] This ideal is obviously frustrated if racial status is a consistent disqualification for such participation simply because whites refuse to work with or vote for a black candidate.

Nevertheless, some commentators argue that judicially imposed remedies to create electoral opportunities for "black representatives" constitute electoral "affirmative action" and disable black voters. The argument is that since whites can, and do, represent black voters, blacks should pursue instead an "integrative" electoral strategy in which white politicians compete for black votes. As long as blacks enjoy formal access to the polling place and intentionally discriminatory statements are suppressed, some commentators contend, blacks should have no special rights to affect an election outcome, even where no black candidate can win because of bloc voting by the white majority. Abigail Thernstrom has advocated a theory of "virtual" representation, in which black interests are taken into account to some extent, but are not actively promoted. Under this rationale, "one can be represented in a political regime in which one has no actual participatory role . . . through the participation of another who is one's likeness."[48]

Virtual representation, which assumes surrogate representation based on common interests, is rooted in the defense by the English Whigs in the eighteenth century of a franchise system in which industrial towns with no representatives in the House of Commons were considered "virtually" represented by members from similar cities. Recent commentators, including Thernstrom, have revived that theory in an attempt to justify monochromatic legislatures on the premise that whites can represent black interests.

Where interests between those "actually represented" are in fact comparable to those "virtually represented," the concept has contemporary relevance. For example, during the 1950's and 1960's, as a young black boy growing up in North Carolina, Frank Ballance, now a member of the North Carolina General Assembly, knew he had a congressman even though no black had been elected to Congress from North Carolina since Reconstruction. His "representative" was Harlem Congressman Adam Clayton Powell, Jr. Ballance did not expect actual representation from the North Carolina congressman elected from his district. Similarly, where majority black single member districts are created within a formerly at-large electoral system to remedy vote dilution, blacks outside the majority black district are considered "virtually" represented.

However, virtual representation theory is not appropriate if the interests of a racial minority are not necessarily fungible with those of the "actual" representatives or of their white constituents. For example, blacks, as a poor and historically oppressed group, are in greater need of government sponsored programs and solicitude, which whites often resent and vigorously oppose. Even a mildly sympathetic white official will not dependably consider black interests if that individual must also accommodate the more dominant views of white constituents.

The theory that white politicians who compete in a majority white district for minority votes also take minority demands seriously is not generally supported by the immediate empirical evidence of the 1988 presidential campaign. To the extent that it has merit, the virtual representation theory requires the active advocacy of minority interests by at least one of the competing parties. Like the swing vote theory, virtual representation presumes inter-party competition. When minority interests are not only distinct but antagonistic to those of the white majority,[49] and when one political party presumes black loyalty while the other panders to racial hostility, such representation is merely symbolic. Thus, black interests are neither actually nor virtually represented.

Blacks are still the pariah group: systematic losers in the political marketplace. Despite visible gains, legislative and executive policy is dominated by white males who lack a sustaining link to black concerns. While commentators critique the representation-reinforcing view of pluralist society, blacks should be supported in their struggle to elect representatives who will advocate a vision which includes their experience. It is unreasonable to expect blacks to allow others to name their reality, especially in the absence of visible reciprocity.

IV. Resurrecting a Voting Rights Agenda

Inflamed racial polarization during the Reagan years rekindled de facto separate and unequal political, economic and social status for African-Americans. The Reagan years have left blacks geographically more concentrated and isolated. Seven states currently have black populations that are over twenty-two percent, yet until 1993 there were no blacks in the United States Senate. Before Douglas Wilder there were no black governors elected by either party in this century, and 1.5% of the elected officials nationwide are black (mostly mayors from majority-black towns with populations under 1000). The potential political influence which concentrations of blacks could wield at the local level has not been combined with a willingness by state and national governments to democratize the voting process. A majority of white voters, in general, has been reluctant to support or contribute to black candidates. In light of the Reagan record of voting enforcement, racial polarization of the electorate and white politicians' limited response, both political parties must affirmatively give black voters a reason to "keep the faith."

A. Immediate Action

An Administration leads not only by rhetoric or good intentions, but also by demonstrating a willingness to enforce existing laws, and a commitment, when necessary, to introduce legislative reforms to remedy continuing inequities. Blacks need presidential leadership in the policy process that will actively implement a voting rights agenda. After all, it was former Attorney General Katzenbach who authored the Voting Rights Act in 1965, at President Johnson's behest. Despite the Reagan Justice Department's attack on race conscious remedies that protect blacks from discrimination, the Act remains the most successfully implemented piece of civil rights legislation and one that has kept abreast of demographic and political changes.

B. Short-term Challenges

A new administration which deems itself eager for black support and a Congress committed to black political participation should approach the present situation with three short-term objectives. First, we should clearly end the civil rights conflict of the Reagan years and replace it with an affirmative and coordinated plan to enforce existing civil rights laws. The

Administration should move quickly to change the Justice Department's prior negative agenda.

Second, both the Administration and Congress must seek out black allies, by supporting—not undermining or patronizing—black and other minority leadership, by appointing a diverse group of black federal officials and by encouraging potential African-American candidates for federal, state and local office. Only if both the Administration and the Congress reach out to diversify their programs will executive and legislative policies be enforced and supported by a diverse, representative and committed group of federal officials.

In light of the Reagan record, the Congress can play an important role in encouraging diversity in the appointment process by withholding its advice and consent until enough nominations have been made to establish a pattern of "affirmative recruitment." For example, if the Bush Administration continued the exclusionary litmus tests of its predecessor, the Senate Judiciary Committee could begin evaluating federal judicial nominations with reference to specific goals for increasing non-white nominees. The Committee could decline to consider any nominee until a sufficient number of nominations—such as twenty or thirty—were made so as to enable the Committee to consider not only the individual qualifications of each, but the impact of these twenty or thirty nominations as a totality on the composition of the federal bench.

Third, the Administration and Congress should consider changes in the civil rights laws and enforcement practices. This does not require fundamental revisions in all regulations or laws. But the president should, at least, endorse and coordinate support for those legislative initiatives which address fundamental flaws in our democracy.

C. Long-range Challenges

By virtue of their continuing status as a racially victimized and insular minority, poor blacks, in particular, still possess a disproportionately small share of political power. It is urgent that the Administration shape a political agenda for the twenty-first century premised upon the plight of this unrepresented group.

To prepare for the future, black voters should demand a White House Summit on Civil Rights in the Twenty-First Century to assess the scope, impact and effectiveness of present laws and to explore new legal remedies to contradictions between American democratic ideology and minority disfranchisement. As an outgrowth of the conference, a task force should be established that includes a substantial number of nonwhite policy analysts, scholars, economists, lawyers, elected officials and public interest leaders. The White House should then propose a plan of action for aggressive federal initiatives and legislative reform.

Conclusion

Twenty-nine years ago President Johnson anticipated that overcoming the "crippling legacy of bigotry and injustice" was necessary, not just for blacks, but for all Americans. In the wake of passage of the Civil Rights Act of 1964, and while the Voting Rights Act was being considered by Congress, President Johnson set the tone for a country with an unfinished political agenda: "We seek not just legal equity but human ability, not just equality as a fact, but equality as a result. And we shall overcome."[50]

Twenty-nine years later we have not yet overcome. The promise of our political system has yet to reach beyond symbols to commitments, beyond token appointments to representative black advocates, beyond electing black candidates to mainstreaming black issues. To keep the faith, blacks expect political fairness. At this moment in history, political fairness for blacks means a fair opportunity to choose their representatives, a fair shake in administrative enforcement that protects minority voting rights, and a fair share of substantive, legislative policy outcomes.

To implement an electoral agenda, African-Americans face the dual challenge of encouraging vigorous enforcement of existing law and restructuring the political process to reflect more fundamentally the sobering reality of inequality. While it is true that under our constitutional system laws have removed most formal barriers to black electoral participation, the Reagan and Bush Administrations did not enforce many of these laws. Blacks do not yet fully participate in the system, even as contemplated by federal statute.

If the voting rights laws are vigorously enforced and the immediate barriers to political fairness are crossed, blacks can obtain a greater degree of actual representation. Even after blacks reach this goal, however, new questions regarding political fairness will certainly arise if blacks remain seen, and not heard. But first, our political system must redress its historical insult to African-Americans by fostering actual representation whenever possible, and thoughtfully considering race issues whenever relevant.

3

The Triumph of Tokenism

The Voting Rights Act and the Theory of Black Electoral Success

In this essay, written in 1990 and 1991, I begin by setting out the assumptions about political participation that animated the Civil Rights Movement. I contrast this vision to the now dominant view of black political success, which puts all faith in electing black representatives. I call this new approach "the theory of black electoral success." This new theory is based on four assumptions about black elected officials: (1) they are authentic psychological and cultural role models; their election (2) mobilizes black voter participation and (3) reduces electoral polarization by transforming cross-racial contact from the anonymity and ignorance of the ballot box to the intimacy and expertise of the legislature; and (4) black representatives respond to the needs of all their constituents, including blacks. I believe that the theory, as well as each of its assumptions, are flawed. The theory of black electoral success supplanted the more transformative and inclusionary vision of the original civil rights activists. The narrowing of the original civil rights movement's goals came in response to pressures from judges and others involved in legal advocacy.

Chapters 3 and 4 were directed originally to an academic audience. The concluding section of chapter 3 and the introductory section of chapter 4 have been deleted so that these chapters, which were written to stand alone, can now be read together.

For almost two decades, the conventional civil rights political empowerment agenda of black activists, lawyers, and scholars has focused on the

41

election of black representatives.[1] The belief that black representation is everything has defined litigation strategy under the Voting Rights Act.[2] Through judicially enforced spurs to black electoral success, black voters gain political self-confidence and legislative influence.

A set of submerged premises and assumptions concerning the goals and strategies for achieving black equality underlie this empowerment agenda.[3] Through use of what I characterize as "the theory of black electoral success," this chapter identifies, organizes, and presents these related propositions. In black electoral success theory, empowerment is obtained through meaningful enfranchisement, which exists where blacks are elected. The theory thus promotes the election of individual black representatives as spokesmodels for political equality.[4] Simply by virtue of election opportunities, black electoral success advances civil rights enforcement, government intervention on behalf of the poor, and black "role-model" development.

Although pervasive and influential, the theory of black electoral success has not been explicitly endorsed as a strategy or articulated as a coherent conceptual model. Neither political science nor legal academic literature has provided voting rights lawyers, courts, or activists with a clear theoretical understanding of their project.[5] Instead, black electoral success has been pursued somewhat unself-consciously as the inchoate rationale and frame of reference for black political and legal empowerment.

In this chapter, my goal is to organize the divergent themes of black electoral success strategy within one conceptual framework in order to give the themes more cogency and attention.[6] Having exposed the existence of a coherent theory, I then argue that the theory posits many of the correct goals but fails to provide a realistic mechanism for achieving them. The article proceeds as follows: In Part I, I develop the ideological and statutory roots of black electoral success theory. In Part II, I analyze the inadequacies of current voting rights litigation and its failure to realize the statute's original goals. I conclude in Part II by arguing that contemporary preoccupation with black electoral success stifles rather than empowers black political participation for three reasons. First, black electoral success theory romanticizes black elected officials as empowerment role models. By ignoring problems of tokenism and false consciousness, the theory promotes black electoral success in order to legitimate the ideology of "equality of opportunity."[7]

Second, even in jurisdictions with proportionate black representation, black electoral success has neither mobilized the black community nor realized the promised community-based reforms. As an empowerment mechanism, electoral control of winner-take-all majority-black districts ignores critical connections between broad-based, sustained voter participation and accountable representation. In addition, although it claims legitimacy as a practical enforcement mechanism of the original goals of the civil rights movement, district based electoral ratification enforces only one of three original goals. While the current approach may result in the election of more black officials, it ignores the movement's concern with broadening the base of participation and fundamentally reforming the substance of political decisions.

Third, the theory assumes that majority winners rule legitimately, even where such rule leads to permanent minority losers. The theory responds to minority disadvantage not by challenging majority rule but by providing a few electoral districts in which blacks are the majority.[8] Consequently, black electoral success theory simply reconfigures winner-take-all electoral opportunities into geographically based, majority-black, single-member districts. Representing a geographically and socially isolated constituency in a racially polarized environment, blacks elected from single-member districts have little control over policy choices made by their white counterparts. Thus, although it ensures more representatives, district-based black electoral success may not necessarily result in more responsive government.

I. The Roots of Black Electoral Success Theory

As both an activist and a litigation strategy, black electoral success theory evolved from the civil rights movement's empowerment vision. The movement viewed broad-based political participation and representation as instrumental to community autonomy and to community-based reform. The theory of black electoral success emerged in response to pressure for judicial supervision of the movement's political agenda. To create a judicially manageable standard to enforce the Voting Rights Act, litigation adopted and modified the theory. By focusing narrowly on electing black officeholders, however, the litigation strategy and the theory eventually eclipsed the movement's wide-angled focus on transformative politics.

The perception that blacks were not effectively represented in majority-white jurisdictions because of racially polarized voting formed the basis of the litigation strategy. Essentially activists holding this view believed that officials elected by a bloc voting white majority ignored the

interests of black voters without suffering any adverse electoral consequences. Where such vote "dilution"[9] was established, black electoral
success theory justified majority-black remedial subdistricts in which
black registered voters exercised electoral control.[10] The litigation strategy posited electoral ratification within majority-black single-member
districts as an appropriate mechanism for ensuring government accountability and responsiveness to black interests.[11]

In this Part, I begin by presenting the civil rights movement's vision of
representation, participation, and legislative reform. I then demonstrate
how the voting rights litigation agenda altered that vision.

A. The Civil Rights Movement's Theory of Political Participation

The civil rights movement's vision of black political empowerment ema-
nated from mass protests to achieve basic enfranchisement. Movement
activists perceived the rights to register and cast a ballot as foundational
for political action, effective social change, and redress from, and representation in, government. These rights were important not only for blacks
but for the advancement of a progressive agenda in general.[12] The movement was based on a redistributive theory of "representation and the
right to participate," which engaged the political empowerment agenda of
both 1960s integrationists and nationalists.[13]

The focus on disfranchisement materialized in the early 1960s, reflecting a major shift from protest to politics.[14] Black voter registration and
political participation gradually became the movement's dominant vehicle for implementation of its legislative agenda.[15] Although some activists
initially failed to appreciate the dramatic potential of voter education and
registration, particularly in light of headlines generated by nonviolent integrated bus rides, electoral participation soon became the way to redeem
southern politics.[16]

The Kennedy administration, preoccupied with incremental reform,
supported voter registration efforts because these efforts appeared to be
less threatening and disruptive.[17] Robert Moses and other black voter registration activists, however, defended their work as the most promising
response to indigenous efforts to transform local reality.

The Voting Rights Act was enacted in 1965 following "sustained national pressure"[18] to include all Americans in the liberal, democratic electoral process. Some commentators have argued that the Act, which was
passed and signed into law barely four months after its formal introduc-

tion, represented the civil rights movement at its most commanding. Critics, however, have suggested that the Act's electoral strategy reflects the triumph of tokenism.

Yet both proponents and critics agree that the Voting Rights Act united the black ideological spectrum. The Act's passage bridged the divergent aims of integration and nationalism[19] in ways that both committed the black community to collective action in pursuit of political power and camouflaged the tension between assimilation and recognition of racial group identity and interests. Through concerted political action, integration and nationalism converged.

For integrationists and many nationalists, the struggle for effective use of the ballot became "the number one civil right."[20] Black activists saw political empowerment as a vehicle for mobilizing the black community, articulating a black social and economic agenda, and electing both authentic black and responsive white officials.[21]

1. POLITICAL PARTICIPATION: MOBILIZING THE BLACK COMMUNITY. The goals of community autonomy and participatory democracy inspired the consensus demanding meaningful access to electoral politics. The idea of community autonomy evolved from a group consciousness that reflected a collective identity shaped by historic conditions and social realities. To differing extents, group identification reflected a shared perception that triggered collective activity. Group solidarity and a general mistrust of the fairness of existing resource allocation increased the likelihood of political activity. Group consciousness connected conceptions of efficacy to political participation.[22] Indeed, both integrationists and nationalists envisioned political struggle as the means to group salvation.[23]

The concept of participatory democracy[24] was the heart of the civil rights "mass movement." Developing a political identity was critical to the movement's efforts to cultivate a grass roots base. Political organizing, particularly in support of black candidates, continued the movement's affirmation of self-worth and human dignity. Electoral politics awakened blacks to their humanity, their heritage, and their potential, as citizens, to participate *equally* in democratic self-government.[25] As one activist observed:

> I think one of the things that made the delegation of the Mississippi Freedom Democratic party so hopeful, so expectant, was the fact that people had made a discovery that there is a way out of much that is wrong with our lives, there is a way to change it, and that is through the execution of this

vote. . . . That's the way we arrived in Atlantic City—really excited about the fact that we were at long last going to be able to participate, to be represented.[26]

The movement's leadership continuously reinforced interaction with and equal participation by its "excited" grass roots base. Behind the movement's protest strategies were civil rights activists, the seminal political campaign workers, with their "tireless enthusiasm for door-to-door persuasion"[27] and their open welcome to "anyone who will work, regardless of affiliation or ideology."[28] Civil rights workers planted themselves in the daily struggles of local blacks. They followed an activist model of continuous community education and political campaigning,[29] as illustrated by attempts of the SNCC workers to teach blacks in the rural south how to pass literacy tests.

For many black nationalists as well, political participation by a self-consciously black community was important. The nationalists believed that a sense of community and group solidarity would potentially broaden political participation and include more blacks in the decisionmaking process.[30] Political enfranchisement would "make participants, not recipients, out of . . . a traditionally excluded [people]."[31]

2. POLITICAL PARTICIPATION: PROMOTING A SOCIAL AND ECONOMIC AGENDA. Although basically engaged in liberal reform to provide a mainstream vehicle for advancement, voting rights activists sought also to expand the liberal vision toward a redistributive agenda premised on equality of condition, and not just freedom from overt discrimination.[32] Rather than a self-limiting movement to assimilate blacks into the councils of government, the original civil rights message endorsed, through the right to vote, broad notions of freedom from hunger, poverty, and discrimination.[33] Both nationalists and integrationists supported a common agenda on issues of civil rights enforcement and social welfare spending.[34]

American principles of equality and democracy were not the only factors compelling the representation of blacks through universal suffrage. Full political enfranchisement also would help complete the movement's "social revolution."[35] Blacks, like Fannie Lou Hamer, advocated "true democracy" and not merely equality within the existing order. By registering and voting, blacks could get people "outa office that [they] know was wrong and didn't do nothin' to help the poor."[36]

Participation in the dominant political system did not necessarily mean assimilating its substantive assumptions or power arrangements. Black nationalists in particular asserted that blacks could gain political power without becoming indistinguishable from other groups in society.[37] Instead of becoming absorbed by the political mainstream, blacks could change it.[38]

Preoccupied with development of group identity and political and cultural expression, the nationalists shifted black activist concerns away from integration and coalition building. The nationalists, however, still supported electoral strategies[39] because they believed, as did the integrationists, that political participation would lead to more responsive, black community-oriented legislation.

3. POLITICAL PARTICIPATION: ELECTING RESPONSIVE OFFICIALS. By concentrating on political participation, black activists hoped to achieve a fundamentally different political reality created in part by responsive government decisionmakers. Because access to the political process was measured, both pragmatically and ideologically, by the authenticity and responsiveness of elected candidates, the energy of the civil rights mass movement became focused on political organizing to elect black officials.

In general, black political leaders would temper the rhetoric and overt racism of white elected officials.[40] In particular, black representatives would, by definition, constitute a progressive force affirmatively promoting black interests. In addition, with blacks in office, white business and political leaders who wanted information about blacks would no longer be dependent on their own menagerie of responsible "Negro leadership."[41] Led by black elected officials, black voters would also be positioned both to articulate their own "interests" and to challenge racially motivated or insensitive legislation.[42] Black elected officials thus ensure black voters a voice in the process of allocating government benefits.

Black electoral success generated interest in and captured the momentum of the first two civil rights concerns: mobilization and reform. The connection between black electoral success and mobilization was demonstrated during voter registration activity in the early 1960s. In Mississippi, some voter registration activists sought to run black candidates for Congress with the expectation not of winning, but of planting the idea of voting in the minds of blacks.[43] In response to local white sheriffs' excessive use of force against civil rights activists, blacks were urged to "Get the vote and pin that badge on a black chest."[44] Even the most inflammatory use in the late 1960s of the slogan, "Black Power," was an organizing tool to inspire political organization, to promote racial pride, and to provide a vehicle for black leadership.[45]

Civil rights activists linked electoral success to community based reform by assuring that black representatives, who were authentic community-based leaders, would be the vanguard for a new social justice agenda.[46] For example, black electoral aspirations stemmed, at least in part, from the belief that a black sharecropper, if *elected* tax assessor, would take a different view of taxing the poor.

Election by a mobilized group of blacks was critical to the black official's legitimacy. The movement's unifying objective was to empower the black community, not simply its representatives.[47] King, in particular, condemned electoral opportunism by black politicians deaf to the demands of their community.[48] In addition, both the nationalists and the integrationists sought to elect descriptively black officials.

For the integrationist, litigation to achieve black electoral success incorporated the preeminent process theory of empowerment: measuring political equality by the fairness of the process through which representatives were elected. Along with other liberal views about individual rights and democratic self-government, integrationists cheerfully argued that a group has its requisite degree of political power if it is able to elect a fair number of representatives.

The nationalists asserted that the community could self-consciously develop a strategy of social and economic transformation by participating in politics on the basis of group power. The nationalists, however, also soon supported the black electoral success strategy as a shortcut to achieving recognition of group identity and to providing a mechanism for channeling group solidarity. Because black representatives were both authentic community leaders and legitimated by black voter support, they compelled greater support than sympathetic white officials. Propelled by the basic "essentialism"[49] of the nationalist position as well as the undeniable reality of ethnic politics and racial group segregation, both the integrationists and the nationalists[50] accepted a theory of representation based on four assumptions about black elected officials: (1) black officials were authentic because of their community and cultural roots; (2) they gained authority from the fact of election; (3) they were legitimate because of community mobilization and enthusiasm; and (4) they were presumptively responsive members of a historically, socially, and politically stigmatized group with strong and cohesive civil rights, redistributive, and community-based agendas.

B. The Evolution of a Legal Strategy of Political Empowerment

The civil rights movement empowerment vision was a statement of strategy and faith. After passage of the Voting Rights Act, that vision collapsed.

Litigation to enforce the Voting Rights Act transformed the original goals of broad-based voter participation, reform, and responsive representation into the shorthand of counting elected black officials. In addition, judicial interpretation of the statute compressed the civil rights movement's capacious conception of political representation, redistribution, and participation into a narrow electoral focus on black representation.

The 1965 Voting Rights Act was a landmark piece of legislation.[51] The Act responded directly to the most urgent claims of activists challenging direct impediments to registration and voting. In drafting the Act, Congress was concerned with eradicating discrimination "comprehensively and finally" from every election in which voters were eligible to cast ballots.[52] Passed[53] and amended[54] to promote black political representation, the Act contemplates the right to vote as the right to meaningful political participation and to an effective voice in government.[55] The right to vote is the right to effective representation: the ultimate instrument of reform.[56]

Yet, within contemporary voting rights jurisprudence, mere electoral control by black voters over their representatives has come to satisfy the Act's conception of representation. In search of a statutory core value and judicially manageable standards, the courts have cobbled from the statute a right to minority electoral success. The courts have ignored statutory language providing for the "opportunity . . . to participate [equally] in the political process" and instead have focused exclusively on language securing the "opportunity . . . to *elect* the representatives of [the protected group's] choice."[57] Especially since 1986, the courts have measured black political representation and participation solely by reference to the number and consistent election of black candidates. The submergence of black electoral potential and the subsequent emergence of black voting majorities capable of electing black candidates have become the preferred indicia of a statutory violation. Issues of voter participation, effective representation, and policy responsiveness are omitted from the calculus.

Given the development of voting rights jurisprudence, current judicial interpretation of the Act is not surprising. Initially, blacks focused primarily on first generation, direct impediments to electoral participation, such as registration and voting barriers.[58] Once these obstacles were surmounted, however, the focus shifted to second generation, indirect structural barriers such as at-large, vote-diluting elections.[59]

With its winner-take-all rules, the at-large election format, instituted by many southern jurisdictions in response to increased black registration, essentially allowed a bloc voting racial majority to control all the elected positions. Fifty-one percent of the population consistently de-cided one hundred percent of the elections. In addition, although every-one had one vote, some votes were qualitatively less important than others because of the voter's or the candidate's race or both. As a result, the black minority was permanently excluded from meaningful participation.[60]

Thus, second generation voting rights litigation focused on "qualitative vote dilution." Voting rights activists sought to elect more black officials, primarily by creating majority-black single-member districts. Indeed, by 1980, the right most closely associated with the Act was that of casting a "meaningful" vote for someone who could get elected.[61]

In 1982, Congress amended the Act to include the right to a meaning-ful vote. A "meaningful vote" became explicitly a vote for a viable minority preferred representative.[62] In addition, the amendments provided that dilution claims could be proved based on discriminatory results alone. Al-though not sufficient to establish a violation, the absence of black elected officials is circumstantial evidence, according to the Act's text, of discrim-inatory results.[63]

From the perspective of its legislative history, the 1982 statute gave litigants a flexible tool and a broad mandate to challenge inequalities in the political process. Moreover, the statutory language seemed vague enough to cover a wide range of political disablements. Indeed, in light of this vagueness, supporters hoped a "core value" would be discovered, dis-tinct from either proportional representation or discriminatory purpose. To those reading the legislative history, it appeared as if Congress had, consistent with the Act's mandate to protect *full* exercise of the franchise by black voters,[64] avoided both finger pointing and finger counting.[65] Within the wide net cast by the statute, no particular factor could govern all cases. Yet, once the statute was enacted, the predictable search began for a justiciable formula, ostensibly structured around a central, measur-able factor. Foreordained by the nature of their adjudicative task, courts attempted to discover which factor could become the first among equals, the center around which to balance the other variables.

The linchpin of pre-1982 constitutional dilution challenges had been unresponsiveness. But unresponsiveness, an obvious metaphor for polit-ical exclusion, was elusive as an evidentiary tool and almost as difficult and divisive as proving discriminatory purpose.[66] Thus, in its place, post-1982 litigators favored evidentiary factors more sensitive to sophis-ticated social science techniques and less malleable by unsympathetic judges. These litigators drew from the one person/one vote quantitative dilution cases, where the issue of impermissible vote dilution was measured by "objective" evidence of numerical deviations from absolute equality.[67]

Because arithmetic had proved useful in the quantitative dilution cases, voting rights activists advanced comparable solutions to their evidentiary quandary. Activists sought an easily identifiable, uniformly enforceable proxy for the judicial inquiry into dilution jurisprudence. Expert witnesses were hired to provide "objective" evidence of racial vote dilution.[68] In particular, the capacity to prove racial bloc voting developed through application of computer technology to precinct by precinct election results. As a result, the "core value" for racial vote dilution cases shifted to reflect the value of social science evidence. The apparent ability of statistics to simplify and objectify racial bloc voting obviated the need for other "gauzy" sociological evidence.[69]

In addition to its evidentiary sensitivity, litigation focusing on racial bloc voting had theoretical appeal. The "extent to which voting in the [jurisdiction was] racially polarized"[70] provided a critical rationale for rejecting election arrangements that diluted and submerged black voting strength. If whites refused to vote for black candidates, and whites were in the majority, then political market failure existed. Although politics involves winners and inevitable losers, pluralist theory depends on a fluid exchange between the two. If one group is permanently excluded, political remedies ultimately will be bypassed in favor of less mainstream alternatives.[71]

That whites and blacks voted in racial blocs ultimately became the preferred evidentiary linchpin. Many courts, however, still felt adrift in a sea of factors. Jurisprudential parameters establishing cause and effect, not just evidentiary anchors, were needed.[72] Courts demanded judicially manageable instructions which dictated where to draw the line between marginal and substantive claims. If dilution was the submergence of minority votes in a racially polarized electorate, then courts needed a mechanism for distinguishing that phenomenon from undilution. The courts looked to the language of the statute for an answer.

Because the key statutory phrase characterized equal opportunity in the political process in terms of being able to elect "representatives of choice," judicial intervention appeared to be limited to claims that racially polarized voting denied blacks the ability to elect viable black candidates. Black electoral success, which apparently defined undilution, became the statutory metaphor for equal political opportunity.[73] The right to a meaningful voice through voting thus became simply the right to elect minority "representatives of choice."

The litigation model's conception of representation produced a very limited vision of the relationship between black voters and black elected officials. Neither the degree of responsiveness of the elected official nor the tendency of the electoral process to depress black participation triggered coverage.[74] The fact of election was the threshold factor.[75] Mere electoral ratification by black voting majorities supposedly assured representational authenticity, authority, legitimacy, and responsiveness.

In addition to proving the existence of dilution, black electoral success also became the preferred remedy. Once a violation was established, the cure was to subdivide larger, heterogeneous electorates into smaller, homogeneous, majority-black districts where black voters could elect candidates of their choice to the governing body.[76]

Full exercise of the franchise was the Act's ennobling goal. But, juridical preference for easy-to-apply, judicially manageable racial vote dilution standards prompted the search for quantifiable and uniform measures of empowerment. Litigators sought standards they could meet by using less costly social science evidence. In addition, Congress' failure to articulate a clear core value for defining political equality prompted voting rights lawyers to advance interpretations of the statutory scheme in response to complaints about the absence of black representation within the context of a viable, judicial remedy.

Voting rights case law thus evolved within a racial justice model that accepted as its premise the fact that people of different races often lived and voted differently from each other. Rather than insisting that such separateness and difference be eradicated, as in the school desegregation context, or that poor blacks, isolated from and stigmatized by an unresponsive government, be afforded equal government services, as in equalization of municipal services litigation, the Voting Rights Act model of racial justice recognized racial difference. Group perspective was valued and legitimated by promoting electoral opportunities for black representation. Using the conjunction of racial identifiability and geographic insularity as a convenient proxy for societal discrimination and political group consciousness, the litigation vision of political equality promulgated four complementary assumptions that eventually became the theory of black electoral success.

First, the litigation focused exclusively on electoral outcomes. The absence of black elected officials became both the symptom and the cause of political inequality. In other words, political equality was defined exclusively in terms of the electoral opportunities afforded a "fair" number of authentic—meaning chosen by the community—black representatives.

Second, the right to political equality was granted as a premise. But as the concept to which the statutory right referred, "political equality" required definition. Ultimately, the phrase was defined in terms of the ability of black voters to elect black representatives in rough proportion to their presence in the population.

Although the voting rights model explicitly rejected "quotas," choosing instead to speak in terms of "results," numerical proportionality sufficed to establish legality. If twelve percent of elected officials nationwide were black, presumably reflective of the percentage of blacks within the population, the litigation model of political equality was satisfied.

Thus, roughly proportionate black representation legitimated the electoral process. The idea underlying this concept was that only after previously excluded groups were successful within the electoral process would the white majority learn to accept black representatives as colleagues in collective governance;[77] only then would blacks invest in the normal channels of electoral mobilization and eschew more activist protest strategies.[78] These themes formed the basis for the authenticity and electoral mobilization assumptions of a black empowerment theory of representation.

Third, majority rule was unquestioned as long as the majority admitted a fair number of blacks to its decisionmaking council. Minority electoral presence "softened the harshness of the principle of majority rule."[79] By virtue of their electoral success within majority-black districts, black representatives had representational presence, which was equated with authority and responsiveness to their distinctive group interests.

Fourth, political equality was judicially enforced by subdividing the electorate into single-member districts, a "fair" number of which were controlled by black voters. Single-member districting was the judicially preferred remedy for electoral discrimination. Moreover, the chosen enforcement mechanism, electoral ratification in majority-black single-member districts, itself became a goal because it appealed as a pragmatic, political tool to both the integrationists and the nationalists.

Both nationalists and integrationists contemplated that small districts, controlled by black majorities, would be the best tool for ensuring minority inclusion, encouraging greater citizen involvement in decisionmaking processes, simplifying organizing efforts, and reflecting residential and social segregationist reality. The emergence of black majority electoral districts became a justiciable proxy for black inclusion in the exercise of government authority. This remedy satisfied the activists, who eventually abandoned a mass movement in exchange for election-oriented litigation campaigns.[80]

As an enforcement mechanism, the black single-member district strategy achieved three separate functions: first, it provided a successful litigation approach to challenge the failure of the election to produce elected black officials; second, it gave courts a justiciable standard to determine the problems and progress that were closely related to the ultimate limits of the voting rights inquiry; and third, as I argue in the next Part, it "inescapably closed the door" on the real goal of the civil rights movement, which was to alter the material condition of the lives of America's subjugated minorities.[81]

II. The Theory of Black Electoral Success

Q: Now, why would you come from Crittenden County to participate in a fundraiser for a county race that was basically a local race to Phillips County?

A: Well, the reason I would come, first of all, there are no blacks elected to a county position in eastern Arkansas and no blacks serving in the House of Representatives in eastern Arkansas and no blacks elected to anything other than school boards in districts that are predominantly black. And I feel like blacks should be elected to public office because they should have a chance to serve.

And I want to help get blacks elected so little black children can see them serving and I want to dispell (sic) the myth that some white kids might have that blacks can't serve or shouldn't be serving at the courthouse. And when my little girl goes to the courthouse or when other little girls go to the courthouse, I want them to be able to see black people working up there.

And if we can get some blacks elected at the local level, eventually we can—blacks will have the expertise and we can groom them to the point where they can run for the state legislature and other positions. . . .[82]

Black electoral success theory defines representation of black people by black legislators as the ultimate empowerment goal of structural reform legislation and litigation. The theory contains four basic assumptions: (1) the authenticity assumption; (2) the mobilization/electoral control assumption; (3) the polarization assumption; and (4) the responsiveness/reform assumption. District-based electoral ratification by black voters is the theory's primary enforcement mechanism.

In this Part, I analyze and criticize each of these assumptions. I conclude that the black electoral success empowerment model fails to provide a realistic enforcement mechanism for establishing either leadership accountability within the black community or representational effectiveness within the legislative deliberation and coalition-building process.

The theory marginalizes black leadership and leads to token representation. Black electoral success theory has failed to comprehend, or even to examine, the nature of representation within collective decisionmaking bodies controlled by prejudice and external inequalities.

My critique of the black electoral success model rests essentially on three claims. First, the status of blacks as a discrete, disadvantaged minority cannot be addressed simply by mobilizing blacks to turn out on election day to elect more black candidates. Black representatives are not necessarily effective advocates for legislative responsiveness.

Second, the prejudice and hostility facing blacks within the political process cannot be eradicated by creating majority-black single-member districts from which black candidates can be elected. Black legislators, especially those representing geographically segregated districts, may be victims of prejudice. Thus, if racially polarized voting results in electoral market failure, then the concept of political empowerment must also address failed legislative decisionmaking. Minority empowerment requires minority legislative influence, not just minority legislative presence. In other words, blacks must develop explicit mechanisms for overcoming majority prejudice in the governing policymaking body.

Finally, the first two claims will not be fully resolved until we focus on the concept of proportionate interest representation, which has received virtually no attention from civil rights lawyers or scholars. By directly undermining the legitimacy of winner-take-all majority rule, proportionate interest representation responds to domination by a hostile, permanent majority.

A. *The Authenticity Assumption: Black Elected Officials Are Authentic Role Models*

Authentic black representation, or "descriptive" representation,[83] is the first important building block for those who believe in black electoral success theory. Authenticity refers to community-based and culturally rooted leadership. The concept also distinguishes between minority-sponsored and white-sponsored black candidates.[84] Basically, authentic representation describes the psychological value for some people of having similarly situated representatives. The term is suggestive of the essentialist impulse in black political participation: because black officials are black, they are representative. Thus, authenticity reflects the importance of race in defining the character of black political participation.[85]

Authentic leadership is electorally supported by a majority of black voters and is, at its best, culturally similar to its constituency base. Thus, authenticity subsumes two separate concepts, the political and the cultural. Black representatives are authentic because they are elected by blacks *and* because they are descriptively similar to their constituents. In other words, they are politically, psychologically, and culturally black.

1. POLITICAL AUTHENTICITY.   Authentic leaders are those elected by black voters. In voting rights terminology, electoral ratification from majority-black, single-member districts establishes authenticity. These facts distinguish the authentic representatives from those officials who are handpicked by the "establishment," or who must appeal to white voters in order to get elected.[86] Establishment-endorsed blacks are unlikely to be authentic where they are not *elected* as the representatives of choice of the black community.[87] In addition, these officials are not "of" the community if they are marginal community members whose only real connection with black constituents is skin color. Electoral support by a majority of black voters is thus a convenient proxy for political authenticity.

2. CULTURAL AND PSYCHOLOGICAL AUTHENTICITY.   In addition to electoral ratification, authenticity refers to a cultural and psychological view of group solidarity. Black representatives are not just physically black. Because they grew up being black, these officials enjoy a cultural and psychic linkage that cuts across class lines. Those who promote black electoral success as an empowerment theory believe that black elected officials, who are physically and culturally similar to their constituents, fulfill the black community's need for self-affirmation through "role models."

From students protesting the absence of black college and law professors, to church leaders ostensibly supporting black community needs, black activists and white sympathizers consistently describe their efforts, at least to some extent, in terms of finding and promoting black role models. By their presence, role models articulate black interests and represent the needs of aspiring young blacks.[88] Role models are living symbols of the equal opportunity process.[89] They reflect the importance of group consciousness to black psychic identity.

Black elected officials are among the most prominent "role models." The election of black representatives affirms that blacks are participating citizens who take an active interest in policy decisions that affect their lives. Authentic representatives also provide psychological uplift by affirming black culture, humanity, and group solidarity.

In the electoral context, role models mediate the paradox of a representative democracy in which all citizens are equal, but some are more equal than others.[90] Including all sectors of society in government operation is consistent with Madison's vision.[91] In a representative democracy, however, all citizens cannot be directly involved in decisionmaking. Some citizens are either "actually" or "virtually" represented.[92] Role model theory justifies the representative principle by referring to a black leadership aristocracy which leads other blacks by virtue of their own achievement and sense of social responsibility.[93] The idea of a black leadership aristocracy was no doubt influenced by W.E.B. Du Bois' repudiated belief in a "talented tenth."[94]

As role models, these black achievers presumptively represent equal opportunity. With few exceptions, their election signals that society's institutions are "color-blind" pure meritocracies.[95] Role models, who convey the message "We Have Overcome," also inspire those not yet overcoming.[96] Thus, in general, black role models are powerful symbolic reference points for those worried about the continued legacy of past discrimination.

Some critics assert that the authenticity assumption is a meaningless cultural and descriptive concept. For example, Abigail Thernstrom, an outspoken critic of the conventional empowerment model, denies the empirical or theoretical validity of culturally similar representatives, because whites can represent black interests.[97] Thernstrom attempts to revive the theory of virtual representation in which black interests are occasionally taken into account even if they are not actively promoted. Thernstrom argues that the single act of voting for any representative legitimates democratic self-government.[98]

Thernstrom's emphasis on color-blind, virtual representation abstracts the black experience from its historical context. Virtual representation ignores the existence of group identity within the black community. Thernstrom's theory reduces electoral participation to the individual unit within the voting booth. At that level, the perception is most acute that one vote will have a negligible effect on the ultimate outcome.[99] Moreover, in neglecting the role of blacks and whites as politically cohesive groups, Thernstrom's electoral self-legitimating focus fails to acknowledge the role that group identity plays in mobilizing political participation and influencing legislative policy.[100] Empirical research also refutes the efficacy of race-neutral theories of virtual representation.[101]

Even when elected officials are unresponsive and voters do not participate enthusiastically, some scholars suggest that voters are still virtually or collectively represented if the legislature as a whole is representative.[102] These scholars suggest that representation is an institutional rather than a personal relationship.[103] Black electoral success proponents dismiss such arguments as self-serving, because "institutional representation" has widened the gap between whites and blacks[104] and has resulted in general voter disenchantment.[105]

I, too, reject the criticism that authentic black representation is meaningless. Authenticity reflects the group consciousness, group history, and group perspective of a disadvantaged and stigmatized minority. Authenticity recognizes that black voters are a discrete "social group"[106] with a distinctive voice. As I argue below, authentic representation also facilitates black voter mobilization, participation, and confidence in the process of self-government.

Authenticity, however, is a limited empowerment tool. As a descriptive matter, authenticity uses the nominally cultural to obscure its substantively political meaning. Although an important source of authority and legitimacy, electoral ratification by black voters fails to furnish a consistent mechanism for establishing community-based credentials or leadership accountability. Electoral success by culturally and ethnically black candidates in majority-white jurisdictions does not necessarily mean that black concerns will be addressed.

For example, where "authentic blacks" are elected by whites with significant black support, electoral ratification by a majority of those blacks voting may not in fact send a recognizable message regarding substantive policies.[107] Especially in winner-take-all electoral systems, "the aggregation device of the election garbles these messages, producing winners while obscuring the reasons for their victories."[108] Thus, even where black support provides a critical margin,[109] successful black candidates in majority-white electorates may not necessarily feel obligated to black voters.[110]

B. The Mobilization Assumption

The mobilization assumption claims that black electoral success directly affects black political participation at the grassroots level.[111] To the extent that blacks can be encouraged to participate in the political process, the possibility of electing a "first" black tends to increase election day turnout.[112] Indeed, the courts and commentators have recognized that the inability to elect black candidates depresses black political participation.[113]

The mobilization assumption measures representational effectiveness based on the ability of black candidates to increase black election day turn-out. Both this assumption and the authenticity assumption presume that black voters will vote for, respect, be affirmed by, and seek services from black elected officials. Neither assumption, however, proposes an ongoing relationship between the representative and the represented. Nor do the assumptions provide a mechanism, other than electoral ratification, for measuring representativeness. In addition, authentic black elected officials may not effectively mobilize sustained black participation, even when measured by the mobilization assumption's own terms.

The mobilization assumption fails to anticipate the difficulties that black candidates in majority-white jurisdictions encounter when they seek simultaneously to appeal to white voters while retaining their black political base. Black voters, who feel neglected and taken for granted by the black candidates "walking the tightrope," may not respond to opportunities for increased black electoral visibility.[114] When blacks are elected by whites with symbolic black support, their victory represents a psychological, but not necessarily substantive triumph.

The mobilization assumption has also depended in large part on empirical evidence supplied by first-time election opportunities. The assumption fails to explain how black electoral success will generate sustained black election day turnout.[115] Reelection opportunities may fail to mobilize voter participation, even in majority-black single-member districts. Because it is the first opportunity to penetrate the previously all-white council that stimulates participation, once the council is integrated, the symbolic importance of electoral visibility is reduced, especially if the representative has become a legislative token, incapable of influencing policy outcomes.

In addition to the above, by focusing exclusively on election day turn-out, the mobilization assumption fails to address any theory beyond symbolic political power.[116] The absence of a concept of representation that demands direct, extended accountability undermines the ability of poor black constituents to participate effectively within geographically insular and politically cohesive districts. The mobilization assumption ignores the need to encourage post election participation by black voters. As a result, voter interests may simply be outweighed by the advantages of incumbency and the perks of patronage.[117]

Even if a black candidate is elected, black voter participation within a relatively homogeneous, insular district may not seem worthwhile because one black representative may not be able significantly to alter public policy. Constituents within isolated single-member districts have little influence over the behavior of representatives from other single-member districts.

Moreover, where blacks form a core but passive electorate, some blacks may simply "manipulate racial symbols and language" to enlist support from the poorest black constituents.[118] Although these elected officials do not respond to constituent needs, under the authenticity and mobilization assumptions, their election and reelection equals black empowerment. Yet, in such circumstances, neither assumption generates sustained, empowering participation in the political process.

C. The Polarization Assumption

The polarization assumption is based on evidence that, absent compelling reasons to do otherwise, whites and blacks vote for persons of their own racial/ethnic background.[119] Thus, in majority-white jurisdictions, racial bloc voting by a white majority inevitably causes the electoral defeat of black candidates. Given racial polarization, black electoral success theory assumes that majority-black single-member districts are needed to overcome black electoral exclusion and to ensure black representational presence. The theory posits that, once elected, black representatives will garner white support and become effective minority participants in legislative negotiations and deliberations.

As a general rule a majority of whites do not vote for blacks. Numerous court decisions,[120] anecdotal reports,[121] surveys,[122] and scholarly studies[123] have confirmed the existence of racial bloc voting. Based on this overwhelming evidence, the polarization assumption concludes that many whites still harbor racial prejudice.[124] Thus, mechanisms to surmount this prejudice and to ensure black electoral success are justified.

According to the polarization assumption, racial bloc voting within the electorate eliminates pluralist bargaining among shifting intergroup coalitions.[125] Where members of the majority consistently refuse to vote for minority-sponsored candidates, blacks are unable to attract enough dissatisfied majority group members to create an effective race neutral majority. White ethnic groups never encountered the problem because, unlike blacks, "an unjust combination of a majority of the whole,"[126] was never so dominant as to silence white ethnic voices over an extended period of time.[127]

While pluralist theories of democracy do contemplate minority losses, they do not necessarily envision a minority that never wins. In other words,

Madison's reliance on checks and balances to control "factions" was both a way to monitor the "special interest" problem *as well as* a hedge against the tyranny of a hostile majority. To fight permanent majority tyranny based on prejudice, voting rights litigation focused on promoting electoral opportunities for black candidates.

The polarization assumption posits that black incumbency tends to diminish prejudice and weaken stereotypes of black incompetence.[128] Black elected officials will assuage white fears by engaging more intimately in legislative deliberations after the election.[129] Black representation is "a crucial lever for obtaining the benefits—patronage, contracts, public services—that must be bargained for in the political arena."[130] Regarding black interests, black representatives will "exert special influence on their colleagues," providing "internal leadership" to which people defer.[131]

Black electoral success advocates assume that prejudice results from ignorance and unfamiliar difference. Once knowledge of similarities is present, or familiarity with differences is facilitated, these advocates contend that black and white elected officials will rationally overcome prejudice and engage freely and equally in pluralistic bargaining or dialogic debate.[132] Particularly on the local level, in small scale, intimate settings, it is hypothesized that black representatives will persuade their colleagues to consider the interests or perspective of black voters.[133]

Black activists have long recognized that blacks cannot become an *effective political majority* without legislative allies. Yet, electing black representatives may simply relocate to the legislature polarization experienced at the polls.[134] Indeed, some political scientists studying "the new black politics" in Cleveland, Chicago, and Atlanta have challenged the working assumption that black electoral success will ultimately reduce polarization.[135] Based on empirical studies of local black officials and city council members, these scholars argue that black representatives often become an ineffective, "seen but not heard" minority in the legislature.[136] Because the individual black elected official may not be able to overcome polarization to "infiltrate the decisionmaking process" at the legislative level,[137] the election of black representatives does not, by itself, translate into intergroup cooperation.

Black representatives may be perceived as tokens or marginalized in the legislative process.[138] Disillusionment produced by such marginality may frustrate attempts at further participation.[139] Without allies, the mere presence of even authentic black representatives does not assure a cooperative environment where normative persuasion and open exchange of ideas prevail.[140]

For example, in Arkansas, blacks successfully challenged a legislative redistricting plan that had produced only four majority-black districts.[141] Black legislators elected from those districts testified that they were an ineffective minority in the overwhelmingly white state legislature.[142] White representatives, including those representing districts with a substantial, extraordinarily poor black constituency, testified that they had no black employees working on their staffs.[143] In addition, these white representatives admitted to using racial slurs to refer to prominent blacks when conversing with other members of the legislature.[144] The presence of blacks in the electorate, one of the bases for the mobilization and polarization assumptions, failed to make these white legislators responsive, even though they represented substantially black constituencies.[145]

Successful black candidates from majority-black districts are also frequently unable to form legislative coalitions that build on and expand their numerical power base. In the Arkansas legislature, the district court found: "Some white members, on being approached by black citizens in their own districts for help, referred these constituents to black legislators representing other areas. And black members have found it difficult to get white members to cosponsor some bills of interest to black voters. . . ."[146] As the most visible members of a stigmatized "out-group," black officials may even be harassed by local officials attempting to suppress black political activity.[147] At least within the black community, the perception is credible that black elected officials are selectively prosecuted.[148]

On the other hand, where black officials are successful in increasing their appeal to white voters, their ability and enthusiasm for advocating on behalf of their black constituents may be undermined.[149] These officials may, for example, attribute their success to individual personality and campaigning rather than issues.[150] These representatives may also be coopted by the dominant majority and thus may effect little substantive change in policy.[151]

Once assimilated into the political mainstream, black officials may define their political agenda without reference to or consultation with a community base.[152] Their reference point may instead become other members of the governing elite with whom they share personal experiences and comparable "rank." With access to prestige rather than power, some black politicians may simply censor themselves in order "to play ball," or characterize political patronage as constituent servicing.[153]

Recognizing that authentic black officials may not be effectively representing the black community does not require that we label all black politicians "as victims of 'false consciousness.' "[154] Authentic representatives are less able to participate effectively in intergroup deliberations primarily because of the dual effects of prejudice and minority status on group dynamics.

To consider effectively all viewpoints, deliberation requires sustained communication and participation among equals.[155] Effective deliberation also demands that group members be receptive to relevant information and willing to compromise.[156] Members of a deliberating body should share information, exchange views, and debate the issues. In addition, the deliberation ideal comtemplates consensus and cooperation derived from honest, good-faith interaction, and not heavy-handed normative pressure.[157]

Testimony from recent cases[158] and research into group processes,[159] however, demonstrate the corrosive power of prejudice on deliberations by collective decisionmaking bodies. Even where minorities are proportionately represented, they may find themselves without allies.

To exert any influence, minority advocates must be consistent and confident. Yet, to advocate consistently and sincerely on behalf of constituents with unpopular viewpoints a representative needs at least one ally.[160] Moreover, absent substantial minority companionship at the beginning of the deliberative process, minority representatives may feel pressured to modify their position in response to the "considerable stress" inflicted by prejudiced majority group members.[161]

Black officials may not be treated with respect in a polarized deliberative process, especially if important debates take place in private, informal, small group settings. Formal rules and sanctions may limit public displays of prejudice and racism.[162] In informal settings, where conduct is less regulated, blatant "microaggressions"[163] against minority victims are more likely. The dynamics of informal groups within the legislature may therefore constrain black/white interaction and deliberation. The number of persons within the deliberative body may also influence the willingness of majority group members to consider minority viewpoints and to counterbalance bias. In smaller groups, minority group members may fail to make critical contributions and are less likely to participate effectively in the deliberation.[164]

In addition, the rules governing the deliberative process may circumscribe a minority group member's influence.[165] Differing decisional rules do not promote fair deliberation to the same extent. Where decisions are made by a simple majority vote, deliberation may be incomplete and less inclusive of minority viewpoints.[166] For example, the "social climate" of deliberation in juries using majority decision rules is more adversarial because members of the majority can reach a decision without responding to opposing arguments.[167]

The presence of members of the minority group often exaggerates in-group solidarity among majority group members. Whether "tokens" or proportionately represented, black elected officials may fail to generate cross-racial alliances. In groups where one race greatly outnumbers the other, group members may treat those in the minority as stigmatized racial tokens. In such "skewed" groups, cross-racial association, laden with cultural and racial overtones, is more difficult to sustain on an issue-by-issue basis.[168] As a result, the numerical minority may be socially segregated and stereotyped even in small, informal deliberative bodies. For example, one black elected official proportionately represented on a small city council operating by majority vote may be isolated and ignored.[169]

Thus, in order for minority groups to participate in winning coalitions, majority group members must be receptive to political bargaining[170] and deliberation. Prejudice against minority group members inhibits admission to the governing majority, ensuring a strategically weak position as a permanent loser.[171] In a racially charged environment, the presence of black representatives may simply increase the value of white membership in the winning coalition.[172] Indeed, the majority may appear to improve its own position by refusing to meet the demands of a minority.

Achieving some degree of reciprocity is essential to sustaining collaborative efforts.[173] Yet, without institutional incentives for cooperation, coalition-building serves only the temporary interests of white allies, who may limit their participation to issues that ultimately promote stability and majority rule. These allies may also choose to leave the coalition.[174] Thus, some scholars, most notably Professor Derrick Bell, have concluded that black rights are recognized only when and to the extent that they coincide with the interests of those in power.[175]

Finally, the mere presence of black officials in the legislature furthers neither the goals of the integrationists nor the nationalists. The integrationists were always concerned with coalition building.[176] They correctly perceived that electoral coalitions affect the ability of representatives to govern.[177] Thus, for some integrationists, coalition building was at the heart of governability. The nationalists also expected more than token representation. For the nationalists black political power meant significant participation in political decisionmaking. Thus, without "more meaningful structures, forms and ways of dealing with long-standing problems," the nationalists felt that political participation did not empower black representatives who enjoyed only a token or proportionate numerical presence.[178]

The polarization assumption ignores these insights. The assumption's hypothesis about the nature of prejudice simply requires blacks to avoid direct electoral competition with whites. Given residential segregation, the assumption supports district election structures to reconfigure a heterogeneous, polarized electorate into a homogeneous one.[179] The assumption correctly perceives that district elections favor black electoral success "because black candidates seeking district seats can steer clear of direct competition with white candidates."[180] District elections also provide greater opportunities to elect people of lower income, education, and status.[181]

Thus, the assumption's predominant enforcement mechanism is black representational control of majority-black districts. This enforcement mechanism enables blacks, through their representatives, to put their case to the legislative majority. Given the prejudices and desires of that majority, however, the mechanism hardly guarantees blacks any real legislative influence.

Although efforts to increase black representation have an independent value, prejudice may simply transfer the "gerrymandering"[182] problem from the electorate to the legislature. Black electoral visibility is useless if district-based electoral arrangements gerrymander legislative decision-making and reproduce in the legislature a mirror image of a racially skewed electorate. With few exceptions, the litigation and activist strategy has thus far failed to anticipate the inevitable third-generation problem: the deliberative gerrymander.[183]

Blacks elected from black single-member districts are less empowered to influence their white colleagues, whose homogeneous white single-member district base enables them to ignore black interests without adverse electoral consequences. For this reason Thernstrom and other conservative critics of the assumption's enforcement mechanism assert that the preoccupation with creating majority-black districts "ghettoizes" black issues.[184] These critics argue that "minority representation might actually be increased not by raising the number of black officeholders [elected from black-districts], but by increasing the number of officeholders, black or white, who have to appeal to blacks to win."[185]

Both conservatives and liberals underestimate the enduring significance of racial polarization to minority empowerment. Thernstrom's call for virtual representation of minority interests by white politicians elected at large reinforces existing unfairness. By ignoring the phenomena of racial bloc voting and white prejudice, Thernstrom rationalizes current distortions in legislative deliberation and bargaining. Similarly, liberal justifications of majority-black districts overlook the negative impact that a prejudiced majority legislative faction may have on the effectiveness of black voters. Black representatives may transcend electoral polarization only to reexperience legislative exclusion because of third generation legislative or deliberative gerrymandering.

Recent voting rights scholarship also fails to consider fully the legislative implications of the polarization hypothesis. For example, Professor Abrams' model of interactive participation suggests that black interests are best represented by aggregating minorities and sympathetic whites within multiracial districts.[186] Abrams' extended, interactive participation model fails to recognize, however, that intergroup cooperation in a polarized environment requires structural support at each stage of the political process if black political influence is not to be contained at every opportunity.[187]

Professor Karlan's cogent process-based civic inclusion theory is also flawed. Essentially the theory would broaden the scope of judicial inquiry from current concerns about geographic districting to more substantive issues such as direct minority participation and decisional responsiveness to minority interests. Enforcement of dilution claims, if based on civic inclusion values, would transcend current judicial preoccupation with majority-black single-member districts and other easy-to-apply mathematical rules.[188]

Karlan's response to the polarization assumption, however, ends with legal protection to ensure minority presence.[189] In this sense, Karlan's vision is as optimistic as Abrams'. Both scholars fail to consider the enduring effect of racism and prejudice on members of both the majority and minority group where racism persists throughout the political process.[190]

D. The Responsiveness Assumption

The responsiveness assumption suggests that black representatives share the original civil rights vision, which targeted the least well off members of the community. In this assumption, black voters gain substantive policy influence by electing racial compatriots with special attachment to and understanding of the black community and its distinctive interests.[191] The assumption also portrays black elected representatives as the first line of defense against racist legislation.

Advocates of the responsiveness assumption believe that black elected officials will discharge their official duties differently from white officials.[192] Black elected officials will intuitively understand the positions favored by their black constituents.[193] Their black constituents also will enjoy a special relationship with black representatives.[194] Thus, increasing the number of black representatives effectively influences legislative policy debates and leads to more favorable substantive political outcomes.

Empirical evidence of racial bloc voting supports the assumption that blacks, to a great extent, are ideologically homogeneous on many issues.[195] Black voting patterns reflect two decades of consensus on the need for greater civil rights enforcement, social welfare expenditures, and government intervention in domestic affairs.[196] Thus, advocates of the responsiveness assumption claim that if more blacks are elected, black voters will be able to reshape the way laws are made and tax dollars are spent to reflect their interests.[197]

Four difficulties exist with the responsiveness assumption. First, the assumption relies too heavily on the singular advancement of authentic individual black officials to transform the status of the group as a whole. Depending on black politicians to shoulder so much of the burden of redistributing resources and power is naive.[198] Even when genuinely concerned, the status of black representatives as "assimilated" members of the political establishment may threaten their commitment to community-based models of reform.[199] Thus, even where feasible, the civil rights movement's goals of government intervention on behalf of the poor may not be generally acceptable to many politicians.[200]

Second, the responsiveness assumption fails because of the message already conveyed to black elected officials by the authenticity assumption. The authenticity assumption converts black elected officials into group spokesmodels without continuously articulating either the basis for a cohesive, community agenda or the responsibility to develop any agenda. The role model is a spokesmodel simply by virtue of being a black elected official.

Yet, as already discussed, black politicians may be electorally successful without being "authentic."[201] The authenticity assumption implicitly encourages black representatives to view their personal advancement as a group advantage and to position themselves to seek higher status based on the attendant privileges of seniority.[202] Elected from "safe" districts, black representatives can afford to spend less time "at home."[203] Thus, black representatives may act even more independently than the responsiveness assumption contemplates.

Third, the vision that prompted the shift from protest to politics may have overestimated the transformative possibilities of electoral activity. Electing individual candidates, even those who are effective and accountable, may fail as a means of creating and redistributing political power and economic wealth.[204] Of course, black electoral success alone cannot transform the depressed political and economic state of the black community, especially given that blacks are concentrated in politically impotent and economically isolated parts of urban metropolitan areas where racial polarization continues.[205] The limitations of black electoral success are also evident when blacks are concentrated in the least influential positions or are elected to posts in largely black municipalities without significant economic resources. The theory is problematic regardless of whether black electoral mobilization positively correlates with white legislative support for black issues.

In response, one might argue that if the goals of poor blacks are restated to appeal more universally to poor and working class whites, then platforms benefiting blacks disproportionately need not alienate whites.[206] Yet, as discussed in conjunction with the polarization assumption, representatives who retain a community-based or generally progressive consciousness may still be ineffective in a polarized legislature. In addition, empirical evidence suggests that race, not class, more often defines political preference.[207]

Fourth, the responsiveness assumption presumes that elections provide the policy issue control postulated by early political scientists of representation.[208] Advocates of the assumption assert that constituents recruit like-minded candidates, who offer descriptive representation. In addition, constituents can vote out officials whose policy views or performance disappoint voter expectations or preferences. This latter assertion assumes that constituents monitor official behavior beyond election day.[209]

The responsiveness assumption adopts this theory of electoral accountability based on the belief that constituents will punish unresponsive representatives at the polls. Where constituents are poor, however, electoral activity may prove too costly, particularly if it involves organizing and campaigning against an incumbent.[210] Even where constituents are not poor, electoral activity inevitably presents collective action problems.[211] In addition, electoral ratification may simply reflect symbolic activity and not any in-depth knowledge of politics.[212] Unless the concept of political participation transcends election day activity, a constituent is not providing much substantive direction simply by casting a ballot.

In addition, election day votes may not adequately convey latent issue conflict within the black community if voters are encouraged to vote for authentic, but not necessarily reformist, black candidates. Although poor and working class blacks may be at the heart of a black electoral majority, they may not form part of the governing coalition put together by middle-class black politicians.[213] Black electoral success theory discourages poor blacks, who may not identify with their middle-class counterparts on every issue, from looking beyond their common racial identity.

In fact, issue cohesion within the black community is generated by common concern about civil rights enforcement, government intervention on behalf of the poor, and increased opportunity for black mobility. On these issues, black representatives may intuitively represent their constituents. But, unless the responsiveness assumption understands the value of sustained voter participation over time and across issues, the emphasis on election day turnout may not forge a common identity if the opponent is also black, or ensure responsive government if the official must contend with countervailing pressures from white business elites.[214]

III. Beyond Black Electoral Success

Black electoral success theory has two major failings. First, the theory abandoned the civil rights movement's transformative vision of politics. In that vision, the purpose of political equal opportunity was to ensure fairness in the competition for favorable policy outcomes, not just fairness in the struggle for a seat at the bargaining table. In addition, legislative responsiveness would not be secured merely by the election day ratification of black representatives. Rather, legislative responsiveness would depend on citizen participation, legislative presence, and legislative success in meeting the needs of a disadvantaged group.

Second, black electoral success theory misses the point of the polarization hypothesis. The theory contains three proceduralist assumptions: one, that technical access usually entails meaningful access to the political process; two, that procedural rules that ensure visibility and technical access draw a neutral line between majority rule and minority rights; and three, that political choices should be made openly and within a process that includes minority representatives. If, however, the majority constitutes itself based on prejudice, as the polarization hypothesis declares, then simply providing technical access for the minority group representatives yields very modest results at best.[215]

Building on these criticisms of black electoral success theory, I propose to shift the analysis of black political empowerment in two ways. First, as a matter of broader democratic theory, voting rights activists and litigators should begin to worry more about the fundamental fairness of permanent majority hegemony in a political system whose legitimacy is based solely on the consent of a simple, racially homogeneous majority. Consistent with fairness, equality, and legitimacy, the original civil rights vision suggests fundamentally different tradeoffs between majority rule and minority rights.

Second, I propose to refocus on the problems affecting marginalized groups within the legislative decisionmaking process. This renewed focus builds on the civil rights movement's view that the values for which our society stands are defined by what we do for the dispossessed. Thus, a theory of representation that derives its authority from the original civil rights' vision must address concerns of qualitative fairness involving equal recognition[216] and just results.[217] For those at the bottom, a system that gives everyone an equal chance of having their political preferences *physically represented* is inadequate. A fair system of political representation would provide mechanisms to ensure that disadvantaged and stigmatized minority groups also have a *fair chance* to have their policy preferences *satisfied*.

In the next chapter, I reexamine the more general theory of majority rule, for we must ask the question that black electoral success theory has ignored at its peril: When does majority rule become the tyranny of the majority?

4

No Two Seats*
The Elusive Quest for Political Equality

This essay, written late in 1991, furthers my critique of current assumptions of black electoral success by examining the weakness of winner-take-all majority rule as generally embodied in single-member districts. As a remedy for political exclusion, districting may fail when electorates are extremely polarized; and districting promotes constituency service but not the higher goal of functional or interest representation. I argue that if we truly hope to represent a diverse set of interests in government, we should in some circumstances consider remedial alternatives to single-member districts. Consideration of these remedies would be triggered by findings of illegal voting discrimination. As alternative remedies, cumulative voting and supermajority rules may open up the political process for politically cohesive minorities, not just racial minorities, and may thereby promote cross-racial coalitions based on mutual interests.

I use these alternative remedies as a baseline for examining the political fairness of both the electoral and legislative decisionmaking process. My exploration of legislative rules focuses on ways to make the process of

---

* "We didn't come all this way for no two seats when ALL of us is tired," Fannie Lou Hamer reportedly responded at the 1964 Democratic National Convention in Atlantic City when the Democratic National Committee offered two seats to the Mississippi Freedom Democratic Party, a grass-roots insurgency group formed to challenge the racially exclusionary practices of the regular Mississippi Democrats. See Frances Lee Ansley, Stirring the Ashes: Race, Class and the Future of Civil Rights Scholarship, 74 Cornell L. Rev. 993, 1049 & n.212 (1989).

legislative decisionmaking more inclusive. If the majority wields dispro-
portionate power based on its prejudices, I conclude that in extreme cir-
cumstances majority domination may become majority tyranny.

The section of this chapter on minority influence districts was origi-
nally written in 1992 and published separately in 1993.

As I explained in the last chapter, the Voting Rights Act was designed to free minority voters from "the near-tyranny of nonrepresentation"[1] and to make state and local government more "responsive."[2] Subsequent amendments confirmed that the statutory goal underlying black empow-erment remains "to help assure adequate representation of all interests"[3] and "to gain the influence that [political] participation brings."[4] Blacks and other statutorily protected minorities are groups whose interests his-torically were unprotected yet were considered by Congress worthy of government attention. To remedy the political system's unresponsiveness the case law under both sections 2 and 5 evolved to protect the group right to vote.[5]

Especially as amended in 1982, the Act anticipates that by exercising the right to elect representatives, blacks as a politically cohesive group will "produce[] fundamental change in state government and affect[] who will represent the people." The Act defined a violation as a denial of an equal opportunity to "participate in the political process and to elect represen-tatives of [the minority groups'] choice." Because entrenched discrimina-tion in the covered jurisdictions persisted, and continues to persist, notwithstanding the Act's passage and reenactments, the United States Supreme Court has consistently interpreted the Act to give it "the broad-est possible scope."

I have argued that the Voting Rights Act was conceived to respond to both political equality and political empowerment visions. The former vi-sion was the realization of the constitutional one person/one vote claim of equal voting weights. Blacks would be afforded the right to vote, and their vote would count as much as that of whites.

The latter vision highlights the moral, as opposed to the arithmetic, proposition implicit in the one person/one vote rule. Political empower-ment means equal voting weight *and* equal voting power. The statutory right to an equally powerful vote reflects the widely shared view that dem-ocratic institutions should provide an equal opportunity to influence po-litical decisions. Derived from the constitutional right to vote, the statutory right is a group right to "full and effective participation" and a voice in government affecting legislative policy. Thus, the statute's broad political equality and empowerment norms, which incorporate both an equality and an empowerment dynamic, focus on the rights of protected voters to limit the extent to which government may disadvantage specific voters, groups of voters, or their interests through voting practices, standards, and procedures.[6] Especially in light of black voters' disadvantaged social and economic status, Congress intended to afford blacks and other statutorily protected groups the opportunity to challenge racial subordination through the political process. Protecting the right to vote furthers the goal of black political empowerment, meaning the opportunity to use the vote to mobilize support within the political process to overcome blacks' depressed and isolated economic and social status.[7]

In this chapter, I use the political equality and political empowerment norms to examine the primary enforcement mechanism of black electoral success theory—the concentration of minority voters within majority minority single-member districts. I evaluate this remedial strategy at the electoral level and at the level of collective decisionmaking within local municipal and county legislative bodies. I conclude that in some circumstances discrete and insular minorities may require protection throughout the political process from the actions of prejudiced, racially homogeneous, local majorities. Where such local majorities exercise power to tyrannize or exclude racial minorities, remedial intervention may sometimes be warranted at the electoral or even the legislative stage. In such extreme instances, alternative decisionmaking rules that embody the ideal of "taking turns" should be considered. These rules are useful primarily as a heuristic to demonstrate the potential unfairness of zero-sum, win-lose voting processes that make some majorities permanent winners and conversely create minorities who are perpetual losers.

I. The Implications of Single-Member Districting for Black Political Influence and Participation

I have already critiqued generally the use made by contemporary voting rights litigation of the second-generation empowerment assumptions. Using both empirical evidence about districting and analytical arguments about majority rule, I now reexamine more specifically the second-generation empowerment model in the particular enforcement context of local county and city government.[8] I evaluate the remedial strategy using the statute's original empowerment goals as modified by black electoral success theory: (1) authentic representation, (2) broad-based, sustained community participation, (3) structurally enforced reciprocity in bargaining or receptivity in deliberation, and (4) accountable policymaking.[9] Although the statute's broad political empowerment norm intends that black voters enjoy an equal opportunity to influence legislative policy, I argue that formally fair voting rules do not all have the same consequence for minority legislative influence and political participation at the local level. To sustain this claim, I fill in the broad outlines of my critique of the contemporary empowerment model by focusing on its primary enforcement mechanism: the subdistricting strategy.

I conclude that the districting model, at least at the local county and municipal level, fails to achieve the political equality and political empowerment objectives of the Voting Rights Act, although it permits physical access to the representative body for minority representatives. First, districting ignores the role of prejudice at the legislative level. Even though such prejudice remains a pervasive problem, the districting model defends majoritarian principles without constraining representatives of the majority to represent, reflect, or accommodate minority interests within local legislative decisionmaking. Second, districting uses a delegate model of representation but fails to ensure substantive accountability to constituents' policy preferences, not just service needs. Third, by focusing on geographic, rather than political, interests, districting depresses the level of political competition and discourages the interactive political organization necessary to mobilize voters to participate meaningfully throughout the political process. In this way, districting fails to realize the moral proposition implicit in the statute's political equality and political empowerment norms that each citizen should have the same chance as every other citizen to influence legislative outcomes.

In Part A, I address the effect of single-member districts on the ability of black representatives to participate effectively in the deliberative and voting process of collective decisionmaking. In two Subparts to that Part, I make first an analytical and then an empirical claim that the subdistricting strategy, to the extent it incorporates winner-take-all majority rule, is not fair. The strategy is unfair because reciprocity and virtual representation, two conditions implicit in the idea of political fairness, are not realized where the majority exercises disproportionate power. Though it can be argued that, as long as some subdistricts are majority-black, black voters are represented whatever the outcome of legislative deliberation and debate controlled by the white majority, subdistricts represent a very poor tradeoff between minority election and minority power.

Thereafter, in Part B, I describe the effect on responsible policymaking of the county or city single-member district representative's relationship with her constituents. Contrary to the tenets of black electoral success theory, it appears that the single-member district strategy may adversely affect black voters' representation. Creating single-member districts does not sustain the electoral participation of blacks, particularly those who are indigent. Disturbingly, this, in turn, reduces the substantive accountability of black representatives to the policy concerns of the black community. Equally troubling is the fact that single-member districts dilute the voting strength of black voters outside the district, as well as the voting strength of other minorities in the district. Lastly, creating single-member districts stifles electoral competition, which further exacerbates the problem of declining voter involvement. From the foregoing, I conclude that the second-generation remedial strategy is ill-advised and that a new remedial focus is needed.

A. *The Districting Model, Virtual Representation, and Majority Rule*

Electing representatives from majority-black, single-member districts may simply transfer the "discrete and insular minority" problem[10] from the polling place to the local municipal or county legislative council. Consider the following recent examples of this phenomenon:

> *Agenda Setting*—After the first Mexican-American woman was elected to the school board in a small Texas county, the board changed its rules for putting items on the agenda. Whereas prior to her election any one member could put an item on the agenda, now it would require a second before issues would be considered.[11]
>
> *Exclusion from Deliberations*—Black legislators within the joint Louisiana senate and house committee for congressional redistricting were excluded from a secret meeting in the subbasement of the senate capitol, where the key members of the committee met with representatives of the governor and *all* other interested parties—except blacks. The result of the closed meeting was a racial gerrymander resembling Donald Duck, including the beak and the webbed feet, slicing with unerring precision through *all* the majority-black districts. When the plan was challenged in court, the reason given for excluding the black legislators was that, in view of the governor's population ceiling for blacks within any congressional district, the black representatives would not have been satisfied with any proposal. Although the plaintiffs' challenge was successful, the three-judge district court declined to reach the question of an intentional,

deliberative gerrymander, notwithstanding the evidence of explicit legislative exclusion and other evidence of discriminatory intent.[12] [" 'We already have a nigger mayor. . . , and we don't need another nigger bigshot.' "[13]]

Denial of a "Meaningful Legislative Vote"—In Etowah and Russell Counties, Alabama, a district court ordered the subdivision of the all-white county commission into single-member districts in response to a Voting Rights Act challenge to the at-large election system. As a result, additional seats were added to the commission, with each commissioner elected from a single-member district. Decisions were made by a simple majority. The white commissioners, who remained on the commission representing majority-white, single-member districts, refused to share the management of road maintenance, which was an important source of patronage in the county. Each of the white commissioners essentially controlled one of the road shops within the county. When the newly elected black commissioners challenged their refusal, the white commissioners in one county offered to delegate the responsibility to a civil engineer, whose decisions would then be approved by a simple majority of the commission.[14]

These examples show some of the myriad ways in which minority representatives can be denied the political clout they would enjoy but for racial prejudice. Minority representatives may be excluded directly from participation, as in Louisiana. Or they may be denied meaningful participation because of changes in agenda-setting rules precipitated by their presence, as in Texas. Or they may experience submergence in majoritarian group voting rules that disproportionately marginalize their status as a permanent, racially homogeneous legislative minority, as in Alabama.

Minority marginalization creates conflict even when caused by the operation of "neutral" decisional rules. The complaints of black students at two predominantly white schools—Brother Rice High School, a boys' Catholic school in Chicago, and Vassar College—that their votes did not count when deciding music playlists and happy hour events serve as a classic example. At Brother Rice High School, the music playlist, determined by giving every student one vote for each of their three favorite songs, shut out black student preferences. Similarly, at Vassar black students who felt "left out and bitter about their experience" broke off and formed their own committee when the senior class commencement committee proposed scheduling "happy hours" at a local bar that has a reputation for being inhospitable to blacks. In a democratic process, even with a few black "voters" on the committee, "your ideas are not necessarily going to be voted on," said Ria Grosvenor, one of the three black former committee members.[15]

Some white students were angry and embittered. They complained that the black students should have gone along with the majority: "The majority makes a decision. That's the way it works." For black students at both schools, however, majority decisionmaking was illegitimate because it shut them out. "For every vote we had, there were eight votes for what they wanted. . . . [W]ith us being in the minority, we're always outvoted. It's as if we don't count."[16]

1. THE ANALYTICAL CLAIM. Simple majority rule assumes that the majority and minority are fungible, meaning that the outcome of voting procedures depends solely on the shape of the distribution of the preferences, and not on which voters hold certain preferences. The scheme assumes further that the minority will support the majority's decision for reasons of stability, efficiency, reciprocity, and accountability. The stability claim is that majority rule reduces conflict because the minority will realize it is outnumbered and, therefore, will accept the majority's decision.[17] Majority decisional rules are also defended as an efficient mechanism for sorting through competing views where the issue can be reduced to two options. The efficiency assumption basically posits that it is easier to get to 51% than 100%; that 51% is less arbitrary than other possible decisional rules; and that the 51% are probably right.[18] Because the majority is probably right *ex hypothesi*, the minority is likely to accept its decision.

The reciprocity claim (also known as the "anonymity" claim) subsumes three related assumptions. First, it presupposes a lack of permanency on the part of the majority. The 51% are legitimate in the eyes of the 49% because the 49% has the opportunity to attract defectors and become the next governing majority. The absence of permanency ensures that the majority will follow the "Golden Rule" (namely, "do unto others as you would have them do unto you") for the simple reason that the majority of today may be the minority of tomorrow. Second, the reciprocity claim subsumes a virtual representation approach. The 51% will look out for the 49% minority as their proxy. The 51% self-interest is essentially public-regarding toward the common good. Third, reciprocity may also operate as a claim for proportionality. The majority will be strong, but it will be unlikely to exercise 100% of the power. Finally, in addition to its reciprocity component majority rule incorporates the electoral accountability assumption that people should rule through electoral ratification. That is, majority rule is a proxy for representative democracy in which those who rule are held accountable through a system of periodic elections.[19]

Without analyzing or contesting these assumptions, many political scientists simply assert that one of the multiple attributes of a fair electoral system is majority rule. Indeed, many merge the concepts of majority rule and democracy. To be legitimate, they argue, a law must have the consent of a majority of the political community. Taking this as the "majoritarian paradigm," democracy becomes synonymous with, and legitimated by, majority rule. Indeed, some argue that the one person/one vote approach of *Reynolds v. Sims*[20] and its progeny constitutionalizes the principle of majority rule.[21]

Yet democracy as majority rule is not self-defining. It could mean control of issue outcomes, voting aggregations to maximize satisfaction, determining the preponderance of opinion, or simply decisionmaking by electorally accountable officials. Indeed, there is an ongoing debate over the existence and possibility of majority rule generally.[22] Some also question directly the presumptive faith in majority rule as quintessentially democratic. Others argue that institutionalizing minority rights is a necessary constraint on the processes of majoritarian democracy.

For the sake of argument, I am prepared for the moment to assume that, under certain conditions, majority rule may be possible. I am also prepared to concede that, as normally understood, the preferences of a bare political majority often are perceived as having greater legitimacy than those of a plurality. But I would argue that majority approval is legitimate *only* if we can assume that neither the majority nor the minority has disproportionate power.[23] To put the point differently: majority rule legitimates a voting procedure, if at all, only to the extent the procedure is fair. To be fair, a procedure must be more than just efficient. It also must comport with the stability, accountability, and reciprocity assumptions.

The claim I press here, but develop later, is that, even in the absence of direct proof of legislative racism, a system in which a permanent and homogeneous majority consistently exercises disproportionate power is neither stable, accountable, nor reciprocal. Proponents of winner-take-all majority rule claim proportionality exists, meaning that the majority is not likely to exercise 100% of the power solely in its self-interest. In my view, however, under the political equality and political empowerment norms of the Voting Rights Act, majority rule is a fair voting procedure to the extent it provides each voter an equal opportunity to influence legislative decisionmaking, or a proportional stake in the legislative outcome. If this is true, then the Voting Rights Act's political equality and empowerment norms are not achieved through the traditional second-generation remedy of creating equipopulous, winner-take-all subdistricts, no matter how much the district lines or district demographics are adjusted, because single-member districts retain majority rule principles but fail to ensure proportional legislative power.

As a remedy, subdistricting primarily attempts to equalize gross population (and therefore votes), without measuring the intensity of voter preferences. In doing so, it equalizes voting weights but not voting power.[24] Even majority-black subdistricts, drawn to compensate for unequally weighted votes at the electoral level, still do nothing to ensure equally powerful, as opposed to equally weighted, legislative votes, for two related reasons. First, it is possible that majoritarian decisionmaking minimizes the legislative power of minorities as a result of their numerical weakness. Second, as I develop in the next Part, the operation of prejudice in a winner-take-all system denies blacks elected from single-member districts the ability to exercise even minimal legislative power.[25] The winner-take-all approach may simply increase the majority's representation at the expense of the representational power of electoral minorities. Even though blacks may win a proportionate share of representation through a single-member districting strategy, the ruling coalition is still one elected by white voters. Indeed, a minority of white voters may elect a bare numerical legislative minority, yet exercise 100% of the power. For example, in a 1000 voter/10 seat jurisdiction, with 750 white and 250 black voters, blacks would be proportionately represented with two majority-black districts. Majority rule tells us, however, that the ruling coalition only needs 6 votes on the legislature to control all decisions. Six white representatives might each actually be elected by bare majorities. In such a case, 306 people (6 districts with 51% majorities) have the potential to decide all issues. Such a ruling coalition would represent neither a majority of the total voters nor even a majority of the 750 white voters.[26]

Yet, just as it would be illegitimate for an advantaged minority to exercise majority power, it is illegitimate for an advantaged majority to exercise disproportionate power. From the excluded minority's perspective, such a system exaggerates its difficulty in winning any power and is unlikely to be stable, accountable, or reciprocal. In sum, to the extent majority rule is associated with winner-take-all voting procedures, it does not ensure minority confidence in the system's fairness. Nor does it comport with the political equality and political empowerment norms of the Voting Rights Act.

The majoritarian paradigm, of course, already includes constraints on the tyranny of the majority through checks and balances, federalism, and judicial review to unblock the political processes and to protect fundamental rights. I will argue, however, that, under the Voting Rights Act, "democratic" enforcement occurs not simply by putting limits on majoritarian democracy in the form of a judicially enforced constitutional or statutory right to group representation, but by inviting fact-specific challenges to the notion that an efficient or technically fair voting process alone supplies majoritarian legitimacy. I will suggest that where it consistently produces disproportionate majority control, an efficient or technically fair voting process simply is illegitimate.

2. THE EMPIRICAL EVIDENCE. Ignoring the analytical and structural aspects of the fairness question, the single-member district solution asks instead the empirical question: are blacks better off with one aggressive advocate or several mildly sympathetic listeners? Forced by its own question to choose, the single-member district model chooses one aggressive advocate. At the state or congressional level, one might argue that one aggressive advocate is a wise choice. Especially where legislative activity is more formal, and involves greater specialization, the presence of an aggressive advocate for minority interests could make a difference. The more informal the setting and the less regulated the conduct, however, the more likely are blatant "microaggressions"[27] against minority victims.[28] The arguments for minority presence, consequently, may be plausible where representatives with seniority and committee specialization who are dependent on the minority community are enabled by formal structures to trade their votes on issues of indifference to that community for the support of other representatives on critical minority issues. In other words, a crucial characteristic of effective minority representation in collective decisionmaking is the formal ability to express the intensity of constituent preferences and to bargain or deliberate accordingly.

Nevertheless, even at the state or congressional level, black representatives from single-member districts do not necessarily realize critical representational components because of legislative racism, which is defined as "racism infecting political judgments about how organized society should allocate scarce resources."[29] Legislative racism describes a pattern of actions persistently disadvantaging a fixed, legislative minority and encompasses conscious exclusion as well as marginalization that results from "a lack of interracial empathy." It means that where a prejudiced majority rules, its representatives are not compelled to identify its interests with those of the African-American minority. Such prejudice obviously impedes the ability of black representatives to influence their white colleagues.

At the level of city and county government, my primary focus in this chapter, the value of one aggressive advocate is quite hypothetical. Because of enduring white prejudice, the single-member district model may contribute to black political visibility but not to black influence on municipal and regional policy. The theory that prejudice is cabined at the local level where small deliberate bodies are less formal, less anonymous, more intimate, and more likely, through continuous voting opportunities, to develop shared values among their participants is not supported by compelling empirical evidence. Instead, studies of small group interaction suggest that minority or dissenting views often are ignored, especially where the decisional rules do not require members of the majority to obtain minority support.

Scientists studying the psychology of prejudice also conclude that, from the perspective of minority constituents, competitive decisionmaking processes fail to produce successful outcomes in a reliable or predictable manner. At the local level, a district system sets up competition between specific interests. This, in fact, is its intended effect to the extent that it assumes territory is a proxy for interest and that specific territorial interests deserve representation. But, where blacks are a numerical minority in a jurisdiction, most districts are drawn not to protect black interests, but to represent white interests. In the absence of any black constituents, white representatives have no accountability to the black community. Thus, it appears that the competitive aspect of local, deliberative bodies disadvantages minority group representatives.

This is particularly disadvantageous to blacks at the municipal or county level. In local governing bodies with a subdistricting structure, a primary goal of each representative is to convince the municipality to spend more money in her district. Many locally districted bodies grant district representatives great discretion in the allocation of money for their area. In order to spend any money in the majority-black district, other than through servicing individual constituents, the black representative, however, needs a majority of legislative votes, not just one or two legislative seats.

At the local level, then, single-member districts may aggravate the isolation of the black representative. Within the council or commission halls, black voters may be denied the political tools to challenge racism or racial insensitivity among white elected officials who have no black constituents.

In addition, even in jurisdictions with substantial black populations, black political participation may be either contained or isolated sufficiently in single-member districts to reduce its political influence,[30] or to disable its electoral success from conversion into a governing coalition.[31]

Consequently, in the conventional litigation model, we can see both progress and paradox. The progress is, of course, the exponential increase in the number of black elected officials and the number of blacks who turn out on election day.[32] The paradox is that by winning, blacks ultimately lose; as soon as they achieve one electoral success, the focus of the discrimination shifts to the legislative arena. By accepting the winner-take-all feature of the prevailing majoritarian paradigm, the subdistricting strategy marginalizes minority legislative presence. In a pluralist society, a winner-take-all approach legitimated by majority rule actually exacerbates marginalization of minorities. It is an especially thin version of pluralism that allows a racially homogeneous majority disproportionate representation at the expense of an historically oppressed racial minority.

B. Single-Member Districts, Black Voters, and the Representational Relationship

Historically, movements for greater minority representation have endorsed single-member districts, which are already common throughout the United States. Studies of the consequences of districting for minority representation focus on comparisons between unmodified at-large and single-member districts to determine which system produces the larger raw number of black representatives. Of the two electoral systems, single-member districts are most closely associated with black electoral success. Based on the delegate theory of representation[33] and the participatory model of local empowerment,[34] second-generation litigation is premised on the assumption that, by increasing the number of black representatives, single-member district voting will ensure that blacks have effective representation.[35]

I argue in this Part that this assumption is in error: effective representation is not just the process of reelection; it is the policy-centered process of governing responsibly.[36] I argue that sustained black voter participation is a necessary condition to ensuring that black representatives remain substantively accountable to constituent policy preferences. Though I concede that the process of election itself, especially in single-member districts, may ensure service accountability to individual constituent demands,[37] several factors suggest that at the policymaking level for municipal and county government the single-member district delegate model fails to ensure that black representatives will be substantively accountable to their constituents. I conclude that local single-member districts do not achieve the representational ideals imbedded in black electoral success theory[38] and that, as a result, a new remedial paradigm is necessary.

First, single-member districts, which facilitate personal campaigning and individual servicing, depress the level of stable, jurisdiction-wide minority political organization. By emphasizing individual candidacies rather than interests, single-member districts promote a locally based network of individual constituents. Though personal contact seems desirable, personal campaigning and networking also tend to minimize emphasis on issues or on the support of organized groups.[39] Even in single-member districts, however, organized, grass-roots efforts are important to facilitate black voter turnout and sustained black voter participation.[40] Yet such efforts may not be cost-effective or even achievable at the local level without the support of community-based political parties. By emphasizing individual candidacies, single-member district structures may consequently accomplish just the opposite: the demobilization of the poorest voters within the black community.[41]

Second, the single-member district model emphasizes only the authenticity and mobilization values encouraged by the ability to elect community-based representatives. It is assumed that the election of such representatives mobilizes black voters to participate and thus legitimates the system, even if these representatives are subsequently reelected by a demoralized electorate in low-turnout contests.

In other words, where each voter has an equal opportunity to become part of the governing coalition in her subdistrict, the second-generation litigation assumption is that a voice backed by a vote enfranchises to the extent it is a vote cast in a majority-black district.

Litigation may be constrained by its own internal dynamics, but it is an especially impoverished strategy when limited to simple election day voting opportunities. In this sense, districting promotes the concept of elections as a single activity, detached from ongoing voter organization and mobilization. Focused primarily on opportunities for electoral ratification and reelection through the enforcement mechanism of majority-black, single-member districts, the litigation model tends to promote a marginal kind of black legislative leadership. Once elected, some politicians—black or white—may define their political agenda without reference to, or consultation with, a community base, except to the extent they view political patronage as constituent servicing.[42]

If, as my first claim suggests, representatives from single-member districts are not particularly dependent on either party organizations or community-based groups for campaign support, they may act independently of their constituents' interests as well. This is particularly damaging at the local level, where media and other intermediary monitors may fail to scrutinize closely the representational relationship.[43]

Third, the districting strategy excludes the possibility of representation for those whose interests are not defined by, or consistent with, those in the geographically defined district. Subdistricting simply assumes a linkage between interest and residence that is not necessarily as fixed as racial segregation patterns might otherwise suggest. At the congressional level, it might be argued that districts work as proxies for interest. On this view, congressional districts, which are already quite large (but not as large as the entire jurisdiction), help voters locate their legislator and reinforce the view that the voter elected a representative to service local, as opposed to state, interests. Indeed, the evidence suggests that representatives elected from single-member districts do more constituency servicing, the demand for which is greater in low-income districts.

But the analysis is different at the municipal or county level. At that level, districting does not create a close fit between interests and residence because the black population may be dispersed throughout the jurisdiction, or some blacks may be concentrated but others merely represented "virtually" through the majority-black subdistricts in which they do not reside and by representatives for whom they do not vote.[44] This is a problem where a so-called majority-minority district lacks a majority of minority registered voters. In such a case, the district is merely "an influence district."[45] I will discuss such districts in subpart C.

Furthermore, the effort to draw districts that have enough members of any one minority group to exert the most influence may dilute the voting strength of other minority groups in neighboring districts. Districting provides no clear theoretical justification for resolving—and may instead exacerbate—conflict between the interests of competing minority groups. For example, subdistricting may set off a "political land grab" in which each minority group has a legitimate but potentially unfulfilled claim to representation.

Indeed, in sorting through the competing claims, the districting process may carve up politically viable communities of interest.[46] Without regard to race, districting arbitrarily limits electoral choices based solely on where particular voters happen to live. A recurrent example, which the Supreme Court confronted in *United Jewish Organizations v. Carey*,[47] is that, in order to create majority-black districts, racially homogeneous white districts are also created on the assumption that white voters are a racially undifferentiated mass. The result often is that moderate white voters are submerged in the resulting majority-white district, separated from blacks who would form coalitions with them but for the subdistricting.[48] Thus, districting limits the options of white, as well as black, voters; this may lead to voter apathy and lack of identity with the "artificial" voting district.[49]

Fourth, districting decisions may simply reflect the arbitrary preferences of incumbent politicians who prefer packed, safe districts to ensure their reelection.[50] Indeed, districting battles are often pitched between incumbents fighting to retain their seats, without regard to issues of voter representation. Because the choice of districts is so arbitrary, incumbents enjoy extraordinary leverage in self-perpetuation through gerrymandering.

Thus, districting strategies often promote noncompetitive election contests, which further reduce voter participation and interest. Even though few political scientists have studied the consequences for voter participation and representation of safe, minority seats, one can certainly argue that safe seats discourage political competition and thus further diminish turnout. For example, black registration and turnout increase in response to first-time election opportunities, but after an initial surge, black voter participation declines in many single-member jurisdictions.[51] Moreover, even where they turn out to vote, black voters often fail to monitor their elected representatives who fail to woo majority political support for a redistributive or even activist government strategy.

Finally, districting tends to promote a two-party system by "avoiding a splintering multiparty development."[52] Although such a system, in which third parties are all but doomed to perpetual defeat, is perceived as more stable than a coalition government, it tends to promote stability at the cost of representing minority interests. In a two-party system, interests are only protected to the extent they garner majority support or merit judicial protection by virtue of the majority's violation of the minority's right to equal protection. Districting, therefore, does nothing to promote active consideration of minority interests; instead, it forces minority voters and representatives to compromise and adjust their interests to the informal constructs provided by one of the two major parties, thereby reducing the representation of minority interests. In this way, districting can reduce the interest representation of minorities to arbitrary, fixed choices.

In fact, it may be that the two-party structure associated with the districting system has disconnected voters from the process of self-government.[53] By disabling political third parties from effective political participation, districting stifles dissent. Without an effective minority party organization to function as the link between local voters and their government, minority political networks are constructed top-down rather than bottom-up. By weakening third political parties, territorial districting thus frustrates an important conduit for interactive voter information, especially among minority voters.

C. Minority Influence Districts[*]

One alternative to creating majority black districts is to disperse the black voting population, creating pockets of electoral influence. A few courts, commentators, and litigators have urged the adoption of districting plans in which blacks are an electoral minority in several districts rather than an electoral majority in just a few. These critics of majority black districts claim that minority influence districts would better integrate minorities into the political process.

For example, some black plaintiffs have endorsed plans that do not maximize the number of districts in which voters belonging to a single racial minority predominate. Their argument is that dispersed electoral influence is preferable to concentrated electoral control.

In its strongest version, an influence district is a district in which minority voters enjoy electoral influence and legislative clout despite the fact they are a numerical minority and voting is racially polarized. For example, an electoral minority may have influence where it can determine the outcome of an election contest between competing majority preferred candidates. Although the minority voters cannot sponsor their own representative, they may influence which majority candidate gets elected.

At the legislative decisionmaking stage, the strong minority influence claim would be that the power of minority voters is superior because minority voters enjoy influence over multiple representatives rather than concentrated control over one or two. Because minority voters must work with other groups in order to enjoy either electoral or legislative power, influence districts arguably mobilize cross-racial alliances in particular and political participation throughout the extended political process, in general.

---

[*]This subpart was written in 1992 and published separately as a section in "The Representation of Minority Interests: The Question of Single-Member Districts." 14 Cardozo Law Review 1135 (April 1993).

There is also a weak influence claim in which influence occurs only *under the right combination of circumstances*. The weak influence claim is based on three alternative assumptions. First, the minority may be influential despite its numerical scarcity *where voting is not racially polarized*. Second, even where the electorate is racially polarized, the racial minority may be influential if there are multiple racial groups that coalesce around a single minority sponsored candidate. Third, even where voting is racially polarized, the racial minority might be influential where there is unusual fragmentation within the white community and the aggregating decisional rule is a plurality not a majority vote threshold.

The first assumption is basically a claim for judicial intervention without the necessary predicate of vote dilution. Vote dilution occurs if a bloc voting majority submerges the voting strength of a minority group. If voting is *not* racially polarized, dilution probably has not occurred and the racial minority may indeed be influential. In such a case, liberal whites might aggregate their votes with blacks to form a "functional majority."

To bring the first assumption within the dilution paradigm, proponents of influence districts might show that whites are a bloc-voting jurisdiction-wide majority. In such a case, a jurisdiction subdistrict composed of liberal whites and blacks might be appropriate where the liberal whites in the influence district are willing to support the interests of the racial minority. If so, blacks might indeed be an influential voting bloc within that particular district because the *district* majority does not predictably coalesce around racial issues. For example, a functional electoral majority exists where blacks plus white cross-over votes are numerically sufficient to exceed the electoral exclusion threshold.

The second assumption also depends on the existence of a "functional majority." In the second assumption, the minority is actually a subset of a multi-racial politically cohesive district majority. For example, blacks who are a numerical minority might join with Latinos to form a functional electoral majority. Voting might be racially polarized between whites and all others within the district. In the second assumption, however, whites are not a numerical district majority.

To bring this second assumption within the dilution paradigm, it would be necessary to demonstrate that whites are a jurisdiction-wide majority that votes as a racial bloc. Within the multi-racial districts, however, whites are the racial minority. As the racial minority in that district, it is whites who presumably enjoy electoral influence rather than control. Whites may be the "swing" vote if the traditional minority groups are fractured. But unless the traditional racial minority groups are politically cohesive, there is no functional majority and thus no influence district. Accordingly, a multi-racial district in which whites are not the majority is less a minority influence district, and more properly termed a multi-racial "minority" majority district.

The third assumption does not build on the concept of a functional majority, but rather on its opposite. In the third case, no group is functioning as a majority; nor do any groups coalesce to form a majority. The racial minority is no worse off than other political minorities. In such a case, the fact that voting is racially polarized brings the district within the dilution paradigm. Whites, in the aggregate, vote as a racial bloc in favor of nonminority sponsored candidates. If the election were held in either the white community or the black community, a different candidate would emerge victorious. Yet, even here, it is probably misleading to term this an influence district. Rather, this is a district in which no group is functioning as a monolithic majority.

The first and second assumptions rely on the existence *within the district* of a functional electoral majority to which the jurisdiction's racial minority belongs. But while these assumptions require a functional electoral majority, the third assumption does not. The third assumption is that a black-supported candidate may squeak through with less than a majority before the white community reunites. This might also happen where a sizable minority plays a role in competitive two-person elections. In such elections, blacks may be the swing vote.

All three assumptions, however, hold a single idea in common. They all require a district in which whites do not function as a monolithic majority. In other words, in its weak version, influence districts depend on some fragmentation within the white community because whites are politically divided or simply outnumbered, albeit not by a single racial majority.

In this sense, the weak version of influence districts is consistent with at least one aspect of the political fairness standard I develop in the next Part. Since there is no majority monopoly of *all* power, racial minorities potentially exercise a fair share of procedural resources. These minorities might have an equal opportunity to influence decisions at the election stage, exchanging information about their preferences, as well as enjoying the capacity to reward or punish candidates.[54]

But where whites function as a cohesive district majority, a numerical racial minority simply cannot be influential. Within the dilution paradigm, the racial minority does *not* have equal access to relevant decisionmaking processes because the white majority exercises disproportionate power.

For this reason, I am not persuaded that the strong version of so-called influence districts achieves political fairness as defined herein. The idea that a racial minority *in a polarized district electorate* has influence or clout is simply inconsistent with the very definition of minority vote dilution.[55]

The strong version of influence districts is therefore incoherent within the dilution paradigm. At the electoral stage, the number of blacks in a minority influence district will simply make no difference. If voting is racially polarized, those elected by the racial majority can ignore the interests of minority voters, even those who supported them, without suffering any electoral consequences.

Where voting is racially polarized, those blacks who support the winning candidate enjoy minimal influence as a swing vote. Black voters may help determine which candidate gets elected, but the successful candidate must first be one who started out with white support. Moreover, once in office, black voters' influence on that candidate's performance is questionable. In a racially polarized environment, white officials are often unaware of black voters' decisive impact or deliberately ignore it because of even more decisive white support. As a consequence, it is hard to imagine a racially stigmatized minority, whatever its size, exercising genuine influence in a racially polarized winner-take-all district.

Even the weak version of influence claims portends a practical difficulty; to describe these as influence claims suggests a point of reference based on some population threshold short of a numerical majority. At what point are blacks better off with two 25% influence districts rather than one 40% influence district and one 10% district? Demonstrating electoral influence within winner-take-all districting is thus problematic as a pragmatic question.

Of course, the answer to this question may itself be pragmatic. One could approach each situation with an intensely factual, local appraisal on a case-by-case basis. The case-by-case approach attempts to discover locally contextualized answers rather than universalizing theories. This is consistent with the empowerment norm, which strives to let voters themselves define their political interests at the local level. It is also consistent with the "functional approach" to the Voting Rights Act taken by Congress and the Court requiring intensely local appraisal of relevant political realities.

If the empowerment norm attempts to enable voters to articulate their own political interests, one method to determine the influence baseline is simply to ask the voters themselves. At what level of population do voting rights plaintiffs consider themselves influential?[56] What benchmark or indicia of influence are the plaintiffs themselves using? To some extent this is what the district court did in *Upham v. Seamon*[57] when it determined that because voting was not racially polarized, minority voters in the Dallas area were better off, in light of local circumstances, with two minority influence districts.

When questioned, black plaintiffs in voting rights class action litigation generally prefer remedial alternatives that ensure an opportunity to elect candidates of their choice. To realize this opportunity, they request relief in the form of districts that provide black electoral majorities. Where majority black election districts are not possible because of demographic or geographic contingencies, they may choose the second best relief, which for these voters is usually a competitive district, otherwise known as an influence district.

Second best, however, still needs to be defined as a matter of judicial manageability. Thus, another approach, still framed conceptually in terms of empowerment, is to ask political scientists what constitutes a competitive district in nonracial terms. If a 60% vote is considered a landslide, then a district in which a minority political party is less than 40% is a safe district for the majority party. Stated in racial terms, a 65% minority population district has been used as a rule of thumb threshold for effective voting equality (defined as realistic potential to elect). If a 65% black district is a safe seat for blacks, then a 65% white district is not an influence district, but probably a safe seat for whites.

Given both these propositions, an influence district may be defined as a district with less than 65% but more than 35% minority population. In such a district, it may make sense to give black plaintiffs the opportunity to prove that they enjoy a realistic potential to influence. This, of course, would depend on the totality of relevant circumstances.

To resolve the practical question of influence thresholds, it is also necessary to define "influence." Thus far the term "influence" has meant electoral or legislative control, or at least, the ability to affect electoral or legislative outcomes. In all of the influence claims, however, minority influence generally means either minority support for a white candidate or minority support for a black candidate who is more directly accountable to the larger white electorate. This is because winner-take-all districting has such a high threshold of exclusion.

Yet, a minority that merely supports, rather than sponsors or elects, its own candidate is still not necessarily influential in the extended political process. Genuine influence requires that the minority voters have the ability at least occasionally to sponsor their own candidates or to punish unresponsive officials whose election depended on minority support. Without this ability, the minority may have limited influence in determining election outcomes, but it does not have any real influence over legislative performance. That kind of extended influence, which depends on reciprocity and mutuality, generally requires a lower exclusion threshold than is permitted by winner-take-all districting.

In sum, the present remedial focus on local municipal and county single-member districts, whether minority black or minority influence districts, tends to reduce functional minority representation. It disengages many minority voters, especially indigents, from both election day turnout and continuous participation in political activity. In so doing, it also reduces the substantive accountability of representatives of single-member districts. Additionally, the strategy lumps together voters with competing interests on the basis of territorial lines, which, if not arbitrary, are drawn strategically to ensure the reelection of incumbents; this dilutes the votes of electoral minorities in the district and of other minorities both inside and outside the district. Lastly, insofar as the strategy strengthens the two-party system, it stifles minority interests.

I conclude from both the analytical claims and the empirical evidence that accountable representation focused exclusively on district-based elections at the local level is too narrow. In response to the question whether blacks are better off with one aggressive advocate or several mildly sympathetic listeners, the single-member district model chooses authenticity and symbolic mobilization values over influence and responsiveness goals. By posing the only choice as between one aggressive advocate or several mildly sympathetic listeners, the single-member district model assumes minimal potential influence as a given. Neither choice will effectively promote the legislative agenda of a disadvantaged minority group. Thus, I would argue that the choice posed by districting—between a few majority-black districts or a few more majority-white "influence" districts—is a false dichotomy.

The single-member district model thus presupposes an unresponsive decisionmaking body and then builds in appropriately limited alternatives, without ever defining what "better off" means. In order to define "better off," we need to reformulate our understanding of equal political participation to emphasize both the political equality and political empowerment norms of the Voting Rights Act. As I show in the next Part, empowerment should contemplate sustained political organization and mobilization leading to fair treatment within and by the council or commission—not merely success in desegregating it.

II. Reconceptualizing Vote Dilution

My primary objective in this Part is to reconceptualize local minority political exclusion. The new conception of exclusion will fit the empirical and structural critique of the single-member districting model and simultaneously will reflect the political equality and political empowerment norms of the Voting Rights Act.[58] Given the observed tendency of the courts to merge the remedy and the liability claim, any reconception should also establish remedial alternatives that can define the violation.

I pursue three lines of argument to accomplish these objectives. First, I argue that we should redefine the unit of analysis from fixed territorial constituencies to voluntary interest constituencies. Dilution should be viewed as the submergence of black voters' politically cohesive and self-identified interests. Second, I argue that once the unit of disempowerment is properly identified, the dilution claim should seek to extend the inquiry from electoral voting rules to legislative decisional rules.

Third, I contend that a properly formulated approach to ascertaining and remedying impermissible vote dilution must compare the challenged system to an alternative that fairly reflects proportionate minority influence. The proportionality principle substantiates the right to fair and effective representation.[59] The proportionality principle delivers what majority rule proponents assume but do not produce: decisional rules that promote reciprocity and accountability without straying too far from the efficiency and stability norms.[60]

The proportionality standard is based on the principle of political fairness or political legitimacy.* Proportionality seeks a reason for implementing a decision that legitimates the decision in the eyes of all voters, even those who may lose. It asks whether the process provides all voters an equal opportunity to be part of the winning coalition. Stated differently, proportionality is a form of political fairness in which no one is entitled to grossly disproportionate influence or a monopoly on control. The majority should enjoy a majority of the power. But in a fair system, a permanent majority should not exercise *all* the power and a permanent minority should not always lose.

Toward this end, I propose a set of remedial aspirations to demonstrate some attributes of a fair electoral system. These aspirations include an interactive, deliberate legislative decisionmaking process that compen-

---

*This definition of proportionality is adapted from my Cardozo Law Review article (id.).

sates for the way prejudice and "neutral" decisional rules encourage unfair political competition, grant the majority disproportionate power, and
distort or marginalize the perspective of minority group representatives.
In particular, I propose an aggregating device for linking voting decisions
at both the electoral and legislative level. Once multiple voting opportunities are consolidated, voluntary minority interest constituencies could
choose to cumulate their votes to express the intensity of their distinctive
group interests.

I derive each of my arguments from a "group-compensating" model of
the Voting Rights Act.[61] This model has four characteristics. First, it reflects the courts' explicit recognition of group voting rights in the context
both of racial vote dilution and partisan gerrymandering. The group is an
appropriate unit for political participation because the "right to elect" is
valueless at the level of the single individual.[62]

Second, it measures the right to fair representation by the extent protected minority groups are provided a meaningful voice in government.
Under this formulation, a meaningful voice is not guaranteed by formal
rules applied uniformly to ensure mere access to the ballot, nor is a meaningful voice ensured by formal rules that aggregate choice, assigning equal
weight to all votes. Rather, a meaningful voice favors aggregating procedures that "minimize the number of people who cast losing ballots" or
"more equitably reflect voting strength."[63] Thus, for example, if policy
decisionmaking is reduced to voting opportunities, minority empowerment requires a proportionality standard for evaluating voting rules.

Third, the group-compensating model also reflects a preference for experimentation and innovation in government, especially at the local level.
The model encourages experimentation with positive-sum solutions in
which everyone stands to benefit from the infusion of alternative viewpoints and from consensus solutions. Finally, the model effects the broad
empowerment goals of the statute. The right to vote for representatives,
standing alone, does not ensure a fair chance of policy influence, or a
chance of winning a fair number of contested policy decisions. The right
to a meaningful voice requires extending the statutory inquiry to examine
legislative decisional rules.[64]

In this sense, the right to vote is a claim about the fundamental right to
express and represent ideas. Voting is not just about winning elections.
People participate in politics to have their ideas and interests represented,
not simply to win contested seats.

Thus, the right to a meaningful voice does not measure participation
simply by counting competitive votes; it examines the extent to which a

system mobilizes broadbased voter participation, fosters substantive debate from a range of viewpoints, and provides and reinforces opportunities for all voters to exercise meaningful choice throughout the process of decision making and governance.

A. Interest, Not Just Voter, Representation

The term "interest" refers to self-identified interests, meaning those high salience needs, wants, and demands articulated by any politically cohesive group of voters.[65] Interest representation emphasizes the importance of voter autonomy divorced from involuntary, fixed territorial constituencies. Using voting patterns, it measures as a politically cohesive group those voters who identify themselves with each other based on their own evaluation of their shared interests. As a statutory approach to vote dilution, interest representation measures the impact of electoral or voting rules on the legislative representation of self-identified minority voters' interests.

Interest representation attempts first to identify a violation of the right to a meaningful vote by locating politically cohesive minority interests that are submerged within winner-take-all voting structures. Interest representation identifies interest submergence by demonstrating the existence of alternative electoral systems that afford greater minority interest representation and satisfaction.[66] Any such alternatives must recognize the intensity, as well as the existence, of minority voter preferences.[67]

For example, in a 25% black jurisdiction with four at-large representatives, the current single-member districting model would assess the fairness of the election system against the potential representativeness of the alternative, a subdistricted system. The relative fairness of the at-large system would be challenged based on the assumption that black voters would be better represented if one majority-black district could be drawn. If blacks are numerous and concentrated enough to be a majority in one single-member district, the subdistricting strategy would use that district alternative to demonstrate the unfairness of the unmodified at-large system.

In contrast, an interest representation model would assess the fairness of the at-large system against the potential representativeness of an alternative voting system that allowed voters to cumulate their votes.[68] I adopt a cumulative voting system because it permits recognition of both the existence and intensity of minority voter preference and allows strategic voting to enforce reciprocal coalitions. Cumulative voting modifies the at-large system to eliminate its winner-take-all characteristic.

In the modified at-large election, candidates would run jurisdiction-wide, but the threshold for election would be reduced from 51% to something less. In the case of a four person at-large council, the threshold for election would be 21%.[69] Voters would each be given the same number of votes as open seats (four in this case) that they could distribute by their choice among the competing candidates. If black voters are a politically cohesive interest constituency, they might use all four of their votes on one candidate. In a 100 voter jurisdiction, where each black voter gave all four of her votes to one candidate, a 25% black minority could elect a representative. The intensity of their interests and their political cohesion would ensure black voters the ability to elect at least one representative.

When measured against the potential representativeness of an unmodified, winner-take-all at-large voting system at the election level, the cumulative voting system promises greater and more authentic black political representation. In addition, it offers the potential for greater black political power than the single-member districting model. The modified at-large system encourages black representation without disabling or diluting the votes of potential allies.[70] By contrast, the single-member districting approach may require submerging Latino voters within majority-black districts or white Democratic voters within majority-white Republican districts.[71]

Depending on strategic voting behavior, a modified at-large system could encourage coalitions of these voters to develop as a result of the choice of election system. Unlike the subdistricting model, the modified at-large system rewards cooperative, rather than competitive, behavior. Thus, interest representation offers black voters both the chance to elect candidates of their choice as well as the chance for their candidates to work in the legislature with potential legislative allies, trading votes to reflect the intensity of constituent preferences.

As an example, assume that in a jurisdiction with 1,000 voters and 10 representatives, blacks are 25% of the population. A subdistrict plan provides roughly "proportionate representation" with 2 majority-black districts of 100 black voters each.[72]

Although the subdistrict plan is a majoritarian approach, a bare majority of 51% in each district can elect a representative. The votes of 49 black voters in each district are unnecessary.[73] In addition, of the 250 blacks in the jurisdiction, 50 of them are not "captured" in either majority-black district but are distributed randomly in the majority-white districts. They are potentially unrepresented in the governing body.[74] Those blacks are not geographically located in the two single-member districts are represented only "virtually," if at all.

Even more damaging, because only 51 blacks are needed to elect a representative, incumbent representatives may be able to control the electorate through political patronage, political contributions, and political control of the district lines. The black voters are not encouraged to participate actively in the political process because a low turnout still benefits the incumbent. Finally, the black voters in the two majority-black districts have no mechanism to encourage representatives from the majority-white districts virtually to represent their interests.

Whereas subdistricts reinforce authenticity and mobilization concerns by clearly removing black candidates from electoral competition with whites, as a matter of legitimacy a "winner-take-only-some,"[75] or interest representation, system actually ensures fewer disaffected voters than the subdistricted majority approach. It allows black voters and their representatives the opportunity to express the intensity of their preference for candidates and for legislative programs. Particular political transactions would depend not just on the number of supporters and opponents but on the relative intensity of preferences. This reflects the insight that if each electoral or legislative vote is insulated from every other, minority interests are consistently disadvantaged. Serial up or down voting permits "a cohesive, well financed majority community to reward itself with enhanced representation, if not outright monopoly" of representation.

In addition, the alternative, nonterritorial approach by its choice of voting arrangement encourages those minority voters or representatives whose votes are not needed to support a single candidate or a particular issue to join with sympathetic white voters to support progressive white candidates or to trade with them votes on issues of indifference. The necessity of strategic voting on salient issues may help identify and shape actual preferences, and coincidentally build cross-racial constituencies.[76] Moreover, by disaggregating the majority, 51% of the people no longer control 100% of either the electoral or the legislative power. Thus, I would argue that the modified at-large, or interest representation, approach promises a more accountable and a more reciprocal voting system.

The interest representation approach I propose is arguably more legitimate and potentially more empowering. For example, in the jurisdiction with 1,000 voters, 250 of whom are black, a modified at-large plan would use a threshold of exclusion of 1/11th based on the formula of one divided by one plus the number of open seats plus one. This means that 1/11th of the voters could not be denied representation. The threshold of exclusion would work out to be 91 voters (91 is 1/11th of 1000 plus 1). Here, there are 250 black voters. Blacks are more than 2/11th, but just short of 3/11th, of the population.

If all voters had 10 votes and could plump them any way they wished, any candidate supported intensely (meaning receiving all 10 votes) by 91 voters would get elected. Each voter could self-identify herself by the way she chose to plump or cumulate her votes. Winner-take-only-some voting reduces the threshold of exclusion from 51% to 1/11th plus 1, yet *more* voters would actually be represented in the governing body. Each representative would need 91 voters to get elected, not just 51. In a fractured electorate, the ten representatives would represent at least 910 voters. Thus only 90 voters would be unrepresented under the most adverse circumstances (compared to 490 using majority rule, winner-take-all subdistricts). On decisions at the policy level, 6 votes could still control (although if the evidence warranted it, a supermajority might be required on issues of concern to the majority, or linkage of issues aggregated over time could also ameliorate racial cleavage). Using a winner-take-only-some electoral system and a majority legislative decisional rule, 6 representatives would at minimum represent 546 voters (6 times 91) or an actual majority.

The winner-take-only-some view is at least as efficacious in ensuring minority representation, but it also potentially leads to greater coalition building. No matter where they reside, two groups of 91 voters are each electing a black representative, assuming they are politically cohesive. The remaining 68 black voters can become a functional interest group if they join with 23 sympathetic whites to elect a third candidate who is also electorally accountable. The extra 68 black voters are not limited in their potential to form cross-racial coalitions by arbitrary, line drawing decisions made on their behalf by incumbents with ulterior motives. And because there is a more complex, interest-oriented electoral system, political organizations might develop to educate and mobilize black voters.

Assuming for the moment that the approach taken by interest representation, if not better than single-member districts, at least effectively ensures black voter interest representation, the meaning of the term "interest" preference itself still requires further explication. My definition of interests refers to voluntary constituencies that self-identify their interests. Unlike a subdistricting system, interest submergence does not depend on a compulsory territorial constituency or on fixed interests. Rather, interest representation acknowledges the existence of intra-group differences as well as the importance of individual choice in choosing group affiliation. Interests, as expressed in group activity and identity, would be recognized in much the same way that geographic, territorial interests are traditionally thought to define distinct communities.

In other words, voluntary constituencies would be recognized to the extent they conceptually organize and attract sufficient numbers of like-minded voters.[77] If the interests of most blacks are fungible with those of most whites, an integrated interest constituency would naturally result. Under such circumstances, it would be impossible to establish impermissible vote dilution.

On the other hand, where black interests are discrete and identifiable, their political salience would define a different, racially identifiable group. The assumption that blacks, wherever they reside, tend to be politically cohesive is supported both anecdotally and empirically. In the words of recent commentators, the empirical evidence consistently shows that "blacks live in a different world from whites."[78] Even disagreements among blacks pale by comparison with the differences in political interest and philosophy between blacks and whites.[79] Studies attempting to take account of intensity of preferences and sustained consideration and deliberation of interest also conclude that the black community is politically cohesive, at least on the interest agenda identified here.[80] That black interest agenda, although necessarily subsuming multiple viewpoints, reflects the fact that historic circumstances have led blacks "collectively [to] define their situations as unjust and subject to change through group action."[81]

In this regard, the interest prong of impermissible vote dilution might be established where a black interest agenda consistently differs from the mainstream emphasis of white working- or middle-class representation. Interest representation would seek to assess in the particular locality the major differences between white and black views of issues.[82] If the core issues of black voters' concern consistently cluster around the racial and economic fault lines of civil rights and poverty, despite class differences, poor and middle-class blacks would be politically cohesive in an interest representation model as measured by their voting patterns.[83]

Yet, interest representation, which requires strategic voting by a politically cohesive group, does not presume that all blacks will submerge their differences to present a monolithic front. Where voting patterns suggest overwhelming majority but not unanimous issue cohesion, interest representation would allow dissenting blacks to cast their votes as they chose.[84] Interest representation is a phenomenon of choices, where the choices protected are the default positions of the black community: from advocacy by authentic representatives for distinctive group interests to advocacy by authentic representatives for the least well-off. Participation by *all* constituents would be encouraged.

Interest representation can, therefore, identify the first prong of a potential vote dilution violation. As a conceptual approach, it also has several remedial implications for recognizing and enhancing the political power of a disadvantaged minority. By defining the violation in terms of interest submergence rather than geographic compactness, appropriate remedies would be measured by their capacity to eliminate "wasted voting,"[85] provide greater leverage in bargaining, recognize the intensity of voter preferences, strengthen incentives for political participation, empower even the most vulnerable members of the black community, and encourage cross-racial alliances.

Although it is perhaps possible that interest representation could inadvertently moderate authentic representatives, alienate black voters by virtue of its complexity, or threaten black community autonomy,[86] these fears are overstated. Interest representation does not nullify existing constitutional prohibitions against illegitimate preferences, such as the Equal Protection Clause. Moreover, the exclusion threshold in most localities will probably be high enough to eliminate real extremist groups. But, to the extent these concerns are substantial, they need to be balanced against the multiple advantages of interest representation.

First, interest representation attempts to produce citizens who are more committed to achieving political solutions to public policy problems. Because interest representation, unlike the districting strategy, depends on high voter turnout, incumbents will not be able to rely on low turnout to ensure their reelection. Instead, incumbents will find it necessary to mobilize voter interest and participation in an election, a task that will require incumbents to develop substantive programs and proposals.[87] To counteract this, challengers will find it necessary to develop counterproposals, thereby heightening the differences between the candidates.

For their part, minorities may participate in election campaigns in greater numbers than they do in single-member districts, because elections will no longer be zero-sum solutions for minority interests.[88] Minorities will finally have good prospects of winning some victories in the political process due to cumulative voting and the absence of territorial divisions of like-minded voters. This aggregate increase in the substantive content of campaigns will facilitate the self-identification of interest constituencies by heightening voter political awareness and participation as a result of the increased discussion and debate about policy issues. Voters who are energized in this way will actively monitor their issues agenda long after election day. Therefore, under interest representation voters may be more involved in the political process, at both the pre- and post-election stages, than are voters under a single-member district scheme.[89]

Second, under an interest representation approach, incumbents are more accountable to constituents because the incumbents are more vulnerable to shifting alliances and regular removal. Because interest representation emphasizes issues, not the personalities of the candidates, incumbents are less likely to ignore the issues in favor of personal networking and campaigning. In addition, after the election, voter interest constituencies may be sufficiently mobilized to monitor the legislative activity of their elected representatives. Thus, interest representation does not simply reproduce the false consciousness or hierarchy of individual incumbents representing safe black districts; instead, incumbents will be constrained to reflect the policy preferences of their constituents—or else.

Third, interest representation generates incentives for community-based organizations to play a more active role in mobilizing the electorate and monitoring the legislature by both protecting and ratifying authentic representatives. In this sense, interest representation requires sustained organization in a campaign to educate, not merely turn out, voters.[90] Representatives, chosen on the basis of shared interests rather than district proximity, would more likely affiliate with organizations or political parties to realize their goals. Strong minority political parties may then better represent minority voters, both substantively and organizationally.[91]

Fourth, the interest representation approach avoids the resentment of race-conscious districting among groups that are not protected under the Voting Rights Act. Although majority-black single-member districts may elect some black representatives, they also submerge the interests of other groups that reside in the district, such as whites or religious minorities. Under the subdistricting strategy, winner-take-all majoritarianism precludes these voters from enjoying direct representation. This form of interest submergence does not occur under interest representation because the modified at-large system ensures representation to any politically cohesive group above the threshold of exclusion. Consequently, the resentment these voters might otherwise feel for their submergence in a single-member district will be ameliorated or eliminated altogether under interest representation.

Interest representation remedies, implemented pursuant to a voting rights claims, allow whites to form interest-based constituencies, too. Interest representation allows politically cohesive groups of voters, such as white women,[92] to organize around their chosen issue agenda, without being limited for at least ten years (that is, until the next census is taken) by their own decisions about where to live or by others' arbitrary districting agendas.[93] If geography fails to define completely the minority group interests, it also pigeonholes whites as well.

Fifth, interest representation promotes the value of consensus in group decisionmaking. As I use the term, consensus does not mean a uniform ideology. Rather, it means that participants who are satisfied a fair number of times are less likely to veto or actively fight decisions with which they may weakly disagree.[94] In other words, because interest representation eliminates the winner-take-all feature of the single-district model, dissenters can expect some victories in the legislature or council. The modified at-large scheme will thus be viewed as fair by dissenters, who will, for that reason, be more likely to accept the majority's decision. Even if the minority loses a given vote, that vote will more likely be public-regarding because it will reflect the infusion of minority viewpoints. As a result, interest representation can produce a more informed consensus.

For the foregoing reasons, the unit of analysis for vote dilution claims should be voluntary interest constituencies, not fixed territorial constituencies. Interest representation aspires to produce better organized and more informed voter participation at all stages of the political process. This ensures that minority interests will be represented in the legislature, because interest representation emphasizes the importance of holding representatives accountable to their constituents. At the same time, however, interest representations avoids the resentment that often flows from the racially charged process of creating majority-black, single-member districts. Because of its intrinsic fairness, participants are likely to regard majority decisions under interest representation as legitimate, promoting consensus.

B. *Interest Representation Within Collective Decisionmaking*

Whereas in the preceding Part of this chapter I argued in favor of interest representation as a remedy for electoral vote dilution, I now move to the collective decisionmaking component of vote dilution. In this Part, I examine the claim that racial prejudice operates in tandem with some legislative voting rules to submerge fair representation of minority interests.[95] I argue that simple-minded notions of majority rule or winner-take-all procedures interact with racial bloc voting to make statutorily protected groups perennial legislative losers. I conclude that wherever winner-take-all majority rule coexists with racial bloc voting, it fails to fulfill the Voting Rights Act promise for a fairer distribution of political power.

The discussion proceeds in three Subparts. In the first, I develop the conceptual claim that majoritarian collective decisionmaking must be evaluated by (1) the proportionality principle of fairness I earlier posited and (2) the statutory norms of political equality, meaning the participation and inclusion of all groups in the political process. Both of these propositions highlight the importance of evaluating collective decisionmaking rules based on their effectiveness in promoting shared power and shared respect.

In the second Subpart, I set out the legal standard for analyzing collective decisionmaking rules: their ability to promote meaningful deliberation,[96] forge consensus, and legitimate the ultimate decision, both from the perspective of the majority and the minority. In the last Subpart, I describe interest representation's remedial ideal of a deliberative process that emphasizes the value of minority political inclusion consistent with the statutory goals. To achieve this ideal, interest representation would remedy violations of the Voting Rights Act by developing procedures to provide equal access to decisionmaking structures and equal power in reaching collective decisions.

1. THE CONCEPTUAL CLAIM. Traditional concern with protecting minority rights in the face of majority rule views some things as so wrong that not even the principle of majority rule can legitimate them.[97] I view the issue differently. I argue that it is not merely a question of whether, on matters of substantive justice, minority rights trump majoritarian democracy. Instead, we ought to question the inherent legitimacy of winner-take-all majority rule.

My claim is that disproportionate majority power is, in itself, so wrong that it delegitimates majority rule. As Alexis de Tocqueville recognized, "[T]he power to do everything, which I should refuse to one of my equals, I will never grant to any number of them."[98] The problem according to attorney Ed Still is that majoritarian systems "create winners who take all rather than winners who share in power, thus making politics into a battle for total victory rather than a method of governing open to all significant groups." Because they do not necessarily recognize the salience or intensity of minority interests, winner-take-all majoritarian systems do not give minority groups a reason to support the ultimate bargain or to believe the outcome is public-regarding or legitimate.[99]

Beyond this, I would argue that majority rule is unfair in situations where the majority is racially prejudiced against the minority to such a degree that the majority consistently excludes the minority, or refuses to inform itself about the relative merit of the minority's preferences.[100] This is because the claim that majority rule is legitimate rests on two main assumptions that do not hold where racial prejudice pervades the majority: (1) that majorities are fluid rather than fixed; and (2) that minorities will be able to become part of the governing coalition in the future. Only by making these assumptions, which essentially mean that the majority will rule in public-regarding fashion (that is, the winners will virtually represent the interests of the losers), is it possible to argue that winner-take-all majority rule is fair.

The documented persistence of racial polarization,[101] however, defeats both of the assumptions supporting the legitimacy of majority rule. Simply put, racism excludes minorities from ever becoming part of the governing coalition, meaning that the white majority will be permanent. Because it excludes minorities from joining the majority, racism also renders the majority homogeneous, comprised of white voters only. The permanent, homogeneous majority that emerges obviously does not virtually represent the interest of the minority. To the contrary, such a majority will "marginalize" or ignore minority interests altogether. Therefore, racial polarization in the electorate and in the legislative body destroys the reciprocity/virtual representation principle and buries it within racially fixed majorities, thereby transforming majority rule into majority tyranny.[102]

Concern over majority tyranny has typically focused on the need to monitor and constrain the substantive outputs of the decisionmaking process. I propose to look more closely instead at the *procedural* rules by which preferences are identified and counted. Although the term "interest," particularly at the level of legislative decisionmaking, might suggest concern with substantive programmatic outcomes, I argue that voting rights litigants need not worry about them because procedural rules, in a very real sense, shape substantive outcomes.

Given the different worlds in which many blacks and whites live, preferences and intensities are dispersed, meaning that different issues may be salient to members of the two interest constituents. Where preferences are dispersed, decisions should not be made according to any single conception of public good. Decisionmaking should instead incorporate a diversity of views[103] to multiply the points of access to government, disperse power, and to ensure a rational, developed dialogue. Such decisionmaking transforms public policy into " 'the equilibrium reached in the group struggle at any given moment.' "[104]

Consequently, interest representation examines procedural rules in collective decisionmaking bodies by raising three interrelated questions: (1) do they make black representatives necessary participants in the governing process; (2) do they disaggregate an otherwise permanent, homogeneous majority faction; and (3) do they give dignity and satisfaction to the strongly held sentiments of minorities? To help answer these questions, I propose a proportionality principle of collective decisionmaking, premised on the belief that deliberation and open communication are critical, or, at minimum, that consensus solutions are generally preferable to those commanded by a monolithic majority. Although a variety of voting arrangements could reasonably attempt to achieve political equality, my claim is that procedural rules that distribute political satisfaction broadly are necessary predicates for procedural legitimacy. Derived from the broad statutory goal of political equality, the proportionality principle strives to meet the legitimacy conditions of accountability, reciprocity, and stability by constantly cycling interests in ways that are fundamentally democratic.[105]

This approach for evaluating decisionmaking rules measures political equality within representative deliberative bodies against a modified standard of fair representation. Political equality within collective decisionmaking bodies would mean "equal access to political influence over a whole pattern of sequence of collective choices."[106] Such a standard incorporates the following principles on behalf of statutorily protected minority groups:

1. that each group has a right to have its *interests* represented, and
2. that each group has a right to have its interests satisfied a fair proportion of the time.[107]

As a conceptual matter, then, interest representation would redefine dilution as the "marginalization" of minority interests. "Marginalization," which expands the definition of vote dilution to include any set of techniques used to dilute or nullify the effects of votes cast by minorities or their representatives,[108] is the third-generation claim of resegregation within the walls of a formally integrated legislature. Marginalization focuses on discrimination in the distribution of procedural resources such as votes, not on the specific outcomes of public policy debates such as the unfair or unequal distribution of resources, including jobs and promotions.

2. THE LEGAL CLAIM. Because marginalization occurs in the legislative body, it is impossible to determine whether it has, in fact, occurred unless the analysis of racial polarization[109] is extended to see if white representatives in the legislature consistently coalesce in opposition to minority voters' interests. By focusing on the voting behavior of these representatives, a court could determine whether the majority used its disproportionate power to reward illegitimate preferences. In making this inquiry, "prejudice"[110] could be inferred from the presence of a majoritarian bloc that consistently exercises disproportionate power to exclude dissenting viewpoints associated with economically disadvantaged, socially isolated, and physically or culturally identifiable numerical minorities. Drawing inferences of prejudice from evidence of disproportionate majority power is justified by the absence of the critical legitimacy conditions, especially reciprocity and accountability,[111] and comports with the Voting Rights Act's broad political equality and political empowerment norms, which define equality as the participation and inclusion of all groups in determining public policy.

In essence, I argue that racial bloc voting that leads predictably to perennial minority losses constitutes a violation of the norms of a fair legislative process, without regard to a litigant's ability to furnish direct evidence of intentional legislative racism. Just as at-large elections put the issue of minority representation "at the discretion of the majority," majority or group decisional rules, such as winner-take-all rules, allow majority discretion to leave minority interests disproportionately—even completely—unrepresented in racially polarized legislative bodies. Also, legislative bloc voting dilutes the voting strength of minority representatives in the same way that bloc voting by a dominant racial group submerges minority voting strength in winner-take-all elections. Finally, just as incumbents can dilute the electoral power of minorities by gerrymandering districts, incumbents can enact decisional rules that deny minority interests political clout.[112]

The goal of interest representation is to desegregate the white majority by minimizing the "threshold of representation" and the "threshold of exclusion" for exercising political power.[113] Interest representation rejects winner-take-all majoritarianism in favor of an "interest proportionality"[114] principle that lowers the threshold for legislative representation from a simple majority and that alters the decisional rule framework from a series of win/lose decisions. Just as one person/one vote cases measure population equality through deviations from the ideal district size, statutory voting rights cases could measure deviations from an ideal proportional power share to determine gross interest representation disparities.[115] Because electoral and legislative voting decisions, distributed proportionately through the voting choices of nonterritorial, voluntary interest constituencies, would provide the results the minority might expect in the absence of discrimination, such a regime would become interest representation's measure of political fairness. Because such electoral or legislative voting rules would more accurately and proportionately represent minority interests, the fact that these alternatives are not being employed becomes a useful indicator of impermissible vote dilution.

To return briefly to an earlier collective decisionmaking example—in the Brother Rice High School prom controversy—instead of each student casting one vote for each of three favorite records, each student would be given ten votes to cast as desired.[116] The black students could then cumulate or plump their votes on the records they preferred. Assuming their musical preferences are cohesive, they could, by voting strategically, express the intensity of those preferences in determining the playlist. Rather than the majority deciding all the songs, the black students could get to pick at least some of the songs played at the prom. In addition, the black students could enjoy the option of trading votes on issues about which they were indifferent (perhaps the prom setting or prom theme, for example) for support on a matter about which they cared a lot (namely, the music).

To summarize, interest representation suggests that impermissible vote dilution should be defined by comparison to a fair voting system in which: (1) neither the majority nor the minority always dominates; (2) each voter has an equal opportunity to cast a "meaningful vote"; and (3) the decisional rules use principles of proportional power to induce consensual approaches to problem solving.

3. THE REMEDIAL IDEAL. Upon the finding of a violation under the approach outlined above, I believe the Voting Rights Act requires the imposition of internal remedial constraints on the decisional process to ensure authentic, accountable, and consensual representation. Both the statutory norms and the enforcement scheme are premised on the need for blacks to use the political process to overcome majority prejudice. Yet, through marginalization, blacks are effectively prevented from using the

political process to that end. Short of policing the substantive outcomes of the political process, the only effective remedy is to adopt procedural rules that force the majority to provide virtual representation to the minority and enable the minority to act effectively on its own behalf.

I propose an aggressive, formal policy that endorses cooperation to modify behavior toward tolerance. Such a policy should require intergroup collaboration for shared goals. It also should provide continuous, formal opportunities for conflict resolution in which individuals have a stake in future interaction.

My proposal envisions restructuring the legislative decisionmaking process on the model of jury deliberations. The analogy is instructive because the process of jury deliberation reveals much about the group dynamics of managing minority and majority viewpoints, developing consensus, and respecting the contribution of individual members. Jurors come collectively to their task under compulsion of law and are instructed to put aside their biases, deliberating only on the basis of the evidence. Their mission is to review the evidence and decide an outcome that is in the public interest, rather than their self-interest. The resulting outcome is supposed to represent the consensus view of all the jurors, as opposed to the ratification of the view of a majority of the jury.[117] Because of these rules and obligations, jurors may tend to respect each others' views to a greater extent than do other members of collective decisionmaking bodies who fail to bond in the same way.

Drawing on both the jury analogy and the group-process research, interest representation attempts to forge a collective contract of deliberation. It seeks to promote the deliberative process by imposing voting rules that reduce the number of up and down votes, instead of inviting consensus through compromise and trading of procedural resources. In this fashion, my proposal pursues the analogy to jury decisionmaking by fashioning local councils in the image of the ideal, consensus-driven jury.

If a violation of the Voting Rights Act occurs, then, at the legislative level, decisional rules other than either simple majority rule or one legislator/one vote may be required in order to ensure equal power, as opposed to equal weight. Collective decisionmaking procedures would be designed to promote positive-sum games to secure the fullest possible participation and consideration of all interested parties and relevant perspectives. Moreover, decisional rules would be fashioned that encouraged the forging of consensus.

If the evidence demonstrated consistent diminution of the black representatives' influence, one innovative and potentially transformative remedial measure would be to reproduce within the council a cumulative voting process. Legislative cumulative voting would discourage voting up or down on individual proposals. Rather, over a period of time and a series of legislative proposals, votes on multiple bills would be aggregated or linked.[118] By linking votes on several issues to allow both weighted and split issue voting, the black representatives could more reliably participate in the legislative process, plumping votes to express the intensity of constituent preferences on some issues and trading votes on issues of constituent indifference. An alternative remedy would be to require a supermajority vote on issues of importance to the majority or its equivalent, a minority veto on critical minority issues. Either alternative would seek to promote the formation of cross-racial coalitions in the legislature.[119]

As United States Assistant Attorney General John Dunne put it, "The whole spirit of the Voting Rights Act is that a particular group cannot gang up to deprive individual members of a protected minority of their rights."[120] Consequently, where the issue involves a change in legislative voting strength, it is appropriate to use the statute both to identify the precipitating problem and then to assess its discriminatory purpose or effect.

The statutory argument would be that a change in the decisionmaking power of an elected official is a change "with respect to voting." Where authority is transferred from individual commissioners to the commission as a whole or to a single engineer appointed by the commissioner, such reallocation of the power of elected officials diminishes the voting power of black voters. Just as the voting power of the black electorate is submerged when at-large elections are used in conjunction with racially polarized voting, a change from individual district decisions to group control over all decisions submerges the political power of black voters.[121] It does so by making decisions that previously were in the hands of each representative dependent upon the votes of all commissioners, the majority of whom are not answerable to the minority constituency.

Even when blacks formally participate as council members or commissioners, they may effectively be excluded from decisionmaking opportunities through the decisions of white representatives to hold clandestine meetings or to debate privately. Whether dramatic or subtle, such informal exclusion is more problematic than an explicit "voting change." Proving the existence of such a practice and that it represents "a voting change" within the meaning of the statute involves many more variables, requires a more refined analysis, and involves the court or the Department of Justice much more deeply in scrutinizing the legislative process. For these reasons, the administrative preclearance route may be closed to some of the more egregious claims of direct legislative exclusion.[122]

Before turning to the discussion of the feasibility of interest representation in the next Part, it is important to bear in mind that even if interest representation is as potentially advantageous in reality as I predict, it is still a limited remediation principle, particularly in local councils and commissions. In those bodies, which have been the focal point of this chapter, the transformative effect of political power is especially questionable. Municipal and county governments in particular, especially in urban metropolitan areas with declining tax bases and increasing resource demands, may be administered by caretakers, not reformers. These limited opportunities for a transformative politics constrain the potential for reform at the local level. In addition, no litigation strategy can mobilize sustained commitment to achieving reform and political justice.[123]

In sum, my purpose is primarily aspirational. I have tried to conceive of a deliberative process in which prejudice does not control all outcomes. By extending my speculative reconstruction of political equality to legislative deliberations, I am not, however, articulating a grand moral theory of politics. Nor do I argue that these proposals are statutorily or constitutionally required. I do not articulate a general principle of judicial review, but have limited my wholly exploratory suggestions to the specific context of a remedial approach to extreme cases of racial discrimination at the local level. Even in those extreme cases, judicial monitoring to remedy inequality of consideration within the legislative process is arguably not desirable. Moreover, I recognize that proposals to deviate from simple majority rule may be contemplated initially only by parties in settlement negotiations or as political initiatives in light of the firmly entrenched mythology surrounding the majoritarian ideal.*

C. The Feasibility of Interest Representation

Some may challenge interest representation as accelerating the momentum toward separatism. To its critics, interest representation, which reinforces minority group interests and creates a hospitable environment for minority political parties, arguably "thickens boundaries" between citizens,[124] transforming elections from "occasions for seeking the broadest possible base of support by convincing divergent groups of their common

---

*The language of this paragraph has been adapted from footnotes and the text of the original version of chapter 3, which parts were deleted to eliminate redundancies between chapters 3 and 4.

interests" into events that "stress the cleavages separating their support-ers from other segments of society."[125]

These critics argue that interest representation inevitably leads to fringe parties, proliferates extremist viewpoints associated with some par-liamentary or other proportionate party systems, or just results in stale-mate.[126] Critics claim all group-based remedies will promote intergroup conflict, balkanizing what instead should be a uniform, national identity built with stabilizing procedural rules. Critics say majority rule, for exam-ple, is necessary as a governing norm to finesse deep and long-standing divisions. In this sense, winner-take-all majority rule is claimed to be both more stabilizing and more efficient than a proportionality principle that promotes deliberation or a "dispersed pluralism."[127] Even if it is stabiliz-ing and accountable and enforces reciprocity and deliberative values, interest representation also may be criticized if it fails to produce substan-tively better outcomes by tending to reinforce fragmentation.

These criticisms essentially incorporate three separate arguments to which I must respond. First, that there is no principled way for iden-tifying legitimate interest representation claims. Second, that my focus on decisionmaking arguably "obfuscate[s] the crisis of liberal constitu-tionalism."[128] Third, that a focus on proportionate interest in decision-making accelerates the momentum toward separatism and ultimately anarchy.

To the first concern, I respond simply that I devised the interest rep-resentation model in the context of a specific statutory enforcement scheme—the Voting Rights Act of 1965—which is itself limited to racial and language minorities. Limiting claims to these statutorily protected groups makes sense because they have succeeded in making a strong, his-torically supported and congressionally mandated case for their claims that a homogeneous, permanent majority has exercised disproportionate power consistently to degrade their influence on the political process as a whole. Nevertheless, other groups need not resent interest representa-tion claims, for once a violation is found, the remedy does not disadvan-tage them and, indeed, advantages them to the extent that they are politically cohesive and sufficiently numerous.

Regarding the second argument, I concede that political equality de-pends ultimately upon a theory of substantive justice. Procedural fairness, however, is not subsumed completely by substantive justice. Procedural fairness means that a legitimate decisionmaking process promotes inde-pendent values of participation, deliberation, and consensus. The deci-sionmaking enterprise can be empowering where it gives participants a stake in the outcome because it promotes both a sense of collective responsibility for the outcome and an individual opportunity to succeed a fair proportion of the time. I would argue that it is, therefore, important to establish the injustice in winner-take-all decisionmaking independent of a full-blown substantive theory.

The third argument requires a more extended response because the separatist critique adopts a number of erroneous assumptions. It suffers first from the false premise that interest representation destroys a preexisting general, common, uniform perspective or cultural understanding. For members of racial minority groups who have been, and continue to be, victimized as a result of their racial identity, a deep consensus that does not acknowledge the pervasiveness of the oppression that some, and the indignity that most, have suffered on account of race is impossible.[129] Interest representation thus does not create conflict where none previously existed.[130]

Moreover, a credible argument can be made that interest representation is, in fact, stabilizing. Although it makes present beneficiaries of electoral or voting rules, such as incumbents, perpetually vulnerable, such "cycling" is arguably desirable for four reasons associated with contemporary pluralist analysis. First, from the perspective of minority interests, interest representation is stabilizing when compared to existing political arrangements. For statutorily protected minorities, the stability ostensibly associated with winner-take-all majority rule is illusory, and its attendant efficiency comes at the cost of ignoring or marginalizing minority perspectives. In this sense, multiple, cross-cutting cleavages are more stabilizing than permanent, deep cleavages because the former better realize the majority rule assumption that shifting alliances are a check against the tyranny of the majority.

Indeed, recognizing the intensity of preferences need not lead to chaos because doing so will create incentives for groups presently alienated by their lack of meaningful political power to work within the political process. By giving such groups proportionate power, and consequently distributing preference satisfaction more widely, it helps compensate for their relative lack of power and legitimates the results of the political process. For example, interest representation may improve the collective decisionmaking process by promoting open discussion among a diverse set of participants and by encouraging strategies of negotiation and coalition-building with the possibility of present alliances as well as future victories. By thus giving minorities a fair share of the power, interest representation's proportionality principle surfaces antecedent racial conflict, which arguably delegitimates prejudice and limits its corrosive effect.[131] In this way, interest representation arguably *moderates* political behavior.

Second, cycling helps reduce the tendency of politically entrenched interests to reproduce themselves or to emphasize the peculiarly transformative effects of their individual prestige and advancement. Such cycling arguably comports with a more participatory view of political power that potentially yields greater accountability or, at a minimum, affirms the importance of constantly renewing community-based ties. Third, interest representation may potentially reduce racial polarization by encouraging whites to identify or converge their interests with blacks. It avoids the polarizing debate about affirmative action, for example, because it does not create or impose external preferences for interests based on presumptions about group solidarity or injury. Interest preferences are voluntary, self-identified needs or wants that must be realized through organizational initiative and cooperation.

Even if a proportionality principle fails consistently to produce consensus, it may be stabilizing nonetheless if it is capable of generating less conflict than current empowerment strategies. Although there will probably still be some conflict, conflict is more likely to dissipate in an interest representation setting than in a subdistricting environment.[132] For instance, because interest representation allows all groups to self-identify their interests with like-minded groups regardless of their location within the jurisdiction, whites are not directly disadvantaged through interest representation, as they may claim to be through majority-black districting remedies that construct districts in which some whites are district minorities who feel politically powerless.

Finally, the winner-take-some-but-not-all approach contemplates "strong democracy," meaning an invigorated electorate that participates (as opposed to spectates) throughout the political process. For example, interest representation could encourage the development of minority political organizations that would mobilize voters directly to articulate preferences and to monitor the legislative process and that would formalize bargains, or at least address issues of intense interest to the minority. Minority voters would thus be empowered to participate interactively through the organization and resources of an accountable, community-based, minority political party, which would have the effect of increasing the accountability of minority representatives.[133]

One need not worry that the development of minority political parties or organizations will necessarily lead to stalemate because stalemate is less probable where, as in interest representation, participants experience continuous opportunities to cooperate and compromise. Indeed, studies of coalition systems do not conclude that stalemate is inevitable. For example, some scholars have concluded from the experience of foreign countries with systems resembling interest representation that long-term government stability can and in fact does exist as a function of the underlying social forces and structural features of such a political system. Furthermore, the argument that multiplication of parties leads to instability, a charge usually levelled against parliamentary systems of government, is less legitimate on a national scale where, as in the United States, the executive is independent of the legislature and certainly is not relevant at the level of local government, which I address here.

In sum, proponents of interest representation posit that changing electoral and collective voting procedures can improve the collective decisionmaking process by including and proportionately reflecting minority interests. Whatever the substantive results, the process can be legitimated and made more deliberative by choosing decisional rules that disaggregate the disproportionate power of the permanent, homogeneous majority. Similarly, conflict between interest groups may be inescapable but need not be unproductive or destabilizing.*

In Part III I explore further the implications of interest proportionality for democratic representation in general and separation of powers in particular. My response here has been limited to the feasibility concern. If it is true, as I have argued, that representatives are equal only if existing distribution of power, resources and prejudices do not play an "authoritative" role in their deliberations, then it is not clear that the remedial goal of equal political participation in the form of a fair and equal distribution of preference satisfaction is realistic, especially within a litigation context.[134]

Even if doctrinally acceptable as a remedial strategy, proportionate interest representation may be politically unsuccessful in a time of retrenchment and regression. The political status quo factors that defeat the traditional electoral success model will predictably dilute any concerted litigation effort to improve legislative performance on behalf of black interests.[135] It may be that no electoral strategy, unaccompanied by a protest-based model of insurgent politics, can mobilize sustained commitment either to incremental reform or to more substantive conceptions of political justice.

---

* The next five paragraphs are adapted from the original language of chapter 3, which was deleted in this collection.

While formidable, these concerns do not alter the proposal's political and doctrinal plausibility at the electoral level and its aspirational value for legislative deliberation. Proportionate interest representation disaggregates the majority to benefit some whites as well as blacks. At the electoral level, lowering the threshold of exclusion potentially empowers all numerically significant groups, including minority political parties, organized groups of women, the elderly, as well as any group of working class or poor people presently politically disadvantaged under a majoritarian model.[136] Retaining at-large elections eliminates the decennial contestation over political power, including the inevitable fight between incumbent politicians and minority groups seeking representation.

At the legislative level, though much more problematic, pursuit of a radically different litigation strategy still may be worthwhile. As applied to legislative decisional rules, these proposals are necessarily fact specific. Given the special historic, social, and political circumstances of a particular case, alternative remedies may be desirable, even preferable.[137] Few courts and voting rights litigators have actually expressed a preference for these alternatives. But, even if litigators approach the *violation* stage of a voting rights case much as they do now, it may still be possible to strengthen, through proofs and briefs incorporating the proportionate interest principle, the remedial side of the judicial inquiry. Moreover, as referenda or ballot initiatives, it may be useful and practical to explore further the qualitative advantages of an interest proportionality principle employed in conjunction with legislative decisionmaking changes.

III. The Constitutionality of Interest Representation

This chapter has thus far demonstrated that interest representation is consistent with the ideals behind the Voting Rights Act. All that remains is to show that interest representation, particularly at the legislative level, is consistent with the Constitution itself. Although there would seem to be several constitutional arguments against interest representation, I address only two of them here, leaving the others to be explored elsewhere.[138] The first of these is the federalism/separation of powers argument. This argument suggests that interest representation would embark the federal courts on a lawmaking enterprise in which they would dictate to state and local government the precise electoral and deliberative systems such governments could employ, issues that should be left to the governments themselves for resolution.

Without exploring more fully than the scope of this chapter permits the federalism and separation of powers issues, I believe an interest-based third-generation approach is justiciable for at least two reasons. First, the focus and basic remedial approach I propose has been mandated by *Congress*. The Voting Rights Act embodies a statutory directive that the courts examine the results or effects of particular voting "standards, practices, and procedures."[139] This mandate is not limited to electoral voting, and, as previously argued, the statute's political equality and empowerment norms require that it not be so limited.

Congress approved several extraordinarily intrusive remedies that establish a broad foundation for the parameters of the approach I propose. The Supreme Court has recognized and deferred to Congress' judgment that such remedies are necessary and appropriate to enforce the Reconstruction amendments to the Constitution.[140] It follows that Congress presumptively viewed possible risks attendant to group-based affirmative remedies as either nonexistent or insufficiently great:

> In [1982] Congress made a deliberate political judgment that the time had come to apply the statute's remedial measures to *present conditions* of racial vote dilution . . . ; that national policy respecting minority voting rights could no longer await the securing of those rights by normal political processes, or by voluntary action of state and local governments. . . . In making that political judgment, Congress necessarily took into account and rejected as unfounded, or assumed as outweighed, several risks to fundamental political values that opponents of the amendment urged in committee deliberations and floor debate. Among these were the risk that . . . reliance upon the judicial remedy would supplant the normal, more healthy processes of acquiring political power by registration, voting and coalition building; and the fundamental risk that the recognition of "group voting rights" and the imposing of affirmative obligation upon government to secure those rights by race-conscious electoral mechanisms was alien to the American political tradition.[141]

Thus, far from actually making law, the federal courts, under interest representation, merely apply a law made, and fashion remedies approved, by four Congresses and Presidents from Lyndon Johnson to Ronald Reagan.

Second, the approach I envision is procedural and not substantive, so that the federal courts, in awaiting interest-representation relief, have nothing to do with the substance of state and local deliberative processes. An interest representation claim does not ask courts to determine what the preferences of the minority are in order to evaluate the merits of particular policy allocations or to enforce substantive policy decisions. Like the vote dilution inquiry at the electoral level, the court's inquiry into whether the legislature is satisfactorily responding to minority interests is limited to an investigation of the voting process itself, an inquiry undertaken in order to determine the racial effects of a challenged voting procedure. The approach, which specifically targets legislative decisional rules, not decisional outcomes, is essentially a process-oriented inquiry into voting patterns.

Furthermore, even if a court found a violation using interest representation techniques, it should reconfigure legislative voting rules only when absolutely necessary. The court should first give the local body an opportunity to correct the violation by adopting rules that do not ensure the defeat of minority interests.[142] If the local body refuses to do so, then the court should order the rule changes itself, limiting its changes to the legislative rules responsible for the violation. Consequently, interest representation's emphasis on racially polarized voting and on giving the implicated legislative bodies the opportunity to correct their violations limits the intrusiveness of judicial review of state and local processes and satisfactorily addresses the federalism argument.[143]

The second constitutional argument is that interest representation violates the principle of one person/one vote. Two features of interest representation may be said to violate that principle: (1) cumulative voting, which gives each voter several votes, and (2) a minority veto, which might be used as an alternative to cumulative voting.

This argument misapprehends interest representation. The one person/one vote principle suggests that each citizen should enjoy equal voting strength; that is, that "one [person's] vote . . . is to be worth as much as another's."[144] Cumulative electoral or legislative voting is clearly consistent with one person/one vote because it ensures that each voter exercises a similarly meaningful vote. It is even more consistent with some notions of one person/one vote than geographically based districting because it equalizes the number of voters each representative represents without gerrymandering or artificially creating communities of interest. Further, under a modified at-large voting system, all voters would have the same number of votes to cast, so that cumulative voting would provide equal voting strength to all voters.

Even where supermajority rules essentially give the minority representative a veto, an argument could still be made that this is consistent with the one person/one vote rule. The argument would be that the rule is designed to ensure each voter an equal opportunity to influence the policymaking process. Because of the dilutive effect of racial bloc voting by the white majority coupled with winner-take-all majority rule, the minority veto would be justified to overcome the disproportionate power presently enjoyed by white voters in certain jurisdictions. In this sense, supermajority rules provide minorities with an equal opportunity to influence the political process and, consequently, comport with one person/one vote. In any event, even if these alternative remedies do not provide perfect equality of voting strength, greater deviations from absolute mathematical equality are tolerated at the local level. Thus, neither the federalism/separation of powers nor the one person/one vote argument against the constitutionality of interest representation is particularly problematic.

Conclusion

In this chapter, I have attempted to move the debate at least beyond symbolic, second-generation conquests to third-generation concerns with effective legislative power exercised on behalf of the minority group's distinctive group interests. Transforming the second-generation litigation strategy is necessary because it has generally failed to produce real empowerment gains for statutorily protected minorities. In most instances, the primary accomplishment has been to effect cosmetic changes in the composition of state and local decisionmaking bodies. As I have argued, this has simply transferred the discrete and insular minority problem from the electorate to the legislative body.

Interest representation, the third-generation strategy, fulfills the dual vision of the Voting Rights Act that minority groups should enjoy equal voting weight *and* equal voting power. Instead of emphasizing arbitrary territorial boundaries, which waste the votes of both minority and majority groups, interest representation favors allowing voters of the same interests to join together in voting for candidates of choice, regardless of where the voters live in the jurisdiction. This at-large system, however, would be modified in one critical respect. The winner-take-all feature of majority rule would be discarded in favor of cumulative voting, which allows voters to cumulate their votes in order to express the intensity of their preferences. In this fashion, interest representation strives to ensure that groups that are politically cohesive, sufficiently numerous, and strategically mobilized will be able to elect a representative to the legislative body.

Unlike the second-generation approach, however, interest representation does not end with electoral reforms. Rather, it looks into the legislative body itself to make sure the discrete and insular minority problem is not replicated there through seemingly neutral rules that have disparate effects on minority representatives. It is important to bear in mind that in its evaluation of the internal legislative processes, interest representation focuses not on guaranteeing that minorities achieve the substantive results desired, but on adopting voting procedures that enhance the quality of the deliberative process. These voting rules help ensure that minority concerns will not be ignored in the deliberative process and that permanent, homogeneous majorities will not dominate by encouraging coalition-building and consensus decisions, perhaps by linking bills of interest to minorities to bills of interest to the majority.

This chapter is part of an ongoing effort to reconceptualize political equality to ensure effective representation of interests, not just voters or territory. At this stage of its incarnation—and in this political climate— neither my emphasis on fair and effective representation nor its attempted statutory application may persuade judicial actors. Nor should my effort be understood primarily as a litigation tool. Nevertheless, it is my hope that the concept of proportionate interest representation will focus attention on the failure of the current voting rights strategy for achieving political empowerment. Once that realization has been made, I hope that interest representation will be seen as a superior ideal for realizing the statutory norms of political equality and empowerment.

5

Groups, Representation, and Race Conscious Districting

A Case of the Emperor's Clothes

This essay analyzes the dominant theory of representation in this country in which the unit of representation is geographic rather than political. Geographic constituencies, which are created through the use of single-member districts, are a form of group representation in which common territory is a proxy for common interests. I argue that the representation of racial groups is valid and desirable given our history and our acceptance of group representation in other forms, although, as argued in previous essays, I claim that representation of either groups or individuals is not well accomplished by single-member districting. I also expand my exploration of cumulative voting, arguing that it is not only consistent with one-person, one-vote, but even better, it embodies one-person, one-vote, one-value in a way that districting systems do not. Yet, cumulative voting is not, in itself, the basis for a grand moral theory of representation or even a panacea for across-the-board voting problems. Instead, I use the idea of cumulative voting as a way to explore and define the unfairness and incoherence of indirect representation of geographic constituencies within winner-take-all territorial units. This essay was written in 1992, and first published in 1993.

[N]ow that the first round of reapportionment has been accomplished, there is need to talk "one man-one vote" a little less and to talk a little more of "political equity," and of functional components of effective representation. *A mathematically equal vote which is politically worthless because*

119

*of gerrymandering or winner-take-all districting is as deceiving as "em-
peror's clothes."*[1]

With voices pitched in the high decibel range, critics of race-conscious
districting[2] are blasting the Voting Rights Act and its 1982 amendments. A
recent *Wall Street Journal* headline declares that voting is now "rigged by
race."[3] Ethnic activists, the writer asserts, are collaborating with GOP op-
eratives in an unholy political alliance to herd minorities into their own
convoluted urban districts in order to improve GOP prospects in majority
white surburban areas. According to such critics, this is a "political one-
night stand" made possible by misguided federal courts and Department
of Justice officials construing the 1982 Act to create majority minority districts, the newest form of "racial packaging."[4]

My students inform me that Cokie Roberts, as part of ABC News's election night coverage, dramatically illustrated the concerns of critics when
she traced on a map of the Chicago area the "earmuff" district, allegedly
carved out of two noncontiguous Chicago neighborhoods joined by a narrow rod to maximize the possibility that the Latino residents would be
able to elect a representative of their choice to Congress.[5] And in June
1993, the Supreme Court discovered a new constitutional right enabling
white voters in North Carolina to challenge, based on its odd and irregular
shapes, a "highway" district that narrowly tracks the path of an interstate,
creating a swatch of voters on either side of the highway from one end of
the state to the other.[6] This fifty-four percent black district, the most integrated in the state, elected Melvin Watt, one of the first two blacks
elected to Congress from that state in this century.[7]

The Voting Rights Act codified the right of protected minority groups
to an equal opportunity to elect candidates of their choice, although its
language disclaims the right to racial representation by members of the
racial group in direct proportion to population. The critics now claim this
is special and unwarranted protection for racial and language minority
groups. In the name of liberal individualism, these critics assert that the
statute effected a radical transformation in the allocation and nature of
representation.[8]

Although race-conscious districting is their apparent target, these critics have fixed their aim on a deeper message—that pressing claims of racial identity and racial disadvantage diminish democracy. We all lose, the
theory goes, when some of us identify in racial or ethnic group terms.

In my view, critics of race-conscious districting have misdirected their
fire. Their emperor has no clothes. Their dissatisfaction with racial-group

representation ignores the essentially group nature of political participation. In this regard, the critics fail to confront directly the group nature of representation itself, especially in a system of geographic districting. Perhaps unwittingly they also reveal a bias toward the representation of a particular racial group rather than their discomfort with group representation itself.[9] In a society as deeply cleaved by issues of racial identity as ours, there is no one race. In the presence of such racial differences, a system of representation that fails to provide group representation loses legitimacy.[10]

Yet these critics have, in fact, accurately identified a problem with a system of representation based on winner-take-all territorial districts. There is an emperor wearing his clothes, but not as they describe. Rather than expressing a fundamental failure of democratic theory based on group representation per se, the critics have identified a problem with one particular solution. It is districting in general—not race-conscious districting in particular—that is the problem.

Winner-take-all territorial districting imperfectly distributes representation based on group attributes and disproportionately rewards those who win the representational lottery. Territorial districting uses an aggregating rule that inevitably groups people by virtue of some set of externally observed characteristics such as geographic proximity or racial identity. In addition, the winner-take-all principle inevitably wastes some votes. The dominant group within the district gets all the power; the votes of supporters of nondominant groups or of disaffected voters within the dominant group are wasted. Their votes lose significance because they are consistently cast for political losers.

The essential unfairness of districting is a result, therefore, of two assumptions: (1) that a majority of voters within a given geographic community can be configured to constitute a "group"; and (2) that incumbent politicians, federal courts, or some other independent set of actors can fairly determine which group to advantage by giving it all the power within the district. When either of these assumptions is not accurate, as is most often the case, the districting is necessarily unfair.

Another effect of these assumptions is gerrymandering, which results from the arbitrary allocation of disproportionate political power to one group.[11] Districting breeds gerrymandering as a means of allocating group benefits; the operative principle is deciding whose votes get wasted. Whether it is racially or politically motivated, gerrymandering is the inevitable by-product of an electoral system that aggregates people by virtue of assumptions about their group characteristics and then inflates the winning group's power by allowing it to represent *all* voters in a regional unit.

Given a system of winner-take-all territorial districts and working within the limitations of this particular election method, the courts have sought to achieve political fairness for racial minorities. As a result, there is some truth to the assertion that minority groups, unlike other voters, enjoy a special representational relationship under the Voting Rights Act's 1982 amendments to remedy their continued exclusion from effective political participation in some jurisdictions. But the proper response is not to deny minority voters that protection. The answer should be to extend that special relationship to *all* voters by endorsing *the equal opportunity to vote for a winning candidate* as a universal principle of political fairness.

I use the term "one-vote, one-value" to describe the principle of political fairness that as many votes as possible should count in the election of representatives. Each voter should be able to choose, by the way she casts her votes, who represents her. One-vote, one-value is realized when everyone's vote counts for someone's election. The only system with the potential to realize this principle for *all* voters is one in which the unit of representation is political rather than regional, and the aggregating rule is proportionality rather than winner-take-all. Semiproportional systems, such as cumulative voting, can approximate the one-vote, one-value principle by minimizing the problem of wasted votes.

One-vote, one-value systems transcend the gerrymandering problem because each vote has an equal worth independent of decisions made by those who drew district lines. Votes are allocated based on decisions made by the voters themselves. These systems revive the connection between voting and representation, whether the participant consciously associates with a group of voters or chooses to participate on a fiercely individual basis. Candidates are elected in proportion to the intensity of their political support within the electorate itself rather than as a result of decisions made by incumbent politicians or federal courts once every ten years.[12]

My project in this chapter is to defend the representation of racial groups while reconsidering whether race-conscious districting is the most effective way of representing these groups or their interests.[13] My claim is that racial-group representation is important, but it is only imperfectly realized through the electoral system based on territorial districting or through the limited concept of racially "descriptive" representation.

In Part I, I describe current doctrinal approaches, such as the jurisprudence of one-person, one-vote, on which some critics of race-conscious districting rely to emphasize the individual rather than the group nature of voting. I suggest that the one-person, one-vote doctrine is consistent with both group and individual conceptions of voting, but in the context of winner-take-all territorial districting, it is a limited principle of political equality. In Part II, I argue that racial-group representation is a natural response to historical and current reality, but it is one best realized in electoral systems employing proportional or semiproportional aggregating rules. Proportional or semiproportional aggregating rules serve as a proxy for the aspirational concept of procedural or political fairness. In such systems, the unit of representation is political rather than regional, and almost all votes count in the election of officials. In this way, systems such as cumulative voting are consistent with principles of both one-person, one-vote *and* one-vote, one-value.

In contrast to winner-take-all districting systems, cumulative voting may—in appropriate, fact-specific circumstances—be an expedient, and more politically fair, election method. Cumulative voting promotes a concept of racial group identity that is interest-based rather than biological.[14] In light of the controversy surrounding race-conscious districting, where circumstances dictate, it is at least worth considering this alternative, thereby attempting to tailor the emperor with some real clothes by putting the principles of political equality into practice.

I

For many liberal reformers, the one-person, one-vote principle is politically fair because its ideal of universal suffrage incorporates the respect due and the responsibilities owed to each citizen in a democracy. The one-person, one-vote cases attempt to equalize the purely formal opportunity to cast a ballot through a system of population-based apportionment. Under this rationale, each district contains approximately the same number of people; each person within the district has the same opportunity to vote for someone to represent the district; and each district representative represents the same number of constituents.

The one-person, one-vote principle thus assures all voters the right to cast a theoretically equal ballot. In this Part, I argue that this theoretical possibility is unlikely to be realized in an electoral system using winner-take-all districts. I further suggest that neither groups of voters nor individuals are fairly represented under such a system.

There are two issues at stake. One raises the question of whether voting is constitutionally protected because it implicates individual rights. If voting is an individual right, the second question asks whether the one-person, one-vote principles that operate within the confines of geographic districts adequately protect the right to vote. I concede that voting has garnered its highest constitutional protection when presented as an individual rights issue, but the widespread use of winner-take-all districts undermines the validity of this characterization. The fact that constitutional rules about voting evolved within a system of regional representation suggests that posing the problem as one of individual rather than group rights has been a distraction. I claim that the heavy reliance on one-person, one-vote jurisprudence to develop a theory of democracy fails both as a theory and as an adequate doctrinal protection of either individual or group rights.

A. *One-Person, One-Vote and the Limits of Liberal Individualism*

In this subpart, I examine the assumption that allocation of representatives through winner-take-all districting is a form of representation of individuals. The heart of this assumption is that citizenship is the ultimate reflection of individual dignity and autonomy and that voting is the means for individual citizens to realize this personal and social standing. Under this theory, voters realize the fullest meaning of citizenship by the individual act of voting for representatives who, once elected, participate on the voters' behalf in the process of self-government.[15] Indeed the very terminology employed in the Supreme Court's one-person, one-vote constitutional principle suggests that voting is an individual right.[16] For these reasons, some assume that the right at stake is the individual right to an equally weighted vote or an equally powerful vote.[17]

The assumption is that constitutional protection for voting is exclusively about protecting an individual right, not necessarily about ensuring equal voting rights. At first, the connection between the two concepts seems plausible because every citizen has the right to vote and every citizen has the right to an equally weighted vote. But the one-person, one-vote principle of voting is primarily about equal, not individual, representation.[18] Under this equality norm, the right to "fair and effective representation" subsumes concerns about equal voting and equal access. As the Court stated in one of its early reapportionment cases, the principle of equal representation for equal numbers of people is "designed to prevent debasement of voting power and diminution of access to elected representatives."[19] Implicit in this equality norm is the moral proposition that every citizen has the right to equal legislative influence. This means an equal opportunity to influence legislative policy.

The assumption that voting is an individual right is also unnecessary for the view that voting rights are a means of political empowerment. One-person, one-vote rules emerged in response to claims about population-based malapportionment and about the right of the majority of people to elect a proportionate share of representatives.[20] In announcing this principle, the Supreme Court recognized that the growing urban majority of the 1960s would never command its *fair share* of legislative power unless the Court intervened. In conjunction with concern about both a fair share of power and developments in the law of minority vote dilution, the Court also adopted an instrumental view of voting. People would participate when and if they thought their vote mattered. Under this empowerment norm, the primary purpose of voting rights is to empower citizens to participate in the political process.

I take the position that the right of the individual to participate politically is a right best realized in association with other individuals, *i.e.*, as a group.[21] As Justice Powell recognized, "[t]he concept of 'representation' necessarily applies to groups: groups of voters elect representatives, individual voters do not."[22] This is a bottom-up view of representation in which voters are empowered by their collective participation in the process of self-government. Under this view, voters engage in collective action to choose someone to represent their interests within the governing body. The representative is charged with influencing public policy on behalf of constituents' collective interests.

The Court's jurisprudence does not consistently express a bottom-up view of representation within either the equality or the empowerment norms. On occasion, though, the Court implicitly assumes the value of collective participation and influence in opinions that do not articulate the bottom-up view. For example, the Court's decision in *Reynolds v. Sims* granting a fair share of representation to population majorities suggests that by equalizing the number of people for whom each representative is responsible, the election of a single individual can fairly represent what are in essence collective interests. Another example is *Baker v. Carr,* where the plaintiffs' original complaint alleged a systematic plan to "discriminate against a *geographical class* of persons."[23]

The bottom-up view of representation is reflected in some of the Court's early language about the importance of having a voice—meaning a public policy vote—in the process of self-government. It also is the basis for the Court's 1986 decision in *Davis v. Bandemer* that political gerrymandering claims are justiciable. In his plurality opinion for the Court in *Davis,* Justice White suggests that the policy decision to represent groups fairly already had been made in the context of racial minorities.[24]

Of course, one could counter that representation is essentially a process of providing individual constituents with individual service and that it is therefore an individual right. This is a top-down view of representation in which the representative reaches back to his or her district to return government benefits to district constituents. In this sense, equalizing the number of constituents equalizes access for individuals, not groups of individuals. Representation becomes the formal opportunity to receive one's fair share of government benefits or to have access to one's representative for individual constituency service. Voting creates "a personal value," or a symbolic statement of belonging, by the mere act of casting a ballot. A vote is meaningful because it is counted, whether or not it actually affects the outcome.

While this top-down view might rest on the assumption that the right to *representation* is an individual right, it does not mesh well with the assumption that the right to *vote* is an individual right. Indeed, a voter need not vote at all to be represented under this understanding. Actually casting a vote is less important than establishing voting status. Representation becomes the process of initiating a relationship in which one need not ever participate except by moving into the district. Even nonvoters are represented vicariously by choices made on their behalf.

Proponents of the philosophy of individualism attempt to use the one-person, one-vote principle to locate voting in the status of individual or constituent. They rely on the fact that every individual has the *opportunity* to cast a potentially winning vote or to be represented vicariously by one who does. This approach camouflages the group nature of voting by emphasizing the personal aspects of representation.

Consistent with their prevailing political philosophy of individualism, some members of the Court have struggled mightily to use one-person, one-vote rules to avoid the concept of group representation. However, even where its nexus to group activity remains disguised, the principle of one-person, one-vote is as consistent with group as it is with individual representation. Similarly, the one-person, one-vote principle is consistent with semiproportional representation systems. Even if voters each were awarded five votes to plump as they choose, the one-person, one-vote principle would be satisfied, since each voter would have the same voting power or voting weight.

In this chapter I argue that despite the efforts of some members of the Court to characterize representation as an exclusively individual notion, the concept of group representation became unavoidable for two reasons. The first, which I develop in Part II, is that the concept of group voting was necessary to understand the political unfairness of excluding racial minorities in a racially polarized constituency. The second, to which I now turn, is that the one-person, one-vote principle was conceived and articulated within a construction of constituencies based on geography. It is districting itself that merges individual representation with the representation of groups of individuals. Thus, it always has been necessary to acknowledge, at least implicitly, the relationship between districts and interests. I already have explored some of the bottom-up interest representation aspects of the equality and empowerment claims in earlier chapters. In the next subpart, I further develop the link between group representation and territorial districting.

B. *Group Representation and Territorial Districting*

In this subpart, I argue that because of our explicit and implicit recognition of constituencies of geography, we have never actually employed a system of individual representation. Indeed, the use of geographic districts as the basis for establishing representational constituencies is at its very heart a system of group-based representation. Moreover, even where districts comply with principles of one-person, one-vote, such districts dilute the voting strength of both individuals and groups.

The concept of representation necessarily applies to groups: groups of voters elect representatives; individuals do not.[25] Representation is more than the individual relationship between constituent and elected representative. Because representation is primarily about political influence, not political service, bottom-up representation becomes the essential link to a genuine voice in the process of self-government. Districting is a form of group-interest representation, albeit an imperfectly realized one.

Districting, by definition, assumes that each voter is a " 'member' of a 'group' comprised of all the voters in her district."[26] As Justice Stewart noted, "The very fact of geographic districting . . . carries with it an acceptance of the idea of legislative representation of regional needs and interests."[27] Regardless of whether other Justices of the Warren Court ever consciously adopted the idea of interest representation, in working within territorial districts they assumed that interests reflect where people live.

The view that geography approximates political interests is not a new idea. Indeed, the idea that geographic units reflect a common or group identity is part of the historical explanation for the winner-take-all system of districts. The American system of winner-take-all districts was adapted from the system in Britain prior to 1832, which in turn can be traced to

Assumes that
systems wants to empower
rather-than divide groups

feudal origins.[28] The feudal tradition helped define the law of the franchise on the theory that "it was the land, and not men which should be represented."[29] It was the community, in theory, that was represented, and therefore the qualification for voting was corporative, with the franchise varying between communities.[30] Functional groupings, not individuals, were the basic units of representation.[31]

The British system also created a link between political representation and geographically based interests. Elected representatives were not seen as representatives of individual constituencies; they were merely equal members of Parliament who represented all of Britain.[32] The parliamentary system of representation had evolved in Britain because of feudal duties and obligations; the lord and his vassals were literally tied to the land, and representation in Parliament was actually part of the lord's feudal service to the king. Similarly, inhabitants of the medieval town were not separate, for representational purposes, from the town itself.[33] The town was a political association, and the status of its inhabitants was defined by the rights of the group to which they belonged, namely the town. This link between political representation and economic or geographic ties was later carried over to the United States during the Colonial period.[34]

By the late Eighteenth Century, towns were directly represented in the American colonial legislatures by representatives with explicit instructions to represent the towns' interests. The relevance of town representation is that colonial towns "exercised power as a group; as a group they had rights, as a group they had powers."[35] Representation by geographic groups became the norm, in part because there was often no practical distinction between occupational and territorial representation.

Indeed, the word "representation" originated as a term used by medieval jurists to describe the personification of collectivities; the spokesperson for a community was its embodiment, the bearer of its representative personhood. Even in its modern form, representation often connotes the activity of furthering the interests of an abstraction rather than of an individual. Although many liberal theorists of American democracy espouse the importance of representation of the rational individual, this claim is at odds with the historical roots of an electoral system that relies on regional rather than political units of representation.

It is also at odds with the practice of districting. The process of geographic districting collects people into units of representation by virtue of certain group characteristics or assumptions about shared characteristics within geographic communities. Geographic districting grounds the representational relationship in the opportunity to vote for a candidate to represent the interests of voters within a regionally defined political unit. It is assumed that those voters who share the homogeneous characteristics that give the district its "identity" (its dominant political, regional, or racial affiliation) are in fact represented. Because *all* voters share at least a common regional identity—they all live within the district's geographic walls—all voters are therefore assumed to be represented without regard to their actual choice of a candidate.

But the geographic unit is not necessarily politically homogeneous or of one mind as to who should represent it. In any contested election, some voters will vote for someone other than the winning candidate. These votes do not lead to the election of any candidate. Although these voters reside in equally populated districts, they have not chosen someone to represent their interests. Their theoretically equal votes are, as a practical matter, wasted in that the casting of their vote did not lead to the selection of their representative. The term "wasted votes," therefore, refers to votes cast for a candidate who does not win. In addition, I use the term to refer to votes cast for someone who does not need the votes to win.

Perhaps for this reason, one commentator refers to the constituency of geography as an "artificial 'group.'"[36] Constituents do not consciously choose to become members of this group, since very few people move somewhere in recognition of their likely voting efficacy within particular election subdistricts. Similarly, when they move, few people know in advance the particular elected officials by whom they are likely to be represented. In other words, voters do not move to an election district; they move to a neighborhood or community.

I am suggesting that constituents within a geographically districted group may be there involuntarily, without sharing the same interests as other community residents, and despite pre-existing hierarchical relationships.[37] In this way, membership in the territorial constituency is like membership in a family, with the former imposed by residence and the latter by kinship. Like family, geographic districts may not reflect conscious choice; as "compulsory constituencies," they nevertheless reflect ties that bind.

Moreover, even if this factual assumption is incorrect, voters who might move based on the likelihood that they will reside within a specific election district are not acting rationally. This is because the imperative of the one-person, one-vote rule mandates continual redistricting. Even motivated voters may rely on existing district configurations for only limited lengths of time.

In addition, the level of mathematical equality now required by the courts makes it hard to claim that many election districts are neighborhoods. The upshot of absolute population equality as the basis for representation is that equipopulous districts are more important than districts that preserve communities of interests or leave neighborhoods intact. In this respect, districting under the one-person, one-vote rule is arbitrary. Indeed, this was Justice Stewart's complaint when he accused the Court of privileging the personal right to vote over the efforts of local government to represent regional needs, communities of interest, or political subunits.[38]

Districting justifies the representation of this artificial group using a theory of virtual representation. "Virtual" representation works like "constructive" in "constructive possession." It means "as if" or "pretended" representation. In contrast to direct representation or bottom-up representation, virtual representation relies on the concepts of (1) *indirect representation,* (2) representation of *similar interests* elsewhere, and (3) *top-down* representation. While the theory of virtual representation could be justified by any one of these concepts, the three assumptions generally are interrelated. Each of these assumptions is critical to the validity of virtual representation.

First, virtual representation assumes that the district winner *indirectly* represents the district losers.[39] For this to hold true, the election winner must do an adequate job of representing all those who reside within the district, including his or her political opponents. This assumption is based on the golden-rule principle that the winner will not tyrannize the losers because the winner may become the loser in the next election. Because the winner realizes the value of political stability, the winner will also represent the losers. Thus, in the long run, the losers' votes are not permanently wasted because they operate to hold the winners in check.

The second assumption of virtual representation is that the district losers technically are represented by *similarly situated* voters elsewhere in the political system. In this assumption, voters are represented when other voters—who are like them—vote in other districts and succeed in electing their candidate of choice. This reasoning assumes that similarly situated voters are fungible. "District voters" are grouped by characteristics they share with "nondistrict voters." Because of these group characteristics, district losers are vicariously represented by winners in other districts for whom they would have voted had they been given the chance. As a result, the second assumption sees voters as represented based on certain "group" characteristics that can be externally predetermined for a ten-year period (between census counts) at the time of reapportionment and that can be measured jurisdiction-wide, rather than district-wide. Again, the district losers' votes technically are not wasted because district losers are represented by someone, albeit not someone for whom they voted.

The third virtual representation assumption is that the district itself is a cognizable group that is represented ultimately as a community of the whole. This incorporates the proposition that a district has some independent existence apart from the discrete individuals who form an electoral majority. This is the historical claim that the district itself has a political or group identity.

This argument relies on a *top-down* view of representation. Living in Pennsylvania, I am represented by two United States Senators even if I am under eighteen years old, mentally incompetent, or disenfranchised based on noncitizenship or a criminal conviction. The assumption is that the district, and hence all its residents, are serviced whenever anyone is elected to represent the district. The key element of representation is equal access to the elected representative who is available to each constituent as a result of her status as a district resident. Each of the voters within the district is represented, even those who voted for a losing candidate *as well as those who did not or could not vote.* Because voting is primarily symbolic of personal status within a coherent community, virtual representation argues that no one's vote is wasted.

Every voter in a district is presumed to be represented simply because her territorial constituency is represented. The voter within a territorial constituency is represented because she has someone to turn to in case of personal constituency service needs. She is presumed to be represented even if she did not vote for the winning candidate. The fact that she wasted her vote is ignored because she is nevertheless "geographically" present within the political subdivision. No stock is placed in the fact that she did not vote for the representative. She is simply represented through the direct representation of her needs and her geographic nexus to the representative's supporters.

If districting is to be justified by virtual representation, the entire theory of districting depends upon the juxtaposition of territorial constituencies and interest constituencies. Drawing district boundaries presumably defines communities of interest. District lines determine a set of associations between the voter and a particular representative as well as among the voters themselves. It is only because voters within a particular district are deemed unlikely to have opposing interests that the notion of a personal relationship between the voter and the representative can survive. Voters are presumed fungible, meaning they are essentially indistinguishable on some critical threshold issue. The representative otherwise would be unable to service disparate personal needs without compromising the interests of other constituents.

These virtual representation assumptions are related to two somewhat inconsistent premises of liberal individualism. One is the value of majority rule. The district majority governs with legitimacy because the district is a coalition of shifting "factions" whose multiplicity of interests will keep any one from dominating. The factions demonstrate that the district is not homogeneous, but the winner will virtually represent the losers because the losers are not permanent; the winner may be the loser at the next election. The first premise thus shares the first premise of virtual representation. It posits that individuals who vote for losing candidates are adequately represented by the winning candidate and have as much opportunity to influence that candidate as do other voters in the district.[40]

The second premise is that representation is primarily a personal relationship between the representative and her constituents. In this context, the representative does not know how a particular constituent voted and will service her needs in the hopes of recruiting or sustaining her allegiance. Adherents of the personal relationship perspective do not deny that the representative is more likely to represent faithfully the interests of those who voted for her; they simply suggest that the *needs* of each constituent also will be met because a district constituency establishes a relationship between the voter and her personal representative without regard to the voter's actual electoral preference.

This premise, however, unlike the majority-rule premise, is based on a view of relative homogeneity within the district. Because the district constituents have similar needs and interests, it is possible for one representative to service adequately all constituents. If the constituency has such common interests, one would expect a relatively unanimous constituency. By contrast, the majority-rule assumption relies on a more fractured constituency to balance the majority's urge to dominate. The personal relationship perspective and the majority-rule premise are, therefore, in some tension. They define voting by reference to competing notions of fungibility and personal access on the one hand and distinct interests on the other.

As a consequence, the virtual representation assumptions do not fit neatly within a one-dimensional view of representation based on liberal individualism. In fact, the rational individual who serves as the focal point of individualism would often take actions that are wholly inconsistent with virtual representation. The most apparent inconsistency is the idea that one's interests can be effectively represented by someone whom the voter, when given the choice, rationally determined did not reflect her interests. There is something distinctly unliberal in the view that indirect representation of interests is preferable to direct representation of groups or interests as defined by the voters themselves.[41] If the voter who goes to the polls is represented by the person against whom he or she votes, then the representation of the majority of the people becomes a representation of the whole people. The voter is defined not by a rational individual choice but by the majority's choice.

Another inconsistency is the notion that the voter will be motivated to participate when she will be adequately represented by whoever is elected. Voting will simply become a habit, a civic duty, although it yields no direct results. In such a scenario, the rational individual might choose not to vote because of the small likelihood of casting the decisive vote.

Yet another inconsistency is produced by the virtual representation assumption that wasted votes—those cast for a losing candidate—do not reflect the absence of representation because the territory defines the community, the group *as well as its interests*. This view suggests that mere geographical subdivisions have interests distinct from those of the people who inhabit them. Because individualism posits that the rational individual will act in her own self-interest, this external determination of the interests represented is inconsistent with individualism.

Perhaps most inconsistent with the theory of autonomous, rational individuals is virtual representation's notion of fungibility. Virtual representation, explicitly in the second assumption and implicitly in the third, assumes that individuals are interchangeable based on some externally observed characteristics. Accordingly, individual choice is subordinated to the choices made by the majority, and the individual must allow someone in another district to act on her behalf.

In these often unstated but related ways, districting conflates the view that territorial constituencies virtually represent discrete individuals who reside therein with the view that territorial constituencies group like-minded voters. Related to each of the virtual representation assumptions, therefore, is the corollary that we can use proxies, in this case geography, for determining voter interests. Such proxies merge voters' own definitions of their interests with the self-interest of political incumbents or with the interests of a homogeneous territorial district majority. The use of such proxies reveals the fundamentally group-based nature of representation—a feature that is inherent to, but inadequately recognized by, our contemporary system of representation.

For example, where representation is only virtual rather than direct, those who vote for the losing candidate may find that their interests are not represented at all. The constituency is presumed to be a group based on a single choice—the decision where to reside. This one choice may not be a real choice for some; for others it may not satisfactorily carry all the weight being assigned. Or the assumption that the geographic constituency is not dominated by a highly organized majority may simply be wrong as a matter of fact.

It is important to recognize, therefore, that the districting debate is not only about representing groups. It also may be about representing groups or individuals unfairly. If voting reflects the voter's conscious choice rather than simply representing the voter's state of belonging, then winner-take-all districting in fact *wastes* votes of both individuals and groups. First, it makes certain there are political losers in each district. Those who vote—as individuals or as a group—for the losing candidate do not obtain any direct political representation. They did not initiate, and they cannot alone terminate, the representational relationship. In response, an individual-rights advocate might argue that the individual who votes for a losing candidate is adequately represented by the winning candidate and has "as much opportunity to influence that candidate as other voters in the district."[42] This, of course, only makes sense if one assumes both that election results count for very little and that representation is exclusively about individual access to representatives chosen by others.

In response, districts could be made more homogeneous to reduce the number of wasted votes. But this alternative demonstrates the second way that winner-take-all districting wastes votes. When more people vote for the winning candidate than is necessary to carry the district, their votes are technically wasted because they were unnecessary to provide an electoral margin within the district *and* they could have been used to provide the necessary electoral margin for a like-minded partisan in another district. In other words, packing voters in homogeneous districts wastes votes because it dilutes their overall voting strength jurisdiction-wide.

The third way districting wastes votes is apparent if we consider voting broadly. I have suggested that voting is not simply about winning elections. The purpose of voting is to influence public policy. Accordingly, I have elsewhere proposed a concept, which I labeled "proportionate interest representation," to describe the importance of an equal opportunity to influence public policy, not just to cast a ballot. This concept reflects both the equality and empowerment norms that I discussed earlier, because the right to cast an equally powerful vote subsumes the right to participate directly in the choice of representatives who then presumably enjoy an equal opportunity to influence legislative policy.

If voting is understood as a means of exercising policy influence, districting tends to limit that influence. Winner-take-all districting gives the district majority all the power. It creates an incentive, therefore, to seek electoral control of a district. But electoral control of a district may isolate minority partisans from potential allies in other districts. In this way, districting wastes votes because it forces minorities to concentrate their strength within a few electoral districts and thereby isolates them from potential legislative allies.

For example, race-conscious districting attempts to provide disadvantaged racial groups the equal opportunity to participate by drawing majority minority geographic districts. Proponents of this strategy assume that electoral control—becoming a district majority—works as a proxy for interest. But creating majority black districts also means creating majority white districts in which the electoral success of white legislators is not dependent on black votes. In this way, race-conscious districting may simply reproduce within the legislature the disadvantaged numerical and racial isolation that the majority minority district attempted to cure at the electoral level.

Where blacks and whites are geographically separate, race-conscious districting isolates blacks from potential white allies—for example, white women—who are not geographically concentrated. It "wastes" the votes of white liberals who may be submerged within white, Republican districts. As a consequence, districting may suppress the development of cross-racial legislative coalition building. Because majority black districts are necessarily accompanied by majority white districts, black representatives may be disenfranchised in the governing body. In this third sense, districting wastes votes because it fails to ensure legislative influence.

The wasted-vote phenomenon makes gerrymandering inevitable.[43] Because winner-take-all districting awards disproportionate power to electoral majorities, it inflates the advantage of district control. This inflated power quotient drives the apportionment process and leads some, myself included, to conclude that on some level all districting is gerrymandering. Gerrymandering is inherent in the districting process, which in essence is the process of distributing wasted votes.

Where incumbent politicians seek safe districts to ensure their reelection, they may be inclined to gerrymander, *i.e.,* waste the votes for their likely opponent. Where political or racial partisans seek legislative control, they may be inclined to gerrymander, *i.e.,* pack the minority party or minority race into a few districts to diminish their overall influence. Or they may fracture the likely supporters of the minority party or minority race, spreading out their votes among a number of districts and ensuring that they do not comprise an electoral majority in any district. These votes are counted, but they are essentially irrelevant in influencing the electoral or governing process.

The gerrymandering phenomenon illustrates once again the group nature of districting. Gerrymandering depends on assumptions about voters' likely behavior based on externally observed or supposed group characteristics or perceived common interests. Although the use of electoral districting has been defended based on the virtues of individual representation, assumptions about the nature of groups likely form the theoretical underpinnings of this election method.

I have tried to show that district representation weakens the connection between the voters' votes and the voters' representative by wasting votes. Unless all the voters in the district vote for the winning candidate, some of their votes are wasted. In addition, if a candidate only needs fifty-one percent of the votes to win, but the district is homogeneous and electorally noncompetitive, then all votes for the winning candidate over fifty-one percent are also technically "wasted." The point is that the voter is deemed represented whether she votes for the losing candidate; is an unnecessary part of the winning candidate's victory margin; or fails to vote at all.

The concept of wasted voting reveals the one-dimensional quality of the virtual representation assumptions. Yet wasted voting is only one of the ways that district representation minimizes the connection between voting and representation. The winner-take-all aspect of territorial constituencies also tends to over-represent the winning party and to deny the losing party a voice on behalf of their specific interests in the legislative forum where public policy is finally fashioned. In addition, territorial constituencies both submerge and subsume the concept of group representation. They also subsume individual definitions of relevant group identity in favor of individual residential decisions.

The artificial nature of these geographic associations suggests the limitations of the view that individual representation is the cornerstone of the right to vote. Territorial constituencies do not realize individual autonomy for at least three reasons. First, many people do not exercise real choice in deciding their place of residence.[44] Second, even where residential decisions are conscious and discretionary, they do not capture the range or salience of interests which voters may hold. Third, the one-person, one-vote requirement of equipopulous districting makes districting even more artificial. If the major constraint on the drawing of district lines is the number of people within each district, district lines cannot conform to naturally occurring areas of common interest. When incumbents exercise enormous control over the districting process, including the custody of census data and the access to computer technology, communities of interest may become mere re-election opportunities. This is the threat to functional interest representation that various Justices have predicted over the years in their dissents to strict population equality principles.[45]

The key point is that criticisms leveled at race-conscious districting as a means of group representation should in fact be directed at the process and the theory of geographic districting itself. In the next Part, I attempt to show that when commentators criticize race-conscious districting, they are really finding fault with the assumptions behind districting in general. It is districting itself which is anomalous, because geographic definitions of group identity, especially within subdistricts, are often so artificial.

II

In this Part, I argue that race is as effective as geography in functioning as a political proxy, but neither is as effective as allowing voters the opportunity to make their own *local* choices about the nature and salience of their interests. Semiproportional systems permit shifting coalitions to form based on voters' own determinations of their interests or their group identity. In other words, geography and race rely on representational assumptions about group association but do not suggest the necessity, standing alone, of either representing or defining group interests a particular way. Modified at-large systems, such as cumulative voting, could be viewed as preferable alternatives that allow members of racial groups, politically cohesive groups, and strategically motivated individuals to be both self-defined and represented, while minimizing the problem of wasted votes for *all* voters.

Race in this country has defined individual identities, opportunities, frames of reference, and relationships. Where race has been of historical importance and continues to play a significant role, racial-group membership often serves as a political proxy for shared experience and common interests. At least to the extent that an overwhelming majority of group members experience a common "group identity,"[46] those who are group members are more likely to represent similar interests. Group members also may share common cultural styles or operating assumptions.[47]

Group members also are more likely to be perceived by their constituents as representing them. This definition of representative as descriptive likeness or racial compatriot has a psychological component. Just as the flag stands for the nation, the presence of racial group members symbolizes inclusion of a previously excluded group. The symbolic role results from both the personal characteristics of the racial-group member and the assumption that, because of those characteristics, the racial-group member has had experiences in common with her constituents. As Hanna Pitkin writes in her groundbreaking work on representation, "We tend to assume that people's characteristics are a guide to the actions they will take, and we are concerned with the characteristics of our legislators for just this reason."[48] Thus, many racial minorities do not feel represented unless members of their racial group are physically present in the legislature.

As a result, traditional voting rights advocates comfortably rely on race as a proxy for interests. For example, in conventional voting rights litigation, election contests between black and white candidates help define the degree of racial polarization, *i.e.*, the degree to which blacks and whites vote differently. The idea is that the outcome would be different if elections were held only in one community or the other. The assumption of difference extends explicitly to the specific candidate elected, and implicitly to the issues that the candidate, once elected, would emphasize.

The assumption of this difference between races rests in part on the claim that where black candidates enjoy protection from electoral competition with whites, black voters can ratify their choices to hold their representatives accountable. In this way, the association between race and interests is modified to the extent that voters are given a meaningful choice in both initiating *and* terminating a representational relationship. Voting rights advocates assume that minority group sponsorship is critical.[49] It is only where minority voters exercise electoral control, or have a meaningful opportunity to retire their representative, that race functions as a representational proxy. Thus, majority-black single-member districts take advantage of segregated housing patterns to use geography as a proxy for racial choice, racial control, and racial representation.[50]

I argued in Part I that the one-person, one-vote cases, with their focus on equalizing individual access through equalizing population, conceal the group nature of representation by districting. The one-person, one-vote rule merges political interests and regional interests under the umbrella of equal access for equal numbers of people. In order to justify placing people with different political interests into one district with only one representative, the wasted vote problem is elided by discussing everything in terms of individual voters. In deference to a tradition of according individual rights a higher value, and relying on the access view of voting, adherents to population-based districting simply skip over geographic districting's implicit assumptions about group attributes.

Race-conscious districting confronts the group nature of representation more directly. It attempts to minimize the wasted vote problem for minority voters whose preferred candidates—because of racial bloc voting by the majority—experience consistent defeat at the polls. Where voting is racially polarized, white voters and black voters vote differently. Where blacks are a numerical minority, racial bloc voting means that the political choices of blacks rarely are successful. To remedy this problem of being a permanent loser, black political activists and voting rights litigants have sought majority black districts in which the electoral choices of a majority of blacks determined the electoral winner.

Yet some commentators challenge race-conscious districting on the grounds that special protection throughout the political process for the rights of minority groups is unnecessary as long as individual minority group members have a fair chance to participate formally by voting in an election.[51] For these commentators, race-conscious districting is illegitimate because the right to vote is individual, not group-based.[52] Relying again on assumptions about fungibility and access, these observers challenge the right of minority groups to representative *or* responsive government.[53]

Given the prominence of racial group identities, I am not persuaded by this criticism to abandon the concept of group representation. I am aware of, but not in accord with, those critics of race-conscious districting who object on moral grounds to the drawing of districts along racial lines.[54] As I suggested earlier, representation is a bottom-up process that ideally recognizes the importance of influencing public policy decisions on behalf of constituency interests. Accordingly, we cannot define political fairness merely as electoral fairness that guarantees nonbiased conditions of voting eligibility and equally counted votes. Nor do I think the only issues are whether blacks have special claims for protection or whether whites can or should represent blacks, although I think they can and do.[55]

Yet, in making the argument that racial groups deserve representation, I do not rely primarily on the political, sociological, or cultural claims involved in racial-group identity, or even on the historic context of group disfranchisement. My principal argument rests on the distinction within the political process between a claim for group rights and a claim for group representation.[56] I argue for the latter based on the historic evidence that representation within territorial districts is implicitly about recognition of group interests, not just individual access. However, the future of such group representation—like the future of the group itself—lies less inside geographic boundaries and more within the cultural and political community forged by group consciousness and group identity. Empowerment— for a group as well as for an individual—comes from active assertion of self-defined interests. A group is represented where it has the opportunity to speak out and not just to be spoken for.

The argument for recognition of group interests makes three assumptions about representation. First, legislators should represent unanimous, not divided, constituencies.[57] Second, each voter's vote should count toward the election of a representative. Third, the unit of representation should be psychological, cultural, and/or political rather than territorial.[58] In other words, groups should be represented, but in ways that permit automatic, self-defined apportionment based on shifting political or cultural affiliation and interests. This would enable voters to form voluntary affiliative districts without the need for prior authorization or formal recognition of the group as one which deserves special treatment. Because such group identity would be affiliative and interest-based, group representation would encourage both coalition building among racial and political factions and grass-roots political organization around issues, not just individual candidacies.

If the decision to represent groups already has been made in the adoption of geographic districting, then group representation based on racial-group association or historical oppression becomes less problematic. Whatever the alleged flaws in racial-group representation, it is racial representation within a system of geographic districts that must be analyzed. As one white Democratic congressman who represents a largely minority constituency is quoted as saying, "I'm torn about it. I do not believe you have to be of the exact same ethnic group to do a good job in representing that community. But, in the end, I think it's that community's choice."[59] Thus, it is important to emphasize the connection between choice, accountability, and group identification. Whoever represents minority interests (just as whoever represents majority interests) should be directly, not merely virtually, accountable to those interests.

Yet some critics of race-conscious districting might attempt to distinguish race from geography as a useful political proxy. Such critics claim that geographic association, unlike race, is temporal, individualistic, and discretionary, at least for some people. There are two problems with this purported distinction. First, geography is neither discretionary nor individualized for members of disadvantaged racial groups.[60] Rather, it reflects the very essence of limitations on choice based on group identity. Race-conscious districting can capture racial communities of interest precisely because residential ghettos are often the result of racial discrimination. As Professor Pamela Karlan writes, residential segregation reflects racial discrimination in both the private and public housing market.[61] Because residential segregation by definition results from the absence of choice, race-conscious districting "can serve as a proxy for a bundle of distinct political interests."[62]

A second problem is that this criticism applies only to race-conscious representation executed within a system of fixed district boundaries. Indeed, the concern can be avoided almost entirely where the voters themselves define their own interests using alternative, modified at-large systems of representation. Representation based on voluntary interest constituencies would unhitch racial-group representation from arbitrary, involuntary assignments.

The voluntary interest constituencies would be comparable to Professor Iris Marion Young's model of a "highly visible" social group with emotional, historical, and social salience defined by a sense of group identity, not just shared attributes.[63] According to Young, groups exist only in relation to other groups. The social processes of affinity and differentiation produce groups. Yet group differentiation is not necessarily oppressive or homogeneous. Group differentiation is created by multiple, cross-cutting, and shifting differences.

The group differentiation of racial minorities is a function of historical oppression, shared experience, and present inequality. Territorial configurations may track this phenomenon to the extent that disadvantaged racial groups are concentrated in substandard housing in urban ghettos, but differentiation by race cuts across geographic lines in many cases. Some racial-group members share a group consciousness without sharing group space. Others are dispersed in small barrios throughout the jurisdiction. Still others may technically be group members in terms of their racial origin or current residence but not in terms of their racial identity.

In addition, group differentiation by race subsumes gender, age, and class differences. A racial group that is politically cohesive on civil rights or welfare policy may have some members with interests that are not shared throughout the group. On these issues, the racial group members may have more in common with group members of another race living outside their immediate geographic area. In other words, racial groups are not monolithic, nor are they necessarily cohesive.

Race in conjunction with geography is a useful but limited proxy for defining the interests of those sharing a particular racial identity. But it is the assumption that a territorial district can accurately approximate a fixed racial-group identity—and not the assumption of a racial-group identity itself—that is problematic. Race-conscious districting—as opposed to racial-group representation—may be rigidly essentialist, presumptuously isolating, or politically divisive. For example, different groups may share the same residential space but not the same racial identity. A districting strategy requires these groups to compete for political power through the ability to elect only one representative.

Yet strategies for race-conscious districting respond to important deficits in a non-race-conscious geographic districting process. Proponents of racial-group representation confront on the jurisdiction-wide level the unfairness of the indirect, virtual representation claims. In justifying race-conscious districting, voting rights activists appropriately employ the concept of racial-group identity. They can demonstrate that members of the racial group have distinctive interests that are often ignored by elected officials who suffer no adverse consequences at the polls. In this way, the activists challenge the view that voters are fungible, especially where minority group voters are consistent losers as a result of racial bloc voting by the jurisdiction majority.

Based on complaints about the way that virtual representation assumptions operate at the macro level to dilute minority voting strength, race-conscious strategies seek to control smaller, majority minority districts. By making the minority a district majority, race-conscious districting seeks to exercise the prerogatives of majority rule on behalf of a jurisdiction-wide minority. But while they challenge the fairness of jurisdiction-wide virtual representation of minority voters by the majority, proponents of race-conscious districts replicate many of the same fairness problems at the micro level.

The same assumptions about virtual representation that were the object of challenge at the macro level are now reproduced within subdistricts that the racial minority controls. The majority minority subdistrict operates on the same winner-take-all, majority rule principles. Even as an imperfect geometric "fractal"[64] of a larger jurisdiction-wide majority, it carries with it the assumptions of virtual representation to justify the minority group's domination. As a consequence, race-conscious districting raises in microcosm the theoretical questions I raised in Part I about districting itself.

An illustration of this fractal problem is a 1992 New York City congressional plan that included a Brooklyn/Queens district to represent the interests of a Latino minority. This district concentrated Latinos in a new 12th Congressional District. Several Latino activists filed as candidates in the Democratic primary. So did Representative Stephen Solarz, a white incumbent whose previous district was consolidated within one-fifth of the new "Latino" district.

The entry of a well-financed, nine-term incumbent from a largely Jewish section of Brooklyn shifted the political expectations. The primary, which had been expected to focus on issues of interest to a poor Latino constituency, turned into a debate over whether a minority group could be represented by someone of a different ethnicity. According to a Latino community organizer, "The community is saying, 'Why is it that this Jewish person who has always represented other interests than ours, comes in now saying he's going to be our savior?' "[65] This complaint—that the white incumbent should not enter the race—rested on a complex, but misinformed, understanding of group representation.

The group is deemed represented where it has electoral control over the winner. The organizer's concern was that the sixteen percent white minority in the district—not the Latino majority—could have electoral control by consolidating their votes and converting their minority status into a plurality win. Since there were at least four Latino candidates, the white candidate would most likely win if the Latino vote were split, even though Latinos are fifty-five percent of the district's voting-age population. If the Latino majority was disaggregated into factions supporting different Latino candidates, it could have been white voters who chose the representative for the new district.

Latino activists complained that this did not give their community the choice they deserved. "The whole idea was to give our community some degree of choice, Latinos or non-Latinos who have some connection with the community. . . . [The well-financed white incumbent] doesn't fit that bill at all."[66] The white candidate answered, "The other candidates fear that I'll win, which somewhat belies their notion that the purpose of this district was to empower the people to make a choice."[67]

The nature of this controversy was captured by a *New York Times* headline that appeared before the primary: "Does Politics of Fairness Mean Only Those from Minorities Should Apply?"[68] I propose restating the problem as follows: Does politics of fairness mean that self-defined groups are best represented by territorial districts, even those they ostensibly control? So stated, the question shifts the issue from the candidate to the constituency. By asking this new question, we can see the three incongruous assumptions inherent in racial control of territorial constituencies.

The first assumption is that because they represent a majority of the district population, the fifty-five percent Latino voting-age population is appropriately empowered to represent the entire district, although eight percent of the district is black, twenty-one percent Asian, and sixteen percent white. This assumption parallels the first virtual representation assumption: the district losers will be indirectly represented by majority winners.

Race-conscious districting is arguably necessary because the jurisdiction-wide majority is organized racially and permanently.[69] This argument suggests that there is nothing inherently wrong with the principles of indirect representation underlying winner-take-all majoritarianism, except where the majority operates based on its prejudices. As long as the current pattern of racial bloc voting continues, the minority cannot become part of the jurisdiction-wide governing coalition. Thus, "special" smaller majorities are warranted.

The second assumption is that a Latino majority in this one district will choose a representative for all Latinos in the city. This tracks the second vicarious representation assumption that similarly situated voters can represent each other. Because Latino interests are underrepresented in other winner-take-all congressional districts, their interests in the city as a whole are now fairly represented by virtue of their electoral control over this one district. Conversely, the Asian, black, and white minorities in this one district are *vicariously* represented by their electoral control over other districts in the city.

Thus, Latinos who do not live in the district are virtually represented by choices made by the Latinos who do live in the district. Race-conscious districting only approximates the diversity of voter identities in the *jurisdiction as a whole,* but not necessarily in each district.

With the second assumption, the race-conscious districting approach does not challenge political representation based on geography; it simply suggests that specific groups should dominate specific districts in proportion to their overall state-wide or jurisdiction-wide percentage. Here, the claim is that political fairness is measured by a jurisdiction-wide baseline rather than by reference to a critique of group rights or majority domination more generally. Majority domination is acceptable as long as each group gets a chance to be represented somewhere in the jurisdiction by its own localized majority.

The third assumption is that the 12th Congressional District is a minority district without regard to the actual intra- or inter-minority conflict within the district. The third assumption presumes political cohesion based on the fiction that the district has an identity independent of the actual constituents. It also presumes equal access for constituency service within the district and relies on the claim that a minority identity ensures a minority ideology. Minority group interests will define the district identity and anyone who represents it.

The Asian, black, and white minorities are presumed to be represented because of their choice to live near Latinos. Stated differently, because Latinos are not as residentially segregated as other racial groups, they can represent the interests of their multicultural neighborhood as a whole. Their neighbors' interests are represented both for personal constituency service and for their territorially defined common interests.

The third assumption is related to the top-down view of representation. Like the virtual representation view that the district has an independent identity, the 12th Congressional District is a "Latino district." As a so-called minority district, it has an identity independent of the actual tensions present, the level of political cohesion, or the political participation rates of its constituents. In this way, race-conscious districting incorporates a static, somewhat monolithic, view of representation that, after the initial drawing of a majority minority district, diminishes the subsequent importance of broad authority from a consenting group of participants.[70]

For example, Latinos within the district arguably are represented by any one of the four Latino candidates, even where a majority of the Latino residents vote for a losing candidate. The issue of choice is submerged within a presumption of ethnic solidarity in the majority Latino population district, even if Representative Solarz did not compete. This is because the district is a Latino district, and the elected representative will therefore service all constituents equally, especially other Latinos.[71]

Yet a top-down view of representation does not encourage broad-based political participation among the district constituency. Nonvoters are represented equally with voters. Because representation is viewed primarily as a means of distributing constituency service and benefits and is primarily based on a common group identity, there is little incentive to monitor actively the public policy positions the representative takes within the governing body. Under this top-down view, elections serve not to initiate an interactive relationship, but to ratify an open-ended one.

In this way, the assumption of "minority district as independent identity" ignores issues of multiple, cross-cutting, and shifting differences.
This is an empowerment strategy designed primarily to increase the proportion of minority-group legislators. Because of the success of individual
minority-group members, the group as a whole is empowered. As I have
argued elsewhere, however, empowerment is not based on assumptions
about phenotypic representation. Voters also must be directly given the
opportunity and the information necessary to define their interests for
themselves.

These three assumptions, of course, invite the criticism that race-
conscious districting arbitrarily reduces voters to their ethnic or racial
identity and then only represents that characteristic in a way that isolates
or balkanizes the population. But the real complaint is not with the race
consciousness of the districting, but with the districting process itself. The
race-conscious districting assumptions simply replay the same virtual representation assumptions that are used to justify territorial constituencies
in the first place.

Thus, the race-conscious districting assumptions are neither unique
nor necessarily contextual. For example, the winning candidate might be
the one Latina who appeals to all the different ethnic and racial groups
within the district, winning with a five-percent plurality of Latino support
and a solid majority of white, black, and Asian votes. Although this individual might be Latina in identity, she would not in fact be elected directly
by Latinos to represent their interests.

In fact, the successful candidate was Nydia Velazquez, a former representative of Puerto Rico to New York, who polled thirty-three percent of
the vote, compared to twenty-seven percent for Mr. Solarz. According to
The New York Times, Ms. Velazquez's margin of victory came from overwhelming Latino support in Brooklyn and from strong support from the
black community.[72] She reportedly benefited from an endorsement by
the city's black mayor, David Dinkins, and from the "firestorm" of criticism that erupted when Mr. Solarz decided to run in the newly drawn
district.[73]

One might argue, then, that Ms. Velazquez's election affirmed the second and third assumptions of virtual representation. Because Latinos supported her within the 12th District, Latinos throughout New York City
are now vicariously represented even though they could not vote for her.
In addition, Ms. Velazquez's black support confirmed the viability of the
third assumption that the 12th District is a bona fide "minority district."
The first virtual representation assumption is not directly implicated by

the election because it depends upon post-election behavior of the elected representative.

Four other Latino candidates competed in the primary. Elizabeth Colon polled twenty-six percent; Ruben Franco polled eight percent; Eric Ruano Mèlendez and Rafael Mendez each received three percent of the vote. Although I do not have the actual precinct totals, these figures do not rebut the possibility that a majority of Latino voters (especially those living in Queens) actually preferred someone other than Ms. Velazquez. Similarly, they do not deny the possibility that blacks, who are only eight percent of the District, may have supported Ms. Velazquez, but Asians and whites may have preferred someone else.

Since Asians, at twenty-one percent, are the second-largest group in the District, it may not be appropriate to presume that interminority political cohesion extends to all of the District's minority voters. The other aspect of the third assumption—that this is a genuine Latino district—is also not clear, since a majority of Latinos may have preferred someone other than Ms. Velazquez.

The validity of the first assumption, that the electoral majority will now indirectly represent *all* the electoral minorities, also remains to be seen. It is currently a theoretical claim based on the operation of golden-rule reciprocity in conjunction with other assumptions about the individual nature of voting and representation. The District's political reality, however, may defy the theory that the district minority—those who wasted their votes—will act as a potent political check on a shifting district majority. For example, the election returns suggest that there are distinct group interests among and within the Asian, black, and white district community. The votes of these subgroups may, as a practical matter, become permanently wasted.

Indeed, over the ten-year term of the District, the Latino majority may act cohesively and return the Latina incumbent to office. Re-election of the incumbent may occur with decreasing turnout as a percentage of all the District's population, but with increasing support among those who do vote simply because she is the incumbent. This is consistent with evidence that minority candidacies generate relatively high voter turnout the first time a viable minority group member competed. Turnout, however, tends to go down when constituents realize that the election of a single minority incumbent changes very little of their day-to-day lives.

But the fact that the Latina is now an incumbent gives her tremendous resource advantages over any future opponents. Some may argue that her continued re-election reduces polarization within the district, as the other non-Latina voters see Ms. Velazquez work on their behalf. On the other hand, her predictable re-election success may exacerbate rather than reduce intergroup conflict. The District's complicated racial, ethnic, and linguistic mix is not reflected in the ethnic or racial group membership of its representative. The fact that the district winner in a multi-ethnic district has a psychological, cultural, and sociological connection primarily to one ethnic or racial group may alienate other groups over time.

If Asians, for example, feel consigned to permanent minority status within the minority district, they may bide their time until redistricting in the year 2000, when the legislature decides how many minority districts should be created and who should control them. The fight to be "the group" who gets the district, and with it all the power, pits minorities against each other. The fact that some members of the other minority groups in the 12th District can only cast wasted votes for ten years encourages each group ultimately to think in terms of its own moral, historical, and pragmatic claims to exclusive or primary district representation. Where representation becomes the lottery of competing oppression, no one wins.

Only the second assumption, at least on the psychological level of vicarious representation, is solidly supported by the election of Ms. Velazquez. This is based on evidence that those minority group members who do not vote for group members nevertheless feel "represented" by them. This phenomenon reflects the continued vitality of racial group identity. Many group members feel most represented by one of their own.

Even if the second vicarious representation assumption is true, one could maintain that people are represented without regard for whom they choose to vote simply because of where they choose to live or who they are. Latinos in Queens living a few blocks outside the 12th District, who cannot vote for Ms. Velazquez, will continue to "waste" their votes within the districts in which they reside. Their votes, which under some other district configuration might help elect an additional, or simply a different, Latino, are submerged within their non-Latino district.

Because their votes will be wasted, nondistrict Latinos are not encouraged to participate directly in the process of self-government. The process of voting itself may become meaningless. Districting ignores this problem with wasted votes by embracing group representation based on territorial contiguity and indirect representation.

Because geographic districting wastes votes, neither minority groups nor majority voters are fairly represented. Districting fails to deliver on its virtual representation assumptions, even where districts are drawn to maximize minority voting strength. Districting is not justified by the individual representation value because each voter's vote does not count to the greatest extent possible toward the election of a representative. Districting is not supported by the group representation value because legislatures do not represent unanimous constituencies, and they therefore find it either hard to govern or easy to excuse unaccountability. The tension—between values of individual and group representation; between direct and indirect representation; between top-down and bottom-up representation; and between wasted and effective votes—permeates virtual representation, even within race-conscious geographic districting.

For this reason, modified at-large systems used in corporate governance, such as cumulative voting, should be considered.[74] Under a modified at-large system, each voter is given the same number of votes as open seats, and the voter may plump or cumulate her votes to reflect the intensity of her preferences. Depending on the exclusion threshold,[75] politically cohesive minority groups are assured representation if they vote strategically.[76] Similarly, *all* voters have the potential to form voluntary constituencies based on their own assessment of their interests. As a consequence, semiproportional systems such as cumulative voting give more voters, not just racial minorities, the opportunity to vote for a winning candidate.

Racial-group interests become those self-identified, voluntary constituencies that choose to combine because of like minds, not like bodies. Legitimate interest constituencies are formed among groups of individuals who share similar opinions or identities. These interest constituencies are less fixed than under territorial districting. Nevertheless, racial minority groups may still choose collectively to elect representatives. But now the minority voters' choices are based on their own conception of identity, which may be defined in racial terms because it is either racially apparent, racially derived, or a function of historical treatment by the numerically superior racial majority.[77]

Thus, even if voting is thought to be a concept of individual autonomy, the recognition of voluntary choices to affiliate or form associations minimizes wasted voting while transcending "artificial groups" based solely on residence or race. On the other hand, if voting is seen as a group-representation concept, representation systems should minimize wasted votes in order to realize maximum influence and empowerment. Under either view of voting and representation, a semiproportional system is preferable because it minimizes wasted votes and defines voting behavior based on election choices exercised by the voters themselves.

Additionally, if racial group identity is a value that deserves representation, territorial constituencies are an imperfect proxy. If racial group
membership is thought to be affiliative yet involuntary in the sense that
history, culture, and social pressures combine to define one's membership, it is equally important to provide openings within the political process for self-defined group representation. Territorial constituencies do
not do this, because they fail to maximize opportunities for group political
empowerment and individual group members' participation and self-
expression.

As a result, whether representation is considered essentially an individual *or* a group activity, the principle of one-vote, one-value is necessary to
protect voters' interests.[78] Everybody's vote should count for somebody's
election. Voters are directly represented only if they actively choose who
represents their interests.

In this sense, I am arguing for a more expansive account of the representational relationship for *all* voters. In order to achieve political equality
and political fairness, an electoral system should give voters the direct
opportunity to initiate and terminate their own representational relationship. It is not enough that some voters choose for everyone or that everyone has an equal chance to be an electoral winner or an electoral loser.
Voting should become a positive-sum experience in which all voters actively participate in selecting their representative.

On the assumption that each participant should enjoy an equal opportunity both to participate and to influence, the concept of one-vote, one-
value describes the idea that each voter should elect someone to represent
her interests. This new view of the representational relationship draws on
the concepts of equal opportunity to participate and equal opportunity to
elect representatives of one's choice that are embodied in the 1982 Voting
Rights Act amendments. It arguably would expand the statutory view of
the representational relationship in a way that benefits all voters.[79]

The courts, however, have been hesitant to employ a one-vote, one-
value system as a remedy under the Voting Rights Act. In Granville
County, North Carolina, black voters challenged the at-large method of
electing the county commissioner. Blacks, who comprised forty-four percent of the county's population, had never been able to elect any person to
the five-member commission. The defendant-commissioners conceded
that black voters were not represented on the county's at-large commission. They also admitted that if the county were districted, *and if two
additional commissioner seats were added,* blacks would be able to elect
one of seven commissioners, giving the forty-four percent black popula-

tion "electoral control" over fourteen percent of the commission. The single-member districting remedy failed to capture much of the black community, which was dispersed throughout the county.

The plaintiffs proposed, and the district court approved, retention of the staggered term, at-large method of election with a threshold lowering, semiproportional modification that allowed voters to cast only three votes for the five open seats. When the modified system was employed, three blacks were elected to the seven-person commission.

The Fourth Circuit in *McGhee v. Granville* reversed and restricted the relief granted based on a narrow definition of the causal relationship between what the plaintiffs challenged and the available relief. The court ruled that single-member districts were the only appropriate remedy. Since the plaintiffs challenged at-large elections that prevented black candidates from getting elected, the exclusive remedy was to create single-member districts in which black candidates were likely to get elected. Even if all or many black voters did not reside in the newly configured majority-black districts, their remedy was limited to the "virtual" representation they received from districts that enjoy black electoral success.

By articulating its analysis of vote dilution exclusively in terms of single-member districts, the courts have tended to promulgate single-member districts as a talismanic liability and remedial threshold.[80] At the same time that courts have moved closer to a single-member district, black electoral success standard, they have clearly established "descriptive" proportional representation as the *ceiling*. The Court in *Thornburg v. Gingles*, for example, reversed a finding of dilution in District 23 where it appeared that black voters enjoyed "proportionate" representation because a black was consistently elected over a twelve-year period. The Court did not discuss the fact that in District 23 black voters had to employ "bullet voting" to elect the black candidate and thus forfeited their chance to influence which whites would be elected.[81] Nor did the Court address the evidence that the black who was elected was actually chosen by the white voters and had to "sail trim"[82] his legislative positions accordingly.[83]

Despite judicial reluctance to adopt alternative remedies, the principle of one-vote, one-value satisfies the representational needs of voters in two ways that districting does not. First, it extracts the unfairness of wasted votes from winner-take-all solutions. Votes that would have been wasted in a winner-take-all system are redistributed to voluntary constituencies consistent with the actual level of their political support. Second, it allows voters to choose their representational identity. Rather than imposing a group identity on a given geographic constituency, this system gives voters the opportunity to associate with the identity that fits their own view of psychological, cultural, and historical reality. Thus, racial and other politically cohesive groups could be represented in proportion to their actual strength in the electorate rather than in proportion to their geographic concentration. As a result of political organization, voter education, and strategic voting, any politically cohesive group that is numerous enough to meet the local threshold of representation could mobilize to gain representation.[84]

Ultimately, what the one-vote, one-value principle does is to transform the unit of representation from a territorial or racial constituency to a political or psychological one. This affirms Iris Young's view of the social group as one based on self- and historical-identification, and it rejects representational groups based simply on the joint possession of externally observable attributes or the choice of a residence.

One-vote, one-value makes the assumption that each voter should enjoy the same opportunity to influence political outcomes. No one is entitled to absolutely equal influence; but by the same token, no one is entitled to grossly disproportionate influence or a monopoly on control. The majority should enjoy a majority of the power, but the minority should also enjoy some power too. Thus, one-vote, one-value measures opportunities for fair participation using a baseline of actual participation and real political strength.

The principle of one-vote, one-value, as realized through cumulative voting, also restores the link between representation and voting by ensuring that legislators represent unanimous, not divided, constituencies. Representation becomes the process of bottom-up empowerment based on self-defined expressions of interest. Moreover, assuming voters vote strategically, votes are not wasted either by voting for losing candidates or by packing voters into safe districts. The legislative body can reflect fairly the range of opinions and interests within the public at large, including racial minorities who can be represented based on their electoral strength. Gerrymandering becomes unnecessary and can no longer be used to enhance the disproportionate power of incumbents to ensure their own reelection or to exaggerate the political control of the party in power. Finally, local political organizations may be given the space and the possibility of success. Such parties can fill the needs for political mobilization, voter education, and legislative monitoring that largely go unfilled in our current system.

Thus, by restoring the link between representation and voting, alternative election systems encourage voter participation. They also can broaden the range of debate by allowing local political organizations to emerge and interest-based political coalitions to form. These coalitions would not be limited to neighborhood communities of interest, certain racial groups, or particular elections, but would contain dynamic possibilities for regional, reciprocal, or cross-racial political cohesion. The race-conscious context of districting might be retained, but only on an election-by-election, issue-by-issue, voter-by-voter basis.

Of course, semiproportional systems of representation can be criticized for their tendency to destabilize the electorate by either promoting stalemate or creating chaos. I have elsewhere identified many of these concerns, some of which still need to be addressed more fully. In brief, alternative election systems raise legitimacy concerns about paralysis, stability, and efficiency, all of which need to be taken seriously. On the other hand, for those who feel excluded, legitimacy is derived from broad-based consensual authority. Self-government by consensus that recognizes the views of minorities is legitimate and enduring.

In balancing the fears of balkanization against observations about existing alienation, I conclude that exclusiveness is a greater evil than controversy, that passivity does not equal contentment, and that differences need not be permanently enshrined in the electoral configuration. Modified at-large election systems encourage continuous redistricting by the voters themselves based on the way they cast their votes at each election. Whatever differences emerge, therefore, are those chosen by the voters rather than imposed externally on the voters based on assumptions about demographic characteristics or incumbent self-interest. These voter generated differences may infuse the process with new ideas; diversity of viewpoint can be enlightening. Finally, the modified at-large system may simply reflect a necessary transition phase from power politics to principled politics. But, whether it succeeds in that respect, it at least has the benefit of infusing the process with more legitimacy from the perspective of previously disenfranchised groups.[85]

I do not mean to denigrate concerns that the proliferation of political interest constituencies may undermine consensus, exacerbate tension, and destabilize the political system. These concerns reflect a preference for conflict resolution that camouflages rather than identifies political differences. My preference, however, is first to recognize salient differences and then to work with those differences to achieve positive-sum solutions. My idea is that politics need not be a zero-sum game in which those who win, win it all. My idea is that where everyone can win something, genuine consensus is possible.

There is, in addition, a concern with one-vote, one-value principles that I have not previously considered. In my focus on wasted votes, I have not yet examined the effect of one-vote, one-value approaches on communities with large numbers of noncitizens, age-ineligible citizens, or people with other conditions that disable them from voting. For example, concerns about the representation of noncitizens are prominent in the Latino community; concerns about the disproportionate number of young citizens are also relevant to the black community. Thus, each of these communities has a special profile in terms of the number of people each voting member of the community ultimately represents. This is a virtual representation problem within the electorate itself.

Since districting is based on population rather than on turnout or registration rates, people who do not vote at all are nevertheless represented. This idea is encompassed by the third virtual representation assumption—that the district identity is independent, yet consuming, of all constituents. Even if one cannot vote, one's interests are presumably represented by those who can. For minority communities whose population is in greater need of government service, access to representatives based on population may be more fair than access to representatives based on turnout. A voluntary interest constituency composed of like-minded voters devalues the interests of elements within the constituency who cannot or do not vote.

Of course, the same criticism can be leveled at safe districting. Although its population base extends top-down representational access to nonvoters, these constituents are stuck with whomever the majority of district voters choose. In other words, safe districting assumes that nonvoters and voters are fungible in that the voters indirectly represent the interests of the nonvoters. Accordingly, children are only indirectly represented by the representatives chosen by adults on their behalf.

Admittedly, changing the structure of electoral units is an incomplete solution even to those problems on which I have previously focused. Because of its potential disruption, it is also a solution worth considering only where the existing election system unfairly distributes political power in a way that is itself disruptive or illegitimate. As for the problem of differential participation rates, I can speculate about three possible responses. First, like districting systems, one-vote, one-value election systems require some subdistricting. Except in very small cities or towns, some multimember subdistricts would be required both to reduce the complexity of the ballot and to promote access for local communities of interest. In

New York City, for example, boroughs might be appropriate multimember districts for borough-wide cumulative voting. This might accommodate the concern that representatives have a local constituency for whom they are responsible without regard to who actually voted for them.

Second, although interest representation based on one-vote, one-value does not directly protect nonvoters any better than districts, it does create an environment in which they, as well as voters, are encouraged to participate directly. By participation I refer to the broad range of bottom-up activity relating to the political process. I specifically disavow an emphasis exclusively on election-day voting. Because semiproportional systems rely on *voluntary* interest-group constituencies, they reward local political organizing efforts more than systems with predetermined constituencies. Representation is earned in proportion to political activity and actual turnout rather than fixed population or majoritarian aggregating rules. This means that local political organizations, with an activated grass roots base, can actually win elections.

Nonvoters can participate in the organizing and monitoring efforts of local political organizations and thus actively assert their own interests. Nonvoters can participate in all the pre- and post-election day activities of the political organization. In this way, one-vote, one-value encourages representation directly of interests, not just of voters. Nonvoters can directly support a local organization that articulates their interests rather than passively rely on the presumption that they benefit from choices made by those who virtually vote their interests.

Third, the commitment to consensus politics implicit in the one-vote, one-value approach benefits voters and nonvoters, majorities and minorities. It infuses the process with receptivity to new ideas. It promotes a new definition of stability based on inclusiveness, not quietude. It creates positive-sum possibilities rather than limiting participation to winners and inevitable losers. With its focus on coalition-building and consensus, it does not assume that conflict is better suppressed than voiced. Nor does it assume that politics need always be zero-sum.

One-vote, one-value represents a new vision of political participation. It assumes that empowerment comes from opportunities for the active assertion of one's own interests—speaking out, not just being spoken for. One-vote, one-value attempts to mediate directly the tension between individual and group representation that characterizes the districting process at each level. Thus it is more fair both to individuals and to groups.

III. Conclusion

The controversy over racial-group representation offers us an opportunity to re-examine the political fairness of our district-based electoral system. I posit that a system is procedurally fair only to the extent that it gives each participant an equal opportunity to influence outcomes. I call this principle one-vote, one-value. This is a measure of procedural, not substantive, legitimacy. According to this principle, outcomes are relevant only to the extent that they enable us to measure degrees of input, not to the extent they achieve some objective, substantive notion of distributive justice.

The challenge to racial-group representation is actually a criticism of a different kind of group representation: representation based on homogeneous geographic constituencies. Race-conscious districting is simply one expression of a larger reality: winner-take-all districting. Both justify wasting votes with often unstated assumptions about the group characteristics of district voters. In other words, the criticism of racial-group representation is, at bottom, a criticism of winner-take-all districting in which the district boundaries and the incumbent politicians define the interests of the *entire* district constituency.

I conclude that group representation is as American as winner-take-all districting; that the two are conflated in criticisms of race-conscious districting; and that consideration of alternative means of representing racial groups can shift the debate about political fairness. By directly confronting the problem of wasted voting, we may make the system more legitimate from the perspective of previously disenfranchised groups, and more fairly representative of issue-based groups who previously have been aggregated and silenced within the majority.

I have proposed a new view of the representational relationship that is more protective of all voters' ability and more conducive to all voters' initiative to choose directly who represents them. By critically examining certain fundamental assumptions about representation, I hope to revive our political imagination. "Change the way people think," said South African civil-rights martyr Steven Biko, "and things will never be the same."[86] Or as Professor Robert Dixon declared about 25 years ago:

> [N]ow that the first round of reapportionment has been accomplished, there is need to talk "one man-one vote" a little less and to talk a little more of "political equity," and of functional components of effective representation. *A mathematically equal vote which is politically worthless because of gerrymandering or winner-take-all districting is as deceiving as "emperor's clothes."*[87]

6

Lines in the Sand

A Review of Charles Fried's Order and Law: Arguing the Reagan Revolution—A Firsthand Account

This chapter concludes the substantive essays of this book with a return to the subject of the Reagan Justice Department. Much of the legal debate over the fate of the Civil Rights Movement centers on the question of the proper role of government intervention. As seen here through the eyes of Reagan's Solicitor General, a self-described revolutionary, the Reagan Justice Department led the charge against judicial and Congressional activism that has recently come to dominate this debate. This essay analyzes the Reagan Revolutionaries' exaltation of the executive branch and their use of so-called neutral principles of adjudication to limit the role of government. Assisted by the metaphors of geometry and line drawing, I seek to reveal the Reagan Revolutionaries' particular preferences for configuring power hierarchies and centralizing decisionmaking authority. I borrow from my criticism of winner-take-all majority rule to show that the Reagan Revolutionaries' zero-sum, adversarial solutions in judicial and executive decisionmaking suffer from similar, exclusionary tendencies. In this way, the idea of majority tyranny itself becomes a more general metaphor to express the way in which hierarchical and competitive systems of decisionmaking may unfairly dominate weaker voices.

I conclude that decisionmaking inclusiveness and accountability are critical to political empowerment and government legitimacy for all citizens. To learn the lesson of the Reagan Revolution, progressives need to

*move from competitive, adversarial approaches toward more coopera-
tive, consensual forms of decisionmaking.*

In 1981 Ronald Reagan staged a revolution, filled with vivid and passionate beliefs,[1] homespun faith,[2] disciplined strategy, a hearty adolescent vocabulary,[3] and a real battleground: the United States Supreme
Court.[4] Harvard Law Professor Charles Fried enlisted in 1985. Invigorated by the robust cadences and vocabulary of war, Professor Fried left
the academic pursuit of moral and social philosophy and contract law. Arguing to a court for the first time in his life, Reagan Solicitor General Fried
summoned his jurisprudential arms to draw *lines in the sand*[5] against the
march of liberal dogma, and what he perceived as its collectivist concept
of equality, its activist legacy on behalf of despised or marginalized groups,
and its fundamental lack of confidence in American society.

In *Order and Law: Arguing the Reagan Revolution—A Firsthand Account,* Fried carefully chronicles his tenure from 1985 to 1989 as Solicitor
General and self-described Reagan Revolutionary. Fried respected Reagan's "deep and fundamental decency,"[6] liked his "simple but understandable version" of principles they shared,[7] and became, as Solicitor
General, the President's principal spokesperson in the United States Supreme Court. There Fried assumed responsibility for articulating the Administration's legal philosophy and theories.

The narrative of the Reagan Revolution in law proceeds on two levels.
At one level, the book packs the punch of good journalism. Fried provides
a revealing personal memoir of the human events at the center of the Reagan legal project of dismantling the liberal judicial legacy of Earl Warren,
of redirecting the courts, and of returning to the president his strong, autonomous hand. At a second, theoretical level, this book offers more than
mere witnessing. Fried attempts to explicate the Reagan legal philosophy.
Neutral, principled reasons, he argues, compel judicial adoption of conservative public policy choices.

Many lawyers, including former Solicitor General Erwin Griswold,
have argued that the Solicitor General's job is to interpret and protect the
Constitution, not an administration's view of it.[8] Holders of the office had
cultivated a tradition that valued independence and legal integrity. Although the Solicitor General is an official of the executive branch who
serves at the pleasure of the President, many perceived the office as an
appendage to the Supreme Court.[9] For the legal establishment, this was a
place where respect for legal precedent should dominate, where an
overtly political discourse was eschewed.[10]

Fried, on the other hand, was aggressively political.[11] He saw his responsibility as advocating the political interests of the executive department, constrained only to the extent those interests could be translated into respectable legal arguments. For Fried, his role as the Solicitor General was to give "principled voice to the concerns of the elected Administration."[12] Consequently, Fried, a conservative activist, was far bolder than his predecessors in urging the Court to depart from its own precedents and to adopt the Administration's view of the law.

Fried's aggressively political stance was controversial. The positions he advanced often were considered extreme. The combination of politics and extremism limited his success during his tenure. At the time, the Supreme Court was still pragmatic, and Fried's ideologically charged arguments were often rejected. According to one scholar, the Administration lost cases it could have won because it acted like just "another interest group."[13]

In the end, it was not, as Fried hoped, the clarity of his arguments that shaped the long-term evolution of the law. His Administration won its revolution by changing the membership, not simply the orientation, of the Court. When power on the Court was held by pragmatists, Fried's arguments failed to win the Court's "triumphant embrace."[14] His views were often rejected. But with a noticeable change in membership, power on the Court shifted dramatically. And "power not reason" became "the new currency of this Court's decisionmaking."[15]

Three themes emerge from Fried's personal and jurisprudential recounting. First, Fried treats ideology as jurisprudence. By taking the Administration's political program as his legal text, Fried candidly reveals the substantive nature of his legal reasoning. Although Fried attempts to neutralize his approach within an interpretative method based on principles of geometric decisionmaking,[16] his explicitly ideological preferences confute such claims.

Second, Fried's book prompts sober reflection about the future of federal court litigation in the period after the Reagan Revolution. Fried's ideology as jurisprudence reminds us that it is time to reevaluate whether a continued focus on judicial solutions to public policy dilemmas makes sense with a Reagan-dominated judiciary. After all, the Reagan Revolution redirected the courts as if they were just another political institution.[17] The great success of this redirection means that progressive reformers are destined to become mere spectators if they focus exclusively on judicial solutions to public policy problems.

Third, Fried's description of his own stewardship illuminates the per-

sonal and institutional cost of using the Solicitor General's office as a revolutionary staging ground. The Administration's radical conception of its
interests often pressured Fried, the lawyer, to take up the gauntlet against
his milder, more traditional set of professional instincts. The friction between Fried's professional role and his revolutionary identity mutes his
professional voice, but does not make it disappear. In these internal duels,
Fried tries gallantly but unsuccessfully to sheath the contradiction of "two
warring ideals in one . . . body."[18]

The Solicitor General's unrelenting campaign on behalf of the Administration's political agenda also played havoc with the Court's own view of
its institutional legitimacy. Members of the judiciary appointed by Ronald
Reagan presumably because of their conservative ideology have shown
signs of battle fatigue in the face of the Solicitor General's sustained political advocacy campaigns. In the classic metaphor of a former Reagan
"warrior," the 1991–92 Term brought forth in a few visible cases a "wimp
bloc"[19] of three Reagan-Bush appointees who resisted, in the name of
institutional legitimacy, insistent volleys against past precedent lodged by
Charles Fried and his successors.[20] Some Supreme Court Justices apparently resist drawing lines in the sand, especially those urged upon them
under an Administration's fire.

Despite its erratic record, Fried's crusade helps contextualize the
courts' clearly conservative tilt and helps crystallize recent developments
in contemporary jurisprudence. If judicial activists of the right now find
merit in Fried's jurisprudence of ideology, they will continue to launch
from the bench a brand of conservative activism that Fried practiced if not
preached. Even the new so-called judicial moderates are cut from a conservative cloth. In either case, from Charles Fried we can learn about the
limitations of ideology as legal method and legal role; we can observe,
firsthand, its effect on the interaction between the Court and at least one
of its coordinate branches; and we can begin to prognosticate about the
future of litigation-based federal law reform.

I. Charles Fried, the Reagan Revolutionary

Through engaging and often frank introspection, Fried tells how a scholar
fused his academic skills with the tough, virulent rhetoric of the Reagan
war against government, against activist judging, and against group entitlements. Fried tells us that the Reagan Revolution associated liberalism
with a cynicism and self-hatred that placed an "exaggerated faith in bureaucracy and government expertise"[21] yet failed to entrust to those who

govern the means or discretion to govern effectively.[22] As a consequence
of this mistrust, liberalism, according to Fried, relied on legal procedures,
Congress, and a permanent bureaucracy to monitor governing elites, especially the Presidency. Liberalism anointed the federal judiciary as the
ultimate guarantor of government accountability and so-called progressive values. Liberalism allowed judges to manipulate rules and remedies
at every level, including the Constitution, and to recast lawsuits as "political struggles" in order to change the fundamental nature of society, to
reorder whole institutions, and to redistribute wealth.[23] In its preoccupation with minority rights, liberalism ignored those in the majority and their
legitimate expectations in knowing where they stand.

The Reagan Revolutionaries fought the campaign against the enemy of
liberal orthodoxy on two fronts. The first objective was to starve liberal
politicians of their redistributive resources through deregulation and tax
reduction. The second was the legal front. As Solicitor General, Fried la-
bored to redefine the boundaries of the second front around his vision of
judicial discipline, presidential autonomy, colorblindness, and geometric
decisionmaking.[24]

Focused on the judiciary, Fried saw himself leading the charge as the
David Stockman of the legal battleground.[25] In particular, Fried would
assist the Administration both in forcing a liberal retreat and in reasserting
Presidential authority, control, and centralized power. Fried saw the administration's real project as "restoring reasonableness and responsibility
to the practice of judging."[26] By changing the membership and orientation of the judiciary, the Reagan Revolution hoped to succeed, where the
political process had failed, in shifting power from the Congress to the
President; from a dispersed, legislative plurality to a centralized majority;
from a chorus of so-called multiple complaining voices to a dominant,
more self-confident hegemony.

A. Doing Battle

The book's first project gives Charles Fried the chance to tell his own
story. This he does with exceptional candor. He recounts the personal
transition from the prominence of an ambitious but abstracted academic
to the heady but mundane duties of a soldier in a jurisprudential war about
public policy. The task of taming liberalism challenges the armchair academic to bend to the demands of a different front; unlike the single authority figure dominating a structured dialogue or solitary researcher
enjoying the quiet and direction of his own imagination, Fried's Solicitor

General as likely takes as gives orders. Fried openly relates the tension between the academic general and the Reagan footsoldier.

By his account, Reagan's Revolution needed academics to give legal teeth, intellectual heart, and judicial soul to the administration's policies.[27] For the Revolution to succeed, it was necessary to recruit sensible, thoughtful support to harness the creative tension of evolving jurisprudence, "disciplined by respect for tradition, professionalism, and careful, candid reasoning."[28] Party loyalty counted less than philosophical commitment.[29]

While Fried claims that the success of the Reagan Revolution depended, in part, on attracting the acumen of men like himself, it was in fact a revolution led by radicals of a different stripe. Hard-line "movement conservatives"[30] such as Attorney General Edwin Meese and Assistant Attorney General for Civil Rights Brad Reynolds fueled the Revolution's ideological engine, apparently energized by the increasingly inflammatory rhetoric of a war against racial minorities, liberal orthodoxy, and government itself. In a contest of wills as well as instincts, Reynolds's missionary zeal pitted him often against the more philosophical Fried. Working with Brad Reynolds became the hardest part of Fried's job.

Reynolds proselytized on behalf of a host of "suicidally radical and unconvincing projects"[31] that Fried was then supposed to argue before the Supreme Court. Reynolds's ruthless, almost religious sense of mission had a "searing" effect.[32] Through carefully developed arguments in the Supreme Court, Fried attempted to give constitutional dignity to Meese and Reynolds's ideological campaigns.[33]

Clashing often with Reynolds's hard edge, Fried discovered his conscience constantly needled by political chores. Although he experienced Brad Reynolds's presence as both "ubiquitous" and "chilling,"[34] Fried worked hard to fit the demands of his position without explicitly capitulating to Reynolds's scornful challenges to his authority.[35] The toughest times came when political superiors pressed positions that Fried did not share or value although he could discern their arguable legitimacy.[36] Here Fried found comfort in technical compromise,[37] in softening as much as possible Reynolds's hard line.

Fried confronted such a dilemma over the principle of federalism as advocated by Brad Reynolds. Reynolds and his deputy, Charles Cooper, wanted to shift the balance of authority to local from national government. They favored strong local government as inherently more democratic and less likely to engage in redistributive policies. Fried, by contrast, who had lived in "the People's Republic of Cambridge," feared the "village tyrant."[38] Although he willingly compromised when the political leadership took sides,[39] he never internalized the position.

In these philosophical tugs of war with the Attorney General or the Assistant Attorney General, Fried relaxed his grip when he found technical legal authority to support the position of his political superiors.[40] For Fried, certain issues were not worth resigning over. Moreover, by resigning he would have no public platform to explain his competing vision.

B. *Defining His Role*

To a great extent Fried's difficulties were of his own making because the role he undertook to serve as Solicitor General differed from that served by many of his predecessors. Fried viewed his office as home to the intellectual vanguard of conservative thought. His overtly political stance eroded the distinction between the President as leader of an ideological campaign and the President as chief executive of a tripartite government.[41] For Fried the Solicitor General was primarily answerable to the former, who commanded loyalty based on a shared political vision.

Fried readily acknowledges the passions and weaknesses of human officeholders, including himself. Yet, he attempts more than a simple narration of his personal crises. Fried offers a conception of loyalty to explain in a predictable way his own particular choices. He devotes an entire chapter to an exegesis on the conflict between loyalty and conscience.

In order to justify following orders while salvaging his independence of mind, Fried claims his choices followed his political principles even when motivated by a political mandate. Fried makes an argument for intellectual autonomy in which the Solicitor General serves as an independent, legal trustee for the President's political program.[42] He adopts a political conscience, in which he is still accountable to conservative principles although he accedes to political opportunities or demands.

But Fried ultimately leaves the reader unsure when he would feel it proper to acquiesce to politically motivated government compatriots' laying on the heavy hand of peer pressure and when the Solicitor should refuse to compromise his conscience. Fried never establishes the fine line he intends between public loyalty and personal conscience.[43]

First, the contours of the line seem to follow Fried's belief that ultimately he, better than Brad Reynolds, represented the President. When confronted by Reynolds, whom he characterizes as the equivalent of a kneejerk ideologue,[44] Fried shielded himself with his own more nuanced understanding. Because Fried intuitively knew the real conservative program, he avoided many tough questions by simply consulting his own conscience. Fried assumes that loyalty to the President was satisfied when Fried acted consistent with his own conscience rather than submitting to Reynolds's orders.

Yet, despite his more sophisticated and intuitive grasp of the political program, Fried often capitulated to Reynolds's demands. His personal conscience becomes quite elastic when necessary to meet political exigencies. Although he ridicules Reynolds as a sinister and crude manipulator, Fried allows himself to be manipulated.

Perhaps he felt he had no choice. Reynolds was not Fried's political mentor or indeed his superior, but Reynolds was more closely tied to the Attorney General's inner policy circle. As a result, Fried frequently relented to Reynolds's bullying. On these occasions, he failed to disclose a principled source for choosing sides between the Solicitor General and the Assistant Attorney General in an overtly political debate.

The need for a principled position helps explain his predecessors' claims that they represented not the President but the Constitution in the Supreme Court.[45] In the past such distinction may have been artificial, but Fried's aggressively political conduct—as well as his overtly ideological conscience—denies him even that way out. Whether politics is spelled with a capital or a small "p," it was politics that got in the way. Unable to seek cover under the claim that the Solicitor General serves the Court, not the President, Fried turns a discussion of what is inherently political into a discussion of what is politic.

Fried cites as a conscience-loyalty dilemma an earlier Solicitor General's controversy over the brief to be filed in the *Bakke* case.[46] Solicitor General Wade McCree, a black former federal court of appeals judge, sat in the Solicitor General's office with two white assistants to defend the government's brief. Joseph Califano, then Secretary of Health, Education, and Welfare, had charged that the brief failed adequately to carry out the Carter Administration policy in support of affirmative action. Califano describes the meeting as "deeply disturbing" because the work of arguing what constituted principles of equality was being orchestrated by technicians (McCree and his assistants), not policymakers.[47]

In replaying this scene, Fried is disturbed more by the fact that a shouting match ensued. For Fried, the problem with Califano's confronting McCree was that he did so in the presence of McCree's assistants. The scene simply "lacks decorum." According to Fried, "[a] famous and powerful Cabinet Secretary should not be getting into a shouting match with another officer's career staff."[48]

This, then, is the second problem with Fried's line-drawing exercise. Fried leaves the reader with a nagging sense that his answer to the conflict between loyalty and conscience is to make human relationships, in particular, and organizational behavior, in general, more a matter of establishing hierarchy and following rules.[49] To reduce the problem somewhat, issues of loyalty are often resolved by politeness, not principle. If Brad Reynolds had just been more respectful of lines of authority, unseemly problems of loyalty might have dissipated.

Fried admits he wrote this book to justify his actions, yet his explanation is ultimately unpersuasive. Despite all the abstract theorizing about accountability, Fried is ultimately unclear as to what he is accountable: his own conscience or the President's. He never reconciles the somewhat existential tension between his responsibilities as a legal professional and his identity as a Reagan Revolutionary.[50] Fried seems content instead to puzzle through the role confusion with a discussion of etiquette.[51] The reader is left untangling lines of authority from spheres of intellectual autonomy and interpersonal comity.

Fried simply skips over arguments that the Solicitor General owes allegiance to any abstract principles distinct from those held by the incumbent administration.[52] Rather than grapple with any model of the Solicitor General's competing obligations, Fried asserts the unitary vision of presidential authority that serves as the source of his political and personal loyalty.[53]

In a manner that parallels Fried's approach to substantive legal problems, he thus tends to conflate problems of loyalty with theorems of geometry. Hierarchy and civility substitute for critical interrogation of his initial premises. Rules resolve what a sustained analysis of the Solicitor General's multiple roles might leave open.[54]

This is a weakness of the book in general. Fried's attempts to theorize tend to oversimplify.[55] He appears attracted more to symmetry than substance. Lines in the sand may reflect Professor Fried's desire to draw on a popular Reagan speechwriter's effective metaphor for political combat.[56] But as a means of staking out clear-cut tests of the Solicitor General's partisanship, they become awash in the murky undertow of ego and the ebb and flow of the tides of Fried's own conscience.

II. Charles Fried: The Reagan Legal Philosopher

The book derives its depth from its evocation of the second theme: the derivation, evolution, and explication of the Reagan legal philosophy. Here Fried's battles were not within himself or with other members of the

Administration, but in the courts with what he terms the judicial bureau-crats who had become complicitous in the liberal project of aggrandizing government unaccountability:

> Egged on by aggressive litigators, the legal professoriate, and the liberal press, the courts had become a principal engine for redistributing wealth and shackling the energies and enterprise of the productive sector.[57]

In analyzing its legal underpinnings, Charles Fried's account thus ex-poses the hidden agendas of the Revolution. First, by packing the courts with young ideologically correct judges, Reagan's Revolutionaries would replace the legislative battleground of temporary political swings and shifting political fortunes with a judicial permanence that endures for sev-eral generations.[58] Although Fried does not discuss court-packing di-rectly, he apparently shared the vision that the Reagan-Bush agenda should become not a temporary, political revolution but a long-term, in-stitutional restructuring. One of the most enduring legacies of the Reagan Revolution has in fact been the rightward tilt of the federal judiciary through the appointment of politically conservative judges.

Second, Fried proposes a grand theory of executive power. Fried's project, at least initially, was to convince the Supreme Court to announce as a "theorem of constitutional law" a rigorous, geometric view of separa-tion of powers.[59] For Fried, a geometric view would make it clear that the executive is unitary and that its functions cannot be usurped by Con-gress.[60] A central premise is that all executive power must be exercised subject to direct Presidential control; related to this premise is the prop-osition that independent regulatory commissions are unconstitutional, because they are not subject to direct executive control.[61] In geometric terms, the president sits at the apex of two upright triangles. In one trian-gle, he asserts unitary executive authority over the independent agencies and cabinet departments. In the second, he enjoys superior positioning relative to the judicial and legislative branches.

The effect on the Administration agenda is clear. Assisted by a now ideologically compatible judiciary, the Republican President would rule majestically as the ultimate and most legitimate power source of govern-ment. The "muscular" presidency,[62] the heart of Fried's geometric theo-rem of constitutional law,[63] would beat in the chambers of young, ideologically committed judicial soldiers for years after the Revolution itself passed.[64] Concern with separation-of-powers symmetry becomes a metaphor to replace legislative prerogative with executive fiat, to develop a federal judiciary that supported the unitary presidency, and ultimately to justify a consolidated executive hierarchy.

Third, multiple perspectives about racism and subordination are reduced to a simple thesis with a single claim: government should be color-blind. If that means that government accedes to a status quo unfairly dominated by a prejudiced or racially fixed white majority, so be it. Fried claims a more subtle view than that held by the hard right, particularly concerning issues of victim-specificity. Yet he argued the hard-line claims in the Court, and enthusiastically supported a firm stand against any tendency toward a "quota society."

Fried's principled defense of the Reagan Revolution becomes a defense of its reasons for particular policy goals—a right to privacy that does not include a right to abortion, protection against intentional discrimination that does not protect against the legacy of past discrimination, and a concept of separation of powers that elevates only the separate powers of a muscular president.

In each of these areas, Fried defends a certain level of governmental intrusion. The right to privacy, like the right to be free of discrimination, amounts to nothing more than a right to be free from a certain level of interference. The task for courts is to look at the type and circumstances of intrusions and decide when and whether they are too great.[65] He writes:

> [I]t is the function of legal doctrine *to develop the lines* separating the rights of individuals to ignore organized society's value judgments from the right of society to make and give life to such judgments.[66]

Here, too, Fried enjoys drawing lines in the sand. His challenge is to tell us how to know independently where to place the lines. He attempts to justify judicial adoption of the Reagan Administration's political platform based on the application of disciplined, restrained legal reasoning. As the following discussion reveals, however, we are ultimately left, as in Fried's individual loyalty-conscience dilemma, with piecemeal adjudications, Fried's own personal view of what is right, and an administration committed to its own perpetuity.

A. Constitutional Interpretation

Fried's central project was to develop an interpretative method that would discern the Administration's main policy themes within the structure and organization of the Constitution. Fried hoped to persuade the Supreme Court that the Constitution mandated long-term institutional restructuring, hierarchical decisionmaking within a centralized, unitary executive, and color-blindness. Fried centers first on describing techniques of constitutional interpretation that provided the jurisprudential anchor for his legal arguments. He rejects both "twist[ing] . . . legal doctrine [and] common sense in order to get to a result [courts] felt was substantively right"[67] as well as the rigid originalist constitutional analysis.[68] He favors instead the "rule of law"[69] and his conception of a constitution that evolves through restrained judicial analogy.[70]

Fried advocates a constitution that is extended through argument from precedent by analogy. He claims that the "Reagan administration's project of judicial restraint" was not about "empirical iron rules," but about reintroducing "a conception of law disciplined by a respect for tradition, professionalism, and careful, candid reasoning."[71] Fried believes that courts could derive correct legal judgments from a few fundamental principles and concepts, analogizing jurisprudence to Euclidean geometry.[72] The comparison appeals to Fried based on the use of inductive reasoning to solve problems and find solutions.[73]

Thus, Fried's rule of law is, in fact, a rule of logic. Logical, abstract thinking allows an intellectual conversation, a respectful discourse that somehow justifies a result in the minds of its participants. For Fried, the rule of logic reasoning is important even where it alone does not ordain particular results. Fried's claim is that the particular results don't always matter; it is the orderly process of leading to the results about which Fried cares.

Fried values the rule of logical reasoning because, if clear, it gives notice and provides stability.[74] Definiteness is important.[75] Consequently, when Fried discusses the rule of reasoning, he starts from the supposition that "men of intelligence and reasonable good will can come to a fair measure of agreement about what the law is, and that our liberty is most secure when in the end it is to the rule of law that government power is responsible."[76] For Fried, order comes before and is the point of law. Order is necessary to enjoy liberty.[77]

But once law establishes order, Fried believes it ceases to function authoritatively. Thus Fried defends an evolutionary process derived from respect for a rule of law with a special antipathy to notions of mandating particular results, particularly equality of result. His rule of law is simply to draw lines in the sand that tell the American people "where we stand."[78] Fried focuses on drawing these lines because they announce reasonable constraints on our conduct, after which we should each be free as individuals to achieve as much as we possibly can for ourselves.

As Fried confesses in his discussion of separation of powers, his arguments are not compelled by the words of the Constitution or the intent of its Framers. He rejects a conception of constitutional jurisprudence based on the overriding righteousness of legislative majorities or on "originalism."[79] Fried criticizes originalism not only because changing circumstances make an historical mode of analysis unwise, but also because originalism fails to deliver on its promises to bring definiteness to decisionmaking and dispose of the need for judicial judgment. Originalism simply results in the finding of general principles, which still need to be applied.[80]

In sum, Fried's primary claim is that the Reagan philosophy could be extended through restrained, logical reasoning. Using an interpretative method that discovers within the structure and organization of the Constitution conservative principles to be applied logically and carefully, Fried defends as a deeply embedded constitutional theme his vision of an orderly, coherent conception of government. His arguments suggest a vision he discerns from the structure of the Constitution as a whole. He supports such a vision because he admires the spider's web: its symmetry is beautiful, its logic perfect.[81]

But like a spider's web attempting to catch a snake, his arguments are often "inadequate to control the dominant facts."[82] Fried relies on abstract logic to marshal legal technique for specific, political ends. This approach to reasoning whittles political tools from the forms and techniques of jurisprudence. As a consequence, his vision is persuasive only to those who have already reached the same conclusions.

Focusing on his explication first of the Reagan vision of separation of powers and second of color-blindness, I suggest that Fried's articulated principles follow his policy preferences.[83] Fried's rule of reasoning is a formalist enterprise that ignores context. It is logical, but only one of several logical modes of analysis. Like the liberal activists Fried condemns, his policy preferences dominate, and apparently precede, the process of legal reasoning. The success of his enterprise thus depends less upon the power of his arguments and more upon their conformity to the ideological and personal preferences of the judges Presidents Reagan and Bush called to the bench.

B. *Separation of Powers*

Fried espouses a rigorous separation of powers theory.[84] This theory holds that the executive power must be kept separate from the other two branches, that the President's power must be firmly unified under his control,[85] and that the executive embodies best the sovereign authority of the nation as a whole.[86] Separation of powers is not just a practical instrument for dividing up government responsibility. For Fried, separation of powers expresses "the deep structure of governmental power over human affairs."[87]

This view of separation of powers is most identified with Justice Antonin Scalia.[88] Under Scalia's analysis, Congress's role in governance begins and ends with the passage of statutes. Once a statute becomes law, the executive and judiciary take over and congressional control has ended. Congress's role is further weakened by Scalia's contention that legislative power can never be delegated,[89] and that legislative history should be given little if any weight.[90]

Unlike his skepticism toward legislative power, Scalia broadly construes executive power.[91] Thus, Scalia's views on separation of powers tilt power toward the executive and away from the legislative branch.[92] Given this tendency, it is not at all surprising that the Administration saw a chance to seize the rhetorical high ground and to reach outcomes supportive of its own enhanced power in Justice Scalia's formalist approach to separation of powers.[93]

Indeed, Fried's defense of Scalia's absolutist views became the administration agenda in the *Morrison v. Olson* case,[94] a challenge to the Independent Counsel law passed in the wake of Watergate.[95] The case made its way to the Supreme Court, where Fried, as Solicitor General, made the structural, constitutional argument against the Independent Counsel law. He argued that the law violated the Appointments Clause of the Constitution and that the law was superfluous, because a special prosecutor appointed by the executive to investigate the executive was still subject to political safeguards.[96]

Like Justice Scalia, Fried focuses—as he did in *Morrison*—on the idea of separateness, locating boundaries between the different branches of government. But unlike Justice Scalia, Fried rests his argument on two explicit assumptions. First, Fried celebrates executive power because it best reflects his yearnings for efficiency and clarity.[97] The government should rule through its executive to avoid legislative tyranny, to ensure that the President is more than ceremonial, and to make government accountable.[98] Fried assumes that the executive is a more efficient manager than large, deliberative bodies,[99] and expresses more completely and directly the will of the majority.[100] In this view, only executive authority most directly serves the principle of democratic accountability.[101]

Fried's second assumption follows from the supremacy of the President over the executive branch, including the independent agencies. Fried uses the rigorous separation of powers theory as part of a strategy to center responsibility within the executive branch. The theory of a unitary executive would limit unconstitutional delegation of legislative authority and reassert executive control over the independent regulatory commissions, the headless fourth branch.[102]

Because the executive commands a huge bureaucracy where power is wielded quietly and massively, Fried wanted to replace the informal network of experienced bureaucrats with their babble of incoherent voices.[103] Diffused responsibility threatens Fried's concept of liberty.[104] The firing squad, for example, is "the ultimate bureaucratic manifestation" because it fails to make responsibility transparent.[105] To deliver accountability, Fried apparently prefers a single executioner.

In sum, Fried's separation of powers discussion is valuable for its clear exposition of the importance to the conservative agenda of a unitary, centralized authority. This authority is present in two guises. First, it is inherent in his fight for neutral principles, the claim that there exist objective standards by which all similarly situated persons can and should be judged. Fried claims that logic and respect for tradition can provide definiteness and common understanding. Thus, Fried invokes the rule of reasoning as an important, unifying authority.[106]

Second, the single, national executive functions to clarify and keep accountable government. Under the rubric of discerning geometric symmetry within the fundamental structure of our government, Fried finds a grand theory of unitary, executive authority. Fried's exposition frankly extols the virtue of centralized control as personified by the direct election of a single, national executive.

But when Fried used this theory to argue that the Independent Counsel law was unconstitutional, few of the Justices were at that time ready to enlist in the project. Fried offers several explanations. The theory itself was not compelled by the words of the Constitution or the Framers' intent. Fried culls the vision from the structure of the document as a whole, "the logic implicit in the arrangement of its parts."[107] The vehicles—cases involving sentencing guidelines and the independent counsel investigating the Attorney General—were, from Fried's point of view, unfortunate.

Most important, the administration had been indiscreet in announcing its intentions. Fried cites Attorney General Meese's speech to the Federal Bar Association, which bluntly questioned the status of the independent agencies.[108] Perhaps, cautions Fried, they would have been more successful had they been more sneaky in their campaign, proceeding step-by-step toward a more rigorous conception of the separation of powers.[109] In the end, only Justice Scalia signed on.

I would suggest an alternative explanation. Fried's real project "had already broken cover"[110] with his willingness to defend aggressively the Administration's ideological agenda. Fried had made no secret that as Solicitor General he told "the Court frankly what he thinks rather than what he thinks it wants to hear."[111] Despite the high sounding rhetoric of separation of powers geometry, geometric symmetry shapes a particular, not a universal, view of governmental organization.

In Fried's organizational chart, the president—the source of governmental power—sits at the apex of two separate power triangles.[112] A geometric vision of separated triangles clarifies for Fried the lines of responsibility within the executive itself and between the executive and the legislative. Even without the Attorney General's premature disclosure, Fried's exposition itself clarifies the implications of the rigorous separation of powers view. Fried's project is to defend presidential authority over that of Congress and to assert presidential control within the executive branch.[113]

The book is subtitled *Arguing the Reagan Revolution—A Firsthand Account,* but its subtitle could just as easily have been *Power,* in particular, *Presidential Power.* Of course, it does not escape notice that the Presidency was the one branch that Reagan Revolutionaries firmly controlled. Fried himself admits that in choosing a judicial battleground and in picking its battles, the Administration acted in response to the Revolution's failure to control both houses of the Congress, and after 1986, either house.

Indeed, Fried claims that the Reagan vision was revolutionary because it was subjected to legal, not just political, battles.[114] The political battles had led to a standoff between the Republican Administration and the Democrat-controlled House of Representatives. Rather than press for legislative change, the Administration decided to seek its solutions through "administrative inactivity," by charging the bureaucrats to deregulate themselves,[115] and by changing the membership and orientation of the courts ultimately charged with resolving conflicts between the executive and the legislature.

With the loss in 1986 of the Republican advantage in the United States Senate, the Supreme Court replaced the legislature as the war zone. The strategy was to enlist conservative lawyers as jurists to soldier on, to "tame"[116] past precedents that attempted "rough justice,"[117] and instead to "stand up"[118] for a conservative agenda in which government is color-blind[119] and minimalistic,[120] and in which the power of the President is "clear and unitary."[121] The objective was to reinterpret and reclaim a "liberal, individualistic"[122] conception of justice, personified in the heightened power of the Presidency.

Fried concedes the ambiguity of his proposed legal solution to the political problem that arises with divided government. After all, the executive is obliged to carry out laws that Congress passes. Indeed, the Constitution commits the President to "take Care that the Laws be faithfully executed."[123] But to avoid stalemate where Congress and the Presidency are controlled by different political parties, the Reagan Administration was attracted by a rigorous or absolutist separation of powers approach that tilts control toward the executive.

Using the theory of the unitary executive, Fried sees the President as the source of government power. But for others, myself included, the legislature, not the President, best represents the people; separation of powers connotes power checking—not separating—power; power-sharing, not power-dividing.[124] For those whose concept of democratic accountability is more participatory and less hierarchical, the theory of checks and balances—of ambition checking ambition, as Madison put it[125]—is equally, if not more, compelling.

For these scholars, the separation of powers represents a commitment to a continual struggle between the branches, not the allocation of fixed, absolute boundaries. The three branches of government are an institutional arrangement resembling a circle, not a triangle. In this view, Madison's checks and balances were an effort to constrain the majority faction, to disperse power, and to ensure that the monarchy against which the American Revolution was fought did not re-emerge in the tyranny of the majority. In Lord Acton's words, "Power corrupts, and absolute power corrupts absolutely." Or as Hamilton put it, when the many are given all the power, "they will oppress the few."[126]

The Madisonian-Hamiltonian solution was to separate legislative, executive, and judicial powers to allow institutional checks and balances, to require each branch to depend in part on powers accorded the others, and to "invest the legislative powers in a democratic body that internally checks the ability of individuals to pursue self-interested ends."[127] Similarly, the Framers established a representative rather than a direct democracy because they thought it would moderate public preferences to avoid majority tyranny.[128]

The American Revolution was fought against the centralized authority of a monarch and an unrepresentative parliament.[129] As victims of what they considered a tyrannical royal prerogative, the Founders were determined to fashion for themselves a Presidency that would be strong but still limited.[130] Experience under the British crown led them to favor less centralization of authority than they perceived in the British monarchy.[131] While it is true that republicanism, the ideology of the American Revolution, was not necessarily intended "to cut off the heads of kings," it represented an effort to enlighten and improve monarchy, not replicate it.[132]

Under this theory, locating all power in an unchanging ruling group, personified by a single executive, is inconsistent with the Framers' original democratic understanding.[133] The possibility of an unchanging group's exercising all the power was a source of fear, not admiration.[134] Alexander Hamilton, one of the strongest proponents of centralized authority, nevertheless referred to the concept of separation of powers as a matter of "joint possession."[135]

History aside, the modern notion that single executives are inherently democratic is peculiarly American. Fried's implicit assumption that government only works in a hierarchical way with a single, unitary authority is questionable. Fried explicitly disavows multiple power centers within the executive. Yet, "even the idea that executive power must be vested in a single individual is contingent."[136]

Other democratic governments choose to disperse power in order to represent better the minority perspectives in a multiethnic or multiracial society.[137] Even within our governing structure, some see the legislature, with its decentralized authority, as the more legitimate source of government power. For example, Fried acknowledges that Justice White, among others, has taken a position antithetical to his.[138] It is a position that, at least in other cases, the pragmatic court had adopted.[139] White posits that the legislative branch is the fundamental building block of government. According to him, Congress has the constitutional authority to determine how each of the branches of government should be organized.[140] According to this understanding, the legislature best embodies the ideals of participatory democracy and democratic accountability.

Indeed, the idea of plural perspectives is also very American.[141] Insistence on a central, unitary authority is under increasing scrutiny from activists and scholars who value a more collaborative environment.[142] This is a project to which I have elsewhere devoted attention, having perceived the tension between two competing "American" traditions: pluralism, on the one hand, and winner-take-all concentrations of power, on the other.[143] Even those preaching entrepreneurial government emphasize the importance of encouraging elastic and responsive results rather than "neutral" and "hierarchical" processes.[144] Especially for those concerned about the perspective of marginalized groups, centralized hierarchy, while appealing in its formality, is frightening in its exclusivity.

Such groups worry about a vision that says political decisions are all win-lose. Fried seems unable to conceive of a politics in which multiple perspectives actually enhance the discourse. While he concedes the evolutionary nature of both the forces of politics and the constitutional response, his vision is purely about efficiency and control rather than change and inclusion. In a society with rapidly changing demographics, competing voices arguably demand a plural, not a unitary, form of power-sharing.[145] Similarly, other choices, such as the one embodied in the 1965 Voting Rights Act, express a vision of a pluralist politics that embodies the richness of diversity, the value of bottom-up rather than top-down empowerment and the legitimacy of heterogeneous institutions in which no one voice arrogates to itself complete control.[146] Participation and the exercise of choice that come from broad-based participation are valued because they enhance citizen autonomy.[147]

Given the different worlds in which so many Americans live, preferences and their intensities are dispersed, meaning different issues are differentially salient to members of different interest constituencies. Where preferences are dispersed, the Voting Rights Act norm suggests that decisions should not be made according to any single conception of the public good. Decisionmaking should instead value and incorporate a diversity of views to enrich the chances that the ultimate decision is both fair and just. Decisionmaking that values diversity multiplies the points of access to government, disperses power, and struggles to ensure a full and developed rational dialogue. Public policy then becomes "the equilibrium reached in the group struggle at any given moment."[148]

In this alternative view, pluralism requires a multiplicity of voices—colorful, not simply color-blind. In a heterogeneous society deeply cleaved by issues of gender and race, centralized authority, by contrast, may reflect a deeply felt need to preserve the control of those in power while ostensibly protecting democratic values.[149]

In Fried's geometric vision, the executive enjoys hegemony over all functions not explicitly assigned to the legislature or the judiciary. Lines of authority, like lines in the sand, separate turf and establish hierarchy. But Fried's logical arguments do not lead to consensus in support of either his rigorous geometric schema or his theory of the unitary executive. Some might perceive his vision itself as counterrevolutionary, given our initial struggle to establish a republic, not a monarchy. For minorities it is counterintuitive. For minority voters, who have little chance to govern when authority is centralized in a single executive, dispersed, plural legislative authority offers the best opportunity to participate meaningfully in the process of self-government.[150]

Fried's centralized authority sits at the apex of two triangles that reduce access and broad-based participation as one gets closer to the top.[151] Centralized authority may serve those in the majority well. But those at the bottom are less interested in clear lines of descending authority; they would like to see fewer lines and more openings. Indeed, "the beautiful symmetry and perfect logic"[152] of Fried's separation of powers theory or other rigorous, clear arguments propounded by his associates do not persuade those at the bottom of his geometric pyramid.

C. Color-Blindness

On issues of race, the rallying cry was color-blindness.[153] A color-blind government would refuse to make contemporary racial distinctions, although in so doing it happily ratifies a status quo that gives whites a "property right" in being white,[154] or at least legitimates expectations derived from participating in a "plantation economy."[155] Evidence of existing racism is just "nasty details,"[156] "ghost[s] to exorcise"[157] (or not).

Like separation of powers geometry, this color-blind concept was lodged in a single, unitary vision of contemporary reality. Whites and blacks were defined by the absence of color, meaning both the neutral principle of being the same, or—as anyone aware of America's history would choose—that they would both be judged as if they were white. As long as formal, overt distinctions based on race were absent, governmental conduct was immunized from challenge.

Just like the separation of power thesis Fried propounds, color-blindness suggests that American democracy is measured by a central, unifying claim. We measure the success of outsiders by the extent to which they assimilate norms identified with a single, nation- or culture-wide majority.[158] Creation of or faith in the ongoing existence of a central unifying norm is necessary to establish a common core in a society riven by racial and ethnic cleavages.[159] Likewise, color-blindness suggests to some that blacks are successful when they become indistinguishable from whites.[160]

Fried distinguishes his personal position from that of others within the Reagan Administration. While he favored withdrawal from the "preference business," he also advocated preferential remedies against those who had been shown to have discriminated.[161] However, according to Fried, Brad Reynolds and his hard-line cohorts "bridled" at any government preferences or race-conscious relief. Color-blindness was an obsession for them, so any relief had to be victim-specific.[162] The latter view carried the day. Although Fried claims that he internally advocated race-based preferences as a remedy for past discrimination, he willingly presented the Reagan Administration policy of victim-specific relief to the Court.[163]

Once the Administration's defeats in several affirmative action cases[164] relieved Fried of his obligation to argue victim-specificity, Fried felt free to formulate Administration policy on race. He concentrated on two things: rejecting quotas and affirming color-blindness as the only permissible government policy except where unusual and compelling reasons exist.[165] Fried perceived the deepest issues at stake to be whether American society is defined in terms of groups, whether rights derive from group membership, and whether individualism is a fundamental conception.[166] While Fried yearns for symmetry in this area as well, he is less sympathetic to the need of Reynolds and others for ideological purity.[167]

Fried saw the task of the Reagan Administration as "ending the drift to a quota society and to dismantling government-imposed racial preferences."[168] For Fried, the problem with quotas is that they "dangerously aggrandize government,"[169] giving it an improper hold over private institutions. Quotas lead to a "sinister" politicization where jobs are handed out not according to market pressures or individual will but "according to membership in a group that has managed to attract political power."[170] Those seeking jobs would come to rely on politics rather than their own capabilities.[171]

Second, quotas, which define everything in terms of groups, threaten the fundamental conception of individual liberty.[172] Racial preferences that are not remedial are "pure social engineering—a kind of racial industrial policy"[173] with negative psychological effects on both the beneficiaries and the white males they displace.[174]

In one of the earliest cases Fried litigated, *Thornburg v. Gingles,*[175] the Supreme Court decisively rejected his vision of pure color-blindness, although it did not embrace "quotas" either. Fried discusses the case only briefly, but, in part because of my own involvement, I went back and re-read the briefs he filed. I discuss the case here because it summarizes much of Fried's thesis about race. It also reveals the connection between his encomium to neutral processes and his vision of what constitutes just results. Finally, Fried's position discloses in the specific context of a concrete case the limitations of his allegiance to a grand, unitary theory of color-blindness.

Gingles was the first case in which the Supreme Court reviewed a trial court's finding of a violation of the 1982 amendment to Section 2 of the Voting Rights Act, an amendment that the Reagan Administration fought unsuccessfully. The amendment was the result of a carefully orchestrated, bipartisan legislative effort to overturn a prior Supreme Court interpretation of the Act in which the Court had declared that a finding of discrimination in the political process required direct proof of invidious intent.[176] The amendment restored a "results" test, prohibiting voting practices, procedures, or standards that resulted in reduced opportunity for minority voters to "participate in the political process and to elect representatives of their choice."[177]

The word "results" was carefully chosen to avoid the controversy over discriminatory effects, which was becoming closely identified with claims of reverse discrimination.[178] Moreover, the effects language was used in another portion of the statute[179] and had been interpreted by the Court to have a particular, narrow meaning. It had been used to refer to "retrogression"—whether the challenged law had minimized the ability of blacks to participate but only in relation to past practices, not relative to an ideal or fair result.[180]

Acting Solicitor General Fried filed a brief at the invitation of the Court. Fried chose to support the state defendants who had lost in the three-judge court. He employed two tactics to support the state. First, he revisited the legislation, engrafting his own definition on the statute. He labeled the amendment "a studied compromise"[181] in which "undue emphasis must not be given to the views of any one faction in the controversy."[182] His brief attempted to undermine the elaborate legislative history accompanying the statutory language. He denigrated the Senate Report, terming it merely the views of "one faction in the controversy."[183] Perhaps because of his single-minded focus on representing the President's program, he urged the Court to interpret the statute in conjunction with the President's signing statement, although the President's role in the legislation had been that of an opponent. As a consequence, Senator Robert Dole and others took the unusual step of filing their own amicus brief in the Court.[184]

Second, he challenged the trial court's interpretation of the facts in light of his narrow reading of the law. He argued that some blacks had been elected under the challenged state districting plan. Since Congress had intended only to guarantee equal access, not equal results, the trial

court had gotten it wrong when it found that black voters had been denied
their right to elect representatives of their choice as a consequence of a
pattern of persistent racial bloc voting, a legacy of overt political exclusion,
ongoing racial appeals, and continued disfranchisement. Although the
statute guaranteeed equal access, for Fried that goal was met if a few black
candidates were successful anywhere.[185] Fried's interpretation measured
the fairness of the process by the episodic election of a few blacks, whose
success may have been aberrational or engineered by whites to undermine the lawsuit itself.[186]

The Republican National Committee, the Republican Governor of
North Carolina and the Republican and Democratic sponsors of the statute in the United States House and Senate all took issue with Charles
Fried's elegy to then-existing politics as color-blind.[187] The Supreme
Court, at that time still willingly enlightened by its own precedents and by
the trial court's extensive factual findings, also refused to go along. The
Court ruled that blacks not only have the right to participate, but that their
right to participate includes a right to elect a representative of their choice,
even if that means a representative of their race.[188] Race consciousness
was a pragmatic recognition of the racial politics the district court had
found evident in each of the challenged districts.[189] Results mattered. The
outcome, not just the process, reflected and provided essential information about a baseline of fairness.

In 1986, the Court rejected Fried's agnostic (or willfully color-blind)
description of contemporary racial politics. By January 1992, however,
the Reagan-Bush Supreme Court had a working majority. In *Presley v.
Etowah County Commission,* not surprisingly, the Court's views converged with those it had repudiated six years earlier.[190] The Court took an
extraordinarily narrow view of another section in the same statute it had
construed in 1986. The Court ruled that blacks may enjoy the right to
vote, but that does not necessarily include the right to govern.[191]

In this case, immediately upon the election of the first black commissioners since Reconstruction, the local white incumbents moved to strip
the black commissioners of their authority. Because they did so within the
closed doors of their legislative chambers, the Court declined to question
either their motives or the effect of their actions. As long as the process of
election allowed blacks to compete successfully, even if meaninglessly,
the processes of government were off limits to judicial scrutiny under certain provisions of the Voting Rights Act.[192]

Of particular relevance, the Court engaged in a line-drawing exercise
worthy of Euclid. If the Court used the Voting Rights Act to examine vot-

ing rules employed by elected representatives, where would they draw the line against federal intrusion in local government affairs? This preoccupation with concerns about drawing lines moved the Court to defy its own precedents that expansively interpreted the statute, to repudiate the Bush Justice Department's carefully constructed arguments supporting the black plaintiffs, and to ignore the statutory scheme Congress extended three times over a seventeen-year period to block strategems that changed the means of discrimination in order to evade full minority political participation.[193]

The Court lifted the case out of its relevant context in which the "unremitting and ingenius defiance" of many of the Southern states had earlier required judicial scrutiny of *all* efforts to maintain local white political hegemony.[194] In dissent, Justice Stevens reminded the majority that the issue was justice and fairness, not symmetry. "A few pages of history are far more illuminating than volumes of logic. . . ."[195]

Had Fried argued in 1992 the same position that he took in 1986, he likely would have won, or at least come closer to predicting the Court's view of Section 2. Like Fried, the 1992 Supreme Court majority assumed a single and universal perspective about racial fairness, which sees racism largely as a thing of the past and color-blindness as current reality and not primarily a heuristic. The Court rejects the possibility of a competing perspective in which race and racism are central to understanding the action of the local white county commissioners.

The outcome of *Presley* reflects the triumph of Fried's geometric approach to decisionmaking; indeed, it was compelled by the application of Friedian principles of legal reasoning. By focusing on the line between federal intrusion and local autonomy, the Court completely overlooked the racial fault line dividing those who govern from those who merely vote. In order to approach judicial decisionmaking logically (as a problem to be solved simply by drawing lines), the Court was willing, according to one conservative commentator, to tolerate a little injustice.[196]

Three lessons emerge. The first is that Fried's arguments in the *Gingles* case reflected his project of constructing universal solutions through the application of logic and reason. In *Gingles,* Fried uses legal reasoning to describe and explain reasonable outcomes that simply ignore the powerful information garnered from a more local perspective.[197] For Fried, it was fair to conclude from the election of blacks in one part of North Carolina that race no longer played a role in inhibiting black political participation elsewhere in the state. In 1986 the Court, on the other hand, was persuaded by the trial court's distinctly local appraisal of the facts in each

district of North Carolina. Rather than seeking to reduce the local political reality to a single common equation, the district court had carefully
weighed the totality of local circumstances in each district as the statute
had instructed.[198]

The second lesson teaches the limits of a rigorous separation of powers theory as applied to the Solicitor General's definition of his own role.
Neither the Court nor the Congress is easily convinced by grand theories
of unitary executive authority, or humbler postulates about single-
minded devotion of inferior appointees, including the Solicitor General,
to the President's program—even when tempered by intellectual autonomy of the loyal subjects. In both *Gingles* and *Presley*, the Court disre-
garded the arguments made by the Reagan-Bush Solicitors General. In
the earlier instance, the Court sided instead with the view articulated by
black plaintiffs and supported by the congressional amici. In the later
case, the Court ignored both the positions Congress had articulated in its
legislative history and the Solicitor General in its brief representing the
Department of Justice, an agency whose expertise in enforcing the statute the Court had previously recognized. Thus, if the Solicitor General
owes no special duty either to Congress or the Court, each branch
apparently feels no comparable allegiance to the Solicitor General's
advocacy.

The third lesson overshadows the first two. It is that the hardball tactics
of those men with "hearty, adolescent vocabularies" ultimately enabled
the law and the courts to accomplish what in de Tocqueville's observation
in other countries would be the subject of ordinary politics.[199] The Reagan Revolutionaries packed the federal judiciary with men[200] based on
their political views, their gender, and their youth.[201] Fried's position,
which in 1986 represented the legal expression of the political reservations of his client, now reflects the judicial philosophy of a majority of the
Court.[202] His former client's political views have merged with and become a commanding jurisprudential force among the judiciary.

The effect of these lessons should not be lost on those who profess a
different, more progressive aesthetic. Fried defends a political jurisprudence in which the Solicitor General, unlike most litigants, is expected to
have a vision that extends beyond the facts of each particular case. Fried
acknowledges as much when he notes how important it is "not to crowd
the Court, since your agenda may not yet be their agenda."[203] Fried seeks
with great modesty to explain his greater success in subsequent Terms.
"Perhaps," he suggests, the later terms were so successful "because we
had figured out where the Court—with Scalia and Kennedy replacing

Burger and Powell—was going to go and had fit our submissions to that disposition."[204]

But Fried gave the Court more than a vision. He treated his job as a political platform. In this revolutionary project, Charles Fried's primary contribution was not his principled reasons or his coherent, legal argument. Rather, he led the way through his willingness to supply legal reasons in defense of the Administration's political policy positions.

Although the Court during his tenure was frequently unpersuaded,[205] the philosophy of law as political jurisprudence has subsequently attracted more judicial adherents. That federal courts have signed on more habitually to the Reagan-Fried agenda seems directly related to Reagan's success in changing the membership of the judiciary. Ronald Reagan and George Bush appointed over half the federal judiciary, many of whose members are former Reagan Administration standard-bearers.[206]

Thus, Fried's overtly political stance cleared the way toward changing the composition of the Court itself. Fried's approach, while claiming neutrality of results, was actually very result-oriented. And the quickest way toward different results was to change the membership of the federal judiciary. In fact, within three years of Fried's departure, the two most liberal Justices, Brennan and Marshall, retired. And not surprisingly they were replaced by two conservatives, one of whom has consistently voted on the same side as the Court's most conservative activist justice.[207]

For those who fought against the Reagan Revolution, this is a most unsettling account of who won what, especially when the Solicitor General—the so-called temporary Tenth Justice—reveals himself to be humbler, more complex, and more thoughtful than some of the actual Justices a Democrat-controlled Senate "advised and consented" to grant life tenure on the bench. Fried, after all, does not insist on complete color-blindness or rigid victim-specificity to remedy past discrimination. A conservative Solicitor General with a geometric approach to decisionmaking is no longer the revolutionary. The revolution succeeded in packing the courts with other, hard-line movement conservatives willing, without questioning and with life tenure, to "enlist in [their] project."[208]

III. Changing Course: A Call to Politics

Fried claims that the liberals used the courts to pursue a manifestly political agenda. He asserts that this was a misuse of the judiciary. He notes de Tocqueville's observation that law and the courts are "the focus of controversies that in other societies are the subjects of ordinary politics."[209]

Others agree: "To a large extent, we have replaced politics with law, or more precisely, ordinary politics with legal politics, turning over most of our important disputes and controversies to courts and lawyers."[210]

Despite his criticisms of the liberal project, Fried deploys the same tactics he condemns. Indeed, in his book Fried carefully describes the ideological nature of his legal campaigns. He concedes, for example, that the Supreme Court became the conservatives' chosen battleground precisely because the administration realized it could not win what it wanted from Congress. "With the loss of the Senate in the 1986 midterm election, legislative relief became unthinkable. . . ."[211] So, like the liberal activists he disdains, the Reagan Revolutionaries treated the Court as offering their only opportunity to secure legislative policy goals.[212]

Fried's openly political stance as Solicitor General, accompanied by a more ideologically compatible judiciary, has revolutionized the entire judicial process. Whereas during Fried's tenure few of the Justices "were ready to enlist in [the conservative] project,"[213] that is no longer true.

The problem for liberals is not simply that the newly reconfigured Court may interpret the Constitution pursuant to a more conservative set of values or using a more restrained, logical set of reasons. If the courts have been successfully politicized, it is not because of judicial restraint. The problem is that the Reagan Revolutionaries have succeeded in politicizing the membership, not just the orientation, of the judiciary. As a consequence, it may be time for Fried's opponents to seek legislative, not judicial, revenge. There are several arguments for changing course.[214]

Professor Gerald Rosenberg articulates the thesis that litigation itself is limiting.[215] The reform model of litigation has relied on a "dynamic view" of courts as powerful, vigorous, and potent proponents of social change. But the dynamic view of courts may overstate their power. It diverts scarce resources from the more important job of political mobilization. It may also disable constituents who become dependent on legal rather than political solutions. Rosenberg sees three problems with the dynamic view.

First, Rosenberg argues that the dynamic view may be popular with lawyers and other participants because it persuades them of their influence. The dynamic view provides a psychological payoff to key actors by confirming their self-image as important members of the governing elite. Courts may serve the ideological function of luring certain actors within movements for social reform to an institution that is structurally constrained from serving their needs, and thus provide only an illusion of change.[216]

Second, legal strategies may weaken the political efficacy of those who prevail. Even an activist court is constrained by its lack of implementation power, by local hostility to genuine reform, and by its inability, except symbolically, to shape preferences. By assuming that courts can overcome political obstacles and produce change without mobilization and partici- pation, public interest lawyers "both reified and removed courts from the political and economic system in which they operate."[217] Crucial re- sources and talent are siphoned off into complex legal actions, which fur- ther weaken political efforts.

Rosenberg describes this as the "fly-paper" model[218] in which litiga- tion attracts activists who are sidetracked by technical legal arguments around which it is difficult to mobilize.[219] Activists are lured by the "law- yers' vision of change without pain."[220] Rosenberg describes this as "a naive and romantic belief in the triumph of rights over politics."[221] Under this view, courts "limit change by deflecting claims from substantive po- litical battles, where success is possible, to harmless legal ones where it is not. Even when major cases are won, the achievement is often more sym- bolic than real."[222]

Third, those who ultimately win Supreme Court victories often become politically lazy. As a result, legal activists fail to sustain political movements to organize and implement real change following legal victories. Legal activists who mistake success in the courts for political reform fail to con- tinue working to change reality. They mistake symbolic accomplishments for substantive ones.[223] In this view, success in court mobilizes the losers, not the winners.[224] In the wake of a Supreme Court victory, it is the op- ponents who may be politically reinvigorated.[225]

Others also suggest that the nature of adjudicative approaches under- mines the prospect of real reform. The politicization of the Court's mem- bership occurred within an institution that depends on the clash of adversaries. In an adversarial win-lose model, court decisions include rea- sons for the important declaration of who wins and who loses. Few people understand the reasons. What is important to the lay public is the bottom line.

Although most litigated cases settle, the adversarial model does not depend on persuading the parties to compromise but simply declares who is right. It oversimplifies the conflict, reducing it to convincing one judge as to who should prevail. A judiciary committed to ideological out- comes is more likely to declare winners, without really listening to the claims of the losers. This is illustrated by Fried's constant invocation of battle metaphors to describe legal debate. Metaphors, such as "lines in the sand," suggest little room for principled compromise and openness to multiple perspectives. Rather, the vocabulary of war portends limited success for those who are outnumbered in the courts.[226] And, Rosenberg would argue, where the court decision does not dissipate the conflict, the losers simply mobilize in another forum.[227] The winners simply disband.[228]

Certainly since the *Brown* decision,[229] the federal courts have been perceived by many activists as a cheaper, more direct way to achieve public policy victories. The judicial imprimatur gives moral force to one side in a public controversy. But if the judiciary is controlled by political renegades, litigants get what they pay for.[230] So if disciplined legal reasoning is not the coin of the realm, it is worth considering other currency.

First, progressive lawyers might begin to identify as aggressive judicial activists the conservatives who dominate the federal judiciary. By identifying or exposing the personal and ideological preferences that inform the decisionmaking of conservative judicial activists, the claim of restrained and responsible judging loses much of its legitimacy.[231] In this project, Fried's candid exposition and "hearty adolescent vocabulary" will be helpful to acknowledge openly the political character of some members of the current federal bench. The goal would be to delegitimize the moral force as well as the philosophical attractiveness of unfair or deeply politicized judicial solutions, and to expose the weak seams in the conservative coalition.[232]

Second, with a Court composed of several young, ideologically committed Justices, Fried's opponents may find themselves longing for the philsophical symmetry and geometric reasoning of the Harvard law professor turned revolutionary. At least the Solicitor General leaves with his Administration. If politics have taken over the judiciary, then some may begin to push for some of the same accountability and transparency that Fried so longs for in the Presidency. Frequent elections are the primary mechanism for ensuring political accountability. Perhaps the fight for term limits has only just begun.[233] At least ways should be found to reduce the "psychic income stream" and the sense of an entrenched, homogeneous elite among federal judges.[234]

Third, some scholars seek to recenter litigation within its narrative tradition, relying on litigants to tell their own stories rather than to score legal points.[235] Within legal academic circles, storytelling is touted as an empowering legal method.[236] Stories are "opposition narratives"[237] that help outsiders remind insiders about a neglected perspective; they establish context for discussion.[238] For outsiders, storytelling helps name reality.[239] For legal advocates, storytelling empowers plaintiffs by giving them a voice in a restructured forum that emphasizes case-by-case conflict resolution by consensus, not fiat.[240]

Finally, it may be time for progressives to articulate a competing vision with a clear political, rather than jurisprudential, dimension. Modern civic republicans argue that legislatures offer a better opportunity than courts to proliferate points of access to government and to enforce a progressive vision.[241] For civic republicans public deliberation in lawmaking institutions is a preferable forum for resolving differences to reach a public-regarding consensus. At least legislative bodies offer a more public, more participatory forum within which to debate and shape collective values.[242] In this understanding, less self-interested outcomes emerge from discussion—even confrontation—with opposing viewpoints. Thus, some civic republicans share Justice White's Congress-centered vision of government in that they view legislative bodies as more authoritative governing organs.[243] Others call for greater legislative responsibility for constitutional values.[244]

Alternatively, Professor Robin West finds merit in political rather than judicial solutions due to her support for a responsibility-centered, rather than rights-centered, account of the relationship between the individual and society.[245] West urges liberals "on and off the Court . . . to concentrate on [the] practice of political and cultural education" of "We the People," rather than "They the Court."[246]

West defends the central importance of personal responsibility for both actions and beliefs. She derives the responsibility-centered vision from a Havelian insistence that each individual "live within the truth."[247] For Havel, freedom is more closely related to empowerment than, as it is for Fried, to liberty.[248] Where freedom is a product of continuous, popular struggle, its proponents must constantly attend to the political process of citizen mobilization and participation. They should always worry about ensuring that leaders act morally and socially responsible.[249]

Others disagree with West's choices.[250] Whatever the merits of the particular vision, it should be a set of political ideas around which to mobilize a grass-roots, not legal, constituency. But whether the issue is conceived in terms of legislative mobilization or litigation as outsider narratives, it is not a question of outmaneuvering the opposition, or of outnumbering them. The shift to politics does not mean just politics as usual. Progressives need to change the metaphors there, too. Politics can become positive-sum in which everyone wins something. Especially in the post–Cold War era, efforts to describe everything in terms of winners and losers may have less appeal.

The issue here is one of procedure and process, not substantive justice. The expectations of political solutions need to shift from winner-take-all battles to power-sharing and deliberative compromises.[251] Political solutions must change focus from anointing leaders to mobilizing a constituency, from technical advances in mass markets to grass-roots advocacy of mass marches, from lawyer-led ideological campaigns to litigation in support of—not instead of—political advocacy.

IV. Conclusion

As Solicitor General, Charles Fried encouraged the Court to engage in a wholesale re-examination of recent precedents in order to correct the errors he perceived in the Warren/Burger Court approach. In the three areas of his principle concern—privacy, race, and separation of powers—the Reagan Revolution was only occasionally successful in getting the Supreme Court to adopt conservative public policy choices. Throughout his tenure, Fried often failed to persuade an essentially pragmatic judicial constituency.

Nevetheless, Fried insists throughout his book on drawing lines in the sand. He articulates carefully and cogently the conservative agenda behind his bellicose metaphors and his preference for grand theories, geometric reasoning, and linear hierarchy in decisionmaking. And where the federal courts themselves enlist in Fried's project, the tides no longer console against the permanence of any lines Fried or his successors may draw.

7

Epilog
*Lessons**

I would like to introduce my husband, Nolan Bowie, and my son, Nikolas Bowie. And I would like to thank them for the support and the love that they have given me over the past month in particular.

I would like to thank the president and the attorney general for the confidence they have expressed publicly and privately in my character and fitness to be assistant attorney general for civil rights. Had I been allowed to testify in a public forum before the United States Senate, I believe that the Senate would also have agreed that I am the right person for this job, a job some people have said I have trained for all my life.

I would also like to thank all the Americans, those who have known me all my life and those who have only just heard of me, for their support and encouragement.

I deeply regret that I shall not have the opportunity for public service in the Civil Rights Division. I am greatly disappointed that I have been denied the opportunity to go forward, to be confirmed and to work closely to move this country away from the polarization of the last 12 years, to lower the decibel level of the rhetoric that surrounds race, and to build bridges

---

* Speech given June 4, 1993, upon the withdrawal of Lani Guinier's nomination to be Assistant Attorney General for Civil Rights.

among people of goodwill to enforce the civil rights laws on behalf of all Americans.

In particular, I had been excited about the possibility of working closely with Attorney General Janet Reno, a woman of outstanding integrity, a woman of principle, a woman whose vision of a more just society has been an inspiration to us all. In many ways, it is her example of strength and courage that has inspired me and has allowed me to remain true to my principles in the difficult days following the announcement of my nomination on April 29.

I have always wanted to be a civil rights lawyer. My father's experience at Harvard College in 1929, as he recounted it to me, was an early lesson in the indignity and inhumanity of racism. My father was denied any financial aid on the grounds that one black student had already been awarded a full scholarship. He was not allowed to live in the dormitories on the grounds that no black, except the relative of a United States senator, had ever resided there. He was the victim of a racial quota, a quota of one.

I have never been in favor of quotas. I could not be, knowing my father's experience.

My commitment to civil rights, to democratic fair play, to cross-racial coalition building were all forged in the crucible of those memories.

I have been fortunate to have had the opportunity to pursue my ideals as a civil rights lawyer, first as a Civil Rights Division attorney and special assistant to Drew Days when he was head of the division in the Carter administration and later as counsel for the NAACP Legal Defense Fund, where I litigated many cases and lost only two.

In all my work, I have been inspired by the civil rights movement of the 1960s, by the Voting Rights Act of 1965 and by the amendments to that act, which I worked with Congress to produce in 1982, and with the vision of those amendments of an integrated legislature in which all of its member work together for the common good.

I have been fortunate to have many heroes and mentors: heroes like Doctor Martin Luther King Jr., Justice Thurgood Marshall, and Judge Constance Baker Motley; mentors like Judge Damon Keith, Solicitor General Drew Days, former Ford administration transportation secretary William Coleman, and Elaine Jones, director-counsel of the NAACP Legal Defense and Educational Fund.

These are people who committed their hearts, their considerable intellectual energy and their professional lives to a vision of a just society, a society in which America makes good on her promise to be a true, generous and inclusive democracy.

I have always believed in democracy and nothing I have ever written is inconsistent with that. I have always believed in one person, one vote, and nothing I have ever written is inconsistent with that.

I have always believed in fundamental fairness, and nothing I have ever written is inconsistent with that.

I am a democratic idealist who believes that politics need not be forever seen as I win, you lose, a dynamic in which some people are permanent monopoly winners and others are permanent excluded losers.

Everything I have written is consistent with that.

I hope that what has happened to my nomination does not mean that future nominees will not be allowed to explain their views as soon as any controversy arises. I hope that we are not witnessing that dawning of a new intellectual orthodoxy in which thoughtful people can no longer debate provocative ideas without denying the country their talents as public servants.

I also hope that we can learn some positive lessons from this experience, lessons about the importance of public dialogue on race in which all perspectives are represented and in which no one viewpoint monopolizes, distorts, caricatures or shapes the outcome.

Although the president and I disagree about his decision to withdraw my nomination, I continue to respect the president. We disagree about this, but we agree about many things. He believes in racial healing and so do I.

Last year, in an interview with Bill Moyers, then-candidate Bill Clinton was asked: Is there one thing on which you would not compromise? He answered, without flinching: Yes, racial equality. I believe that he and Attorney General Janet Reno will use the opportunity of this presidency to act on that commitment, to act affirmatively to move this country forward, to work with and for all Americans, to go beyond the polarization and divisiveness of the past few years and the poison of racism that has so infected our society.

There are real problems affecting real people in this country, people who are still the victims of unlawful discrimination on the basis of their race, their ethnicity, their gender, their sexual orientation or their disability. I hope that despite the unfairness of the way that I have been treated by the political process, that people will nevertheless work within that system to resolve the more important unfairnesses that others continue to suffer in their daily lives.

We have made real progress towards Dr. Martin Luther King's vision of a society in which we are judged by the content of our character, not by the color of our skins. But we are not there yet. And we need real presidential leadership, action, not just words, to heal the racial hemorrhaging and to realize Dr. King's dream, which is my dream too.

Notes

Chapter 2. Keeping the Faith

1. Most blacks interpreted Reagan's victories in 1980 and 1984 as "damaging to their political interests." *See, e.g.,* T. Henderson, Jr., *Black Politics and American Presidential Elections,* in The New Black Politics 3 (1982).

2. Generalizations about the concerns of African-Americans or blacks are not an attempt to describe a single, monolithic viewpoint, but reflect the consistent political cohesion that black voters display. The observations in this chapter may also describe concerns of other minority groups, such as Hispanics and Native Americans. However, the conclusions are explicitly drawn from experience, scholarship and information about blacks.

3. See L. Williams, "Black Voter Trends," 14 JCPS 80, 87 (Nov.–Dec. 1986). The black community has always viewed the right to vote as "the number one civil right." Black leaders, including Dr. Martin Luther King, Jr., supported this view: "Give us the ballot, and we will no longer have to worry the federal government about our basic rights. . . . [G]ive us the ballot and we will fill our legislative halls with men of good will. . . . Give us the ballot and we will help bring this nation to a new society based on justice and dedicated to peace." Dr. Martin Luther King, Jr., *reprinted in* Charles V. Hamilton, Foreword, The New Black Politics xviii (1982).

4. Arguing that the answer to discrimination is not new discrimination, the Administration aimed its civil rights resources at the "problem" of "reverse discrimination," i.e., race-conscious goals and timetables to remedy historic discrimination against blacks. A. Freiwald, *William Bradford Reynolds,* The American Lawyer, Mar. 1989, at 149 (citing B. Landsberg, former career Civil Rights Division attorney and head of its Appellate Section during Reagan's first term). *See, e.g.,* City of Richmond v. J.A. Croson, 109 S. Ct. 706 (1989): Local 28, Sheet Metal Workers v. EEOC, 478 U.S. 421, 444 n.24 (1986) (noting Justice Department challenge to affirmative action goal provision). The Reagan Department of Justice attempted to reopen 50 consent decrees on the grounds, subsequently rejected by the Court, that Firefighters Local Union No. 1784 v. Stotts, 467 U.S. 561 (1984), forbade all racial or gender affirmative action goals, even if those goals were designed to overcome prior discrimination. *Nomination of William Bradford Reynolds to Be Associate Attorney General of the United States: Hearings Before the Senate Comm. on the Judiciary,* 99th Cong. 1st Sess.

(June 5, 1985), 562–63, 570–72, 574–75 (statement of J. Lichtman) [hereinafter *Reynolds Nomination Hearings*].

5. *Reynolds Nomination Hearings,* at 589–90, 593–96 (statement of P. McClure). Commentators have criticized the Reagan Administration enforcement policies across the spectrum of civil rights issues. *See, e.g.,* Days, *Turning Back the Clock: The Reagan Administration and Civil Rights,* 19 Harv. C.R.-C.L. L. Rev. 309 (1984); Selig, *The Reagan Justice Department and Civil Rights: What Went Wrong,* 1985 U. Ill. L. Rev. 785; Chambers, *Racial Justice in the 1980's,* 8 Campbell L. Rev. 29, 31–34 (1985). Although this chapter focuses on black interests, similar complaints have been voiced by Hispanics and other activists. *See, e.g., Reynolds Nomination Hearings,* at 196 (statement of R. Fajardo, for the Mexican American Legal Defense and Education Fund); *id.* at 562 (statement of J. Lichtman, for the Women's Legal Defense Fund).

6. Berry v. Reagan, 732 F. 2d 949 (D.C. Cir. 1983); *see also* Comment, *The Rise and Fall of the United States Commission on Civil Rights,* 22 Harv. C.R.-C.L. L. Rev. 449, 476–80 (1987).

7. *See* Johnson, *Reagan Vetoes Bill That Would Widen Federal Rights Laws,* N.Y. Times. Mar. 17, 1988, at A1. col. 6.

8. One commentator has argued persuasively that the very success of the civil rights laws of the 1960's and 1970's helped nurture public support for the Reagan agenda in the 1980's. "The narrow focus of racial exclusion (the belief that racial exclusion is illegitimate only where the 'Whites Only' signs are explicit) coupled with strong assumptions about equal opportunity, makes it difficult to move the discussion of racism beyond the societal self-satisfaction engendered by the appearance of neutral norms and formal inclusion." Crenshaw, *Race, Retrenchment and Reform,* 101 Harv. L. Rev. 1384 (1988). The conflict in the 1960's that inspired the civil rights movement emphasized the gap between the promised privileges of American citizenship and the practice of racial subordination. That inconsistency was narrowly addressed through formal changes in both laws and rhetoric. In part because of these formal changes, people were more sympathetic to Administration claims that enough had been done, just at the point when civil rights advocates began to explore the need for deeper institutional reform.

9. *See, e.g.,* Memorandum for Heads of Department Components. 22 February 1988, from Wm. Bradford Reynolds, assistant attorney general and counselor to the attorney general. I ("In addition, we must polarize the debate. We must not seek 'consensus,' we must confront.") [hereinafter *Reynolds Memorandum*]: *see also* A. Freiwald *supra* note 4, at 151 ("In carrying out his agenda, Reynolds has polarized what has long been a bipartisan consensus on civil rights"). Overt racial hostility increased over the Reagan years and was reflected in incidents of racial violence and unrest. *See* Note, *Combatting Racial Violence: A Legislative Proposal,* 101 Harv. L. Rev. 1270, 1270 & n.1 (1988). The Reagan legacy, for many blacks, was not judicial but instead took the form of "heightened racial tension arising from rhetoric. . . ." Johnson, *Deciding What to Do Next About Civil Rights,* N.Y. Times, March 12, 1989, at E5, col. 4.

10. Wygant v. Jackson Bd. of Educ., 476 U.S. 267 (1986) (negotiated race-based layoff program violates 14th amendment; City of Richmond v. J.A. Croson, 109 S. Ct. 706 (1989) (minority set-aside unconstitutional unless justified by compelling government interest and narrowly tailored to accomplish remedial purpose).

11. While the initial focus was on black registration, southern ingenuity to "offset the

gains made at the ballot box" prompted congressional efforts to "achieve full participation for all Americans in our democracy" by renewing the Act in 1970, 1975 and
1982 to cover a "broad array of dilution schemes . . . employed to cancel the impact of
the new black vote." S. Rep. No. 417, 97th Cong., 2d Sess. 4–9, 81–87 (1982) [here-
inafter *Senate Report 417*]. In both 1970 and 1975, Congress renewed Section 5 of the
Voting Rights Act "with full awareness of its interpretation by the courts to include
dilution . . . as well as outright denials of the opportunity to register or vote. . . .
Seventy-five of the members of the Senate who acted . . . in 1970 [to ratify a broad
interpretation of Section 5] had also been members in 1965 when Section 5 was first
enacted." *Id.* at 7 n.8. Key provisions of the 1965 Act would have expired in 1970;
seven of the original sponsors of the 1965 Act joined three other members of the
Senate Judiciary Committee in 1970 to sponsor a five-year extension. Their views,
which have been accepted as the committee report on the 1970 extension, *see, e.g.,*
City of Lockhart v. United States, 460 U.S. 125, 140 n.4 (1983) (Marshall concurring
in part and dissenting in part); *Senate Report 417,* at 7, cite approvingly the Supreme
Court's expansive reading of the 1965 statute in Allen v. State Bd., 398 U.S. 544
(1969), as "clarifying the scope" of the 1965 Act, and recommend extension of the
Act's temporary provisions to cover a wide range of discriminatory election laws—
including "obstructionist tactics . . . such as boundary lines [which] have been gerrymandered, elections [which] have been switched to an at-large basis . . ."—passed in
the wake of the 1965 Act to exclude blacks "from the southern political process." Joint
Views of Ten Members of the Judiciary Committee, 91st Cong., 2nd Sess., *reprinted
in* 115 Cong. Rec. 5517, 5520–21, 5529 (March 2, 1970). Again in 1975, 20 days of
hearings confirmed the continued need for the preclearance remedy in light of massive evidence that the covered jurisdictions were switching to discriminatory dilution
schemes. S. Rep. No. 295. 94th Cong., 1st Sess. 16–17 (1975) (report on the Voting
Rights Act Extension, by the Senate Committee on the Judiciary).

12. The drafters of the 1965 Act were committed to enacting expansive legislation to correct historic disfranchisemen of black voters. *See, e.g.,* H. Rep. No. 439, 89th Cong.,
1st Sess. 10, 15 (1965); S. Rep. No. 162, Pt. 3, 89th Cong., 1st Sess. 5 (1965) (pointing
to racial gerrymandering as an example of the variety of means employed to "bar Negro voting and the durability of these discriminatory policies"); *id.* at 14 (correlating
registration barriers with the absence of a "public policy against racial discrimination"); *id.* at 15 (expressing concern with "other tactics of discrimination" to which
state and local election officials might resort). Even Republican opponents of the particular form of the federal statute acknowledged a "consensus that a departure from
traditional legislative method must be made" to "free those of our citizens who now
endure the near-tyranny of nonrepresentation." *Id.* at 37, 38, 53. *See also id.* at 62; *cf.*
J. Ely, Democracy and Distrust, 116–25 (1980) (blacks are one group everyone agrees
should be extended special protection).

13. As Frank Parker of the Lawyers Committee for Civil Rights testified in 1985:

> Despite the fundamental importance of the right to vote, Mr. Reynolds, as Assistant At-
> torney General for civil rights has adopted policies and taken positions which have failed
> to protect, and which have undermined, the right to vote. He has opposed voting rights
> legislation designed to strengthen the statutory protections for minority voting rights, he
> has defaulted in numerous instances in his sworn duty to enforce statutory voting rights
> protections, and he has placed his imprimatur on racially discriminatory redistricting

plans and other discriminatory voting law changes which diluted minority voting strength.

Reynolds Nomination Hearings, at 450 (testimony of Frank Parker, director of the Lawyers Committee for Civil Rights, Voting Rights Project).

14. The Leadership Conference on Civil Rights (LCCR) is the central lobbying group of over 150 organizations which monitors congressional and administrative civil rights activity. The organization was founded in the early 1950's by a group of 50 national organizations united in support of civil rights legislation, S. Lawson, Black Ballots 144–45 (1976).

15. Leadership Conference on Civil Rights, Without Justice: A Report on the Conduct of the Justice Department in Civil Rights in 1981–82, at 68–69 (1982).

    In one incident, Assistant Attorney General Reynolds reversed himself and decided not to join in a voting rights enforcement suit in Edgefield County, South Carolina—Senator Strom Thurmond's childhood home—after talking with the Senator about the case. This decision was reached after the brief had been prepared by the staff of the Voting section and sent for filing to the local United States attorney's office. *Id.*

    In another incident, after the Justice Department had filed a complaint in an important voting rights case alleging a history of official action to maintain "white supremacy" in Mobile, Alabama, Republican Senator Jeremiah Denton protested. The attorney general directed the filing of an amended complaint to delete the phrase. Veteran lawyers could not recall another instance when a complaint already filed was changed to accommodate a political protest. *Id.*

16. 446 U.S. 55 (1980).

17. Statement of William Bradford Reynolds to the NAACP Legal Defense Fund Civil Rights Institute in New York City (May 20, 1983).

18. F. Parker, director of the Voting Rights Project, Lawyers' Committee for Civil Rights Under Law, *Voting Rights Enforcement in the Reagan Administration,* in Citizens' Commission on Civil Rights Report 2, 10 (Jan. 1989) (citing U.S. Department of Justice, Voting Section, Civil Rights Division, Voting Cases at District Court Level in Which the United States' Participation Began After January 20, 1981). Parker noted that, given its resources during the Reagan Administration's eight-year tenure, the Division filed "relatively few substantive lawsuits" to enforce the nondiscrimination requirements of the Voting Rights Act, since most cases were interventions in existing private lawsuits, friend of the court briefs (often opposing positions of minority voters), Section 5 defensive lawsuits, and settlements involving other statutory provisions. He estimated that during the same period private groups with more limited resources filed 10 times more voting cases than did the Division. *Id.*

19. Brief for the United States as *Amicus Curiae* Thornburg v. Gingles, 478 U.S. 30 (1986). The Department's position was opposed by North Carolina Governor James Martin, the Republican National Committee, and the principal congressional cosponsors of the 1982 amendments all of whom filed *amicus curiae* briefs in the Supreme Court supporting the position of the black plaintiffs. As a result of the dilution of minority voting strength at the time that the lawsuit was filed in 1980, only four black members of the North Carolina General Assembly had ever been elected, although blacks represented 24% of the state's electorate. Black voters also constituted

significant percentages within each of the challenged multi-member legislative districts; they were unable to elect black candidates to the North Carolina General Assembly because, as the experts for both sides agreed, the white at-large majority consistently voted as a racial bloc to defeat black office-seekers. *See id.* at 66–67.

Using the recently amended Section 2, black voters opposed the state's legislative apportionment plan because it used large, multi-member conglomerations to submerge minority neighborhoods. At-large election schemes and racially gerrymandered districts—perhaps the most prevalent dilution methods—submerge or fracture into a larger bloc-voting white majority cohesive and geographic concentrations of black voters. If these black voter concentrations were retained within a neighborhood-based single member district, there would be enough black voters to elect a black representative; but because they are diluted in district fragments or city and county-wide electorates that are white dominated, black voters are unable to elect representatives of their choice if voting is racially polarized. After the 1965 Act was passed, the use of such dilution techniques reached epidemic proportions. *See* Derfner, *Racial Discrimination and the Right to Vote,* 26 Vand. L. Rev. 523, 554 n.126 (1973).

20. Rogers v. Lodge, 458 U.S. 613 (1982). This case was the first in which the Supreme Court specifically held, on the basis of circumstantial evidence, that black plaintiffs had demonstrated that an at-large system was being maintained with a discriminatory racial purpose. No black person had *ever* been elected to the Burke County, Georgia, Commission, although blacks were a majority of the county population, and 38% of the registered voters. Some of the court findings were that roads were not paved as soon as they reached the black community and that a "nigger hook" still hung in the courthouse.

21. *Reynolds Nomination Hearings,* at 887–88 (testimony of the nominee). "[I]t was my view that the at-large system was not one that was in place and being maintained for a racial purpose." *Id.* at 891. When questioned about this decision, Mr. Reynolds responded less than candidly about a "resource problem." *Id.* at 887.

22. In addition to the nationwide prohibition against discrimination in the electoral process, the Act also establishes a "preclearance" process administered by the Attorney General or designee. The Civil Rights Division is responsible for conducting the statutory preclearance review. All "covered jurisdictions," that is, those with a history of discrimination as defined by the statute, are required to submit any "standard, practice or procedure affecting voting" for advance federal approval. The Division has 60 days to determine whether the election change has a discriminatory purpose or effect. 42 U.S.C. § 1973c (1982).

23. The Act places the burden of proof in a Section 5 proceeding on the submitting jurisdiction, which must demonstrate that its proposed election law change has neither a discriminatory purpose nor effect. *Id. See also Reynolds Nomination Hearings,* at 999–1000 (colloquy between Sen. Joseph Biden and the nominee).

24. South Carolina v. Katzenbach, 383 U.S. at 326–27.

25. 574 F. Supp. 325 (E.D. La. 1983) (three-judge panel). I was one of several attorneys representing the black plaintiffs in this case. The three-judge district court, convened in Louisiana, ultimately invalidated the plan. The court found that the redistricting plan was racially discriminatory because the duck-shaped gerrymander sliced through every predominantly black precinct in New Orleans with unerring precision.

26. The image superimposed on a map of New Orleans closely resembled that cartoon

character, including the webbed feet. One of Mr. Reynolds' predecessors during the Nixon Administration, Jerris Leonard, testified under oath that the Donald Duck plan was one of the most blatant gerrymanders he had ever seen. He compared it to the infamous case of Gomillion v. Lightfoot, 364 U.S. 339 (1960), "where the Board of Supervisors in Tuskegee, Alabama, annexed territory to increase the size of the city, but in doing so excluded all the blacks around the city from the annexation. I would put Major v. Treen into that category of a blatant intentional racial gerrymander." *Reynolds Nomination Hearings,* at 379–80.

The three-judge district court which heard the case following the Section 5 administrative review found:

> Act 20's jagged line dissects a large concentrated community of black voters residing in Orleans Parish, dispersing that community into the First and Second Congressional Districts. With unerring precision, this line slices through the City's traditional political subunit, the ward, in a racially selective manner, leaving intact predominantly white wards, while carving up those densely populated by blacks. Homogeneous black precincts are separated: white precincts are not.

574 F. Supp. at 353.

27. *Id.* at 394, 398, 404–05 [Testimony of Lani Guinier; exhibits provided by Gerald W. Jones, chief, Voting Rights Division, U.S. Dept. of Justice. Notes taken during Reynolds' meetings with Governor Treen, Jan. 11, 1982, and May 31, 1982]. Governor Treen had threatened to veto any congressional redistricting plan which contained a majority black district. He instead proposed three alternatives, none of which had a district with more than 45% black population. Major v. Treen, 574 F. Supp. at 331, n.10. The sequence of events in the reapportionment process indicates that Governor Treen, however, was not exclusively responsible for the enactment of the disputed plan. Racial considerations of individual legislators also played a significant part in the legislature's acquiescence to the Governor's refusal to support any plan with more than 44.7% black population in one district. One prominent legislator was quoted as stating his opposition to a majority black district centered in New Orleans with the explanation that, "We don't need another 'nigger' bigshot. We already have one 'nigger' mayor."

28. Major v. Treen, 574 F. Supp. at 384.

29. *See* Record at 87, Major v. Treen (Testimony of Baer, March 9, 1983). The accuracy of that perception was made clear during the trial by the Secretary of the Louisiana Senate:

> JUDGE POLITZ: Am I hearing you say that the principal motivating factor, as you came to an attempt to work out a compromise that would pass muster, meaning, be adopted by the Legislature, is a determination to satisfy the incumbents?
> WITNESS: Yes, sir.
> JUDGE POLITZ: Number one?
> WITNESS: Yes, sir.
> JUDGE POLITZ: Draw plans that would satisfy the incumbent?
> WITNESS: Yes, sir.

See also id. at 19–20, 26, 60; *id.* at 75–76 (Testimony of Treen. March 10, 1983) (Governor's opposition prompted primarily by perceived adverse impact on Republican congressman).

30. Speech of William Bradford Reynolds at Amherst College 19 (April 29, 1983).

31. Mr. Reynolds' failure to act in this situation is particularly significant because of the Administration's strong endorsement of the intent test as a reasonable approach to ferreting out discrimination. The *Treen* case casts further doubt on the sincerity of those endorsements since the evidence of racial purpose was so compelling. *Reynolds Nomination Hearings* at 387–90.

32. From January 1981 through September 30, 1986, the Division reviewed over 72,000 changes pursuant to its administrative preclearance responsibilities. Parker, *supra* note 18, at 27 (Table of Justice Dept. Statistics). The large number of changes, however, did not by itself reflect aggressive enforcement of the statute. First, the statistics which the Department used masked the actual number of submissions because each aspect of a state's law, however technical or incidental to the critical change, was being counted separately. Second, preclearance review did not mean investigation. By law, the assistant attorney general had the submission for 60 days. If he did nothing, that also constituted a "review." Department of Justice Procedures for the Administration of Section 5 of the Voting Rights Act as Amended, 28 C.F.R. § 51.42 (1987 ed.).

    Finally, there was no period in any prior Administration with which to compare the performance of the Division. The preclearance provision had never been applicable to the same number of jurisdictions (e.g., the State of Texas with hundreds of counties and political subunits, each of which had to submit separately its voting changes, first came under the Division's authority in 1975), nor had it been enforced following a decennial census with its redistricting mandate. In 1971, the Division was just getting started enforcing the statute because the previous six years had been spent in litigation against the southern states which were challenging the constitutionality of the 1965 Voting Rights Act and the types of changes that had to be submitted. Allen v. State Bd. of Elections, 393 U.S. 544 (1969); Perkins v. Matthews, 400 U.S. 379 (1971).

33. *See* Parker, *Voting Rights Enforcement in the Reagan Administration,* at 12–13. *See also* J. Selig, *The Reagan Justice Department and Civil Rights: What Went Wrong,* U. Ill. L. Rev. 12–13 (1985) at 830. ("Behind many a case or brief is an untold story of a struggle within the Division to persuade Mr. Reynolds to enforce the law. Mr. Reynolds has not hesitated to take public credit either in these instances or when the Department has overruled the Division and taken a 'pro-civil rights' position over his vigorous objection.")

34. Strenuous enforcement of black rights to representation is also to the advantage of the white majority. Rights like these are "critical to the functioning of an open and effective democratic process" and cannot be left to the process itself to correct since white incumbents have a vested interest in the status quo. J. Ely, *supra* note 12 at 105, 117. *See also* Bell, *And We Are Not Saved* (1987), ch. 2 (arguing that whites are the primary beneficiaries of civil rights enforcement).

35. Overwhelming black support has helped Democrats in Louisiana, Georgia and North Carolina defeat conservative Republicans, and in California, provided the critical margin of victory for Alan Cranston's re-election bid. *See, e.g.,* Williams, *Blacks Cast Pivotal Ballots in Four Key Senate Races, Data Show,* N.Y. Times, Nov. 6, 1986, at A33, col. 3 (Democratic majority due in large part to crucial black vote); Dionne, *Voting Produces Strong Evidence of Importance of Race in Politics,* N.Y. Times, Nov. 5, 1987, at A1. col. 1.

36. *Senate's Roll-Call on the Bork Vote,* N.Y. Times, Oct. 24, 1987, at 10, col. 1 (two

Democrats, only one from the South, joined 40 Republicans in supporting confirmation; opponents included conservative southern Democrats such as John C. Stennis, and Republicans such as John W. Warner who were elected from constituencies with significant black populations); *see also* Dowd, *Winning One from the Gipper,* Time Magazine, Nov. 9, 1987, at 125 (coalition of black, labor, environmental and feminist groups instrumental in Senate rejection of Bork nomination).

37. In June 1988, national polls gave Michael Dukakis, then the probable Democratic nominee, a 10-point lead over Republican George Bush. Yet, among white males, Dukakis only barely led Bush, doing slightly better among white women. It was when the votes of blacks—the most loyal Democrats—were added, that Dukakis' lead became formidable. Dionne, *Democratic Strength Shifts to West,* N.Y. Times, Nov. 13, 1988 at 32, col. 1. This is consistent with voting behavior in past presidential elections. In close elections, the black vote has been pivotal. *See, e.g.,* Henderson, *supra* note 1, at 4, 10–16.

38. Hamilton, Foreword, The New Black Politics xix (1982); *see also* Abrams, *"Raising Politics Up": Minority Participation and Section 2 of the Voting Rights Act,* 63 N.Y.U. L. Rev. 449, 502 (1988) ("Exclusion from meaningful participation may eliminate incentives for any participation"). According to Basil Patterson, a black former New York secretary of state, "One way of putting blacks back in their place is to vote against anyone who has any relationship with them, whether it is Jesse Jackson or Michael Dukakis," quoted by Michael Oreskes, *In Racial Politics, Democrats Losing More Than Elections,* N.Y. Times, Nov. 20, 1988, E5. Other black leaders express their anger at "rainbow coalitions" in which "black folks coalesce and white folks get power," and in which "blacks get all the rain and white folks got all the bows." Thomas N. Todd as quoted by Johnson, *Racial Politics: Chicago's Raw Nerve,* N.Y. Times Magazine, Feb. 19, 1989 at 34, col. 1.

39. Focus Magazine, Trendletter 2 (1988) (supplement to Vol. 16, No. 4) (reporting results of the 1987 Joint Center for Political Studies/Gallup survey). "Fifty-five percent of whites for example said that in a contest between a black and a white for mayor of their city, they would vote for the white candidate based on race regardless of qualifications." *Id.*

40. *See, e.g.,* Louis Harris and Associates, A Study of Racial Attitudes, Behavior, and Tensions in the United States, Vol. 1 (Jan. 11, 1989) (finding, by an overwhelming 91% majority, that blacks would prefer to see the nomination of more blacks to high office than for blacks to remain a "swing vote"). *See infra* note 49. Although black voters who are a sizable minority may be "influential" in the election of candidates, the theory of a powerful swing vote has not been empirically demonstrated. White political beneficiaries of the swing vote are often unaware of its decisive impact or deliberately ignore it because of even more decisive white support. Davidson, *Minority Vote Dilution,* at 9–11.

   As the district court found in Smith v. Clinton, 687 F. Supp. 1310, 1318 (E.D. Ark. 1988), when faced with a challenge by black voters to a multi-member legislative district, "candidates favored by blacks can win but only if the candidates are white." This is the contemporary analogy to the all-white Democratic primary after Smith v. Allwright, 321 U.S. 649 (1944). Although the Supreme Court in *Smith* extended fifteenth amendment coverage to Democratic Party primaries, local and state parties quickly enacted rules to retain whites-only party membership, explicitly limiting to party members the right to run as candidates. Arkansas Democrat, April 5, 1944; Arkansas Gazette, Sept. 17, 1944 (reproduced as plaintiffs' exhibit 15, Whitfield v. Democratic Party, 686 F. Supp. 1365 (E.D. Ark. 1988). *See also* Terry v. Adams, 345 U.S. 461 (1953) (striking down whites-only pre-primary selection process).

41. Whites elected by a majority black constituency can and do represent minority interests. However, there is little evidence of whites, elected by a white majority constituency with black support, as aggressive advocates of black interests. *See infra* note 49. *See* Karnig & Welch, Black Representation and Urban Policy 108–09 (1980) (black elected official provides descriptive, though not necessarily substantive, representation for the black community); H. Pitkin, The Concept of Representation (1972) (descriptive representation matches racial and social class attributes of constituents).

42. B. Grofman, Representation and Redistricting Issues 58 (1982); *see also* M.D. Morris, *Black Electoral Participation and the Distribution of Public Benefits,* in Minority Vote Dilution 277 (C. Davidson ed. 1984) (black elected officials are the focus of black expectations for a more responsive government; black voters gain influence by selecting racial compatriots with special attachment to and understanding of the black community). Ultimately, the right to representation attempts to protect minorities from denials of equal concern as subjects of legislative policy. *See* J. Ely, *supra* note 12, at 86–87.

43. P. Karlan, *Maps and Misreadings: Going Beyond Single-Member Districts in Section 2 Cases,* 24 Harv. C.R.-C.L. L. Rev. 173 (1989). *See also* M.D. Morris, *supra* note 42, at 275 (political efficacy and level of trust in government affect black turnout).

44. White ethnic groups used politics to legitimize, not transform, social and economic assimilation. J. Ely, *supra* note 12, at 80–81 (discussing strategy of pluralism). White ethnic groups could employ a pluralist strategy because, unlike blacks, "an unjust combination of a majority of the whole," The Federalist No. 51, at 357–58 (J. Madison), was never so dominant as to silence white ethnic voices over an extended period of time. Madison's theory that no one group would wield majority control fails to comprehend racial discrimination and polarization. Because of extreme racial polarization within the electorate, the pluralist model does not work for blacks. The possibility of forming coalitions with like-minded allies to aggregate minority political power into an electable majority fails where members of the majority consistently refuse to vote for minority sponsored candidates. Abrams' theory, *see supra* note 38, of an extended political process also fails to account for this weakness.

Blacks' view of political participation as a means of transforming and redistributing political and economic goods may simply be unrealistic. Of course, black electoral success alone cannot transform the political or economic position of the black community. Barnett, *The Congressional Black Caucus: Illusions and Realities of Power,* in The New Black Politics 49 (1982). *See also supra* note 3. Moreover, electing black representatives may simply relocate to the legislature the polarization experienced at the polls. As Abrams suggests, black representatives may be perceived as tokens or treated as marginal to the legislative process. Abrams, *supra* note 38, at 502. But, as Karlan points out, the nature and process of legislative deliberation may be less hospitable to overt racism. Karlan, *supra* note 43, at 173. This does not require one to accept Ackerman's repudiation of Ely's "pariah" model, *see* Ackerman, *Beyond Carolene Products,* 98 Harv. L. Rev. 732–35 (1985), although it does suggest that familiarity may diminish hostility. *Cf.* J. Ely *supra* note 12, at 161. Black elected officials may assuage white fears during their incumbency. The power of incumbency is supported by studies which suggest that black incumbents are in fact re-elected with more white support. See L. Cole, Blacks in Power 4–5 (1976); see also Johnson, Racial Politics: Chicago's Raw Nerve, N.Y. Times Magazine, Feb. 19, 1989, at 37, col. 1:

> Among the white Cassandras who saw in a black man's election the impending ruin of their city, hate turned to mere dislike, and perhaps even to grudging respect, as the garbage still got picked up and the streets still got plowed. During his brief second term, Washington began to make peace with white politicians. In November 1987, he endorsed a slate of Democratic Party candidates running for Cook County offices: one black, one Hispanic and two whites, among them Daley. Washington said the ticket was "made in heaven" and warned his supporters, "Anyone who does not vote for this ticket is not my friend."

45. City of Petersburg v. U.S., 354 F. Supp. 1021, 1029 (D.D.C. 1973), aff'd 410 U.S. 962 (1973).

46. The acquisition of access to electoral politics on an individual, and perhaps "vicarious" basis through black elected officials is criticized by some commentators because the individual black elected official may not be able to "infiltrate the decision making process" at the legislative level. See M. Coleman & L. McLemore, Black Independent Politics in Mississippi: Constraints and Challenges, in The New Black Politics 131, 151 (1982). Nevertheless, coalition politics within the legislature is more likely to be effective than attempts at the electoral level to break down racially polarized voting. For this reason, it is important that representation be "actual," to lend the greatest legitimacy to the representative body, and to ensure that the body is more "deliberative." See Sunstein, Beyond the Republican Revival, 97 Yale L.J. 1539 (1988).

47. Relying primarily on a pluralist jurisprudence of political participation, Professor Kathy Abrams has argued that electoral success is merely one way of measuring political participation; important political goals such as discussion, lobbying and coalition building should also be addressed in voting rights enforcement.

48. Michelman, The Supreme Court Term 1985—Foreword: Traces of Self-Government, 100 Harv. L. Rev. 4, 51 (1986). Thernstrom, Whose Votes Count? Affirmative Action and Minority Voting Rights (1987); see also Schuck, What Went Wrong With the Voting Rights Act, The Washington Monthly, Nov. 1987, at 51, 55 (minority voters better served by white politicians competing for minority votes).

49. Although black voters who are a sizable minority may be "influential" in the election of candidates, this theory of the "swing vote" has not been empirically demonstrated. White political beneficiaries are often unaware of black voters' decisive impact or deliberately ignore it because of even more decisive white support. Davidson, Minority Vote Dilution: An Overview, in Minority Vote Dilution 9–11 (C. Davidson ed. 1984).

50. Public Papers of Lyndon Johnson, at II, p. 284 (1965).

Chapter 3. The Triumph of Tokenism

1. I use the terms "black" and African-American interchangeably. I prefer the term "black" for two reasons. First, many of my observations about black political empowerment apply to other racial groups. The term "black" succinctly describes a racial

identity and status based on color that is shared, to some degree, by other people of color with different ancestral lineages. *See* Matsuda, *Looking to the Bottom: Critical Legal Studies and Reparations,* 22 HARV. C.R.-C.L. L. REV. 323, 335 n.50 (1987). Similarly, the black community is a convenient proxy for an insular group that is politically cohesive, historically stigmatized, economically depressed, and socially isolated.

Second, although I also use the term "minority," especially to convey the numerical status of blacks in this society, as Patricia Williams observes, minority "implies a certain delegitimacy in a majoritarian system." Use of the term "black" eludes this problem. *See* Williams, *Alchemical Notes: Reconstructing Ideals From Deconstructed Rights,* 22 HARV. C.R.-C.L. L. REV. 401, 404 n.4 (1987); *cf.* Graves v. Barnes, 343 F. Supp. 704, 730 (W.D. Tex. 1972) (three-judge court), *affd. in relevant part and revd. in part on other grounds sub nom.* White v. Regester, 412 U.S. 755, 769-70 (1973) (protected minority does not have a merely numerical denotation; rather it refers to an identifiable and specially disadvantaged group).

2. 42 U.S.C. § 1973 (1988). Section 1983 codifies as amended the Voting Rights Act of 1965, Pub. L. No. 89-110, § 2, 79 Stat. 445. The Voting Rights Act of 1965, § 2, was amended in 1975, Pub. L. No. 94-73, 89 Stat. 402, and in 1982, Pub. L. No. 97-205, 96 Stat. 134. Amended § 2 of the Act, which provides a nationwide private right of action, states:

> (a) No voting qualification or prerequisite to voting . . . shall be imposed or applied . . . in a manner which results in a denial or abridgement of the right of any citizen of the United States to vote on account of race or color . . . as provided in subsection (b) of this section.
> (b) A violation of subsection (a) of this section is established if, based on the totality of circumstances, it is shown that the political processes leading to nomination or election in the State or political subdivision are not equally open to participation by members of a class of citizens protected by subsection (a) . . . . in that its members have less opportunity than other members of the electorate to participate in the political process and to elect representatives of their choice. The extent to which members of a protected class have been elected to office in the State or political subdivision is one circumstance which may be considered: *Provided,* That nothing in this section establishes a right to have members of a protected class elected in numbers equal to their proportion in the population.

The term "representatives of choice" refers to "black" representatives. *See supra* note 1. The House Report accompanying the amendments defines representatives of choice as "minority candidates or candidates identified with the interests of a racial or language minority." H. Rep. No. 277, 97th Cong., 1st Sess. 30 (1981).

3. Although not synonymous, the terms empowerment, political equality, and effective representation are used here interchangeably to convey the concept of "full enfranchisement."

4. Spokesmodels are role models who also speak in a representational capacity on behalf of others. *Cf. Star Search* (Television Program Enterprises 1991) (contestants compete for best "spokesmodel" based on their physical attributes, poise, and ability to talk). In general, the notion of spokesmodels seems to apply only to the black community. *See* Reed, *The "Black Revolution" and the Reconstitution of Domination,* in RACE, POLITICS AND CULTURE: ESSAYS ON THE RADICALISM OF THE 1960s, 61, 67-68 (A. Reed ed. 1986)("No 'white leaders' were assumed to represent a singular

white population; social category 'black leaders' meant "certain blacks were declared opinion-makers and carriers of the interests of an anonymous black population.").

5. Black politics, unlike issues concerning employment or schools, is considered "offbeat," or worthy of only occasional interest. *See, e.g.,* D. PINDERHUGHES, RACE AND ETHNICITY IN CHICAGO POLITICS 253-55 (1987) (noting the absence of substantial body of research addressing paradoxes in American black politics); Walton, Foreword to J. ELIOT, BLACK VOICES IN AMERICAN POLITICS at xi–xii (1988).

6. I also position black electoral success theory within current voting rights legal scholarship. *See e.g.,* Abrams, *"Raising Politics Up": Minority Political Participation and Section 2 of the Voting Rights Act,* 63 N.Y.U. L. REV. 449, 472–75 (1988) (theory of a "jurisprudence of political opportunity"); Karlan, *Maps and Misreadings: The Role of Geographic Compactness in Racial Vote Dilution Litigation,* 24 HARV. C.R.-C.L. L. REV. 173, 179-82 (1989) (theory of "civic inclusion").

7. *See infra* note 154 (describing false consciousness). The legitimating power of black electoral success was articulated, in the general context of civil rights law, by Professor Alan Freeman in his essay, *Antidiscrimination Law: A Critical Review,* in THE POLITICS OF LAW 96, 110–14 (D. Kairys ed. 1982).

8. The theory also assumes continued residential segregation. As developed *infra,* not all blacks presently reside within majority-black districts.

9. See *infra* note 59 for a definition of vote dilution.

10. Voting rights litigants noted that black electoral success usually depends on black electoral control of small, majority-black subdistricts within a jurisdiction.

11. Such geographically configured districts would ensure government responsiveness through the election of black representatives. The theory also posits that white elected officials would become at least minimally responsive to their newly voting black constituents. *See, e.g.,* T. BRANCH, PARTING THE WATERS: AMERICA IN THE KING YEARS 1954–63 893 (1988) (one of the primary goals in winning the right to vote was to drive the white segregationist politicians from office).

12. Give us the ballot, and we will no longer have to worry the federal government about our basic rights. . . . Give us the ballot and we will fill our legislative halls with men of good will. . . . Give us the ballot and we will help bring this nation to a new society based on justice and dedicated to peace.

Dr. Martin Luther King, Jr., *quoted in* Hamilton, *Foreword,* in THE NEW BLACK POLITICS xviii (M. Preston, L. Henderson & P. Puryear eds. 1982). In suggesting that the most important step blacks could take was "that short walk to the voting booth," the NAACP, SCLC, and Dr. Martin Luther King, Jr., anticipated that the development of "[a]n alert, independent, and aggressive Negro electorate" would become an important progressive political factor. *Cf.* H. MOON, BALANCE OF POWER: THE NEGRO VOTE 9, 11 (1948).

13. *See, e.g.,* Barnett, *A Theoretical Perspective on American Racial Public Policy,* in PUBLIC POLICY FOR THE BLACK COMMUNITY 3, 39 (M. Barnett & J. Hefner eds. 1976) (nationalists, calling for black ethnic group unity, and black integrationists each pursued interrelated goals despite often heated rhetoric). For the nationalists the right to vote necessarily meant the right to constitute an "essential ingredient . . . of the sovereign principle," delegable only to "true representative[s]." *See* Delany, *The Political*

Destiny of the Colored Race, in The Ideological Origins of Black Nationalism 195, 197–98 (S. Stuckey ed. 1972).

14. *See* S. Lawson, Black Ballots (1976); *Negro Vote Surge Expected in South—Administration Experts Sure of a Political Break Through as Result of Recent Gains,* N.Y. Times, June 26, 1961, at 1, col. 6 ("The Rev. Dr. Martin Luther King Jr. and other leaders of the new militant movements—the sit-ins and Freedom Riders—have come around to agree that the vote is the key."); *see also* Nelson, *Cleveland: The Rise and Fall of the New Black Politics,* in The New Black Politics, *supra* note 12, at 187 (since the mid-1970s, the black community has accepted the idea "that electoral politics provide[s] the best avenue for advancing black interests."); Preston, *Black Politics and Public Policy in Chicago: Self-Interest Versus Constituent Representation,* in The New Black Politics, *supra* note 12, at 159–61 (politics in now the "cutting edge" of the civil rights movement).

15. T. Branch, *supra* note 11, at 479 (voter registration defended during the early 1960s as a priority in order to build political protections for the movement, especially when the religious zeal faded); *see also* Williams, *Black Political Progress in the 1970's: The Electoral Arena,* in The New Black Politics, *supra* note 12, at 74–75.

16. *See, e.g.,* S. Carmichael & C. Hamilton, Black Power: The Politics of Liberation in America 87 (1967) (SNCC started its first voter registration project in 1961 because it believed that political power organized around the right to vote was the key to dismantling southern racism).

17. T. Branch, *supra* note 11, at 482. Some of the earliest efforts to change tactics from protest to politics were engineered by the Kennedy Justice Department "to coax [civil rights activists] out of precisely the kind of confrontational actions [such as the Freedom Rides] around which they were shaping their identities." *Id.* at 479. The Kennedy Administration pushed the merits of voter registration, extending promises of draft exemptions, foundation grants, lawsuits, newspaper coverage, prosecution of obstructionist white Southern officials, and federal protection for voter registration activists. *Id.* at 480–81, 619–20. *But cf. id.* at 680–83, 713, 787 (FBI failed to investigate certain complaints or simply gathered information for subsequent civil cases without enforcing criminal protections against harassment or intimidation of voters).

18. R. Weisbrot, Freedom Bound: A History of America's Civil Rights Movement 150, 152 (1990) ("despite [the Voting Rights Act's] far-reaching implications, the legislation enjoyed broader, more sustained public support than any previous civil rights measure.").

19. Integration and nationalism were the most salient characteristics of the African-American intellectual and political agenda in the 1960s. *See* J. Grant, Black Protest 9, 13 (J. Grant ed. 1968) (although integration in American political and economic mainstream has been main tendency in fight for black rights, demand for positive assertion of blackness also persistent thread); Marable, *A New Black Politics,* The Progressive, Aug. 1990 at 18, 20 (black protest movements all based on fundamental racial ideologies of either integration or black nationalism).

   Compare M.L. King, Jr., The Trumpet of Conscience 10 (1967) (integration a basic aspect of freedom, meaning the freedom to choose where to live, to eat, to attend school) *and* Marable, *supra,* at 18 (racial integrationists consistently advocate elimination of all restrictions that keep blacks from participating fully in society's mainstream) *with id.* (black nationalists reject integration as a hoax, are suspicious of alliances with whites, and advocate self-help community based empowerment); C. LINCOLN, THE BLACK MUSLIMS IN AMERICA 45 (1961) (nationalism an involuntary, defensive response to escape hostile forces) *and* S. CARMICHAEL & C. HAMILTON, *supra* note 16, at 47, 54–55 (black liberation lies in group action acknowledging race as an overwhelming fact of life; goal is to build and strengthen the black community with its racial and cultural integrity intact and to obtain "an effective share in the total power of the society").

20. *See, e.g.,* King, *Civil Right No. 1—The Right to Vote,* N.Y. Times, Mar. 14, 1965, § 6 (Magazine), at 26. Many black nationalists played an important role in the fight for the franchise, reflecting their "admiration" for America's "free institutions." THE IDEO-LOGICAL ORIGINS OF BLACK NATIONALISM, *supra* note 13, at 21, 146–48.

21. *See, e.g.,* J. GRANT, *supra* note 19, at 427 (independent black politics added economic power to concepts of freedom and political action); M.L. KING, JR., WHERE DO WE GO FROM HERE: CHAOS OR COMMUNITY 37–38, 149–50 (1967); M.L. KING, JR., WHY WE CAN'T WAIT 166 (1963). King advocated full political participation by an enlightened electorate to elect blacks to key political positions, to liberalize the political climate in the United States and to influence the allocation of resources; *see also Voting Rights: Hearings Before Subcomm. No. 5 of the House Comm. on the Judiciary,* 89th Cong., 1st Sess. 377–80 (1965) (statement of Roy Wilkins, Executive Director, NAACP, and Chairman, LCCR) (eliminating voting restrictions means elected officials will become responsive to the will of all the people).

22. Miller, Gurin, Gurin & Malanchuk, *Group Consciousness and Political Participation,* 25 AM. J. POL. SCI. 494 (1981); Shingles, *Black Consciousness and Political Participation: The Missing Link,* 75 AM. POL. SCI. REV. 76 (1981); *see also* S. CARMICHAEL & C. HAMILTON, *supra* note 16, at 46 (group identity mobilizes participation; where blacks have a majority they will seek control; when they lack a majority they will seek proper representation and sharing of control). Stokely Carmichael's views are particularly interesting because he worked in the civil rights movement doing voter registration work in the early 1960s. Toward the end of the decade, identifying with a black nationalist ideology, he became one of the foremost advocates of "Black Power." According to Carmichael, even blacks associated with an integrationist ideology approved notions of group power.

> America has asked its Negro citizens to fight for opportunity as *individuals,* whereas at certain points in our history what we have needed most has been opportunity for the *whole group,* not just for selected and approved Negroes. . . . We must not apologize for the existence of this form of group power, for we have been oppressed as a group not as individuals.

Id. at 49 (quoting paid advertisement by black church members affiliated with National Council of Churches).

23. For the former, salvation would come as the result of a perpetual engagement to make America true to its stated principles, extended on behalf of "the Negro people." For the latter, group salvation would result from the development of group identity, expression, and independence. *See, e.g.,* S. CARMICHAEL & C. HAMILTON, *supra* note 16, at 49; R. WEISBROT, *supra* note 18, at 206, 216; *see also* Delany, *supra* note 13, at 196–97 (right to vote must include right to constitute essential part of the ruling element).

24. The focus on equality and universal suffrage was greatly influenced by the one person/ one vote language of Reynolds v. Sims, 377 U.S. 533 (1964). Some of the marchers from Selma to Montgomery in March 1965 carried "one man/one vote" signs. *See, e.g., Eyes on the Prize* (videotape segment five). John Lewis was arrested for carrying a "One Man /One Vote" sign outside a Selma, Alabama, courthouse. T. BRANCH, *supra* note 11, at 900; *cf. id.* at 587–88, 733 (describing predictions that the Supreme Court's reapportionment decisions would transform black voting the way *Brown v. Board of Education* changed education).

25. The capacity to participate made integration meaningful. *See, e.g., Black Power*, N.Y. Times, July 31, 1966, at E5, col. 1 (a paid advertisement by influential blacks affiliated with the National Council of Churches), *cited in* S. CARMICHAEL & C. HAMILTON, *supra* note 16, at 48–49. Political power, for nationalists as well, meant black people making decisions that affect their lives. *Id.*

26. VOICES OF FREEDOM: AN ORAL HISTORY OF THE CIVIL RIGHTS MOVEMENT FROM THE 1950s THROUGH THE 1980s 197–98 (H. Hampton & S. Fayer eds. 1990) (quoting Victoria Gray) (emphasis added) [hereinafter VOICES OF FREEDOM]. Approximately 80,000 blacks participated in "Freedom Vote," helping to dispel illusions about black political apathy. *Id.* at 181.

27. R. WEISBROT, *supra* note 18, at 194; *see also* S. CARMICHAEL & C. HAMILTON, *supra* note 16, at 103–08 (describing SNCC organizing efforts).

28. Zinn, *The Old Left and the New: Emancipation from Dogma*, NATION, Apr. 4, 1966, at 385, 387.

29. Although the march from Selma to Montgomery directly preceded congressional action on the Voting Rights Act, the mass direct action efforts to achieve the ballot were not based on a single march but were built from extended campaigns and were accompanied by nightly mass meetings. Watters, *Why the Negro Children March,* in BLACK PROTEST IN THE SIXTIES 96 (A. Meier & E. Rudwick eds. 1970) (Selma voting rights campaign involved prolonged siege of demonstrations and mass meetings, day after day, week after week). Of course, the most famous mass meeting was the August 1963 March on Washington for Jobs and Freedom. *See, e.g.,* T. BRANCH, *supra* note 11, at 840–49, 874; *see also id.* at 689 (describing blueprint for the Birmingham, Alabama, campaign combining small-scale sit-ins, boycotts, mass marches and other organized efforts to publicize efforts, enforce economic pressure and overflow the jails).

30. S. CARMICHAEL & C. HAMILTON, *supra* note 16, at 39, 43, 47 (broadened political participation means blacks choosing their own leaders and holding them responsible; it also means more black people becoming politically active; goal of black self-determination is full participation in decisionmaking processes); *id.* at 44 ("The concept of Black Power rests on a fundamental premise. *Before a group can enter the open society, it must first close ranks.* By this we mean that group solidarity is necessary before a group can operate effectively from a bargaining position of strength in a pluralistic society."); *see also* Carmichael, *What We Want,* N.Y. REV. BKS., Sept. 22, 1966 (black consciousness provides the basis for political strength).

31. Hamilton, *An Advocate of Black Power Defines It,* in BLACK PROTEST IN THE SIXTIES, *supra* note 29, at 156.

32. *See, e.g.,* S. CARMICHAEL & C. HAMILTON, *supra* note 16, at 37 (integration and nationalism both mean improving the lives of blacks both politically and economically); M.L. KING, JR., *supra* note 19, at 11, 14, 53, 61, 62 (political agenda involves economic jus-

tice, including a minimum annual income). Even the Urban League, one of the more conservative civil rights groups, projected a reformist view of democracy. Whitney Young, in his address at the League's 1963 national conference, expressed the group's underlying philosophy:

> . . . democracy is more than a convenient institution through which privileges and material products flow to [white citizens]. For both [whites and blacks] democracy is a way of life, an ideal in which all share its rewards, as well as its responsibilities. . . . For the public official—whether city, state or federal—witnessing means greater concern for broad, democratic promises and human rights, rather than preoccupation with technical, constitutional details and states' rights.

Young, *For Protest Plus "Corrective Measures,"* in M. BRODERICK & A. MEIER, NEGRO PROTEST THOUGHT IN THE TWENTIETH CENTURY 287, 289–90 (1965).

From the time of the Niagara Movement, and the founding of the NAACP in 1910, black activists have adopted a protest platform that included: the right to equal treatment, increased public high school and college facilities, judicial reform, health care, and vigorous enforcement of the post Civil War Amendments. M. BRODERICK & A. MEIER, *supra,* at 48–50.

33. R. WEISBROT, *supra* note 18, at xiii (civil rights leaders demanded equality of condition not just desegregation); *see, e.g.,* S. CARMICHAEL & C. HAMILTON, *supra* note 16, at 39–41 (political modernization emphasizes human dignity, not sanctity of property, "free people," not "free enterprise."); Matsuda, *supra* note 1, at 357 (Martin Luther King's version of rights would require radical transformation of existing social structures; King was concerned with ending poverty and closing the gap between the rich and the poor); *see also* VOICES OF FREEDOM, *supra* note 26, at 180 (quoting Unita Blackwell who attended a voter registration meeting held in a church in Sunflower County, Mississippi, during Freedom Summer 1964):

> I was only told when I started off that if I registered to vote, I would have food to eat and a better house to stay in, 'cause the one I was staying in was so raggedy you could see anywhere and look outdoors. My child would have a better education. . . . It was the basic needs of the people. The whites, they understood it even larger than that in terms of political power. We hadn't even heard that word, "political power," because it wasn't taught in the black schools. We didn't know there was such a thing as a board of supervisors and what they did, and we didn't know about school board members and what they did.

Id.

34. *See* THE NEW BLACK POLITICS, *supra* note 12, at 17 (civil rights is a consistent black interest-group value and preference). For example, at the National Black Political Convention in Gary, Indiana, in 1972, Coretta King and Black Panther Bobby Seale shared the platform at which a "Black Agenda articulated a revolution of values, a social transformation placing 'community before individualism, . . . a living environment before profits, . . . justice before unjust order, and morality before expediency.' " Poinsett, *Unity Without Uniformity,* EBONY, June 1972, at 45, 52. The Black Agenda contained eighty-eight recommendations, including proportional black political representation, reparations, free education through college, guaranteed annual income, national health insurance and a National Black Political Assembly to sponsor candidates, lobby for black issues, and make recommendations to the black community generally. *Id.* at 52, 54.

35. T. Branch, *supra* note 11, at 880.

36. H. Raines, My Soul Is Rested: Movement Days in the Deep South Remembered 249 (1977) (quoting Ms. Hamer).

37. Indeed, black nationalists offered racial pride and solidarity as a means of transforming the social, economic, *and* political conditions of black people. In this sense, black electoral success theory fit within a nationalist imagery that borrowed from the ethnic experience of group unity and determination to reinforce individual aspirations. S. Carmichael & C. Hamilton, *supra* note 16, at vii, viii (black power means, *inter alia*, psychic control by blacks over their own lives; black consciousness involves a sense of "peoplehood" that relies on group pride and communal responsibility); *see also* R. Weisbrot, *supra* note 18, at 201, 206. Even Dr. King saw group solidarity as part of his creative endeavor to reach the "Beloved Community" of interracial brotherhood and harmony. *Id.* at 206.

38. *See, e.g.,* S. Carmichael & C. Hamilton, *supra* note 16, at vii (black power will "contribute to the development of a viable larger society"); L. Killian, The Impossible Revolution, Phase II: Black Power and the American Dream 113, 125, 161–63 (1975); Hamilton, *supra* note 31, at 156; Jennings, *Boston: Blacks and Progressive Politics,* in The New Black Vote 208–18 (R. Bush ed. 1984) (political participation can mobilize voters to alter the dominant substantive agenda while still retaining group consciousness).

39. From the 1960s through the 1980s, black nationalists supported voter registration and electoral activity. Nationalists, interested in preserving racial-cultural differences, pushed for separate *and* equal black representation to give blacks greater self-consciousness and pride. By 1972, when the National Black Political Agenda was passed by a convention of black delegates in Gary, Indiana, group representation was openly perceived by most activists as critical to effective voting rights. *See, e.g.,* D. Pinderhughes, Race and Ethnicity in Chicago Politics 232 (1987) ("[b]lack nationalists of cultural and political dimension" actively involved in 1983 political campaign for black mayor); Voices of Freedom, *supra* note 26, at 225 (in 1964 Malcolm X offered to assist with voter registration and committed to work with the Mississippi Freedom Democratic party); *Worry for Democrats: "Black Power Drive,"* U.S. News & World Rep., Mar. 27, 1972, at 82 (National Black Political Convention met Mar. 10–12, 1972, in Gary, Indiana, attended by 3500 delegates to set up an independent black political movement backed by the voting strength of black registered voters) *supra* note 37. Some groups, such as the Nation of Islam, went through a temporary period of electoral isolation that ended at least by 1984 when Jesse Jackson ran for President. *See, e.g.,* Joint Center for Political and Economic Studies, *Muslim Politics,* Focus Magazine, Political Trendletter 3 (June 1990).

40. *See, e.g.,* Cutler, *Using Morals, Not Money on Pretoria,* N.Y. Times, Aug. 3, 1986, at E23, col. 2 (Mississippi Sen. James Eastland, noted segregationist, apparently confided, "When [blacks] get the vote, I won't be talking this way anymore."); *see also infra* notes 193–97 and accompanying text.

41. In 1963, for example, rather than consulting directly with the black civil rights leaders involved, Attorney General Robert Kennedy relied on a haphazard group of black entertainers and academics to explain events in Birmingham, Alabama. T. Branch, *supra* note 11, at 809–11. Even more typical was Birmingham's Mayor Thompson's effort to appease civil rights requests for negotiations by announcing "he would meet

with a biracial committee of his own choosing, specifying Negro members who had praised his stand on segregation." *Id.; see* Wolman & Thomas, *Black Interests, Black Groups and Black Influence in the Federal Policy Process: The Cases of Housing and Education,* in BLACK POLITICAL ATTITUDES 183, 193–94 (C. Bullock & H. Rodgers eds. 1972) (describing indirect representation through practice of "consulting a few well-known black leaders or enlisting them in formal and highly visible advisory capacities").

42. Black representation would thus obviate difficult equal protection constitutional challenges to discriminatory policies. *See* J. ELY, DEMOCRACY AND DISTRUST 86–87 (1980) (the right to representation attempts to protect minorities from denials of equal concern as subjects of legislative policy).

43. T. BRANCH, *supra* note 11, at 560; *see also* S. CARMICHAEL & C. HAMILTON, *supra* note 16, at 100–20.

44. R. WEISBROT, *supra* note 18, at 200 (quoting Hosea Williams on the "Meredith March" in Greenwood, Mississippi, June 1966); *see also* S. CARMICHAEL & C. HAMILTON, *supra* note 16, at 46 (a black sheriff can end police brutality; a black tax assessor can channel tax monies to improve services for black people).

45. S. CARMICHAEL & C. HAMILTON, *supra* note 16, at 44–46, 98–120 (describing Black Panther Party efforts in Alabama to run blacks for office in a manner that would serve as a "model for democracy"); R. WEISBROT, *supra* note 18, at 204.

46. Indeed, it is not mere coincidence that many prominent black elected officials and black candidates were once active in the civil rights movement. From Andrew Young to beleaguered former D.C. mayor Marion Barry, to Harvey Gantt, the 1990 Democratic nominee for U.S. Senator from North Carolina, many black political aspirants had their roots in civil rights struggle. *See, e.g.,* Smothers, *North Carolina Democrat Sets Strategy in Taking on Helms,* N.Y. Times, June 7, 1990, at B7, col. 1.

47. *From Gary to Miami Beach,* EBONY, Sept. 1972, at 142 (national black assembly "would force white politicians to deal with the entire black community instead of with a few hand-picked black politicians"); Poinsett, *supra* note 34, at 27, 45 (people work to create black politics to empower all of black America—instead of only representatives).

48. King noted that simply electing blacks was not enough. "Negro politicians can be opportunistic as their white counterparts if there is not an informed and determined constituency demanding social reform." M.L. KING, JR., *supra* note 21, at 49.

49. *See* S. CARMICHAEL & C. HAMILTON, *supra* note 16, at 46–47. Black electoral success theory reflects the basic "essentialism" of the nationalist position. The theory locates meaning in the concept of racial identity as a social-cultural, historically derived structure. For some nationalists, racial identity also has biological significance. For black power nationalists of the 1960s and early 1970s, however, essentialism meant recognition of their group identity as a source of pride, culture, and as a politically animating force.

50. THE BLACK POLITICIAN: HIS STRUGGLE FOR POWER (M. Dymally ed. 1971) [hereinafter THE BLACK POLITICIAN] (diverse black leaders all stressed black political organizing); Clark, *Foreword* to *id.* (black power movement is an "effective smokescreen" behind which quest for "genuine direct political power for blacks could proceed with minimum interference").

51. Commemorating the Voting Rights Act's 25th anniversary, Governor Douglas Wilder

of Virginia, the first black elected governor this century, credited the important symbolism of his own election to the Act, one of "two landmark events which literally changed the face of this nation." Lewis, *They're Wild About Wilder*, Phil. Inquirer, May 28, 1990, at A9, col. 1.

52. S. Rep. No. 417, 97th Cong., 2d Sess. 5 (1982); *see also* 42 U.S.C. § 19731(c)(1) (1988).

53. Some quarrel with the original legislative understanding of the right to vote. For example, Abigail Thernstrom writes that the 1965 Act was concerned exclusively with registration and voting, and later was transformed unwittingly into a statutory mandate for black electoral success, or "job corps" for black elected officials. *See* A. Thernstrom, Whose Votes Count? Affirmative Action and Minority Voting Rights 11, 18, 22–30 (1987). Even Thernstrom, however, concedes that by 1970 Congress, the judiciary, and voting rights plaintiffs all acknowledged the importance of a meaningful right to vote, meaning the right to elect representatives of choice. *Id.* at 22, 31. Without engaging in a semantic exercise or an extensive legislative history of the 1965 Act, it is nevertheless significant that in his message to a Joint Session of Congress transmitting the proposed 1965 legislation, President Johnson referred to the right of citizens to have a voice in electing their leaders as the *cornerstone* concern of the legislation. *See* 111 Cong. Rec. H5059 (1965) (equal right to vote affirms dignity of man because it rests, *inter alia*, on most basic right of all, the right to choose one's own leaders). Even Republican opponents of the 1965 Act acknowledged the consensus "to free those of our citizens who now endure the near-tyranny of nonrepresentation." *See, e.g.,* H.R. Rep. No. 439, 89th Cong., 1st Sess. at 37–38, 53, (1965).

54. *See* 115 Cong. Rec. 5517 (1970) (joint view of ten members of the Judiciary Committee). The Senate sponsors of the 1965 Act supported its renewal in 1970 in part because the Act was so successful in encouraging blacks "running for office in Southern states to help assure adequate representation of all interests." *Id.* at 5520.

55. For example, the Act defines "voting" to include "all action to make a vote effective." 42 U.S.C. § 1971(e) (1988); *see also supra* note 53. As the Supreme Court announced one year before the Voting Rights Act was passed, "[E]ach and every citizen has an inalienable right to full and effective participation in the political processes of his State's legislative bodies." Reynolds v. Sims, 377 U.S. 533, 565 (1964); *see also* Terry v. Adams, 345 U.S. 461 (1953) (striking down whites-only preprimary selection process on the ground that the right to vote is a right to an effective voice in governmental decisionmaking); *cf.* City of Richmond v. United States, 422 U.S. 358 (1975) (Brennan, J., dissenting) (blacks should enjoy the opportunity to elect responsive officials and have a significant voice in conduct of government affairs). President Lyndon Johnson allegedly told Hubert Humphrey during the legislative struggle for the 1964 Civil Rights Act:

> Yes, yes, Hubert, I want all those other things—buses, restaurants, all of that—but the right to vote with no ifs, ands, or buts, that's the key. When the Negroes get that, they'll have every politician, north and south, east and west, kissing their ass, begging for their support.

M. Miller, Lyndon: An Oral Biography 371 (1980); *cf.* F. Piven & R. Cloward, Why Americans Don't Vote 4 (1988) (right to vote is core symbol of democratic ideal that ordinary people would have a stake in government and their grievances addressed through the right to elect representatives).

56. As President Johnson declared when he signed the historic 1965 Act, "But only the individual Negro, and all others who have been denied the right to vote, can really walk through those doors, and can use that right, and can transform the vote into an instrument of justice and fulfillment." 111 Cong. Rec. 19649, 19650 (Aug. 6, 1965).
57. *See supra* note 2.
58. The first generation of voting litigation, and the 1965 statute which represented the congressional response, were concerned with the complete and total exclusion of blacks from the electoral process. The initial structure of the Act itself focused on the suspension of literacy tests, the deployment of federal registrars, and federal administrative review of local registration procedures in covered jurisdictions. Success under the Act was immediate and impressive. The number of blacks registered to vote rose dramatically within five years after passage. *See* Karlan, *supra* note 6, at 183–84.
59. "[D]ilution is a process whereby election laws or practices, either singly or in concert, combine with systematic bloc voting among an identifiable group to diminish the voting strength of at least one other group." Davidson, *Minority Vote Dilution*, in Minority Vote Dilution 1, 4 (C. Davidson ed. 1984); *see* Gingles v. Edmisten, 590 F. Supp. 345 (E.D.N.C. 1984), *modified sub. nom.* Thornburg v. Gingles, 478 U.S. 30 (1986), where the court considered:

> the essence of racial vote dilution . . . is this: that primarily because of the interaction of . . . racial polarization . . . with a challenged election mechanism, a racial minority with distinctive group interests that are capable of aid or amelioration by government is effectively denied the political power to further those interests that numbers alone would presumptively give it in a voting constituency not racially polarized . . .

590 F. Supp. at 355 (citations omitted). Structural barriers, such as at-large elections, dilute minority voting strength and make voting a futile gesture where the electorate is racially polarized. *See, e.g.,* Nevett v. Sides, 571 F.2d 209 (5th Cir. 1978); Zimmer v. McKeithen, 485 F.2d 1297 (5th Cir. 1976). At-large elections have been struck down under a constitutional theory of discriminatory effects, White v. Regester, 412 U.S. 755 (1973), a constitutionally compelled intent test, Rogers v. Lodge, 458 U.S. 613 (1982), and a statutory results standard, Thornburg v. Gingles, 478 U.S. 30 (1986).
60. While pluralist theories of democracy contemplate minority losses, they do not envision a minority that always loses. *See infra* notes 125–27 (principle of "minority acquiescence"—that minorities are supposed to lose—does not contemplate systematic bloc voting).
61. Encouraged by the Supreme Court's reapportionment decisions as popularized by the slogan, "one person/one vote," a meaningful vote became a vote undiluted by discriminatory, though facially neutral election schemes. *See* City of Mobile v. Bolden, 446 U.S. 55, 103 (1980) (Marshall, J., dissenting); Allen v. State Bd. of Elections, 393 U.S. 544 (1968); Reynolds v. Sims, 377 U.S. 533 (1964). Blumstein, *Defining and Proving Race Discrimination: Perspectives on the Purpose vs. Results Approach from the Voting Rights Act*, 69 Va. I. Rev. 633, 649–58 (1983), refers to this as a "substantive effects test," which he concedes may be appropriate for fundamental constitutional rights.
62. As amended, the statute states that a violation is established if blacks have "less opportunity than other members of the electorate . . . to elect representatives of their choice." 42 U.S.C. § 1973 (1988) (as amended). By codifying the language of White

v. Regester, 412 U.S. 755, 766 (1973), proponents sought to embrace a line of cases with an established, judicially manageable set of standards for ascertaining abridgement of minority voting rights. Blacks would henceforth enjoy the statutory right to elect candidates of their choice based on a functional view of their political circumstances as reflected in local historic, social, and economic relationships. Dillard v. Baldwin County, 686 F. Supp. 1459 (M.D. Ala. 1988); *cf.* Note, *Defining the Minority-Preferred Candidate Under Section 2 of the Voting Rights Act,* 99 YALE L.J. 1651, 1665–67 (1990).

63. *See supra* note 2. The statutory disclaimer stated that "[t]he extent to which members of a protected class have been elected to office" is relevant, *"provided* [t]hat nothing in this section establishes a right to have members of a protected class elected in numbers equal to their proportion in the population." 42 U.S.C. § 1973(b) (1988). The *Senate Report* also identified minority electoral success as a probative factor. *See* S. REP. NO. 417, 97th Cong., 2d Sess. 16, *reprinted in* 1982 U.S. CODE CONG. & ADMIN. NEWS 177, 193 (presence of minority elected officials is a "recognized indicator of access to the process") [hereinafter 1982 SENATE REPORT].

64. South Carolina v. Katzenbach, 383 U.S. 301 (1966); *see also* 128 CONG. REC. 14,302–341 *passim* (1982).

65. *See* Gingles v. Edmisten, 590 F. Supp. 345, 355 (E.D.N.C. 1984), *modified sub. nom.* Thornburg v. Gingles 478 U.S. 30 (1986); Major v. Treen, 574 F. Supp. 325 (D. La. 1983).

66. Unresponsiveness was initially perceived as a "core value" since it was the unwillingness of the governing body to respond to the needs and interests of the minority community that prompted judicial concern in the first place. *See, e.g.,* Blacksher & Menefee, *From* Reynolds v. Sims *to* Mobile v. Bolden: *Have the White Suburbs Commandeered the Fifteenth Amendment?* 34 HASTINGS L. REV. 1, 43 n.283 (1982). Proving unresponsiveness involved the awkward task of identifying specific pieces of legislation sponsored and supported by particular legislators antagonistic to minority group interests. The claim also could be conclusively rebutted with evidence of peripheral and insignificant "minority interest" legislation. Because unresponsiveness was judicially unmanageable, litigators convinced Congress to demote unresponsiveness to optional rebuttal. Unresponsiveness became a relevant factor only to the extent plaintiffs chose to prove it. *See* 1982 SENATE REPORT, *supra* note 63, at 29 n.116, *reprinted* at 207 n.116.

67. *See* Karcher v. Daggett, 462 U.S. 725, 738–39 (1983).

68. One of the most successful efforts involved the analysis of election returns using both the "interocular" test and "bivariate regression" to demonstrate polarization in the electorate, although sophisticated racial bloc voting analyses did not surface in dilution litigation until the late 1970s. *See, e.g.,* Nevett v. Sides, 571 F.2d 209 (5th Cir. 1978), *cert. denied,* 446 U.S. 951 (1980). After the 1982 amendments, however, proof of racial bloc voting assumed primary importance. *See* Thornburg v. Gingles, 478 U.S. 30, 55 (1986).

69. *See* City of Mobile v. Bolden, 446 U.S. 55, 71 n.17 (1980) (dilution claim rejected based simply on gauzy sociological evidence).

70. S. REP. NO. 417, 97th Cong., 2d Sess. 29 (1982) (listing typical, evidentiary factors to be considered within a totality of circumstances analysis).

71. *See* City of Mobile v. Bolden, 446 U.S. 55, 141 (1980) (Marshall, J., dissenting) (warn-

ing that political second class status for blacks provides short-lived, superficial tranquility because, without a reasonable judicial remedy, "the victims of discrimination" could not be long expected "to respect political channels of seeking redress"); *see also infra* note 78.

72. Although racial bloc voting was relatively easy to prove, it seemed omnipresent; every election system in every jurisdiction with some black population was vulnerable. Yet, judicial intervention would not halt the private racial preferences of individual voters. Whereas racial bloc voting might explain political market failure, it failed to identify which election schemes in particular were responsible and remediable.

73. The absence of proportional representation alone was not evidence of a violation. This absence, however, was still useful as a rhetorical device and to establish a baseline definitional floor of political inequality. At the same time, the presence of roughly proportional black representation defined the limits of equality. As Justice O'Connor observes, proportionate representation is an inexact concept. In a jurisdiction that is 40% black, a governing body with either 30% or 50% black representation would be sufficient to establish "undilution." Thornburg v. Gingles, 478 U.S. 30, 88–89 (1986) (O'Connor, J., concurring). As predicted by the 1982 amendments opponents, both the tool and the mandate became confined by judicial interpretation to the right to elect black representatives. But, contrary to opponents' claims, proportional representation was a ceiling rather than a floor. Even successful plaintiffs did not necessarily enjoy black representation proportionate to the black voting strength in the community. McGhee v. Granville Cty., 860 F. 2d 110, 120 (4th Cir. 1988). The phenomenon of the floor becoming the ceiling is not unusual in legal and other prescriptive discourses. *See* letter from Frank Michelman to author (Dec. 19, 1990) (on file with author). As long as black electoral success was consistent and proportionate, further scrutiny of black representation was discouraged. Thornburg v. Gingles, 478 U.S. at 77, 80 (remanding House District 23 because blacks enjoyed consistent, proportionate representation). The quality of black representation was not investigated. *Id.* (describing black voters' unexamined claim in Durham that a black elected through single shot voting was not adequately representing their interests because he was more directly beholden to white voters in the multimember district).

74. I make this claim notwithstanding the language in the legislative history accompanying the 1982 amendments which recognizes the relevance of a "depressed socioeconomic condition" to judicial enforcement of the Act. *See* 1982 SENATE REPORT, *supra* note 63, at 29 & n.114, reprinted at 206–7 & n. 114. The role of the representative has simply not been explored. The only discussion in the case law, for example, of the nature of representation involves some recent cases discussing judicial coverage under the Act based on the judicial "function." *See* League of United Latin Am. Citizens Council No. 4434 v. Clements, 914 F.2d 620 (5th Cir. 1990) (en banc), *cert. granted sub. nom.* Houston Lawyers' Assn. v. Attorney Gen. of Texas, 111 S. Ct. 775 (1991) (judges are not electorally accountable and are therefore not representatives subject to the Voting Rights Act). *But cf.* Martin v. Allain, 658 F. Supp. 1183, 1200 (S.D. Miss. 1987), *cited with approval in* Chisom v. Edwards, 839 F.2d 1056, 1063 (5th Cir. 1988), *vacated,* 853 F.2d 1186 (5th Cir. 1988), *cert. denied,* 488 U.S. 955 (1988), *overruled,* League of United Latin Am. Citizens Council No. 4434 v. Clements, 914 F.2d 620 (5th Cir. 1990), *cert. granted,* Houston Lawyers' Assn. v. Attorney Gen. of Texas, 111 S. Ct. 775 (1991).

75. The statute tracks the electorally triggering approach taken by the Supreme Court in one person/one vote cases. *See, e.g.,* New York City Board of Estimate v. Morris, 489 U.S. 688 (1989) (fact of election subjects board to constitutional scrutiny under the fourteenth amendment). According to the Eleventh Circuit, "The language [of Section 2] is only and uncompromisingly premised on the fact of nomination or election." Dillard v. Crenshaw Cty., 831 F.2d 246, 251 (1987).

76. *See, e.g.,* Connor v. Finch, 431 U.S. 407, 414 (1977); McGhee v. Granville County, 860 F.2d 110 (4th Cir. 1988); *accord* Chapman v. Meier, 420 U.S. 1, 18–21 (1975); Mahan v. Howell, 410 U.S. 315, 333 (1975); Connor v. Johnson, 402 U.S. 690, 692 (1971); *see also* Parker, *Racial Gerrymandering and Legislative Reapportionment,* in MINORITY VOTE DILUTION, *supra* note 59, at 85, 111–13.

77. The model assumes that in majority-white jurisdictions, whites must overcome the lasting legacy of Reconstruction era stereotypes to vote for black candidates. *See infra* notes 119–32 and accompanying text.

78. *See* T. BRANCH, *supra* note 11, at 880 (quoting John Lewis, then head of the Student Nonviolent Coordinating Committee (SNCC), at the August 1963 March on Washington); S. KARNIG & A. WELCH, BLACK REPRESENTATION AND URBAN POLICY 15 (1980) (until blacks given fair share of political power, danger of continued widespread violence); U.S. COMMN. ON CIVIL RIGHTS, THE VOTING RIGHTS ACT. UNFULFILLED GOALS 63 (1981); Note, United Jewish Organizations v. Carey *and the Need to Recognize Aggregate Voting Rights,* 87 YALE L.J. 571, 590 n.106 (1978). *See generally* City of Mobile v. Bolden, 446 U.S. 55 (1980) (Marshall, J., dissenting).

79. *See* letter from Jim Blacksher to author (Aug. 15, 1990) (on file with author).

80. J. CONYERS & W. WALLACE, BLACK ELECTED OFFICIALS: A STUDY OF BLACK AMERICANS HOLDING GOVERNMENTAL OFFICE 20 (1976) (89% of black officials surveyed believed court actions very important in achieving real progress); C. STONE, BLACK POLITICAL POWER IN AMERICA 10 (1970) (age of demonstrations has passed to age of the ballot).

81. *See* letter from Samuel Issacharoff to author (Sept. 24, 1990) (on file with author).

82. Whitfield v. Democratic Party, 686 F. Supp. 1365 (E.D. Ark. 1988), *affd. by equally divided court,* 890 F.2d 1423 (8th Cir. 1989) (en banc) (trial transcript at 654–55) (testimony of black state legislator Ben McGee, who was elected to the Arkansas House from a majority-black single-member district created as a result of a successful voting rights challenge in Smith v. Clinton, 687 F. Supp. 1310 (1988)).

83. Descriptive representation is representation by culturally and physically similar persons. *See* H. PITKIN, THE CONCEPT OF REPRESENTATION 60–91 (1967); Grofman, *Should Representatives Be Typical of Their Constituents?* in REPRESENTATION AND REDISTRICTING ISSUES (B. Grofman ed. 1982). Descriptive representation assumes that voters are best represented by people who look like or physically "describe" their constituents.

84. Authentic representatives need not be black as long as the source of their authority, legitimacy, and power base is the black community. White candidates elected from majority-black constituencies may therefore be considered "black" representatives. Nevertheless, the term usually connotes a minority group member. *See, e.g.,* Citizens for a Better Gretna v. City of Gretna, 834 F.2d 496, 504 (5th Cir. 1987) ("black preference is determined from elections which offer the choice of a black candidate"). Although some civil rights advocates acknowledge that whites who are sponsored by and elected within a *majority-black constituency* can and do represent minority interests, very few would support as authentic leaders whites who are elected within a

majority-*white* constituency with some black support. Others claim that even minority-sponsored white candidates elected within a majority-black jurisdiction, while sympathetic, are not generally perceived as aggressive advocates of black interests. As discussed *infra,* the real ambivalence asserts itself regarding the election of black representatives outside majority-black districts with some black support.

85. *See, e.g.,* C. STONE, R. WHELAN & W. MURIN, URBAN POLICY AND POLITICS IN A BUREAUCRATIC AGE 17 (1986) (few factors are more important to contemporary urban politics than race or ethnicity); Fainstein & Fainstein, *The Racial Dimension in Urban Political Economy,* 25 URB. AFF. Q. 187 (1989) (arguing that race plays a critical independent role in determining political outcomes and political roles for blacks). *But cf.* Marable, *supra* note 19, at 20 (race-based strategy for social change minimizes growing class differences within black community).

86. *See* Gingles v. Edmisten, 590 F. Supp. 345 (E.D.N.C. 1984), *modified sub. nom.* Thornburg v. Gingles, 478 U.S. 30 (1986) (trial transcript) (blacks elected from majority-white multimember districts sail trim, meaning they defer to other blacks to introduce and promote controversial legislation that would affect black constituents).

87. Defendant jurisdictions are challenged when they attempt to get credit for establishment endorsed black leaders, unless they produce evidence that a majority of black voters also supported the candidate. *See* Collins v. City of Norfolk, 883 F.2d 1232 (4th Cir. 1989); *Gingles,* 590 F. Supp. at 345. The litigator's approach is to examine voting patterns to determine whether the election system enables the black community to elect its own candidates or whether black officials are chosen instead by white voters.

88. For example, some blacks claim that as teachers they have "a clear, racial representational function," meaning that they both "comprehend" and "represent" the needs and interests of all black students. *See* Bell, *Statement, reprinted in* MINORITY GROUPS NEWSLETTER 18 May, 1990 (section on AALS) (advocating on behalf of black women role models and mentors); *see also* Austin, *Sapphire Bound!* 1989 WIS. L. REV. 539, 574 (Many role models are "black people who have achieved stature and power in the white world because they supposedly represent the interests of the entire black community. Such role models gain capital (literally and figuratively) to the extent that they project an assimilated persona that is as unthreatening to white people as it is (supposed to be) intriguing to our young.").

89. For example, minority faculty assist minority student recruitment by suggesting the opportunity to provide mentors for minority students and "hint[ing] at a culturally and ethnically heterogeneous campus environment." *Minority Issues in Legal Education,* LAW SERVS. REP., May–June 1990, at 4, 13; *see infra* notes 95–96.

90. B. BARBER, STRONG DEMOCRACY: PARTICIPATORY POLITICS FOR A NEW AGE 145–47, 291 (1984) (principle of representation that rescues democracy from the problems of scale is itself inherently oligarchical; representation is incompatible with equality and social justice); *cf.* Abrams, *supra* note 6, at 479 (representative democracy embodies unresolved tension between equality of all citizens and the greater participation of a few as important policy decisionmakers).

91. *See, e.g.,* THE FEDERALIST No. 39 (J. Madison) (rejecting elitist plutocracy).

92. *See* Michelman, *The Supreme Court, 1985 Term—Foreword: Traces of Self-Government,* 100 HARV. L. REV. 4, 50–55 (1986); *see also supra* chapter 2. (actual representation involves direct election by constituents; virtual representation consists

of representation by someone elected by another constituency with common interests and sympathies).

93. *See* Du Bois, *The Talented Tenth,* in THE NEGRO PROBLEM 31, 45 (Arno Press ed. 1969) (1903). In Du Bois' view, the "talented," whose own ability would be maximized, would make racially unique contributions, thus raising up the level of the race they represented. J. DEMARCO, THE SOCIAL THOUGHT OF W.E.B. DU BOIS 46 n.61, 48, 51 n.73 (1983). The ideal political system would enfranchise the talented tenth whose own empowerment and sense of social responsibility would benefit the masses. Du Bois advanced a theory of self-development, voluntary self-segregation, and personal intellectual achievement to create an avant-garde that convinced whites blacks were worthy of help. E. RUDWICK, W.E.B. DU BOIS: A STUDY IN MINORITY GROUP LEADERSHIP 291 (1960).

94. *Id.* Even though Du Bois ultimately abandoned his early proposals for a talented tenth, the concept remained influential to the advancement of middle-class aspirations and opportunity. In many ways, treatment of the talented tenth became a barometer of the degree to which blacks had overcome racism, both as a direct measure of equal opportunity for individual black achievers and as an indirect measure of the lowered racial barriers for those disadvantaged blacks still suffering disproportionate levels of poverty and deprivation. *Cf.* Brooks, *Life After Tenure: Can Minority Law Professors Avoid the Clyde Ferguson Syndrome?* 20 U.S.F. L. REV. 419, 423 (1986) (arguing that black middle class is in position to speak on behalf of black problems in general).

95. In the electoral context, promoting black role models is important to convince other blacks that the system is working. *See* Delgado, *The Ethereal Scholar: Does Critical Legal Studies Have What Minorities Want?* 22 HARV. C.R.–C.L. L. REV. 301, 310 (1987); Freeman, *supra* note 7, at 96, 110.

96. Black elected officials are not only important role models, but their election, even in a majority-white electorate, also legitimates them as group spokespersons. The spokesmodel theory of empowerment affirms the status of blacks as full citizens who can not only vote but can also hold elective office. The individual advancement of black elected officials inspires black constituents to believe in the system, and the individual elected official, as a racial spokesperson, attests reliably to the soundness of that belief. Especially since it was assumed that black role models were meaningful cultural symbols, then spokesmodels were even more meaningful bridges to those less fortunate. *See, e.g.,* A. RAMPERSAD, THE ART AND IMAGINATION OF W.E.B. DU BOIS 81 (1976) (Du Bois recognized the need for a process of "natural selection" of indigenous black leadership); *see also* W.E.B. DU BOIS, THE SOULS OF BLACK FOLK (1973); Austin, *supra* note 88, at 575 ("By their sheer visibility, [role models] are of service to those left behind. They are functionally useful in providing images for emulation. . . .").

97. Thernstrom's theory of representation is essentially that representation is a neutral outcome reflecting voter preference. In the absence of intentional discrimination, efforts to ensure "black" representation promote legislative set asides or electoral "quotas." A. THERNSTROM, *supra* note 53, at 237–38. Thernstrom's theory of voting rights has received considerable attention, in part because its proponent utilizes effectively the inflammatory language of quotas. *See, e.g.,* Greenhouse, *The "Quota" Dispute Battle Over Civil Rights Bill Involves Larger Debate Considering Race,* N.Y. Times, July 21, 1990, at A10, col. 5 (in issues of race, no word is "more emotionally

loaded or universally shunned than 'quota' "); *see also* Wright v. Rockefeller, 376 U.S. 52, 63–67 (1964) (Douglas, J. dissenting) (condemning "racial electoral registers" and race conscious districting which encourages racial partisans).

98. Actual participation by group members in an extended political process becomes superfluous because nondiscriminating representatives are responsive to their *electoral* constituency regardless of race. The assumptions supporting this hypothesis have already been carefully dissected elsewhere. *See, e.g.,* F. PARKER, BLACK VOTES COUNT (1990); Abrams, *supra* note 6, at 481–88 (individual preferences not easily aggregated nor translated into governing policies); Guinier, *supra* chapter 2. Karlan & McCrary, *Without Fear and Without Research: Abigail Thernstrom on the Voting Rights Act* (Book Review), 4 J. L. & POL. 751, 776–77 (1988).

99. *See* B. BARBER, *supra* note 90, at xiii (citing "crisis in participation"); Ackerman, *The Storrs Lectures: Discovering the Constitution,* 93 YALE L.J. 1013, 1034–35 (1984) (citing problems of apathy and uninformed voting); Brennan & Buchanan, *Voter Choice: Evaluating Political Alternatives,* 28 AM. BEHAV. SCI. 185, 187 (1984); *cf.* S. VERBA & N. NIE, PARTICIPATION IN AMERICA; POLITICAL DEMOCRACY AND SOCIAL EQUALITY 31 (table 2-1) (1972).

100. Most significantly, virtual representation is one step further removed from vicarious representation through political spokesmodels. At least the possibility of electing a descriptively similar representative mobilizes black voter turnout. Virtual representation, by contrast, offers nothing to animate participation. To the contrary, virtual representation undermines the fundamental values of participation in a democracy. *See infra* note 111 and accompanying text.

101. For example, studies suggest that House members are most responsive to their most supportive constituency. R. FENNO, HOME STYLE: HOUSE MEMBERS IN THEIR DISTRICTS 234 (1978); *cf. infra* notes 111–12, 115 and accompanying text.

102. Weissberg, *Collective vs. Dyadic Representation in Congress,* 72 AM. POL. SCI. REV. 535 (1978).

103. *Id.;* H. EULAU & K. PREWITT, LABYRINTHS OF DEMOCRACY: ADAPTATIONS, LINKAGES, REPRESENTATION, AND POLICIES IN URBAN POLITICS (1973) (voters may in fact be better represented by legislators outside their district); *cf.* United Jewish Orgs. v. Carey, 430 U.S. 144 (1977) (white voter in majority-black district with nonwhite representative will be represented by legislator elected from other majority-white districts to the extent voting is along racial lines).

104. *See* A COMMON DESTINY 6 (G. James & R. Williams eds. 1989); R. FARLEY & W. ALLEN, THE COLOR LINE AND THE QUALITY OF LIFE IN AMERICA (1989).

105. Oreskes, *As Problems Fester, Voters Send Pink Slips,* N.Y. Times, Sept. 23, 1990, at E5, col. 1; *see also supra* note 99; Oreskes, *Low Voter Turnout in Primaries, Once Again,* N.Y. Times, Oct. 4, 1990, at B16, col. 4 [hereinafter Oreskes, *Low Voter Turnout*] (Committee for the Study of the American Electorate reports widespread decline in voter turnout).

106. Young, *Polity and Group Difference: A Critique of the Ideal of Universal Citizenship,* 99 ETHICS 250, 259–61 (1989) (concept of social group is distinguished from simple aggregate or association of people by its special history, identity, values, and expressive style; social group is defined primarily by members' sense of personal identity derived from group affinity and relational differentiations from other nongroup members); *see also infra* notes 195–96. To say, however, that blacks in general

have a distinct or shared experience is not to say they are monolithic. This idea is developed further in subsequent chapters.

107. Where electoral ratification is imprecise because, for example, the black elected role model is elected in a majority-white jurisdiction, cultural authenticity alone often substitutes as a mechanism for defining and validating the "black" leaders. *See infra* notes 149–53.

108. Abrams, *supra* note 6, at 487. Even where an electoral majority sends a clear message, the representative may have difficulty translating this message into substantive policy. She may be unable to persuade her legislative colleagues or she may feel obliged to support initiatives opposed by those who elected her. She may be subject to pressure from constituent groups or other organized interests not responsible for her election. Alternatively, a representative's incumbency may so insulate her from electoral pressures that she feels little need to respond to constituent demands.

   Id. Cf. Barnes, *Into the Mainstream,* 22 NATL. J. 262 (1990) (Virginia black governor Wilder "may become less accessible and less accountable politically to blacks whose demands will be competing for attention against those of Virginia's white-majority constituency—and those of Wilder's large campaign contributors").

109. The black "swing vote" is not usually critical unless there is a close split in the white vote. *See* Williams, *Blacks Cast Pivotal Ballots in Four Key Senate Races, Data Show,* N.Y. Times, Nov. 6, 1986, at A33, col. 3. Moreover, white political beneficiaries of the swing vote are often unaware of its decisive impact or deliberately ignore it because of even more decisive white support. Davidson, *supra* note 59, at 9–10; *see also* Stodghill, *After the Victory Party, Frustration in the Black Community,* BUS. WK., Jan. 8, 1990, at 49.

110. In Virginia, where Douglas Wilder is the first black elected Governor since Reconstruction, some commentators have interpreted his victory as a "new black politics." *But cf.* Ayres, *Virginia Governor Baffles Democrats With Crusade for "New Mainstream,"* N.Y. Times, Oct. 14, 1990, at A22, col. 1 (Wilder considers himself "a governor who happens to be black, not a black who happens to be governor."); Smothers, *supra* note 46, at B7, col. 1. Others see Wilder's win as the triumph of a single-issue constituency in the wake of recent Supreme Court decisions on abortion. In either case, given the narrow margin of victory, Wilder's ability to govern on other issues important to the black community is considerably vitiated. *Cf. infra* notes 125, 213 and accompanying text.

111. Abrams, *supra* note 6, at 501 (Black election is a crucial aid to political morale "demonstrating to minority voters that defeat is no longer inevitable, and that there is someone in the government who will respond to their interests."); *see* L. COLE, BLACKS IN POWER 110–18, 221–23 (1976); J. CONYERS & W. WALLACE, *supra* note 151, at 6–7; Montague, *The Voting Rights Act Today,* A.B.A. J., Aug. 1, 1988, at 56 (statement of B. Grofman); Morris, *Black Electoral Participation and the Distribution of Public Benefits,* in MINORITY VOTE DILUTION, *supra* note 59, at 275, 277 (political efficacy and level of trust in government affect black turnout); *see also* A. THERNSTROM, *supra* note 53, at 122 (quoting Rolando Rios, legal director, Southwest Voter Registration Education Project) ("When Hispanic candidates do not get elected, he said, they cease to run, and without minority candidates, Hispanics do not vote.").

112. D. PINDERHUGHES, *supra* note 5 at 245 (quoting G. McWorter, D. Gills & R. Bailey, Black Power Politics as Social Movement: Dialectics of Leadership in the Campaign

to Elect Harold Washington, 8–9 (1984) (unpublished manuscript, Afro-American Studies and Research, University of Illinois, Urbana)) (black organizations worked so closely not everybody knew "what group they were working under. Everybody seemed just to know what they were working for: *the election of Chicago's first Black Mayor.*") (emphasis added); *id.* at 244–47; Pettigrew, *Black Mayoral Campaigns,* in URBAN GOVERNANCE AND MINORITIES (H. Bryce ed. 1976) (black turnout declined second time a black candidate ran); *see also* S. KARNING & A. WELCH, *supra* note 78; D. MCADAM, POLITICAL PROCESS AND THE DEVELOPMENT OF BLACK INSURGENCY 51 (1982); *cf.* Johnson, *Racial Politics: Chicago's Raw Nerve,* N.Y. Times, Feb. 19, 1989, § 6 (Magazine), at 37 (The night in 1983 Harold Washington was elected Chicago's first black mayor, "black people literally danced in the streets of Chicago. They had voted in record numbers, charging to the polls by car, by bicycle, by foot, by wheelchair. There were elderly blacks who said they had never voted before. Now, finally, they had a reason to vote.").

113. *See, e.g.,* McMillan v. Escambia County, 748 F.2d 1037, 1045 (11th Cir. 1984); Hendrix v. McKinney, 460 F. Supp. 626, 631–32 (M.D. Ala. 1978); Citizens for a Better Gretna v. City of Gretna, 636 F. Supp. 1113, 1119 (E.D. La. 1986), *affd.,* 834 F.2d 496 (5th Cir. 1987); *see also supra* note 111.

114. Smothers, *Omen for Young: Low Black Turnout,* N.Y. Times, July 19, 1990, at B6, col. 4 (Andrew Young neglected black vote in appeal to moderate whites; as a result he received fewer black votes in Georgia precincts than Jesse Jackson did in 1988 running for the Democratic nomination for President).

115. *Cf.* R. FENNO, *supra* note 101, at 184 (elected office becomes a way of life not just a job; incumbents enjoy the prestige, the policy influence, and name recognition); *id.* at 178 ("The first term is the hardest. If you win election a second time, you're in for quite a while."); *id.* at 172, 174 (elected officials are more involved with their constituency both before and immediately after their first election); *id.* at 191–93 (once their electoral base is solidified, their interaction with constituents decreases significantly, dwindling to providing access to a core group of constituents; at the end of a lengthy career in Congress, for example, one representative did not even maintain a district office).

116. Black electoral success both within and without majority-black districts rewards black voters with "prestige" rather than "policies." *See, e.g.,* A. REED, THE JESSE JACKSON PHENOMENON: THE CRISIS OF PURPOSE IN AFRO-AMERICAN POLITICS (1986); Reed, *A Critique of Neo-Progressivism in Theorizing about Development Policy: A Case from Atlanta,* in THE POLITICS OF URBAN DEVELOPMENT 199 (C. Stone & H. Sanders eds. 1987) [hereinafter Reed, *Neo-Progressivism*]; (political power often ineffective in delivering to core constituency where based simply on electoral strength) Reed, *The Black Urban Regime: Structural Origins and Constraints,* 1 COMP. URB. & COMMUNITY RES. 1 (1988) [hereinafter Reed, *The Black Urban Regime*].

117. Especially for established incumbents, tension often develops between representing constituent interests, on the one hand, and pursuing personal influence within the legislature, on the other. R. FENNO, *supra* note 101, at 215, 216, 218 (long-term incumbent experiences gradual erosion of local orientation in exchange for perception of governmental influence; legislative influence offered as a substitute for constituency access; allocation of resources to the reinforcement of constituency support declines over length of representatives' service). Representatives in general tend to

perceive a conflict between their role as ombudsman and lawmaker. M. JEWELL, REP-RESENTATION IN STATE LEGISLATURES 2 (1982). On the other hand, for some representatives, interaction with constituents is a "security blanket." R. FENNO, *supra* note 101, at 218. The conflict between political responsiveness and career development is one that a passive, economically depressed electorate is incapable of resolving.

118. Marable, *supra* note 19, at 21 ("These charlatans rely on the old nationalist rhetoric of racial solidarity, but lack any progressive content and fail to deliver on a substantive agenda because they are detached from any social protest movement for empowerment or resistance.").

119. For purposes of racial bloc voting, white ethnics are considered white. *See, e.g.,* United Jewish Orgs. v. Carey, 430 U.S. 144 (1977) (Hasidic voters proportionately represented by white elected officials). Although blacks may prefer black candidates, they often do vote for white candidates, especially where no black candidate runs. At the local level Carl Eggleston, the first black elected to the Farmville, Virginia, city council following a successful § 2 lawsuit in 1984, experienced racial bloc voting after he rose to prominence in the State Democratic Party, and tried without success to gain reelection to the council from a majority-white district when he moved his residence. Mr. Eggleston explains his defeat as follows:

> I really thought I had a chance. . . . There were a lot of issues in the campaign, and the incumbent had voted wrong on a number of them and in general had lost touch. But I found out that the only issue people were interested in was race. Whites voted against me not on the issues, not on any stand I had taken, but just because I'm black. . . . People would come to the polls and talk out loud—I mean out loud—saying, "We've got too many blacks on council."

McDonald, *Votes of Confidence,* Found. News, Sept./Oct. 1988, at 27, 31.

120. Rogers v. Lodge, 458 U.S. 613, 623 (1982); Gomez v. City of Watsonville, 863 F.2d 1407, 1417 (9th Cir. 1988); Jeffers v. Clinton, 730 F. Supp. 196, 198 (E.D. Ark. 1989); Brown v. Board of Commrs. of Chattanooga, Tenn., 722 F. Supp. 380, 393 (E.D. Tenn. 1989); McNeil v. City of Springfield, 658 F. Supp. 1015, 1027 (C.D. Ill. 1987); Busbee v. Smith, 549 F. Supp. 494, 495 (D.D.C.) (Young deposition at 9).

121. *See* Applebome, *Blacks and the Election: What Was the Message?* N.Y. Times, Nov. 18, 1990, at A30, col. 2 [hereinafter Applebome, *Blacks and the Election*] (racially charged contests bring out white voters; white incumbent in North Carolina injected racial issues into the campaign in final days to win a massive white turnout that swamped black opponent); *The 1990 Elections State by State,* N.Y. Times, Nov. 8, 1990, at B8, col. 5 (poll of North Carolina voters showed that 65% of whites supported Jesse Helms while 93% of blacks supported his black opponent); Applebome, *Racial Politics in South's Contests: Hot Wind of Hate or a Last Gasp?* N.Y. Times, Nov. 5, 1990, at A1, col. 5 (campaign commercial used white hands crumpling rejection letter as part of racial appeal against black opponent); *see also* Toner, *Unseating Helms: Rival Charts Uphill Climb,* N.Y. Times, July 16, 1990, at A12, col. 6 (although survey suggests 35% of whites backed a black candidate in the North Carolina Senate race, many preelection surveys in other states found whites often reluctant to admit to unknown interviewer their prejudice against black candidates); Applebome, *Drama Is Past Tense in Georgia Race,* N.Y. Times, July 16, 1990, at A12, col. 1; *Breakthrough in Virginia,* TIME, Nov. 20, 1989, at 54.

122. *Attitudes in Black and White,* TIME, Feb. 2, 1987, at 21 (survey of attitudes); *see also* Guinier, *supra* chapter 2 (citing 1987 Joint Center for Political Studies/Gallup survey in which 55% of whites said they would not vote for a black mayor regardless of qualifications).

123. Hahn, Klingman & Pachon, *Cleavages, Coalitions, and the Black Candidate,* 29 W. POL. Q. 507 (1976); Halley, Acock & Greene, *Ethnicity and Social Class: Voting in the 1973 Los Angeles Municipal Elections,* 29 W. POL. Q. 521 (1976); Walton, *Black Politics in the South: Projections for the Coming Decade,* in PUBLIC POLICY FOR THE BLACK COMMUNITY, *supra* note 13, at 77–100; *see also* F. PARKER, *supra* note 98, at 136 n.13; Bullock & Campbell, *Racist or Racial Voting in the 1981 Atlanta Municipal Elections,* 20 URB. AFF. Q. 149 (1984); Hero, *The Election of Hispanics in City Government: An Examination of the Election of Federico Pena as Mayor of Denver,* 40 W. POL. Q. 93, 94 (1987); Hero, *Multiracial Coalitions in City Elections Involving Minority Candidates: Some Evidence from Denver,* 25 URB. AFF. Q. 342, 344–46 (1989) [hereinafter Hero, *Multiracial Coalitions*]; Hero & Beatty, *The Elections of Federico Pena as Mayor of Denver: Analysis and Implications,* 70 SOC. SCI. Q. (1989).

124. Despite increased acceptance of blacks in social settings, many whites still harbor racial prejudice. *See* Delgado, *supra* note 95, at 316 n.87 (citing, *inter alia,* G. ALLPORT, THE NATURE OF PREJUDICE 79–80, 197–202 (1954)); Lawrence, *The Id, the Ego, and Equal Protection: Reckoning with Unconscious Racism,* 39 STAN. L. REV. 317, 339 n.91 (1987) (social stereotypes can and do create their own social reality; racism as a product of the unconscious is more complex than either the conscious conspiracy of a power elite or the simple delusion of ignorant bigots; racism is part of common historical experience and, therefore, culture, arising from learned assumptions as well as from patterns of fundamental social activities); Pettigrew, *New Patterns of Racism: The Different Worlds of 1984 and 1964,* 37 RUTGERS L. REV. 673, 688–89 (1985); *Poll Finds Whites Use Stereotypes,* N.Y. Times, Jan. 10, 1991, at B10, col. 2 (whites believe blacks are less hardworking, more violence-prone, less intelligent, and less patriotic). The Reconstruction era specter of black political control continued to fuel white antipathy during the Mississippi voter registration drive of 1963. T. BRANCH, *supra* note 11, at 718; *see also* A COMMON DESTINY, *supra* note 104, at 11 (despite substantial consensus, in the abstract, on the broad goal of achieving an egalitarian society, white resistance to equality continues, especially when contemplating frequent interracial contact of long duration); *cf.* C. BULLOCK & H. RODGERS, RACIAL EQUALITY IN AMERICA 154–55 (1975); A. CAMPBELL, WHITE ATTITUDES TOWARD BLACK PEOPLE ch. 7 (1971) (citing evidence of unfavorable stereotypes of blacks).

125. *See, e.g.,* J. ELY, *supra* note 42, at 135; Davidson, *supra* note 59, at 5–10 (hostile white majority has "panoply of weapons at its disposal"; even if minority exercises electoral influence, winning candidates do not always pay attention to minority interests after the election; postelection pressure from white constituents may nullify minority "influence"); *cf.* Goodman, *De Facto School Segregation: A Constitutional and Empirical Analysis,* 60 CALIF. L. REV. 275, 315 (1972) ("Race prejudice divides groups that have much in common (blacks and poor whites) and unites groups (whites, rich and poor) that have little else in common than their antagonism for the racial minority. Race prejudice, in short, provides the 'majority of the whole' with that 'common motive to invade the rights of other citizens' that Madison believed improbable in a pluralistic society.").

126. THE FEDERALIST No. 51, at 346 (J. Madison) (P. Ford ed. 1898).
127. *See, e.g.,* B. RINGER & E. LAWLESS, RACE-ETHNICITY AND SOCIETY 151–69 (1989) (duality of qualitatively different political treatment of racial minorities and white immigrants structured by constitutional underpinnings sanctioning two separate political-economic systems); *see also supra* notes 59–60.
128. Black elected officials, by virtue of their status and tenure, tend to assuage white fears during their incumbency. The power of incumbency is supported by studies which suggest that black incumbents are in fact reelected with more white support. *See* L. COLE, *supra* note 111, at 4–5; J. CONYERS & W. WALLACE, *supra* note 80, at 143–45; *see also* Johnson, *supra* note 112, at 37 ("among the white Cassandras who saw in a black man's election the impending ruin of their city, hate turned to mere dislike, and perhaps even to grudging respect, as the garbage still got picked up and the streets still got plowed").
129. Ackerman, *Beyond* Carolene Products, 98 HARV. L. REV. 713, 732–735 (1985) (black representatives not necessarily pariahs since familiarity may diminish hostility); Karlan, *supra* note 6, at 216–18 (local governing bodies are intimate groups with ongoing relationships that enable a single black legislator to build legislative bridges; continuous, open voting opportunities also foster accommodation; institutional setting with debates, amendment processes and hearings encourages active participation of minority representatives); *see also* L. COLE, *supra* note 111, at 222 (the presence of black elected officials sensitizes white associates); Abrams, *supra* note 6, at 500 (increasing number of black representatives creates opportunities for greater cross-racial interaction and requires white officials to hear black officials articulate black interests).
130. Montague, *supra* note 111, at 58; *see also* Morris, *supra* note 111, at 277.
131. In recent interviews, members of the House of Representatives have acknowledged the importance of black elected officials. Roberts, *Letter Critical of Israel Stirs Political Fallout,* N.Y. Times, Mar. 25, 1988, at B8, col. 4; *see* M. JEWELL & S. PATTERSON, THE LEGISLATIVE PROCESS IN THE UNITED STATES 197–98, 211–12 (4th ed. 1986) (both national and state legislators take direct cues for decisionmaking from other legislators with specialized information); *see also* Barnett, *The Congressional Black Caucus: Illusions and Realities of Power,* in THE NEW BLACK POLITICS, *supra* note 12, at 28 (black representatives seek to influence congressional legislation on behalf of blacks at every step; black elected officials are an "authority structure" within the black community).

   Some proponents of the polarization assumption go even further and suggest that coalition politics within the legislature may be more effective than attempts at the electoral level to break down racially polarized voting, especially because legislators have more voting opportunities to further the process of accommodation. These scholars hypothesize that the legislative process itself may maximize opportunities for a strong proponent of black interests to persuade sympathetic but less informed colleagues.
132. Robinson & Preston, *Equal Status Contact and Modification of Racial Prejudice: A Re-examination of the Contact Hypothesis,* 54 SOCIAL FORCES 911 (1976); Michelman, *Conceptions of Democracy in American Constitutional Argument: The Case of Pornography Regulation,* 56 TENN. L. REV. 291, 293 (1989) (deliberative politics suggests an openness to persuasion by reasons; deliberation involves argumentative

interchange among equals); Michelman, *Conceptions of Democracy in American Constitutional Argument: Voting Rights,* 41 Fla. L. Rev. 443, 448 (1989) [hereinafter Michelman, *Conceptions of Democracy*] (strategic interaction, or classic pluralist interest-group politics, seeks coordination rather than cooperation based on self-interested bargaining, not good-faith argument); Michelman, *Law's Republic,* 97 Yale L.J. 1493 (1988); Sunstein, *Interest Groups in American Public Law,* 38 Stan. L. Rev. 29 (1985); *cf.* Abrams, *supra* note 6, at 500 ("Collegiality requires . . . that [white officials] give a hearing to the interests articulated by minority officials."); Sunstein, *Beyond the Republican Revival,* 97 Yale L.J. 1539, 1548 (1988) (civic republicans emphasize rationale deliberation covering ends as well as means); *see also infra* note 133 (assuming, first, *a critical mass of allies for moral support and resonance* and, second, *a disaggregated majority,* even a lone black may effectively rely on normative persuasion or on bargains within a pluralist exchange, especially in a small body where a face-to-face encounter is an unavoidable fact of life).

133. *See supra* note 129 and accompanying text; *see also* F. Michelman, Justice Marshall's *Bolden* Dissent 5–6 (Nov. 28, 1990) (unpublished manuscript) (classical interest-group pluralist account would claim that racial bloc voting is "harder to sustain within the face-to-face dealings among a commission of three members than in the mass-political conditions in which members are elected"; politically salient issues may split two white members and encourage alliance with lone black; from a less strategic, dialogic perspective, "immediacy of . . . Black presence . . . [and] Black voice . . . in . . . daily encounters and public deliberations . . . make the difference"; *see also* letter from Frank Michelman to author (Dec. 19, 1990) (on file with author) (despite distinctions between normative persuasion and pluralist exchange, within either perspective a single black may be effective within a dialogic understanding or hold critical swing vote, especially in a small legislative body where critical mass of allies more likely). *But cf. infra* notes 138, 155–59, 166–75 and accompanying text.

134. Abrams, *supra* note 6, at 502 n. 269 (contemporary record of intergroup cooperation is mixed); Karlan, *Undoing the Right Thing: Single-Member Offices and the Voting Rights Act,* 77 Va. L. Rev. 41–43 & n.159 (1991) (giving blacks some seats on a multimember body poses no immediate threat to continued white predominance in the political process; voluminous literature on "tipping points" suggests gulf between black presence and influence); *cf.* Apodaca v. Oregon, 406 U.S. 404, 412–14 (1972) (having minority group representatives on jury does not assure outcome because they may simply be outvoted by majority).

135. Nelson, *supra* note 14, at 187 (black political influence in Cleveland moving in reverse); Preston, *supra* note 14, at 159, 163 (black political representation in Chicago fairly large but ineffective); Stone, *Race and Regime in Atlanta,* in Racial Politics in American Cities 125 (R. Browning, D. Marshall & D. Tabb eds. 1990); Reed, *Neo-Progressivism, supra* note 116, at 199.

136. S. Carmichael & C. Hamilton, *supra* note 16, at 7; J. Wilson, *The Negro in American Politics: The Present,* in The American Negro Reference Book 453 (1966) (the larger the black population, the greater the perceived threat, and thus the greater the resistance to intergroup participation and dialogue).

137. *See* Coleman & McLemore, *Black Independent Politics in Mississippi: Constants and Challenges,* in The New Black Politics, *supra* note 12, at 131, 151 (blacks may

enjoy individual, vicarious access through black representatives but not meaningful political access in which demands are authoritatively decided upon).

138. Abrams, *supra* note 6, at 502, *see also* Michelman, *Law's Republic, supra* note 132, at 1523–24, 1530–32; Michelman, *supra* note 92, at 50–55; *see also infra* notes 152–54 and accompanying text.

139. *See* Oreskes, *Blacks in New York: The Anguish of Political Failure,* N.Y. Times, Mar. 31, 1987, at B1, col. 3 (failure of black elected officials to penetrate governing coalitions may reduce morale and participation within the black community in general).

140. In a collective decisionmaking body, decisionmaking generally proceeds from public discussion and debate of policy issues to enactment of proposals using agreed upon mechanisms or decisional rules for ascertaining collective preference. Because of prejudice and inequality, black representatives may not participate meaningfully in either the deliberative or voting stages of collective decisionmaking.

141. Jeffers v. Clinton, 730 F. Supp. 196 (E.D. Ark. 1989) (three-judge court).

142. Trial transcript at IV-20, IV-30, 730 F. Supp. 196 (no. 89-004). Senator Jewell sought public office to "try and come in and see if I could do something inside and do so with complete integrity"; because black concerns meet a "very negative response." Representative McGee, unable to initiate legislation on the "real issues" of black concern such as "teenage pregnancy, housing, and education reforms," "decided that [his] role should be just to try and stop bad legislation.").

143. Trial transcript at IX-51, 730 F. Supp. 196 (No. 89-004) (trial testimony of Nancy Balton, Rep. from Mississippi County).

144. Trial transcript at 178-79, 730 F. Supp. 196 (No. 89-004) (trial testimony of Senator Paul Benham, Jr., who referred to Jesse Jackson as a "coon" in conversations with other state legislators); *see also* Major v. Treen, 574 F. Supp. 325 (E.D. La. 1983) (three-judge court) (white state legislator voted against creating a majority-black Louisiana congressional district because "we already have one nigger bigshot" in reference to the black mayor of New Orleans); *cf.* Busbee v. Smith, 549 F. Supp. 494, 500 (D.D.C. 1982) (identifying a prominent member of the Georgia legislature as a "racist").

145. Jeffers v. Clinton, 730 F. Supp. 196, 214 (E.D. Ark. 1989) (Rep. Nancy Balton of Mississippi County voted against bill exempting very poor people from paying taxes to appease white middle-class constituents who felt that "poor people on welfare were living better than they were." In Mississippi County, per capita income is $5685 for whites and $2426 for blacks; 45% of black families, compared to 13.4% of white families, live in poverty.). *But cf. infra* note 181 (black constituency size has positive impact on legislative support for black issues).

146. 730 F. Supp. at 214.

147. *See* 730 F. Supp. at 210–11 (felony charges instigated by the county sheriff against a black lawyer and political candidate, the court concluded, were "designed to discourage [the black candidate] in particular and black political activity in general"); 730 F. Supp. at 212 (black attorney running for county judge threatened by "individuals wearing hoods," and subjected to official harassment by the county, which, after he lost, reduced its business with his funeral home, and paid premium rates to a "white" funeral home to bury black paupers). Even when blacks are elected by a landslide, they are often the victims of hostile gerrymandering to eliminate their

districts. Buskey v. Oliver, 565 F. Supp. 1473 (M.D. Ala. 1983); Busbee v. Smith, 549 F. Supp. 494 (D.C. 1982).

148. Mathews, *Hooks Says Prosecutors "Overzealous,"* Phila. Inquirer, July 10, 1990, at 10A, col. 1 (NAACP convention delegates unanimously condemned unfair treatment of black elected officials by white prosecutors, citing as examples Mayor Tom Bradley of Los Angeles, Rep. William H. Gray (D. Pa.), Atlanta Mayor Maynard Jackson and former Atlanta Mayor Andrew Young; Executive Director Benjamin Hooks criticized as overzealous even the notorious prosecution of D.C. Mayor Marion Barry for perjury and drug possession); *see also* Farber, *U.S. Dismisses Charges Faced By Rep. Flake,* N.Y. Times, Apr. 4, 1991, at A1, col 3 (many blacks viewed case as latest example of selective prosecution against black elected officials); Kaplan & Miller, *Persecution or Prosecution?* NEWSWEEK, July 23, 1990, at 21 (enough high-profile cases make the perception of racial prosecution credible).

149. A. KARNIG & A. WELCH, BLACK REPRESENTATION AND URBAN POLICY 112 (1980); Reed, *Neo-Progressivism, supra* note 116, at 199; *see also* Applebome, *As a Mayor Returns, Atlanta Is Rich and Poor,* N.Y. Times, Jan. 7, 1990, at D4, col. 3 (black civic and political leaders claim Atlanta's black mayor Andrew Young "squandered" opportunity to help the poor, who are overwhelmingly black; Young "helped the rich get richer, but the poor just got poorer"; Young's record and agenda were not much different from that of Atlanta's white business-oriented mayors); *cf. infra* notes 199–214 and accompanying text.

150. *See* C. GREEN & B. WILSON, THE STRUGGLE FOR BLACK EMPOWERMENT IN NEW YORK CITY: BEYOND THE POLITICS OF PIGMENTATION 85–113 (1989); *cf.* R. FENNO, *supra* note 101, at 241 (House members believe that voters are "equally or more interested in using issue presentations as an opportunity to judge representative as a person"; treatment of persons, not issues, is centerpiece of representational relationship); M. JEWELL, *supra* note 117, at 14; W. RIKER, THE THEORY OF POLITICAL COALITIONS 207–8 (1962); Freedman, *One Struggle Over, Attention Turns to Guilt,* N.Y. Times, Oct. 29, 1989, at H5, col. 1 (black elected officials consumed by "cult of personality"); Marable, *supra* note 19, at 18, 20–21 ("post-black politicians," recruited from the professional classes, favor programs with little kinship to traditional civil rights agenda).

151. R. BROWNING, D. MARSHALL & D. TABB, PROTEST IS NOT ENOUGH: THE STRUGGLE OF BLACKS AND HISPANICS FOR EQUALITY IN URBAN POLITICS 56–61 (1984) ("access to mayor's office did not lead to full minority incorporation into city bureaucracy"); A. KARNIG & S. WELCH, *supra* note 78, at 14; C. STONE, REGIME POLITICS: GOVERNING ATLANTA, 1946–1988, at 242 (1989) (Atlanta white business interests secured place in governing coalition to safeguard special privilege; business elite exercised preemptive power over black middle-class politicians); Fainstein & Fainstein, *supra* note 85, at 189 (while black elected officials produce more government jobs and contracts for middle-class blacks, they fail to redirect government programs to benefit poor blacks); *see generally* Nelson & Van Horne, *Black Elected Administrators: The Trials of Office,* 34 PUB. ADMIN. REV. 526 (1974).

152. *See* Nelson & Van Horne, *supra* note 151, at 529. Even where elected from majority-black districts, black officials may be rewarded for individual achievement in unrelated fields. Gingles v. Edmisten, 590 F. Supp. 345 (E.D.N.C. 1984), *modified sub. nom.* Thornburg v. Gingles, 478 U.S. 30 (1986) (testimony at trial that only black

elected to county office was former football star in Wake County, North Carolina). They may be effective public speakers but not spokespersons. *See* telephone interview with Norman Lockman, black journalist in Wilmington, Delaware (May 22, 1990) (black city council members in Wilmington are social workers, not power brokers); interview with Jerome Mondesire, Chief of Staff for the Philadelphia office of Rep. William Gray (May 6, 1990) (blacks often elect blacks to celebrate a cause, not to advocate a legislative platform). They may become preoccupied with individual rather than group opportunity. *Id.; see also* THE NEW BLACK POLITICS, *supra* note 12, at 204 (Detroit mayor Coleman Young's political alliances and policy preferences shaped by patronage and economic gain, not community service). To the extent assimilation is a legal strategy for diffusing the redemptive force of citizen's movements, coopting local leadership, and ultimately maintaining existing power arrangements, it is inconsistent with the original aspirations of voting rights activists. *See generally* F. PIVEN & R. CLOWARD, POOR PEOPLE'S MOVEMENTS: WHY THEY SUCCEED, HOW THEY FAIL 181 (1979).

153. W. Singham, The Political Socialization of Marginal Groups (1966) (paper presented at American Political Science Association annual meeting), *cited in* S. CARMICHAEL & C. HAMILTON, *supra* note 16, at 15 n.4 (position within party hierarchy does not necessarily mean inclusion within decisionmaking process; blacks often "go along with all that talk" to make sure of continued access); *see also* S. CARMICHAEL & C. HAMILTON, *supra* note 16, at 12–14 (criticizing black elected officials who "play ball" to promote benefits of status and material gains for individual black constituents); R. KANTER, MEN AND WOMEN OF THE CORPORATION 208–9 (1977) (where minority group members are numerically dominated in a "skewed" grouping—less than 15% of an institution in which an overwhelming preponderance of another type is represented—they often have difficulty gaining peer acceptance and difficulty behaving "naturally"); C. SILBERMAN, CRISIS IN BLACK AND WHITE 204–6 (1964) (describing cooptation of black Chicago congressman).

154. Ackerman, *supra* note 129, at 735–37. Ackerman defines false consciousness as minority group members' belief in unfavorable group stereotypes. I use the term to refer to tokenism in which individual advancement defines empowerment. False consciousness rationalizes the privileged position of some minority group members. Ackerman's critique of a "social-psychological" approach to analyzing minority legislative power may simply reflect a differing view of false consciousness or the still primitive development of legal analysis of group processes.

155. Cohen, *Deliberation and Democratic Legitimacy,* in THE GOOD POLITY 17, 22–23 (A. Hamlin & P. Pettit eds. 1989); *see* Sturm, *Toward a Jurisprudence of Public Law Remedies,* 79 GEO. L. J. (1991). In shifting coalitions with no repeated and continual losers, all potential participants must be "acceptable role partners." S. KASSIN & L. WRIGHTSMAN, THE AMERICAN JURY ON TRIAL: PSYCHOLOGICAL PERSPECTIVES 172 (1988) (first component of dynamic deliberation is one of independence and equality; indeed, in context of jury deliberations, courts often exclude from service people who might exert disproportionate influence); W. RIKER, *supra* note 150, at 162.

156. *See, e.g.,* Lempert, *Uncovering "Nondiscernible" Differences: Empirical Research and the Jury-Size Cases,* 73 MICH. L. REV. 643, 679–80 (1975); Ballew v. Georgia, 435 U.S. 223, 232–34 & n.21 (1978) (likelihood of compromise important phenomenon for fulfillment of jury common sense function); S. KASSIN & L. WRIGHTSMAN,

supra note 155, at 173 (openness to informational influence is second component of deliberation ideal).

157. *See* S. KASSIN & L. WRIGHTSMAN, *supra* note 155, at 173; *see also* Allen v. United States, 164 U.S. 492, 501–2 (1896); Michelman, *Conceptions of Democracy, supra* note 132, at 448. I do not mean to imply, however, that all forms of pressure are coercive and necessarily opposed to honest interaction. Indeed, impassioned, personal, or dramatic appeals are consistent with fair political deliberation. *See, e.g.,* I. Young, Justice, Democracy and Group Difference 10 (Sept. 1, 1990) (unpublished manuscript prepared for presentation at American Political Science Association) (deliberative process does not require emotional detachment or rigorous adherence to specific rules of argumentation; formal rules of argument may silence just as much as physical, economic, or political domination).

158. *See, e.g.,* Jeffers v. Clinton, 730 F. Supp. 196 (E.D. Ark. 1989); Major v. Treen, 574 F. Supp. 325, 334 (E.D. La. 1983) (three-judge court) (black legislators excluded from critical redistricting meeting).

159. *See* Latanè, *Psychology of Social Impact,* 36 AM. PSYCHOLOGIST 343 (1981); Latanè & Wolf, *The Social Impact of Majorities and Minorities,* 88 PSYCHOLOGICAL REV. 438 (1981). Some of the most important research is in studies of juries. The process of jury deliberation reveals much about the group dynamics of managing minority and majority viewpoints, developing consensus, and respecting the contribution of individual members. *See, e.g.,* H. KALVEN & H. ZEISEL, THE AMERICAN JURY 462 (1966) (substantial minority viewpoint presence of 4 or 5 jurors out of 12 at beginning of deliberations usually necessary to influence jury outcome); S. KASSIN & L. WRIGHTSMAN, *supra* note 155, at 169–88).

160. Psychologists experimenting on the effect of group pressure in a deliberating body conclude that the presence of allies is critical to minority members' integrity and influence. *See* R. KANTER, *supra* note 153; Asch, *Effects of Group Pressure Upon the Modification and Distortion of Judgments,* in READINGS IN SOCIAL PSYCHOLOGY 2 (G. Swanson, T. Newcombe & E. Hartley eds. 1952); *see also* Williams v. Florida, 399 U.S. 78, 101–2 & n.49 (1970) (citing Asch's conformity experiments, Court reasons that in the context of jury deliberations, jurors in the minority are likely to be influenced by the proportional size of the majority aligned against them). *But cf.* S. KASSIN & L. WRIGHTSMAN, *supra* note 155, at 197 (it is the absolute, not proportional size that enables minorities to withstand normative pressure; the presence of a single ally is powerful determinant of ability to maintain independence).

161. Maass & Clark, *Hidden Impact of Minorities: Fifteen Years of Minority Influence Research,* 95 PSYCH. BULL. 428 (1984); Nemeth, *Differential Contributions of Majority and Minority Influence,* 93 PSYCHOLOGICAL REV. 25 (1986) (high degree of stress may affect performance among minority group members); Nemeth & Wachtler, *Creative Problem Solving as a Result of Majority vs. Minority Influence,* 13 EUROPEAN J. SOC. PSYCHOLOGY 45 (1983) (majority assumes differing minority is incorrect and manifests outright "derision" towards minority).

162. This is the view presented in recent legal and political science literature. Delgado, Dunn, Brown, Lee & Hubbert, *Fairness and Formality: Minimizing the Risk of Prejudice in Alternative Dispute Resolution,* 1985 WIS. L. REV. 1359, 1385–87; Lind, Thibaut & Walker, *A Cross-Cultural Comparison of the Effect of Adversary and Inquisitorial Processes on Bias in Legal Decisionmaking,* 62 VA. L. REV. 271 (1976);

Thibaut, Walker & Lind, *Adversary Presentation and Bias in Legal Decisionmaking*, 86 HARV. L. REV. 386 (1972). Yet, "it is also true that demands for order, quiet, and 'civility' can also protect racism against effective, passionate challenge." Letter from Frank Michelman to author (Dec. 19, 1990) at 4 (on file with author).

163. Delgado, *supra* note 95, at 305 n.30 (citing C. Pierce, Unity in Diversity: Thirty-Three Years of Stress, Solomon Carter Fuller Lectures, American Psychiatric Assn. Meeting, Washington, D.C. (May 12, 1986)) (describing microaggressions as those "subtle, minor, stunning automatic assaults . . . by which whites stress blacks unremittingly and keep them on the defensive, as well as in a psychologically reduced condition").

164. *See, e.g.,* Ballew v. Georgia, 435 U.S. 223, 231 n.10, 233 (1978) (citing social science literature). Progressively smaller groups are less likely to engage in effective deliberation. R. HASTIE, S. PENROD & N. PENNINGTON, INSIDE THE JURY 228 (1983) (members of small dissenting factions "participate at lower rates in majority rule juries and are less satisfied with the jury verdict"). *But cf.* W. RIKER, *supra* note 150, at 51, 55 (in small groups, "considerations of maintaining the solidarity of the group and the loyalty of members to it probably often dominate considerations of maximum victory"; local governing bodies "are often operated as small groups in which considerations of loyalty and local solidarity outweigh rational calculations of advantage"; for example, in the South the zero-sum gain is between whites inside the system and blacks outside of it).

165. Some commentators have noted that public voting may pressure group members to join the majority and generally to behave less cooperatively. *See* S. KASSIN & L. WRIGHTSMAN, *supra* note 155, at 203–4 (public ballot prompts "verdict-driven style" of deliberation; formal commitment to a position creates advocates, not factfinders); J. NAGEL, PARTICIPATION 72–75 (1987) (voting enables an internally conflicted group to act and recognizes that legitimate differences exist within it; yet where conflict persists, use of other adversary decision procedures besides majority rule voting may be less divisive; majority rule balloting may produce a permanent minority; more inclusive would be a rule of proportionate outcomes, distributing goods on the basis of the numerical strength of competing factions or other appropriations formula, or decisional lotteries).

166. *See, e.g.,* R. HASTIE, S. PENROD & N. PENNINGTON, *supra* note 164, at 228–30 (dissenting or minority viewpoints are disadvantaged by nonunanimity rules); S. KASSIN & L. WRIGHTSMAN, *supra* note155, at 201–2; M. SAKS, JURY VERDICTS (1977); Davis, Kerr, Atkin, Holt & Mech, *The Decision Processes of 6- & 12-Person Mock Juries Assigned Unanimous and Two-Thirds Majority Rules,* 32 J. PERSONALITY & SOC. PSYCH. 1 (1975); Nemeth, *Interactions Between Jurors as a Function of Majority Vs. Unanimity Decision Rules,* 7 J. APPLIED SOC. PSYCHOLOGY 38 (1977).

167. R. HASTIE, S. PENROD & N. PENNINGTON, *supra* note 164, at 112; *see also* Nemeth, *supra* note 166 (majority rule appears to suppress robust conflict, reduces the number of informational and opinion comments, shortens functional deliberation time, and undermines confidence in the outcome).

168. Some legislators resist alliance with minority group members because they fear their constituents will permanently identify them with "black" issues. *See, e.g.,* Polman, *"Black Party" Image Splits Democrats,* Phila. Inquirer, Jan. 14, 1990, at A1, col. 1 (white party activists complain that Philadelphia's Democratic Party is now seen by

white voters as the "black party" since the city's black mayor is a black Democrat); *see also* R. Kanter, *supra* note 153, at 209 (in racially imbalanced groups, racially dominant group controls both the group's culture as well as the group; proportional representation of the minority, or at least 35% minority representation, is necessary to empower a minority within a working group); F. Parker, *supra* note 98, at 135–36 (blacks have difficulty forming coalitions with white legislators on measures identified as black issues; bills identified with black caucus sponsors failed; only when white legislators take lead can blacks provide votes necessary to win).

169. *See* A. Karnig & S. Welch, *supra* note 78, at 14 (Blacks usually hold office as "one of a small minority unable to take decisive action—certainly not unilateral action."); *see also supra* notes 164–67.

170. The model described here is essentially a pluralist one, because it remains the dominant political science explanation of contemporary political participation. *See, e.g.,* B. Barber, *supra* note 90, at 143–44 (pluralist model of "mainstream American political science" relies on self-interested groups formulating and aggressively pursuing private interests within a framework of competitive legislative bargaining); D. Pinderhughes, *supra* note 5, at 253–55 (pluralist theory presumes equivalence between all political and economic demands, and incremental decisionmaking based on bargainable issues).

171. *See* W. Riker, *supra* note 150, at 179–80 (where blacks excluded by systematic agreement among whites, no whites defect; no white factions so dissatisfied as to attempt to bring blacks into controlling coalition; black participants unable to attract dissatisfied whites because of intense fear shared by all white participants that breakup of white hegemony would yield devastating results).

172. *See* W. Riker, *supra* note 150, at 95–96 (size principle reflects tendency of winning coalitions to minimize size in order to divide gains among fewer persons; role of minority opposition is to create value in coalition of the whole). Empirical studies suggest that black candidates frequently seek to create electoral coalitions with white liberals, but often fail. *See, e.g.,* R. Browning, D. Marshall & D. Tabb, *supra* note 151; *see also* Johnson, *supra* note 112, at 34, col. 2 (For blacks, the inevitable outcome of a rainbow coalition that does not emphasize black representation is that " 'black folks get all the rain and white folks get all the bows.' ") (quoting Thomas N. Todd); Holloway, *Negro Political Strategy: Coalition or Independent Power Politics?* 49 Soc. Sci. Q. 534 (1968); *cf.* S. Carmichael & C. Hamilton, *supra* note 16, at 7 (white groups solidify when confronted with black demands).

173. *See, e.g.,* C. Stone, *supra* note 151, at 8 (in the absence of coercion, achieving cooperation requires constant effort, most often through mechanisms to ensure reciprocity). Especially where they are also dependent on support from the white majority, coalitions between minority groups may also be tenuous and susceptible "to disintegration in the crucible of day-to-day governing." Hero, *Multiracial Coalitions, supra* note 123, at 349; *see also* Guinier, *supra* chapter 2 ("reciprocity in bargaining requires the active promotion of black interests, not just occasional subvention" of civil rights issues; "black legislative issues can be ghettoized from the Left as well as the Right").

174. *See* Matsuda, *supra* note 1, at 348 (volunteers from the ranks of the privileged can leave a cause with the same privilege of choice with which they joined); *supra* notes 168, 172; *see also* W. Martin, The Mind of Frederick Douglass 25 (1984) ("whites became abolitionists out of choice; blacks were abolitionists out of necessity").

175. *See, e.g.,* D. BELL, AND WE ARE NOT SAVED (1987); D. BELL, RACE, RACISM AND AMERICAN LAW (1980); Bell, Brown v. Board of Education *and the Interest-Convergence Dilemma,* 93 HARV. L. REV. 518 (1980).

176. *See, e.g.,* M.L. KING, JR., *supra* note 21, at 150; Rustin, *"Black" Power and Coalition Politics,* COMMENTARY, Sept. 1966, at 35; Rustin, *From Protest to Politics: The Future of the Civil Rights Movement,* COMMENTARY, Feb. 1965, at 25. Dr. King consistently acknowledged the importance of coalition building. M.L. KING, JR., STRIDE TOWARD FREEDOM 34 (1958); T. BRANCH, *supra* note 11, at 875; 884 (quoting Walter Reuther).

177. C. STONE, *supra* note 151, at xi–xii (electoral coalition not equivalent of governing coalition; political regime dependent on getting strategically positioned people to act together); Hero, *Multiracial Coalitions, supra* note 123, at 343; *see also* B. FERMAN, GOVERNING THE UNGOVERNABLE CITY (1985); J. MOLLENKOPF, THE CONTESTED CITY (1983); T. SWANSTROM, THE CRISIS OF GROWTH POLITICS (1985) (arguing importance of coalition building and political struggle).

178. Some nationalists anticipated the arguments advanced here. *See* S. CARMICHAEL & C. HAMILTON, *supra* note 16, at 173–77 (mere election of a few blacks will not solve problem of political representation; black visibility within present institutions of political representation is not black power).

179. F. PARKER, *supra* note 98, at 136, 147 (black representation limited by number of majority-black legislative districts); Note, *Law and Racial Geography: Public Housing and the Economy in New Orleans,* 42 STAN. L. REV. 1251, 1265 nn.79–80 (1990) [hereinafter Note, *Racial Geography*] (black physical/geographic solidarity necessary for political power). *But cf.* Gomez v. City of Watsonville, 852 F.2d 1186 (9th Cir. 1988) (for geographically dispersed minority living in pockets of residential segregation, minority districts may not capture all, or even most, minority voters; those outside the district are merely "virtually" represented). *Compare* Gingles v. Edmisten, 590 F. Supp. 345, 383 (E.D.N.C. 1984), *modified sub. nom.* Thornburg v. Gingles, 478 U.S. 30 (1986) (no judicially manageable way to measure black influence in majority-white districts). In a residentially segregated community, district elections use a territorially defined constituency as a proxy for interest representation. The use of single-member districts is also premised on the "ubiquity of territorially based representation in American government"; *see* F. Michelman, Justice Marshall's *Bolden* Dissent 9 (Nov. 28, 1990 draft) (unpublished manuscript).

180. A. KARNIG & S. WELCH, *supra* note 78, at 29. Most research reveals significant links between district elections and greater black electoral success. *See, e.g.,* Davidson, *supra* note 59, at 5–6; *see also* Campbell & Feagin, *Black Politics in the South: A Descriptive Analysis,* 37 J. POL. 129, 143 n.28 (1975); Engstrom & McDonald, *The Election of Blacks to City Councils: Clarifying the Impact of Electoral Arrangements on the Seats/Population Relationship.* 75 AM. POL. SCI. REV. 344 (1981); Gelb, *Blacks, Blocs and Ballots,* 3 POLITY 45 (1970); Jones, *The Impact of Local Election Systems on Black Political Representation,* 11 URB. AFF. Q. 345 (1976); Karnig, *Black Representation on City Councils,* 12 URB. AFF. Q. 223, 223 (Dec. 1976); Karnig, *Black Resources and City Council Representation,* 41 J. POL. 134 (1979); Kramer, *The Election of Blacks to City Councils: A 1970 Status Report and a Prolegomenon,* 1 J. BLACK STUD. 443, 449 (1971); Robinson & Dye, *Reformism and Black Representation on City Councils,* 59 SOC. SCI. Q. 133, 133–34 (1978); Taebel, *Minority Repre-*

sentation on City Councils: The Impact of Structure on Blacks and Hispanics, 59
Soc. Sci. Q. 142, 151 (1978).

181. *See, e.g.,* F. Parker, *supra* note 98 (single-member districts dramatically increased
number of black elected officials in Mississippi); S. Welch & T. Bledsoe, Urban
Reform and Its Consequences 35–36, 42–46, 50 (1984) (district electoral system
helps new urban forces of ethnic-minorities, neighborhood-based groups, and those
groups most spatially segregated, such as blacks, to balance political power of conservative urban organizations; at-large systems disproportionately favor those with
greater financial resources); *cf.* Ackerman, *supra* note 129, at 726–28 (discrete, insular minorities enjoy district-based organizing advantages).

182. As generally used, the term "gerrymandering" refers to political manipulation that
unfairly excludes or disadvantages a distinctive group within the process of drawing
district boundaries. *See* Gomillion v. Lightfoot, 364 U.S. 338 (1960) (classic gerrymander altered municipal boundaries, created uncouth 28-sided figure and removed
all but 4 blacks from city limits); McDonald & Engstrom, *Detecting Gerrymandering,* in Political Gerrymandering and the Courts 178 (B. Grofman ed. 1990).

183. Deliberative or "legislative gerrymander" is a term suggested to me by my col-
league Seth Kreimer to describe deliberate exclusion and diminution of black legislators from critical policymaking meetings or from sharing critical appropriations
authority.

184. A. Thernstrom, *supra* note 53, at 7; Schuck, *What Went Wrong With the Voting
Rights Act,* Wash, Monthly, Nov. 1987, at 51, 55; Thernstrom, *"Voting Rights" Trap,*
New Republic, Sept. 2, 1985, at 21, 23. This same argument was made by congressional opponents to the 1982 amendments. *See* S. Rep. No. 417, 97th Cong., 2d Sess.
103 (additional views of Sen. Orrin Hatch) (arguing that majority-black single-
member district would be nothing more than "political ghettos for minorities" in
which "minority influence [would] suffer enormously").

185. Thernstrom, *supra* note 53, at 21.

186. For example, Abrams promotes minority sponsored white candidates, elected from
within a geographically splintered districting plan, to represent blacks. But these
representatives may experience, despite the multiracial nature of their constituency,
the same hostility from their colleagues as do black representatives. As a result, such
coalition candidates may fail to advocate aggressively on behalf of their least popular,
namely black, constituents. Instead, they may compromise the needs of the more
stigmatized members of their electoral base in order to obtain any success on behalf
of the coalition. *See* J. Conyers & W. Wallace, *supra* note 80, at 144–45 (some black
officials elected by multiracial coalitions feel obligation to satisfy white constituents).

   For Abrams, the "generation of cooperative political behavior" is independent of
black representation, and a development that voting rights enforcement should pursue without prerequisites. This unwillingness to recognize the polarization hypothesis undermines her otherwise important contribution.

187. For blacks, in whose embryonic political life each gain has been both hard fought and
ultimately evaded, special protection from normal political behavior is considered
necessary before they can answer the question Abrams asks—"How do those who
exert themselves effectively within the system behave?" Abrams, *supra* note 6, at 490
n.218. Without structural support to protect blacks from majority prejudice and to
ensure effective representation of black interests, Abrams' interactive model of political influence is indeterminate and inaccessible.

188. Informed by the value of civic inclusion, Karlan's vision of voting rights litigation is interactive like Abrams' but more committed to minority sponsored representation. Karlan, *supra* note 6, at 218 (promoting diversity of representation to ensure fuller deliberation based on a richer perspective and to legitimate the governing body as a democratic instrument).

189. Karlan attempts to answer the wrong question: whether blacks are better off with several mildly sympathetic whites or one aggressive "black" representative. In casting her vote with the "authentic" black representative, Karlan maneuvers around the implications of the deliberative gerrymander. For Karlan, a process in which black voters elect black representatives who fail, because of majority prejudice or minority cooptation, to advocate forcefully on behalf of their constituents can still be a fair process as long as black representatives are allowed to participate within legislative deliberation and dialogue.

190. Abrams denies its influence on voter choice. Karlan understands profoundly the pervasiveness of polarization within the electorate, and she also takes important preliminary steps to address structural barriers that deny black representatives civic legislative inclusion. Karlan, *supra* note 6, at 237–48 (discussing supermajority decisional rules and the rotation of powers as potential remedies to legislative exclusion). But Karlan still tends to measure success by the number of blacks elected. Although Karlan acknowledges the Voting Rights Act's goal to reconstruct society, a civically inclusive society would be more open, more accessible, but not necessarily more equal. Legislative inclusion, although critical, does not produce equal outcomes dependably, especially when relying primarily on the ameliorative role of familiar, intimate association in small, collegial decisionmaking bodies. *Id.* at 240: "[W]hile the claim for equal political access is always legitimate, the claim for a particular substantive outcome to the governing process is not."

191. *See* Hamilton, *Public Policy and Some Political Consequences,* in PUBLIC POLICY FOR THE BLACK COMMUNITY, *supra* note 13, at 237; *see also Extension of the Voting Rights Act: Hearings on H.R. 3112 Before the Subcomm. on Civil and Constitutional Rights of the House Judiciary Comm.,* 97th Cong., 1st Sess. 365–80 (1982) (testimony of Henry Marsh, Mayor, Richmond, Va., and Michael Brown, Coordinator, Va. St. Conf. of NAACP); *id.* at 590–742 (testimony of Laughlin McDonald, Director, Southern Regional Office, ACLU); J. Ely, *supra* note 42, at 86–87; D. GLASGOW, THE BLACK UNDERCLASS: POVERTY, UNEMPLOYMENT, AND ENTRAPMENT OF GHETTO YOUTH 22 (1980). Thus, membership in the "victimized" group suggests a special sensitivity and loyalty to a victim perspective. T. BRANCH, *supra* note 11, at 895; S. WELCH & T. BLEDSOE, *supra* note 181, at 23 (issue of concern to most black city council members appears to be civil rights); Matsuda, *supra* note 1, at 326, 333–35 (black Americans are the paradigm victim group of our history with distinct normative insights); Morris, *supra* note 111, at 277.

192. *See, e.g.,* F. PARKER, *supra* note 98, at 134–35; *see also* Applebome, *King Holiday Observances Point Out Both Pain and Triumphs,* N.Y. Times, Jan. 16, 1990, at B4, col. 1 (first black mayor of New York City greeted marchers observing the Martin Luther King, Jr., National Holiday, while marchers critical of white predecessor had been stopped by barricades holding them at the edge of City Hall Park; quoting march leader, "Today we marched as the included. The last time we marched in protest. Today we march to participate."). The core idea of the black advocacy perspective is that doing something about the problem of racial discrimination means

attention to issues from the perspective of those experiencing discriminatory conditions. Freeman, *supra* note 7, at 98; *see also* Ackerman, *supra* note 129, at 733 n.35, 735, 744–45.

193. L. COLE, *supra* note 111, at 114, 233. Black representatives themselves acknowledged special insights. "If you are a minority person you know what's needed. And what you do is go about the business of trying to fill that need." *Id.* at 89.

194. M. JEWELL, REPRESENTATION IN STATE LEGISLATURES 94 (1982) (black constituents do have special relation to black representatives, who represent a broader constituency than electoral district); *see also* Gingles v. Edmisten, 590 F. Supp. 345 (E.D.N.C. 1984), *modified subnom.* Thornburg v. Gingles, 478 U.S. 30 (1986) (trial testimony of Frank Ballance; black in North Carolina considered his own representative in the 1950s to be Harlem's black congressman Adam Clayton Powell, Jr.). J. ABERBACH & J. WALKER, RACE IN THE CITY (1973); Sears, *Black Attitudes Toward the Political System in the Aftermath of the Watts Insurrection,* 13 MIDWEST J. POL. SCI. 515 (1969) (blacks believe that black elected officials more trustworthy than white elected officials); *see also* Jeffers v. Clinton, 730 F. Supp. 196 (E.D. Ark. 1989), *modified* 756 F. Supp. 1195, *affd.* 111 S. Ct. 662 (1991) (three-judge court) (some white state legislators refer black constituents from their electoral districts to black legislators representing other areas); L. COLE, *supra* note 111, at 109, 111; Lee, *The Black Elected Official and Southern Politics,* in THE BLACK POLITICIAN *supra* note 50, at 85–86 (black elected official effective because of identification with frustrations of blacks who "know what it feels like to want someone in government who can be trusted"). *But cf.* Joint Center for Political and Economic Studies, FOCUS MAGAZINE, TRENDLETTER, 2 (Apr. 1988) (reporting results of 1987 Gallup survey) (blacks write letters and lobby to a much lesser extent than whites).

195. *See e.g.* C. Hamilton, *Measuring Black Conservatism,* in THE STATE OF BLACK AMERICA 47–51 (ed. J.D. Williams 1982); Seltzer & Smith, *Race and Ideology: A Research Note Measuring Liberalism and Conservatism in Black America,* 46 PHYLON 98 (1985); Welch & Combs, *Interracial Differences in Opinion on Public Issues in the 1970's,* 7 WEST. J. BLACK STUD. 136 (1983). Black voting patterns reflect near unanimity in contests in which a viable black candidate competes and in presidential contests in which blacks overwhelmingly support the Democratic candidate. *See* T. CAVANAGH, INSIDE BLACK AMERICA (1985).

196. *See* Thornburg v. Gingles, 478 U.S. 30, 51, 57 n.25 (1986) (black representatives are those black-community-sponsored candidates whose election reflects the community's "distinctive minority group interests"); S. WELCH & T. BLEDSOE, *supra* note 181, at 23 (civil rights is issue of concern to most black city council members). Some social science studies tend to support the assumption of consensus. *See* R. BROWNING, D. MARSHALL & D. TABB, *supra* note 151; N. NIE, S. VERBA & J. PETROCIK, THE CHANGING AMERICAN VOTER 253–55 (1979) (no other group as distinctly liberal as blacks as a group in terms of position on central issues).

197. *See* Herring, *Legislative Responsiveness to Black Constituents in Three Deep South States,* 52 J. POL. 740 (1990); Marable, *Foreword* to THE NEW BLACK VOTE, *supra* note 38, at 1; Morris, *supra* note 111, at 271. *But cf.* Bullock, *Congressional Roll Call Voting in a Two-Party South,* 66 SOC. SCI. Q. 789 (1985); Whitby, *Effects of the Interaction Between Race and Urbanization on Votes of Southern Congressmen,* 10 LEGIS. STUD. Q. 505 (1985).

198. A. KARNIG & S. WELCH, *supra* note 78, at 13–14 (some people have clung to unrealistic hopes about black elected "supermen and superwomen" who could "cure the ills of three centuries overnight").
199. *See generally* Reed, *supra* note 4, at 67; Austin, *supra* note 88; J. Bond, Winning the Ballot, Losing the War: The Paradox of Minority Empowerment, HARV. C.R.-C.L. L. REV. Symposium, Mar. 3, 1990, at 3 (transcript on file with author) (lack of mobilized constituency base to provide "will" for change causes black elected officials to limit their agenda; in addition, class of locally elected black officials has been captured by black entrepreneurs rather than black community based activists).
200. A. KARNIG & S. WELCH, *supra* note 78, at 14; *see also* D. PINDERHUGHES, *supra* note 48, at 109 (to serve constituents' interests black politicians in Chicago in the first decades of this century faced paradox of highlighting issues that provoke strong resistance from other organized groups).
201. This is consistent with game theories of leadership incentives. *See, e.g.,* W. RIKER, *supra* note 150, at 203–8 (pluralist system devises reward structure that encourages opportunism; system prefers leaders who want absolute power, prestige and maintenance of position). The benefits of incumbency may insulate the beneficiary from electoral pressure, undermining the assumption that electoral ratification ensures substantive policy advocacy. Abrams, *supra* note 6, at 487 n.214; *see* W. RIKER, *supra* note 150, at 207–8. The promotion of professional political careers, exemplified in the 98% reelection rate of incumbents to Congress, affects white as well as black politicians; but then whites' expectation for government attention is lower. Even within state legislatures, the trend is toward longer tenure and professionalization of their positions. *See* M. JEWELL, *supra* note 117, at 5.
202. This is similar to the critique of the message conveyed by black middle-class success as that of individual advancement at the expense of social and group consciousness.
203. *But cf.* S. WELCH & T. BLEDSOE, *supra* note 181, at 24 (black city council members appear more conscious of constituents and are more likely than whites to schedule regular meetings with them; casework may simply be more important to more needy black constituents).
204. *See* Barnett, *supra* note 13, at 41 ("hodge-podge of well-meaning but limited social programs [cannot] actually end poverty"). White ethnic groups are often cited as successful models for political empowerment. But these groups used politics to legitimize and enhance preexisting social and economic assimilation. They viewed political participation as a primary means of assisting and facilitating the redistribution of economic and social goods that was already ongoing. *See* J. ELY, *supra* note 42, at 80–81; Barnes, *supra* note 108, at 264 (difference in assimilation for whites and blacks is that "other ethnic groups haven't felt as deprived socially and economically as the blacks," (quoting Professor Seymour Lipset, Stanford University)); *cf.* Pohlmann, *Race-Ethnicity and Society* (Book Review), 105 POL. SCI. Q. 165 (1990) (urban political machines had diminished as assimilation agents when racial minorities attempted to press for political power). White ethnic groups, who were not as deprived socially and economically as are blacks, relied on politics for symbolic status recognition, not wealth redistribution. Barnes, *supra* note 108, at 264 ("What these other groups were looking for is sort of symbolic status recognition—'We've made it in America.' The blacks are looking for more," (quoting Professor Lipset)).

205. Blacks are concentrated in inner cities in which, as a result of continued white prejudice and white flight, the resident "managerial" class of politicians administer a declining tax base in a crime infected urban environment. *Cf.* Freedman, *supra* note 150, at H5, col. 1 (black elected officials, with few exceptions, have become bureaucrats and caretakers).

206. Some black activists, consistent with their protest roots and civil rights philosophy, have begun to promote a black political agenda of resource allocation that suggests certain social goods—health care, housing—are recognized as basic entitlements. *See* Hamilton, *supra* note 12, at xix–xx; *cf.* Cavanaugh, *South Politics After Super Tuesday* (rights to basic social services an integral part of public policy in other industrial democracies). Many of these programs would also benefit poor whites, although a black agenda might target spending as "reparations" or geographically to benefit majority-black, inner city neighborhoods.

207. A. Glazer, K. Brace, B. Norrander, R. Griffin, V. Campagna, D. Brady & L. Handley, *Three Variations on a Theme by V.O. Key: Race and Politics, Race and Politics, and* (the ever popular) *Race and Politics* (paper presented at Annual Meeting of Am. Pol. Sci. Assn., Sept. 1988) (describing decline of class and the rise of race as fundamental cleavage line in American politics).

208. (*See, e.g.,* Miller & Stokes, *Constituency Influence in Congress,* 57 Am. Pol. Sci. Rev. 45 (1963).

209. This is consistent with political science literature finding incentives for individual members of Congress to respond disproportionately to constituent monitoring. *See* Fitts, *The Vices of Virtue: A Political Party Perspective on Civic Virtue Reforms of the Legislative Process,* 136 U. Pa. L. Rev. 1567, 1605–7 (1988).

210. Contemporary empirical evidence suggests that most voters are ignorant of their representatives' policy preferences and are insufficiently motivated even to participate in elections. *See, e.g.,* Preston, *Black Politics and Public Policy in Chicago: Constituent Representation,* in The New Black Politics, *supra* note 12, at 167; Polman, *U.S. Election Fund Drops as Public Abstains,* Phila. Inquirer, July 29, 1990, at A1, col. 1; *Primary Results: Setting the Stage for November,* N.Y. Times, June 7, 1990, at B6, col. 3; Reinhold, *As Primary Victor, Feinstein Becomes Democrats' Hope,* N.Y. Times, June 7, 1990, at B6, col. 1; *see also* Oreskes, *Low Voter Turnout, supra* note 105, at B16, col. 4.

211. *See generally* M. Olson, The Logic of Collective Action (1971).

212. Empirical observations about the electoral process suggest the electorate is guided not by enforcing representative responsibility—the classic view that electoral ratification is the main technique for holding the representative responsible—but by vague moods about public policy in general. *See, e.g.,* Eulau, *Changing Views of Representation,* in The Politics of Representation 49–50 (H. Eulah & J. Wahlke eds. 1978); Wahlke, *Policy Demands and System Support: The Role of the Represented,* in *id.* at 74–75 (few citizens think about, communicate, inform themselves or are interested in legislative functioning and do not realize that voting is an opportunity for making policy demands or choices). Spokesmodels, for example, reflect the growing involvement of elected representatives in candidate-centered activities, promoting personal trust rather than an issue-based reason for voting. *See supra* note 150. Thus, even if black election turnout exceeds that of their socioeconomic cohorts, voting for a candidate, without more finely tuned issue identification, pro-

vides primarily symbolic ratification. Electoral ratification is also an empty gesture if the representative does not seek reelection or faces only token opposition or opposition that does not focus on the representative's record. Of course, some political theorists would argue that the failure to vote, or to cast an educated vote reflects contentment with the status quo, and performs the same function as extended political participation might.

213. C. STONE, *supra* note 151, at 205–7, 241 (challenge for black politics is finding a way to bring the poor into a coalition of the white business leadership and the black middle class; instead of promoting redistribution toward equality, Atlanta governing coalition of middle-class blacks and white business elites perpetuates inequality).

214. C. STONE, *supra* note 151, at 189–91, 195, 216 (selective incentives and business control shape Atlanta governing coalition; effectiveness of business centered civic network possible because voter contact shallow and ephemeral); Nelson *supra* note 14, (black regimes adopt "corporate center" development strategy that undermines reform platform); Reed, *The Black Urban Regime, supra* note 116, (political institutions and entrenched patterns of political behavior constrain black mayors' impact on budgetary allocations, including service delivery patterns and composition of public employment; black regimes unable to affect high levels of poverty and unemployment); Reed, *Neo-Progressivism, supra* note 116, at 212–13 (proposals to reformulate allocative element of business development agenda to include niche for blacks are not redistributive; consensus around development policy derives from political processes in which interests of black poor are not represented).

215. *Cf.* Baker, *Neutrality, Process, and Rationality: Flawed Interpretation of Equal Protection,* 58 TEXAS L. REV. 1029, 1044–45, 1048–50 (1980) (process-based approach does not require equalization of political influence; decisions to continue subordination of minorities can occur even if political process considers their interests); Tribe, *The Puzzling Persistence of Process-Based Constitutional Theories,* 89 YALE L.J. 1063, 1077 (1980) (protecting minorities requires theory of substantive rights).

216. By "equal recognition," I mean equal status as full participants in politics. *See* Baker, *supra* note 215, at 1079 (describing equality of respect model).

217. Beitz, *Equal Opportunity in Political Representation,* in EQUAL OPPORTUNITY 155, 167–68 (N. Bowie ed. 1988) (any satisfactory doctrine of political equality must simultaneously address three concerns of democratic decisionmaking about public policy: (1) its value by virtue of public cooperative enterprise, (2) the content of legislation it produces, and (3) its contribution to political education of its citizens). The ultimate aim would be the promotion of just legislation:

> Although it may be too much to expect that by manipulating the structure of representation just legislation can be systematically promoted, it may at least be possible to minimize some of the familiar dangers to which representation schemes have historically been prone. . . . [especially] the danger that the majority in the legislature will pay too little attention to the interests and rights of popular minorities.

Id. Young, *Polity and Group Difference: A Critique of the Ideal of Universal Citizenship,* 99 ETHICS 250, 261 (1989) ("[A] democratic public . . . should provide mechanisms for the effective representation and recognition of the distinct voices and perspectives of [disadvantaged constituent groups].").

Chapter 4. No Two Seats

1. H.R. Rep. No. 439, 89th Cong., 1st Sess. 53, *reprinted in* 1965 U.S.C.C.A.N. 2437, 2482.
2. Id. at 37, *reprinted in* 1965 U.S.C.C.A.N. 2466.
3. 115 Cong. Rec. 5520, 5531 (1970) (Joint Views of Ten Members of the Senate Judiciary Committee, including Senator Hart, one of the original sponsors of the 1965 Act). See also 121 Cong. Rec. 24,720 (1975) (remarks of Sen. Tunney) (stating that when blacks get equal access to the political process, they will "hold [ ] their heads up higher . . . [and feel] more a part of the system. They [will] feel their Government is more responsive to them.").
4. U.S. Comm'n on Civil Rights, The Voting Rights Act: Ten Years After 8 (1975).
5. See Metro Broadcasting v. FCC, 110 S. Ct. 2997, 3019 (1990) (citing voting rights cases that "operate on the assumption that minorities have particular viewpoints and interests worthy of protection"). Both the statutory and the constitutional right have come to embrace a group sense of the right to vote. See, e.g., Davis v. Bandemer, 478 U.S. 109, 124-25 (1986); Thornburg v. Gingles, 478 U.S. 30, 48-51 (1986); *Reynolds,* 377 U.S. at 576; Terry v. Adams, 345 U.S. 461, 463-64 (1953). But cf. Daniel H. Lowenstein, Bandemer's Gap: Gerrymandering and Equal Protection, *in* Political Gerrymandering and the Courts 64, 72 (Bernard Grofman ed., 1990) (arguing that in early reapportionment cases the constitutional right to vote was an individual and personal right and that the fair and effective representation language did not announce a constitutional right but a legitimate state purpose).

   Whatever the source and scope of the constitutional right, it is clear that the statutory right with which I am concerned is a group right. See infra notes 61–62. Under section 5 of the Act, for example, the inquiry "focuses ultimately on 'the position of racial minorities with respect to their effective exercise of the electoral franchise.' " United Jewish Orgs. v. Carey, 430 U.S. 144, 164 (1977) (quoting Beer v. United States, 425 U.S. 130, 141 (1976)). Because the political process comprehends more than the ballot box and the formal right to enter the polling place, nonrepresentation for any group of voters is the evil to be eradicated where the claims are brought by plaintiffs whose influence on the "political[process as a whole" is "consistently degrade[d]." *Davis,* 478 U.S. at 132. In this way, both the constitutional and the statutory claims are ultimately reconciled.

   Under the Constitution, the Court has explained the consequences of electoral exclusion in terms of the black community's inability to address its policy concerns within the legislature:

   > [E]lected officials . . . have been unresponsive and insensitive to the needs of the black community, which increases the likelihood that the political process was not equally open to blacks. This evidence ranged from the effects of past discrimination which still haunt the county courthouse to the infrequent appointment of blacks to county boards and committees; the overtly discriminatory pattern of paving county roads; the reluctance of the county to remedy blacks complaints, which forced blacks to take legal action to obtain school and grand jury desegregation; and the role played by the County Commissioners in the incorporation of an all-white private school to which they donated public funds for the purchase of band uniforms.

   Rogers v. Lodge, 458 U.S. 613, 625–26 (1982) (footnote omitted).
6. As laudable as the statement of the political equality norm is, it nevertheless remains

an incomplete definition of political equality generally. For example, it fails to account directly for inequality in politically relevant private resources or in access to public resources. On the other hand, the statutory scheme does consider that such inequalities are not distributed randomly, but tend to be disproportionately associated with those suffering the legacies of past discrimination. See S. Rep. No. 417, 97th Cong., 2d Sess. 29, *reprinted in* 1982 U.S.C.C.A.N. 177, 206–7.

7. As one senator put it:

> [t]he importance of the right to vote is recognized by those who want to participate in the democratic process and by those who have so bitterly and persistently opposed that participation. *Both sides realize that the vote for any minority means some degree of significant political power—power that will lead to better lives.*

116 Congress Rec. 6,642 (1970) (remarks of Sen. Tydings) (emphasis added).

8. I focus on city and county governing bodies because their tradition of experimentation and innovation, the absence of monitoring by intermediaries (such as local television stations with regional, as opposed to municipal, audiences), the desirability of bottom-up rather than top-down approaches to empowerment, and the existence of actual examples as a result of contemporary voting rights litigation make local governing bodies the appropriate unit of analysis. Many of my conclusions, however, may apply at the state and federal level.

9. I derive these goals from the statute's legislative and contemporaneous political history. Although these empowerment objectives focus on the goals of government from the perspective of minority representation or oppressed minority interests, they mirror to some extent the majority group's perspective of traditional goals of government. See generally Robert Dixon, Democratic Representation: Reapportionment in Law and Politics 23–57 (1968) (discussing various theories of representative government).

10. The "discrete and insular minority" problem is used here to refer to a legislative minority against whom members of the majority, even within the legislature and often simply reflecting the outlook of their constituents, are prejudiced. See United States v. Carolene Prods. Co., 304 U.S. 144, 152 n.4 (1938).

11. Rojas v. Victoria Indep. School Dist., Civ. A. No. V-87-16, 1988 U.S. Dist. LEXIS 11049 (S.D. Tex. Mar. 29, 1988), aff'd, 490 U.S. 1001 (1989). The Department of Justice did not object under the Voting Rights Act to this change on the grounds that the "change did not affect the range of matters over which the school board could make decisions. Nor did it affect the power of individual members to influence those decisions, since decisions of the board required a majority vote both before and after the change." Brief for the United States as Amicus Curiae Supporting Appellants at 18 n.7, Presley v. Etowah County Comm'n, Nos. 90-711 & 90-712; 1991 U.S. LEXIS 4190 (U.S. Sept. 20, 1991).

12. Major v. Treen, 574 F. Supp. 325, 334, 353–55 & n.39 (E.D. La. 1983) (three-judge court). I use this example even though it draws on the experience of black representatives in a state legislature because, as one of plaintiffs' trial counsel, I had unusual access to internal legislative documents and testimony. Moreover, it reinforces the extent of the problem of minority legislative exclusion even where a committee structure and more formal rules apply.

13. Nomination of William Bradford Reynolds to be Associate Attorney General of the United States: Hearings Before the Comm. on the Judiciary, 99th Cong., 1st Sess. 440 (1985) (reporting testimony of Lawrence Chehardy, a local tax accessor, alleging

these comments to have been made by State Rep. Charles Emile Bruneau of New Orleans).

14. Mack v. Russell County, No. 90-712 (M.D. Ala. Aug. 1, 1990), prob. juris. noted, 111 S. Ct. 2007 (1991).

15. Lisa Foderaro, At Vassar, Expanded Role for Blacks at Commencement, N.Y. Times, May 13, 1991, at B6.

16. Isabel Wilkerson, Separate Senior Proms Reveal an Unspanned Racial Divide, N.Y. Times, May 5, 1991, §1, at A36.

17. The stability claim also relates to the proposition that majority rule maximizes the number of people who can exercise self-determination in collective decisions—that majority rule permits more people to live under the laws they desire. See Robert A. Dahl, Democracy and Its Critics 138–39 (1989). I refer to this as the accountability claim. See infra note 19 and accompanying text.

18. This is essentially the Condorcet principle. See Marquis de Condorcet, Essay on the Application of Mathematics to the Theory of Decision-making, *in* Condorcet: Selected Writings 33 (Keith Michael Baker ed., 1976) (1785); see also Jeremy Waldron, Rights and Majorities: Rousseau Revisited, in Majorities and Minorities: Nomos XXXII (John W. Chapman & Alan Wertheimer eds., 1990) at 63–64 (stating that if issue is one where rational argument is possible, dynamics of argument may sustain average competence at a level where Condorcet's theorem produces favorable results). Closely related to the efficiency assumption is the view that majority rule is "morally reliable." See e.g., Elaine Spitz, Majority Rule at 149, 151, 157 (1984). As a result, majority rule is able to sustain cohesion, maximize rationality, and simultaneously ensure action. Id. at xiv.

19. The electoral accountability component represents the historical roots of majority rule as a Revolutionary War–era challenge to England's power to legislate for the American Colonies. See Gordon S. Wood, The Creation of the American Republic 1776–1787, at 162–63 (1969); see also Ian Shapiro, Three Fallacies Concerning Majorities, Minorities, and Democratic Politics *in* Majorities and Minorities: Nomos XXXII 79 (John W. Chapman & Alan Wertheimer eds., 1990) (referencing some historical purposes of majority rule).

20. 377 U.S. 533 (1964).

21. See, e.g., Lucas v. Forty-Fourth General Assembly of Colorado, 377 U.S. 713, 748 (1964) (Stewart, J., dissenting); James V. Blacksher & Larry T. Menefee, From *Reynolds v. Sims* to *City of Mobile v. Bolden:* Have the White Suburbs Commandeered the Fifteenth Amendment? 34 Hastings L.J. 1, 5–17, 64 (1982). I would argue, however, that *Reynolds v. Sims* simply voided minority rule, meaning a system in which a minority actually decides a majority of the decisions, without necessarily constitutionalizing a particular decisionmaking alternative. See Reynolds v. Sims, 377 U.S. 533, 568–69 (1964).

22. The assertion that majority rule does not exist comes from two distinct areas of economics: public choice theory and social choice theory. Although public choice theorists do not explicitly argue that a majority cannot exist, they contend that special interest groups are able to organize and block out the will of the majority. See Robert A. Dahl, A Preface to Democratic Theory 124–31 (1956); Mancur Olson, The Logic of Collective Action 143–44 (2d ed. 1971); Gary Becker, A Theory of Competition Among Pressure Groups for Political Influence, 98 Q.J. Econ. 371, 392 (1983). In

contrast, social choice theorists argue that there is no such thing as a majority in a democratic system. They suggest that whenever at least three individuals are voting on at least three options, a well-defined majority preference does not necessarily exist. Although one option may win, over time these different options are merely recycled. See Kenneth Arrow, Social Choice and Individual Values 2–3 (1951); Condorcet, supra note 18, at 43–48. The implication of both is that the majority does not rule. Public choice and social choice theory may be powerful analytical tools in other contexts, but I would argue that neither theory accounts for the discrete and insular minority problem documented by empirical evidence. See also Michael Fitts, The Vices of Virtue: A Political Party Perspective on Civic Virtue Reforms of the Legislative Process, 136 U. Pa. L. Rev. 1567, 1616 & n.163 (1988) (collecting political science and economic sources challenging the existence of true majority preference or stable majority-rule outcomes).

23. I use the terms "legitimate" and "legitimacy" throughout this chapter to describe the extent to which a process follows valid rules to produce results that, even from the perspective of adversely affected parties, are acceptable because of the perceived fairness of the process. This claim of legitimacy is based on a procedural conception of justice, which raises the question of whether officials have a reason for implementing a certain decision, not whether the decision itself is justified on the merits. See Thomas Christiano, Political Equality, *in* Majorities and Minorities: Nomos XXXII 150, 171–74 (J. Chapman & A. Wertheimer eds., 1990). Procedural justice defends majoritarian procedures not because they necessarily produce substantively just outcomes, but because the process of decisionmaking itself helps legitimate the outcome. Id. at 174–75. But cf. Anthony Cook, The Postmodern Quest for Community: An Introduction to a Symposium on Republicanism and Voting Rights, 41 U. Fla. L. Rev. 409, 411 (1989) (emphasis on process assumes substantive value choices); Heidi Hurd, Challenging Authority, 100 Yale L.J. 1611, 1665 (1991) (procedural theory of justice collapses into substantive theory of justice). Consequently, procedural fairness requires structuring political institutions or allocating political power through laws that "provide a just framework within which the diverse political groups in our society may fairly compete." Washington v. Seattle School Dist., 458 U.S. 457, 470 (1982) (quoting Hunter v. Erikson, 393 U.S. 385, 393 (1965)); see also Alan Howard & Bruce Howard, The Dilemma of the Voting Rights Act—Recognizing the Emerging Political Equality Norm, 83 Colum. L. Rev. 1615, 1619 (1983) (arguing that the legitimacy of law is a function of the fairness of the process creating it and that a law can be legitimate only where all eligible voters have an equal and fair chance to participate.).

24. The two concepts—voting weight and voting power—are not synonymous because votes may be counted equally but may not have an equal ability to influence the outcome. A common illustration of this proposition hypothesizes a committee of *A*, *B*, and *C*, where *A* has 50 votes, *B*, 49, and *C*, 1. Their actual power, meaning their potential to form minimal winning coalitions as the pivot, is ⅔, ⅙, and ⅙, respectively. Even though the voting weight of *B* and *C* equals that of *A*, *A* has ⅔ of the voting power.

Even if the mathematical model that produces these power scores is flawed, it illustrates the basic principle that the number of votes is not necessarily proportionate to the amount of power, however it is coded. See William H. Riker and Lloyd S. Shapely, Weighted Voting: A Mathematical Analysis for Instrumental Judgments, *in*

242 Notes to Chapter 4

Representation: Nomos X 200–7 (J. Roland Pennock and John W. Chapman eds., 1968) (describing Shapely-Shubik power index to measure decisive source of influence in voting bodies). This is the insight behind qualitative vote dilution strategies that challenge at-large elections despite perfect population equality.

25. Whereas the power scores in the preceding footnote are ⅔, ⅙, and ⅙, respectively, if B, with 49 votes, is a stigmatized minority, prejudice diminishes its actual power score to zero because A or C will form coalitions with each other rather than join B on issues of importance to B. By eliminating completely the minority's proportionate share, the exercise of majority power becomes illegitimate in the eyes of the minority and under the political equality and empowerment norms of the Voting Rights Act.

26. This is the social choice insight that powerful interest group minorities exercise power in the name of the majority. See WMCA, Inc. v. Lomenzo, 377 U.S. 633, 647 (1964) (34.7% of population elected majority of New York state assembly and 41.8% of population elected majority in New York state senate); Reynolds v. Sims, 377 U.S. 535, 569 (1964) (due to lack of redistricting in half-century, rural electors elected majority of representatives in Alabama house of representatives). For example, second-generation remedies could magnify the legislative strength of the Republican Party if concentrating blacks in a few districts gives the Party a statewide electoral advantage. If this occurs, then Republicans, even if a minority of the electorate, may elect a bare numerical majority of representatives yet wield 100% of the power in the legislature.

27. Microaggressions are "subtle, minor, stunning automatic assaults . . . by which whites stress blacks unremittingly and keep them on the defensive, as well as in a psychologically reduced condition." See Richard Delgado, The Ethereal Scholar: Does Critical Legal Studies Have What Minorities Want? 22 Harv. C.R.-C.L. L. Rev. 301, 305 n.30 (quoting C. Pierce, Unity in Diversity: Thirty-Three Years of Stress, Solomon Carter Fuller Lectures, Amer. Psychiatric Ass'n Meeting, Washington, D.C. (May 12, 1986)). For a compilation of contemporary examples of racial insensitivity, see Guinier, supra chapter 3.

28. This is because prejudice flourishes in informal settings. See Richard Delgado, Chris Dunn, Pamela Brown, Helena Lee & David Hubbert, Fairness and Formality: Minimizing the Risk of Prejudice in Alternative Dispute Resolution, 1985 Wis. L. Rev. 1359, 1388–91. Formal rules assist in exposing the contradiction between behavior and norms. Irwin Katz, Stigma: A Social Psychological Analysis 109 (1981); Allan Lind, John Thibaut & Laurens Walker, A Cross-Cultural Comparison of the Effect of Adversary and Inquisitorial Processes on Bias in Legal Decisionmaking, 62 Va. L. Rev. 271, 282–83 (1976); John Thibaut, Laurens Walker & Allan Lind, Adversary Presentation and Bias in Legal Decisionmaking, 86 Harv. L. Rev. 386, 399–401 (1972). Similarly, the "confrontation" theory posits that formal public settings are relatively safe for minorities. See generally Delgado, supra note 27, at 314–18 (arguing that formal public structures are needed to protect minority group members from subtle manifestations of prejudice).

29. Legislative racism encompasses intentional, conscious discrimination, as well as the consistent willingness to ignore black preferences and the inability to apprehend the intensity of those preferences. James S. Liebman, Desegregating Politics: "All-Out" School Desegregation Explained, 90 Colum. L. Rev. 1463, 1572 & nn.470–72. A recurring example of legislative racism is the necessity that black representatives in state legislatures get white legislative sponsors, not just allies, to initiate bills for them in

order for the bills to be taken seriously. See, e.g., Frank R. Parker, Black Votes Count 134–36 (1990); Telephone Interview with black elected official from Virginia (March 13, 1991) (stating that minority groups need a legislative sponsor to bring up a bill and to push it to final passage).

30. See, e.g., Susan S. Fainstein & Norman I. Fainstein, The Racial Dimension in Urban Political Economy, 25 Urb. Aff. Q. 187, 188–89 (1989) (arguing that on economic issues, even where black population is heavily concentrated, blacks are sufficiently politically isolated "to become irrelevant to aggregate growth").

31. Id. at 189 (citing scholarship on the effects of black electoral victory on government and on the condition of the black population). But cf. Richard F. Bensel & M. Elizabeth Sanders, The Impact of the Voting Rights Act on Southern Welfare Systems, *in* Do Elections Matter? 509–63 (Benjamin Ginsberg & Alan Stone eds., 1986) (arguing that black political activity forces politicians to recognize voters' political clout); Mary Herring, Legislative Responsiveness to Black Constituents in Three Deep South States, 52 J. Pol. 740, 753 (1990) (suggesting that responsiveness to needs of black community rests in part on continued election of black representatives).

32. As of 1990, in the seven Southern states with the largest black populations as a percentage of the voting age population, ranging from 18% to 33%, blacks had won nearly 3400 elected positions. Joint Center for Political and Economic Studies, Black Elected Officials: A National Roster (1990), at 10–11. But there are nearly 32,000 elected officials in these same seven states. Id. Blacks thus had a mere 11% share of the total seats. Of the 7,335 black elected officials nationwide, most are municipal officials. Doug Wilder's election is the exception, albeit a promising one.

33. The models—the constituency servicing, the power broker or the facilitator—all revolve around policy responsiveness, appropriate allocation of resources, and constituent servicing. See Robert A. Dahl, Democracy in the United States: Promise and Performance 115 (4th ed. 1981) (legislative decisions should not embody preferences of minority, whether electoral or legislative); Malcolm E. Jewell, Representation in State Legislatures 18–19 (1982). See generally Hanna Fenichel Pitkin, The Concept of Representation 60, 92, 113 (1967) (identifying the "descriptive," "symbolic" and "substantive" roles of delegate representation). The delegate model assumes a representative who is both legitimate and responsive as a result of her descriptive qualities and her incumbency. As a descriptive representative, she naturally intuits and reflects the default position of the constituency on issues in which blacks are politically cohesive. Moreover, as an incumbent, she is electorally ratified by a majority black constituency. This is the delegate view of accountability. See infra note 35.

34. A significant number of political theorists argue that a smaller political unit is best able to preserve participatory democracy. These authors do not necessarily argue the merits of single-member districts as such, but do suggest that smaller political units provide opportunities to citizens that larger political units such as multimember districts cannot. The two main benefits from small political units include increased identification of political leaders by their constituents and increased political participation by the citizenry. In smaller political units, political candidates are more like the people they represent and can therefore empathize more with their constituency. See Robert A. Dahl & Edward R. Tufte, Size and Democracy 84–86 (1973); Jane J. Mansbridge, Beyond Adversary Democracy 280 (1980). See generally Sidney Verba & Norman H. Nie, Participation in America: Political Democracy and Social Equality 229–47

(1972) (discussing the interaction of the size of the political unit and political participation).

35. The delegate model assumes that the representative is substantively accountable to her constituents, an advocate for constituent views, and a servicer of constituent needs who is reinforced by electoral ratification. The model also values local participation within small units of representation to situate the representative in a community of like-minded persons and to enable the voter to realize her individual or local service needs. See Robert A. Dahl, The City in the Future of Democracy, 61 Am. Pol. Sci. Rev. 953, 959–60 (1967); Silva, supra note 107, at 767–68. Local districts are presumed to heighten the citizen's awareness of and reason to participate in electoral activity. See Mansbridge, supra note 34, at 278–80; Verba & Nie, supra note 34, at 237–47. Some political theorists also suggest that small districts encourage consensus, and, therefore, political debate. See, e.g., Benjamin R. Barber, Strong Democracy 248 (1984); Mansbridge, supra note 34, at 278.

36. In other words, the representational relationship encompasses more than the way representatives are elected (authorized) or terminated (held to account). It involves the way representatives measure and evaluate both the articulated demands and unarticulated interests of their constituents. See Pitkin, supra note 33, at 164–66. But cf. Chisom v. Roemer, 111 S. Ct. 2354 (1991) (holding that the fact of election defines the representative).

37. This is the traditional view of representation as a structural relationship measured by the congruence between constituent needs and representative decisions. See Richard F. Fenno, Jr., Home Style: House Members in Their Districts 240–41 (1978).

38. The comparison I present is not between single-member and multimember districts. Rather, I assess how well local single-member districts realize the subdistricting theory's delegate and participatory models of representation.

39. See Charles Green & Basil Wilson, The Struggle for Black Empowerment in New York City: Beyond the Politics of Pigmentation 85–113 (1989); cf. Jewell, supra note 33, at 14 (citizens often vote based on the candidate's personality and not the issues). Smaller, homogeneous districts, which enhance a representative's physical and ideological proximity, also generate less contest around issues. By contrast, in at-large districts, obtaining group endorsements and the assistance of political parties is important because, due to the size of the electorate, it is impractical for candidates themselves to concentrate on door-to-door campaigning. See Malcolm E. Jewell, The Consequences of Single- and Multimember Districting , in Representation and Redistricting Issues 131 (Bernard Grofman, Arend Lijphart, Robert B. McKay & Howard A. Scarrow eds., 1982).

40. Indeed, in terms of organizing black voters, they may be crucial. See Paul Carton, Mobilizing the Black Community: The Effects of Personal Contact Campaigning on Black Voters 13–14 (1984); Joint Center for Political Studies, Race and Political Strategy: A JCPS Roundtable 47 (Thomas E. Cavanagh ed., 1983) [hereinafter Race and Political Strategy]. The critical contact is not between the candidate and the voter but between grass-roots organizers and potential voters. See, e.g., Organizing and Educating for Successful Mobilization, in Strategies for Mobilizing Black Voters 137, 140–43 (Thomas E. Cavanagh ed., 1987).

41. Cf. James P. Thompson, III, The Impact of the Jesse Jackson Campaign on Local Black Political Mobilization in New York City, Atlanta, and Oakland 385, 388, 396

(1990) (unpublished Ph.D. dissertation, City University of New York) (stating that low-income blacks are habitually organized to elect blacks but are then allowed to disaggregate and that black representatives resist "over-organizing" such constituents) (on file with the Virginia Law Review Association).

More generally, poverty depresses participation. See S. Rep. No. 417, 97th Cong., 2d Sess. 29 n.114, *reprinted in* 1982 U.S.C.C.A.N. 177, 207 n.114. As a district court recently observed, "[b]lacks tend to have fewer telephones and fewer cars. If a person has no phone, cannot read, and does not own a car, the ability to do almost everything in the modern world, including vote, is severely curtailed." Jeffers v. Clinton, 730 F. Supp. 196, 211 (E.D. Ark. 1989) (three-judge court); see also Guinier, supra Ch. 2 (voter registration rules requiring the initiative of voters work hardship on blacks, who are more likely to be without cars or telephones). But cf. Dianne M. Pinderhughes, Race and Ethnicity in Chicago Politics: A Reexamination of Pluralist Theory 114–18 (1987) (noting that blacks participate at rates higher than whites of comparable socioeconomic status).

42. See Fainstein & Fainstein, supra note 30, at 189; Albert K. Karnig & Susan Welch, Black Representation and Urban Policy 14, 112 (1980); William E. Nelson, Jr., Cleveland: The Rise and Fall of the New Black Politics, *in* The New Black Politics 204 (Michael B. Preston, Lenneal J. Henderson, Jr. & Paul Puryears eds., 1982); William E. Nelson, Jr. & Winston Van Horne, Black Elected Administrators: The Trials of Office, 34 Pub. Admin. Rev. 526, 529 (1974) (describing black constituency as too weak politically to exert pressure in the decisionmaking process); Adolph Reed, Jr., A Critique of Neo-Progressivism in Theorizing about Local Development: A Case from Atlanta, *in* The Politics of Urban Development 199 (Clarence N. Stone & Heywood T. Sanders eds., 1987). See generally Fenno, supra note 37, at 215–18 (discussing the conflicts between congressional representatives' legislative and constituent duties). But cf. Bensel & Sanders, supra note 31, at 59–63 (suggesting that many black representatives remain responsive to constituent needs).

Especially for black representatives, this phenomenon may reflect historically determined false consciousness, see supra Ch. 3 or the natural response to the decline of a "demand-protest activity" following the election of black representatives. See Thompson, supra note 41, at 385, 388, 396.

43. One major problem for grass-roots organizations is the high cost of access to local television, especially when the community or neighborhood is located within a much larger media market. See Bernard R. Berelson, Paul F. Lazarsfeld & William N. McPhee, Voting: A Study of Opinion Formation in a Presidential Campaign 258 (1954); Herbert J. Gans, Deciding What's News 276, 307 (1979) (media fails to get to underlying political issues); Sidney Kraus & Dennis Davis, The Effects of Mass Communication on Political Behavior 64-66 (1976) (media depresses local turnout); Jewell, supra note 39, at 133.

44. See Howard M. Shapiro, Note, Geometry and Geography: Racial Gerrymandering and the Voting Rights Act, 94 Yale L.J. 189, 202–3 (1984); see also infra Ch. 5 (defining virtual representation). This is a particular problem for Latino and Asian voters who are less likely than blacks to be residentially concentrated in only one compact, contiguous territory. See Robert Pear, Council Map Makers Argue It Mirrors New York 'Mosaic,' N.Y. Times, July 19, 1991, at B5 [hereinafter Map Makers]; Robert Pear, 'Problems' Arise in New York Map, N.Y. Times, July 18, 1991, at A1 [hereinafter

Map Problems]. This does not mean that Latino or Asian voters do not live in segregated or impoverished circumstances but that they may be distributed in segregated pockets throughout the jurisdiction.

45. An "influence district" has a significant minority population but not enough to exert electoral control. In an influence district, minorities exercise their clout by influencing who gets elected. For minorities to be influential, however, two conditions must exist. First, the district must be competitive, meaning that both parties compete for black votes. Second, the population of the district must be racially fluid, in the sense that: (1) voting is not racially polarized, (2) blacks and whites perceive their common interests, and (3) interracial coalitions are reciprocal. Where these conditions are present, blacks have what Professor Allan Lichtman terms a "functional majority" district because of white cross-over voting. See Telephone Interview with Allan Lichtman (Sept. 27, 1991).

   Where these conditions do not hold, influence districts are presently nonjusticiable because, without electoral control, courts lack an identifiable or quantifiable means of assessing "influence." Courts are thus left without a compass in this political thicket. See, e.g., Gingles v. Edmisten, 590 F. Supp. 345 (E.D.N.C. 1984) (three-judge court); Major v. Treen, 574 F. Supp. 325 (E.D. La. 1983) (three-judge court). In addition, minority voters worry that a claim for influence districts will have serious repercussions on the 65% rule. See infra subpart C. As a political matter, influence districts require intense local scrutiny to predict the impact of a minority "swing vote." See Armour v. Ohio, No. C88-1104Y (N.D. Ohio, Sept. 4, 1991) (three-judge court) (finding impermissible dilution where political boundaries were drawn in a way that failed to protect black voters' ability to elect white candidates of their choice); Upham v. Seamon, 536 F. Supp. 931 (E.D. Tex. 1982) (three-judge court) (stating that black voting strength was not diluted when Texas created two minority influence districts rather than one majority-black district).

46. See, e.g., Charles H. Backstrom, Problems of Implementing Redistricting, *in* Representation and Redistricting Issues 43, 47 (Bernard Grofman, Arend Lijphart, Robert B. McKay & Howard A. Scarrow eds., 1982); Bernard Grofman, Criteria for Districting: A Social Science Perspective, 33 UCLA L. Rev. 77, 87 (1985) (stating that preserving communities of interest may conflict with other criteria). For example, according to a Texas state Senate Redistricting Committee staff member, divergent socioeconomic Latino communities in Dallas, Texas, were packed into one district, in which there is "no community of interest between them except they are all brown." Heard by the author on All Things Considered (National Public Radio broadcast, July 29, 1991). See also Daniel H. Lowenstein & Jonathan Steinberg, The Quest for Legislative Districting in the Public Interest: Elusive or Illusory?, 33 UCLA L. Rev. 1, 3–5 (1985) (arguing that there are no coherent, neutral, public-interest criteria for districting); Lee Papayanopoulos, Compromise Districting, *in* Representation and Redistricting Issues 59, 60 (Bernard Grofman, Arend Lijphart, Robert B. McKay & Howard A. Scarrow eds., 1982); David Wells, Against Affirmative Gerrymandering, *in* Representation and Redistricting Issues 77, 84-86 & n.29, 89 (Bernard Grofman, Arend Lijphart, Robert B. McKay & Howard A. Scarrow eds., 1982).

47. 430 U.S. 144 (1977).

48. This is apparently the Republican districting strategy for the 1990s. By supporting

majority-black districts, they drain potential Democratic allies and create majority-white districts in which conservative whites are the majority. See supra note 26.

49. See Martin Gottlieb, New York's Democratic Experiment, N.Y. Times, Sept. 15, 1991, § 4, at 18 (quoting criticism of districting as a strategy that does violence to neighborhood coherence, disconnects voters from the legislative body, and erodes civic participation). An "artificial" district is one that reflects geographic compactness but not communities of interest. See Morris Collins, The Atlanta Metropolitan Area, *in* Evolving Issues and Patterns of State Legislative Redistricting in Large Metropolitan Areas 3, 21 (Morris W.H. Collins, Jr., Manning J. Dauer, Paul T. David, Alex B. Lacy, Jr. & George J. Mauer eds., 1966). Or it might be grossly gerrymandered to protect incumbents without regard to geographic and representational integrity. It may waste votes in that not all district residents vote for the winner. See Peter Schuck, Partisan Gerrymandering: A Political Problem Without Judicial Solution, *in* Political Gerrymandering and the Courts 240, 244–46 (Bernard Grofman ed., 1990). This may lead to resentment at affirmative, race-conscious action for racial, but not religious, minorities. See United Jewish Orgs. v. Carey, 430 U.S. 144 (1977).

50. See, e.g., David Wells, Against Affirmative Gerrymandering, *in* Representation and Redistricting Issues 77, 79–80 (Bernard Grofman, Arend Lijphart, Robert B. McKay & Howard A. Scarrow eds., 1982). Incumbents apparently believe that single-member districts improve their prospects for reelection despite the fact that name recognition, which gives incumbents the advantage in both at-large and single-member districts, is more helpful in the larger jurisdiction-wide contest. See Jewell, supra note 39, at 132; see also Bruce E. Cain, Assessing the Partisan Effects of Redistricting, 79 Am. Pol. Sci. Rev. 320, 331 (1985) (redistricting tactics more likely to include incumbency considerations "in era when party loyalty counts for less and incumbency counts for more"); Wells, supra note 148, at 85–86 (stating that the current districting approach may freeze composition of legislature, virtually assuring individual incumbent of continued reelection). But cf. Charles Backstrom, Leonard Robins & Scott Eller, Establishing a Statewide Electoral Effects Baseline, *in* Political Gerrymandering and the Courts 145 (Bernard Grofman ed., 1990) (suggesting an alternative measure and standard of partisan gerrymandering); Gordon E. Baker, The "Totality of Circumstances" Approach, *in* Political Gerrymandering and the Courts 203 (Bernard Grofman ed., 1990) (elaborating eight indicators of political gerrymandering that address the evidentiary burden of the Voting Rights Act); Richard Morrill, A Geographer's Perspective, in Political Gerrymandering and the Courts 212, 238 (Bernard Grofman ed., 1990) ("If the technique of gerrymandering can be demonstrated to have a high probability of resulting in a sense of misrepresentation . . . then gerrymandering, like malapportionment earlier, must be seen to frustrate the intent of the Constitution."); Richard G. Niemi, The Swing Ration as a Measure of Partisan Gerrymandering, *in* Political Gerrymandering and the Courts 171 (Bernard Grofman ed., 1990) (setting forth alternative approaches to identifying gerrymanders that establish formal criteria for evaluating the structures of districting plans).

51. There are several possible explanations for this decline, all of which suggest that when blacks do win office, the excitement generated by that symbolic success is soon supplanted by frustration over the symbol's inability to govern or to participate effectively in a governing coalition. The decline in voter participation is particularly problematic when leaders of insurgent political organizations become part of the government. See

Sam Roberts, Gadflies of Today Parcel the Blame Among Old Allies, N.Y. Times, July 1, 1991, at B1; see also Vanessa Williams, Political Setback for Blacks, Phila. Inquirer, June 23, 1991, at A12 (reporting black voter turnout levels). Thus, black electoral success may actually "kill" the transformational potential of black political organization: "You [become] that body that you actually used to organize against. We became government." Id. (quoting local political analyst).

52. Robert G. Dixon, Jr., Representation Values and Reapportionment Practice: The Eschatology of "One-Man, One-Vote," *in* Representation: Nomos X 167, 173–74 (J. Roland Pennock & John W. Chapman eds., 1968); see also V.O. Key, Jr., Politics, Parties and Pressure Groups 208–9 (5th ed. 1964) (arguing that single-member districts and plurality elections lead to a two-party system); E.E. Schattschneider, Party Government 69–84 (Phillips Bradley ed., Greenwood Press 1977) (1942) (arguing that the American two-party system is a direct result of single-member districts and plurality elections, both of which tend to exaggerate the strength of the plurality winner); Maurice Duverger, Duverger's Law: Forty Years Later, *in* Electoral Laws and Their Political Consequences 69, 70 (B. Grofman & A. Lijphart eds., 1986) (linking plurality voting and the two-party system).

53. See Americans Not Politically Apathetic, But Disillusioned, 19 Focus, Political TrendLetter at 2 (supplement to July 1991) (reporting that citizens perceive the political system to be "spiraling beyond their control") (citing Kettering Foundation Report, Citizens and Politics: A View from Main Street America (1991)); David S. Broder, More and More, the Citizenry Feels Governmental Politics Is Beyond Redemption, Phila. Inquirer, June 6, 1991, at A18 (concluding from study that legitimacy of our political institutions more at issue than leaders imagine) (citing Kettering Foundation Report, Citizens and Politics: A View from Main Street America (1991)).

54. On the other hand, the weak version of the influence district claim may be equally vulnerable as is the majority minority district to failures regarding voter mobilization and legislative accountability.

55. Minority vote dilution refers to electoral or voting practices or procedures that predictably submerge minority voting strength because of the bloc voting by the racial majority. The premise of dilution claims is that where the majority votes as a racial bloc, the interests of the minority inevitably will be ignored. The very reason for creating majority minority districts in the first place is to give minorities an opportunity to participate in a political process that is not dominated by the racial bloc voting majority.

56. This, of course, assumes the plaintiffs are adequate class representatives.

57. Upham v. Seamon, 456 U.S. 37 (1982).

58. My ultimate goal is to realize the original statutory vision of a "transformative politics." Among other things, a transformative politics gives disadvantaged groups a substantive basis for lending their consent to government decisions. A transformative politics contemplates empowerment as making government more responsive to minority interests, not just integrating legislative bodies. A transformative politics also envisions a mobilized electorate that not only votes on election day, but also continuously monitors and holds its leadership to account.

59. Proportionality compares the ratio of votes cast by black voters or their representatives to successful outcomes, meaning the number of times voters or their representatives are part of minimum winning coalitions. See infra text accompanying notes 105–7. Proportionality is primarily aspirational in that decisions are not always mea-

sured in binary win/lose terms, but may include compromise alternatives in which participants all gain something. With a proportionality principle, the whole is distributed so that the winners do not win all. Proportionality is a qualitative standard of fairness, embodying the "taking turns" approach described in ch. 1. It builds on the definition of political legitimacy discussed earlier in this chapter.

60. In particular, a principle of proportionality moderates the political environment away from a model of two-party competition to one in which third political parties and community-based organizations can play a more active role in mobilizing voter participation to enforce representational accountability.

61. The group compensating formulation is developed from Bruce Cain's hierarchy distinguishing group rights to representation, such as those conferred by the Voting Rights Act, from the individual formalist approach to representation and participation. See Bruce E. Cain, Perspectives on *Davis v. Bandemer:* Views of the Practitioner, Theorist, and Reformer, *in* Political Gerrymandering and the Courts 117, 128–31 (Bernard Grofman ed., 1990).

62. The reason is that a single individual can only achieve political representation by acting in concert with others. By embracing a group-rights or group-compensating model, however, neither the courts nor I seek to trump individual rights or autonomy. The group-rights model simply recognizes and takes into account the political and sociological theory of pluralism supporting the autonomy and value of group identification and collective participation. See Frank I. Michelman, Super Liberal: Romance, Community, and Tradition in William J. Brennan, Jr.'s Constitutional Thought, 77 Va. L. Rev. 1261, 1308–9 (1991); see also Iris Marion Young, Justice and the Politics of Difference 42–48, 183–85 (1990) (discussing the concept of the social group and concluding that group representation encourages expression of individual and group needs). Indeed, my preference for voluntary interest constituencies as the unit for representating groups reflects the value of individual autonomy and choice.

63. Cain, supra note 61, at 131. In this way, the group-compensating model evaluates voting standards, practices or procedures by the extent to which they minimize wasted voting, measure salience and intensity of preferences, respect voter autonomy, and take into account "informal" inequalities of politically relevant resources, such as wealth on the one hand and ability to become part of the governing coalition (the absence of prejudice) on the other.

64. I recognize that some may criticize this claim as outcome-oriented jurisprudence that improperly invades the province of the local legislature. I believe that my focus on legislative decisional *rules*, not decisional *outcomes*, adequately answers this criticism. See infra notes 103–8 and accompanying text. I propose to conceptualize the problem as an equal opportunity to influence legislative decisionmaking, regardless of race. Outcomes are relevant only as evidence whether the decisionmaking process is fair.

   Outcomes are considered, but only in a procedural justice sense to measure degrees of participation by eligible voters in the decisionmaking process. The term influence is used to include opportunities to exchange information about, as well as capacities to reward or punish compliance with, preferences and intentions.

65. Interest representation does not attempt to distinguish between interests and desires, between advantages and needs, or between short-term and long-range interests. However, interest representation *does* distinguish between voters: first and foremost, interest representation is a claim on behalf of statutorily protected minorities who

have endured, and continue to endure, consistent disadvantage throughout the political process despite apparent gains. Interest representation takes the statutory mandate to mean that the political process is suspect when statutorily protected groups are denied meaningful participation, which occurs, for example, where minority interests are consistently ignored or discounted due to prejudice or winner-take-all majority rule.

66. The existence of alternative systems establishes the basis for unfair dilution because submergence and dilution are comparative concepts. For example, in oral argument before the Supreme Court in Chisom v. Roemer, 111 S. Ct. 2354 (1991), Justice Antonin Scalia asked the litigants to define dilution, suggesting that dilution, like "watered beer," is a relative concept. See Lyle Denniston, Split Argument Pays Off in Voting Rights Case, Am. Law., Sept. 1991, at 103; see also Grofman, supra note 46, at 145 (stating that "vote dilution is inherently a *comparative* concept.")

67. Intensity is the degree to which voters want or prefer an alternative. See Dahl, supra note 22, at 91.

68. Modified at-large voting, which allows voters to cast their votes in any combination they choose, reduces the exclusion threshold to promote proportional or plurality representation. Limited and cumulative voting are judicially approved techniques for implementing such modifications. See Karlan, Maps and Misreadings, 24 Harv. C.R.–C.L. L. Rev. 173, 223–36 (1989). Edward Still, Voluntary Constituencies: Modified At-Large Voting as a Remedy for Minority Vote Dilution in Judicial Elections, 9 Yale L. & Pol. Rev. (1991); Delbert A. Taebel, Richard L. Engstrom & Richard L. Cole, Alternative Electoral Systems as Remedies for Minority Vote Dilution, 11 Hamline J. Pub. L. & Pol. 19, 26–29 (1990).

69. The threshold for election is calculated mathematically using the formula one divided by one plus the number of open seats plus one. The formula determines the minimal number of votes necessary to elect a candidate. In this case, the formula tells us that one-fifth plus one of the voters cannot be denied a representative.

70. Because the threshold for election under the modified system in the four-person council is 21%, any politically cohesive interest constituency sufficiently numerous to organize at least 21% of the voters cannot be denied representation. White women or moderate white voters normally subsumed by the majority or Latino voters sufficiently numerous but dispersed may also gain representation without straining their political alliances with blacks.

71. This is certainly the source of concern among some commentators about "the unholy alliance" between Republicans and blacks seeking greater representation in which Republicans are accused of draining black voters from potential white Democratic districts to create safe black districts. Republicans admit their interest-convergence with blacks seeking majority-black districts. See Daniel H. Lowenstein and Jonathan Steinberg, The Quest for Legislative Districting in the Public Interest: Elusive or Illusory? 33 UCLA L. Rev. 340 (1985); Jack Quinn, Donald J. Simon & Jonathon B. Sallet, Redrawing Political Maps: An America of Groups? Wash. Post, Mar. 24, 1991, at C1; see also supra note 26 (noting advantages in some instances to Republican Party of concentrating black voters in a few districts).

72. Assuming two of the districts of 100 voters each were in fact 100% black, then 51 voters in each 100 voter district could elect a representative. Assuming equal population subdistricts of 100 people (all of voting age), 51 voters in each district would be

able to elect their preferred candidate. A total of 510 voters would be, at minimum represented in the legislature. A minority of 490 would be potentially unrepresented.

If the unrepresented minority of 490 were racially homogeneous with the 510 voter majority or its interests were fungible with those of the majority, we would proclaim majority rule that was consistent with the reciprocity/virtual representation principle. If the unrepresented minority of 490 were instead racially diverse but a "fair" number of subdistricts were majority black, second-generation voting rights litigation would also claim success. At least some of the elected representatives would represent black voters who were a majority in a particular subdistrict. Even those blacks outside the majority black subdistricts would be virtually represented by the black subdistrict majority representatives.

73. One way of looking at the subdistrict plan is to emphasize the way it wastes votes. Only 51 blacks are needed to elect a representative, yet 100 blacks are "packed" into the subdistrict. This is in part based on the 65% rule. Wasted, too, are the votes of whites who may be a minority within a majority-black district or who may be a minority of moderate voters within a conservative, Republican dominated district.

74. 51 voters in each district, of 510 voters, control the legislative body. That means a total of 490 voters of both races voted for losers and are not represented.

75. As I develop below, I use the "winner-take-only-some" phrase to refer to a positive-sum election mechanism in which the threshold of representation or exclusion is less than 50% and probably considerably less.

76. Cf. Kathryn Abrams, Kitsch and Community, 84 Mich. L. Rev. 941, 948 (1986) (reporting de Tocqueville's observation that "by working with others with whom one feels salient similarities, one develops the understanding of and confidence in collective action that permits later cooperation with those who are dissimilar to oneself"). The model I propose here suggests that people learn their interests in interaction with others. Their interests are not based solely on fixed, territorial interests but are formed through deliberation and participation. On the other hand, some commentators have criticized the view that voting preferences necessarily reflect the objective interests of the voter. See Isaac D. Balbus, The Concept of Interest in Pluralist and Marxian Analysis, 1 Pol. & Soc'y 151 (1970); S.I. Benn, "Interests" in Politics, 60 Proc. Aristotelian Soc'y (n.s.) 123 (1960); William E. Connolly, On "Interests" in Politics, 2 Pol. & Soc'y 459 (1972). To these commentators, existing preferences are "shifting and endogenous" and a function of "current information, consumption patterns, legal rules, and general social pressures." Cass R. Sunstein, Preferences and Politics, 20 Philo. & Pub. Affs. 3, 10 (1991). On this view, voting for representatives, or even the votes of representatives may not constitute the best occasion to test interest preferences.

77. This, however, is not an argument for "influence districts" in which black voters are a district minority *presumed* to exercise influence as a critical "swing" vote. See Part C at 86–91.

78. Jennifer L. Hochschild & Monica Herk, "Yes, But . . .": Principles and Caveats in American Racial Attitudes, *in* Majorities and Minorities: Nomos XXXII 308, 319 (John W. Chapman & Alan Wertheimer eds., 1990) (collecting and reviewing survey data).

79. See, e.g., Parker, supra note 29, at 226 n.13; Pinderhughes, supra note 41, at 110; Fainstein & Fainstein, supra note 30, at 188; Charles V. Hamilton, Measuring Black Conservatism, *in* The State of Black America 1982, at 113, 124–39 (J.D. Williams ed.,

1982) (annual report by the National Urban League); Richard Seltzer & Robert C. Smith, Race and Ideology: A Research Note Measuring Liberalism and Conservatism in Black America, 46 Phylon 98, 105 (1985); Susan Welch & Michael W. Combs, Interracial Differences in Opinion on Public Issues in the 1970's, 7 W. J. Black Stud. 136, 139–41 (1983). Even efforts by the Bush Administration to promote the views of black conservatives succeeded only in identifying a handful of prominent black Republicans whose views, while presently visible, are not supported by a majority of blacks. See Dwight Ott, Blacks Who Are Taking a New Path, Phila. Inquirer, July 28, 1991, at 1A; Louis Harris, Doubts on black-conservative link, Phila. Inquirer, Oct. 18, 1991, at 19A (describing as "patent nonsense" claim that black support for Justice Clarence Thomas reflects new conservative coalition; polling data gathered during Thomas' nomination hearings suggest blacks supported Thomas because of his race, not his views). See also Gallup Poll, May 1991, reporting that only 8% of college educated blacks agree with the views expressed by black conservatives that things got better in the 10 years between 1981 and 1991.

80. See Rufus P. Browning, Dale R. Marshall & David H. Tabb, Protest Is Not Enough: The Struggle of Blacks and Hispanics for Equality in Urban Politics 132–35 (1984); Norman Nie, Sidney Verba & John Petrocik, The Changing American Voter 253–55 (1979); Susan Welch & Timothy Bledsoe, Urban Reform and Its Consequences 23 (1988); Mary Herring, Legislative Responsiveness to Black Constituents in Three Deep South States, 52 J. Pol. 740 (1990). See generally Guinier, supra Ch. 3 (collecting sources). On issues other than civil rights and aid to the poor, it may be difficult to articulate a uniform, across-the-board consensus. Even on the issue agenda identified, intrablack conflict must be acknowledged.

81. Doug McAdam, Political Process and the Development of Black Insurgency 1930–1970, at 51 (1982); see also Thompson, supra note 41, at 389 (stating that "[b]lack politics exists as a unique entity in American politics precisely because all classes of blacks are still trying to overcome the effects of centuries of exclusion from economic and political development"); cf. Welch & Bledsoe, supra note 80, at 23 (stating that civil rights appears to be the issue of primary concern to most black city council members). From the time of the Niagara Movement and the founding of the National Association for the Advancement of Colored People (NAACP) in 1910, blacks have adopted a protest platform that included: the right to equal treatment, increased public high school and college facilities, judicial reform, health care, and vigorous enforcement of the post–Civil War Amendments to the Constitution. See Francis L. Broaderick & August Meier, Negro Protest Thought in the Twentieth Century 49–52 (Francis L. Broaderick & August Meier eds., 1965). Of course, to say that blacks experience group consciousness and a collective identity that shapes their world view does not mean or imply that blacks are monolithic in their approach to particular issues.

82. Obvious issues as to which there are differences in viewpoint among the races include social programs and advocacy for the poor; see James E. Conyers & Walter L. Wallace, Black Elected Officials: A Study of Black Americans Holding Governmental Office 31 (1976) (arguing that black officials are much more likely than their white colleagues to favor social programs such as housing); Martin Tolchin, $50 Billion Plan Is Called for to Train Minorities, N.Y. Times, Jan. 10, 1990, at A22 (Urban League proposes an "urban Marshall Plan" and is awaiting action from Bush Administration),

affirmative action, see James A. Barnes, Into the Mainstream, 22 Nat'l J. 262, 262 (1990) (observing that blacks support affirmative action), the proper extent of government involvement, see id. at 264 (reporting that whites, unlike blacks, prefer limited government involvement in their everyday lives), and war and peace. See, e.g., An Observer, The Gulf War and the Wounds of Race, 1 Reconstruction 6 (1991) (observing that 80% of general population, but only 50% of blacks, supported the recent Gulf War). Whites and blacks also assess racial progress quite differently. See Hochschild & Herk, supra note 78, at 308, 312, 315–17 (finding that since the late 1970s, 67% *or more* of whites "expect further racial progress or complete racial equality soon," as compared to between 30% and 45% of blacks).

83. Indeed, an interest representation approach would seek to encourage the support and potential leadership of the more upwardly and residentially mobile members of the community. Interest representation, which relies on voluntary, not territorial, constituencies, would be defined by class and geographic cleavages within the black community only to the extent black voters chose an exclusively class- or neighborhood-based interest constituency. My intuition is that this is unlikely. See, e.g., Lucius J. Barker & Jesse J. McCorry, Jr., Black Americans and the Political System 26 (2d ed. 1980); Bernard Grofman, Amihai Glazer, Kimball Brace, Barbara Norrander, Robert Griffin, Janet Campagna, David Brady & Lisa Handley, Three Variations on a Theme by V.O. Key: Race and Politics, Race and Politics, and (the ever popular) Race and Politics (Aug. 28, 1988) (unpublished paper presented at Annual Meeting of American Political Science Association Sept. 1988) (on file with the Virginia Law Review Association). But cf. William Wilson, The Declining Significance of Race (1978) (arguing that class, rather than race, is the relevant distinction).

84. For example, black Republicans would be free to express their issue preferences by plumping their votes on the Republican candidate.

85. I use the term "wasted votes" consciously, although it may be imprecise. See Schuck, supra note 49, at 244–45. My claim that interest representation reduces wasted voting is also somewhat controversial. Id. at 246. Similarly, not all agree that interest representation would promote coalition-building even after elections. Id.

86. For example, a remedy that promotes cross-racial or intraracial, cross-class alliances may pressure community-based black representatives to censor their views to appeal to white or middle-class black allies. This is a concern both in terms of electing in the first place black representatives whose constituency is jurisdiction-wide and in terms of monitoring black representatives who remain accountable to a community-based agenda. In addition, proposals that empower reciprocal alliances between blacks and white moderates may likewise produce reciprocal alliances between conservatives and equally numerous white extremists. Moreover, I readily acknowledge that some hold a strong presumption against wholesale changes in the electoral system, especially where those changes may be confusing for the ordinary voter. I attempt to address concerns about voter mobilization and strategic voting through the mechanism of third political parties.

87. See Enid Lakeman, The Case for Proportional Representation, *in* Choosing an Electoral System: Issues and Alternatives 41–51 (Arend Lijphart & Bernard Grofman eds., 1984); supra notes 49–50. Unlike negative campaigning, which simply gives voters a reason not to vote for a candidate's opponent, interest representation encourages an affirmative vote for a candidate. See, e.g., Leon Weaver, The Rise, Decline, and Res-

urrection of Proportional Representation in Local Governments in the United States, *in* Electoral Laws and Their Political Consequences 139, 150 (Bernard Grofman & Arend Lijpharts eds., 1986).

Another reason why voter education is important in interest representation is the relative complexity of cumulative voting. Instead of having just one vote to cast, voters will cast as many votes as seats on the decisionmaking body being elected. Because of the strategic considerations involved in plumping votes, see supra note 70, it will be to the candidates' advantage to educate voters about how to make their votes most effective.

88. See, e.g., V.O. Key, Jr., Politics, Parties, & Pressure Groups 587–89 (5th ed. 1964). Interest representation promotes perceptions of political efficacy because voters have a heightened sense of their ability not just to affect election outcomes but to influence the process of legislative decisionmaking.

89. This suggests that interest representation may be even *more democratic* in the traditional sense of more people actively participating in politics. Rates of political participation in this country are the lowest of any Western democracy. Although there are many competing explanations for low voter turnout, from registration barriers to rational withdrawal in recognition of futility, Michael Parenti, Democracy for the Few 208–13 (1977); Abrams, "Raising Politics Up," 63 N.Y.U. L. Rev. 449, 491 (1988); Bruce Ackerman, The Storrs Lectures: Discovering the Constitution, 93 Yale L.J. 1013, 1034 (1984); Geoffrey Brennan & James Buchanan, Voter Choice: Evaluating Political Alternatives, 28 Am. Behav. Scientist 185, 187 (1984), to expression of contentment with the status quo, Seymour Lipset, Political Man 181 (1960); Heinz Eulau, The Politics of Happiness, 16 Antioch Rev. 259 (1956), participation as part of group expression can have an ameliorating effect, whatever the preferred answer.

Thus, I would argue that increased political participation is not a function of the size of the political unit. See Barber, supra note 35, at 209, 249; Verba & Nie, supra note 34, at 234–35. If this is so, then a decentralized political environment in which winner-take-all majoritarian controls are modulated may increase the opportunity for broad-based participation. See Barber, supra note 35, at 267–73; Richard B. Stewart, Federalism and Rights, 19 Ga. L. Rev. 917, 918 (1985).

Of course, it may be unrealistic to mobilize politically poor people beset by other problems, but in conjunction with its potential to activate community-based organizations, see text accompanying infra notes 86–87, this interest representation scenario is not implausible. For example, once socioeconomic status is taken into account, blacks may actually participate at a *higher* level than whites. See, e.g., Verba & Nie, supra note 34, at 232–35; Arthur H. Miller, Patricia Gurin, Gerald Gurin & Oksana Malanchuk, Group Consciousness and Political Participation, 25 Am. J. Pol. Sci. 494, 500 (1981) (stating that groups whose members feel that their group lacks comparable, relevant resources are more likely to be politically active); Richard D. Shingles, Black Consciousness and Political Participation: The Missing Link, 75 Am. Pol. Sci. Rev. 76, 77–78 (1981) (stating that black mistrust and efficacy, along with group consciousness, are related to various forms of political participation).

I claim, however, that as a discrete and insular minority, blacks may be able to take maximum advantage of interest representation, in part because, as a small group with group consciousness, they are better able to organize collectively. See Katherine Tate, Protest to Politics: The New Black Voters in American Elections 7 (Mar. 1990) (stating that, in addition to group consciousness, organizational strength may be an equally important determinant of black participation) (unpublished manuscript) (on file with the Virginia Law Review Association); Ronald W. Walters, Black Presidential Politics 26 (1988) (direct advocacy of black interests will spark greater black electoral participation that will increase black political participation).

90. Interest representation would revive the civil rights movement's metaphor of sustained marching as an "army for justice." Taylor Branch, Parting the Waters: America in the King Years 880–81 (1988). However, mobilizing and sustaining black political activity will require more than protest politics and the attendant emotional appeals. See Stokely Carmichael & Charles V. Hamilton, Black Power: The Politics of Liberation in America 119 (1967). Therefore, interest representation would encourage candidates to develop programs and issues that motivate voters to participate actively in an extended political process, pursuing a more active model of continuous community education and political campaigning.

91. See Robert A. Dahl, After the Revolution? Authority in a Good Society (1970); Alexis de Tocqueville, Democracy in America 195–99 (Henry Reeve trans., 3d ed. 1838); Verba & Nie, supra note 34, at 209–28; James Q. Wilson, Political Organizations 95–96 (1973); Thomas E., Cavanagh, Understanding Black Voter Turnout: The Strategic Context, *in* Strategies for Mobilizing Black Voters 3 (Thomas E. Cavanagh ed., 1987); Michael Fitts, The Vices of Virtue: A Political Party Perspective on Civic Virtue Reforms of the Legislative Process, 136 U. Pa. L. Rev. 1604 (1988). This may be particularly critical in small, rural communities where mobilization of minority voters is most difficult. See Hurumia Ahadi, An Independent Black Political Party: Posing an Alternative to Asses, Elephants and Rainbows, 11 Nat'l Black L.J. 117, 140 (1989); Dianne M. Pinderhughes, Legal Strategies for Voting Rights: Political Science and the Law, 28 How. L.J. 515, 529 & n.62 (1985); Paul J. Stekler, Electing Blacks to Office in the South—Black Candidates, Bloc Voting and Racial Unity Twenty Years After the Voting Rights Acts, 17 Urb. Law. 473, 476–77 (1985).

Alternatively, voters might turn to campaign consultants and run even more intensely candidate-centered campaigns. In this case, destructive competition between allies could be transferred from once-a-decade redistricting conflicts to regular election battles. Professor Dan Lowenstein suggested this critique of interest representation to me. Although Lowenstein's critique is a serious one, its force depends on the viability of organizational alternatives, such as minority political parties.

92. The assumption that women are politically cohesive turns on whether there is credible evidence substantiating the so-called gender gap. Even if the evidence of a gender gap were substantiated, however, that fact would not be enough to establish a claim under the Voting Rights Act. Nonetheless, if an interest representation system were implemented for statutorily protected groups, that assumption of political cohesiveness would be a promising basis for organizing women who believed that they did have, as women, "distinctive group needs."

93. Interest representation is both more efficient and less rigid or essentialist than the compulsory constituencies of fixed, territorial subdistricts. By representing interests rather than geography, interest representation wastes fewer votes. It also allows for direct representation of voter interests, unlike subdistricts that presume virtual representation by the racial majority of both territorially connected voters living inside the district and racially bonded voters living outside the district.

94. A principled consensus finds a solution that is persuasive or acceptable to the participants in the deliberations. Consensus has been defined as "general agreement," which means that "no party dissents significantly from the shared position." Susan Sturm, A Normative Theory of Public Law Remedies, 79 Geo. L. Rev. 1355, 1423 n.367 (1991).

95. In arguing that interests are the appropriate unit of analysis for identifying electoral vote dilution, I hypothesize a salutory, though necessarily indirect, effect on black legislative influence and accountability. In order to remedy more completely third-generation legislative disenfranchisement, however, it may be necessary to challenge directly, at the legislative decisionmaking level, access-based empowerment strategies. For example, where single-member districts have been previously imposed to remedy electoral dilution claims or where single-member districts are preferred by poor, strapped communities that seek representational refuge in a majority-black district, those single-member districts could be seen as continuing the violation. By reinforcing and assuming racially polarized voting, single-member districts may thereby encourage legislative racism, which taints the collective decisionmaking process. Consequently, as both a theoretical and empirical matter, I discuss here the potential danger for minority interests wherever a racially homogeneous majority exercises disproportionate legislative power, despite the presence of black representatives.

96. "Deliberation" consists of the process of framing the issues to be resolved, proposing alternative solutions, examining the reasons for and against the proposed solutions, and settling on an alternative. See Barber, supra note 35, at 178–79; Joshua Cohen, Deliberation and Democratic Legitimacy, *in* The Good Polity 17, 22 (Alan Hamlin & Philip Pettit eds., 1989); Bernard Manin, On Legitimacy and Political Deliberation, 15 Pol. Theory, 338, 345 (Elly Stein & Jane Mansbridge trans., 1987). See also Harold Lasswell & Myres McDougal, Legal Education and Public Policy: Professional Training in the Public Interest, 52 Yale L.J. 203, 217–26 (1943) (arguing that institutions can be evaluated to determine if they promote democracy based on three related criteria: shared power, shared respect, and shared knowledge).

97. Discussion usually revolves around the existence of a system of checks and balances, judicial review, and the Bill of Rights, particularly First Amendment principles that guarantee that the majority is subject to ongoing criticism. See Whitfield v. Democratic Party, 686 F. Supp. 1365, 1373 n.3 (E.D. Ark. 1988), aff'd on reh'g by an equally divided court, 902 F.2d 15 (8th Cir. 1990) (en banc), cert. denied sub nom. Whitfield v. Clinton, 111 S. Ct. 1089 (1991); Robert A. Dahl, Democracy, Liberty, and Equality 15 (1986); Stephen Holmes, Rethinking the Liberal Tradition 13 (April 12, 1991) (unpublished manuscript presented to the University of Pennsylvania Legal Studies Workshop) (on file with the Virginia Law Review Association). Because of these protections, it is assumed that the majority will not dominate the minority but will actually represent the interests of the minority. To civic republicans, another reason for majority restraint is civic virtue, which exists when each individual votes for what she regards as best for the community. See Waldron, Rights and Majorities: Rousseau Revisited, supra at 64.

98. Alexis de Tocqueville, Democracy in America 240 (Henry Reeve trans., spec. ed. 1835); see also The Federalist No. 10 (James Madison) (arguing that it should be the goal of government to avoid domination by any particular interest group); John Stuart Mill, Representative Government, *in* On Liberty, Representative Government and

The Subjection of Women: Three Essays by John Stuart Mill 248–49 (1974) (arguing that a majority cannot legitimately exercise all of the power). Or, as Alexander Hamilton put it, when the many are given all the power, "they will oppress the few." 5 The Debates on the Adoption of the Federal Constitution in the Convention Held at Philadelphia in 1787, With a Diary of the Debates of the Congress of the Confederation as Reported by James Madison 203 (Jonathan Elliot ed., 1968).

99. Consequently, winner-take-all collective desisionmaking frustrates the fundamental goal of political stability, which is "to induce losers to continue to play the political game, to continue to work within the system rather than to try to overthrow it." Nicholas R. Miller, Pluralism and Social Choice, 77 Am. Pol. Sci. Rev. 734, 742 (1983). Because any form of less-than-unanimous voting introduces the danger that the majority will consistently exploit the minority, the potential for instability exists where any significant group of people end up in the minority. See Robert Sugden, Rules for Choosing Among Public Goods: A Contractarian Approach, 1 Const. Pol. Ec. 63, 69 (1990). See generally Dahl, supra note 22, at 90–103 (arguing that decisions carried by the relatively indifferent majority against the relatively strong preference of the minority may undermine stability). Where the minority experiences the alienation of complete defeat, it lacks incentive to respect laws passed by the majority over its opposition.

100. This is the essence of "legislative racism," see supra note 29, or the tyranny of the majority. See The Federalist No. 51, at 349–51 (James Madison) (Paul Ford ed., 1898).

101. Proof offered in voting rights cases and empirical studies demonstrate that voting is persistently racially polarized. See supra notes 78–82 and accompanying text; supra text accompanying notes 10–14; Samuel Issacharoff, supra note 60 at 3. Polarized Voting and the Political Process: The Transformation of Voting Rights Jurisprudence, 90 Mich. L. Rev. 1833 (1992).

102. I intend to develop a more general critique of majority rule as a principle of political process elsewhere. In this chapter I simply claim on behalf of statutorily protected minorities that 51% of the voters exercising 100% of the power loses legitimacy when the generic assumptions of stability, reciprocity, efficiency, and electoral accountability are voided by the permanence and homogeneity of the majority.

103. In the words of James Madison: "Extend the sphere and you take in a greater variety of parties and interests; you make it less probable that a majority of the whole will have a common motive to invade the rights of other citizens; . . ." The Federalist No. 10, at 61 (James Madison) (Carl Van Doren ed., 1945).

104. Miller, supra note 99, at 735 (quoting Earl Latham, The Group Basis of Politics: Notes for a Theory, 46 Am. Pol. Sci. Rev. 376, 390 (1952)). Interest representation attempts to normalize, rather than economize, consensus. It seeks contemporary parallels to James Madison's checks and balances and separation of powers. See The Federalist No. 47 (James Madison). In this sense, interest representation may be the "functional analogue of the institutions of checks and balances and federalism, recognizing the creative functions of disagreement and multiple perspectives for the governmental process." Cass R. Sunstein, Preferences and Politics, 20 Phil. & Pub. Affs. 34 (1991).

105. The proportionality principle illuminates the irony in defending majority rule for its stabilizing propensity. The historical use of majority rule had been to "destabilize

institutions" in a society where political power was based on inherited wealth and privilege. See Wood, supra note 19. The paradox is that, as a paradigm of democracy, majority rule might be more successfully defended from the minority perspective not as an ideology of government and stability but as "fundamentally an ideology of opposition" in which democrats welcome the "perpetual instability" of dominant coalitions. Shapiro, supra note 19, at 116. In this sense, democracy is about "displacing entrenched elites, undermining the powerful, empowering the powerless." Id.

106. James M. Buchanan, Contractarian Presuppositions and Democratic Governance, *in* Politics and Process: New Essays in Democratic Thought 180–81 (Geoffrey Brennan & Loren E. Lomasky eds., 1989).

107. This formulation reflects the implicit understanding of the Court in articulating the one person/one vote rule of Reynolds v. Sims, 377 U.S. 533, 565 (1964), that each citizen should have the same chance as each other citizen to influence legislative outcomes. In a subsequent Article, I intend to argue that political equality also contains a political justice component that could be summarized as "3. everyone has a right to have basic interests acted upon."

108. This definition extends to votes cast by representatives the definition of dilution proposed by Stephen Wasby. See Wasby, Vote Dilution, Minority Voting Rights and the Courts at 1 (vote dilution is the result of a set of "techniques for reducing or nullifying the effects of the votes that minorities do cast).

109. If the outcome of a set of important yet controversial legislative issues would be different if voting were held exclusively among the white- rather than among the black-sponsored representatives, then the legislative voting is racially polarized. In racially polarized voting, the white representatives can use their numerical strength consistently to defeat the interests associated with, or promoted by, the black minority.

110. I use the term "prejudice" to include both the controversial meaning of group stigma and bias as well as the new meaning of disproportionate majority power that I develop below.

111. Contrary to the majority rule assumptions, where prejudice exists, minority interests do not cycle through the majority. This suggests that where there are permanent majorities, only the majority exercises self-determination. The minority is subject to external determination or majority determination. Dahl, supra note 17, at 147, 161.

112. In this sense, the proportionality principle recognizes the traditional one person/one vote qualitative dilution charge that residents in larger districts exercise disproportionate power. Unlike some one person/one vote remedies, however, interest representation attempts to equalize voting strength at both the electoral and legislative levels. The claim for legislative majority disaggregation derives from the mathematical argument that nonequipopulous districts can submerge the voting strength of residents in smaller districts, especially given the propensity of the representatives of the larger districts to vote as a bloc. See John F. Banzhaf, III, Multi-Member Electoral Districts—Do They Violate the "One Man, One Vote" Principle, 75 Yale L.J. 1309, 1319–24 (1966).

113. These thresholds, which are two sides of the same analytical coin, represent the dividing line between representation and nonrepresentation for a given group of voters. That is, any politically cohesive group of voters that constitutes a percentage of the electorate equal to, or greater than, the threshold of representation is ensured

representation. Mathematically, the threshold of representation is defined as $[1/(1+n)] + 1$, where n is the number of seats in the legislative body. See Bernard Grofman, Alternatives to Single-Member Plurality Districts: Legal and Empirical Issues, *in* Representation and Redistricting Issues 113 (Bernard Grofman, Arend Lijphart, Robert B. McKay & Howard A. Scarrow eds., 1982).

Similarly, any such group whose percentage of the electorate equals, or is lower than, the threshold of exclusion will not be represented. The threshold of exclusion is expressed mathematically as $[1/(1+n)] - 1$.

114. I use the term interest proportionality to refer to winner-take-only-some voting, in which decisionmaking procedures are designed to enable all groups to share in the decisionmaking process. It suggests that a fair shake is approximated by a fair share, meaning that 51% of the voters should enjoy approximately 51% of the power; likewise, 49% of the voters should exercise close to 49% of the power.

115. This is an elastic rather than rigid concept, modeled in that sense after the equal protection rule the Supreme Court developed to adjudicate post–*Reynolds v. Sims* reapportionment cases at the local and municipal levels. In local reapportionment jurisprudence, a range of deviations is tolerated, with a presumption that deviations of less than 10% are de minimus. See Connor v. Finch, 431 U.S. 407, 418 (1977). Population equality is most commonly measured by total deviation and average deviation. See Grofman, supra note 46, at 81–82.

116. The number ten reflects the exclusion threshold. Although it is perhaps an arbitrary number, it is no more so than the number three, and it still consists with one person/one vote notions of fairness because each student has an equal number of votes.

117. See, e.g., Parker v. Hoefer, 100 A.2d 434, 447–48 (Vt. 1953). The jury model's emphasis on achieving consensus in jury deliberations is consistent with the group process research, which suggests that a majority decisional rule tends to weaken the process of deliberation. See Reid Hastie, Steven Penrod, & Nancy Pennington, Inside the Jury (1983); Saul M. Kassin & Lawrence S. Wrightsman, The American Jury on Trial: Psychological Perspectives 201–2 (1988). According to group process theory, majority decisional rules are especially effective in "nullifying the potency of minority viewpoints." Hans Zeisel, . . . And Then There Were None: The Diminution of the Federal Jury, 38 U. Chi. L. Rev. 710, 722 (1971).

For example, the process of voting itself may polarize the debate, particularly when there are only two options, such as guilty or not guilty. With more options, such as degrees of homicide, compromise is possible. Also, where the objective is to reach a consensus result, voting may be less effective than direct persuasion. See Joan B. Kessler, The Social Psychology of Jury Deliberations, *in* The Jury System in America 69, 85–86 (Rita James Simon ed., 1975) (citing C. Hawkins, Interaction and Coalition Realignments in Consensus-Seeking Groups: A Study of Experimental Jury Deliberations 106–7 (1960) (Ph.D. dissertation, University of Chicago)). In addition, the size of the group may encourage factions, which then withdraw from the deliberation process, especially if the majority faction has disproportionate power. See Kassin & Wrightsman, supra, at 199, 201. *Any* decisional rule dependent on zero-sum voting may have the same effect. See, e.g., Harry Kalven & Hans Zeisel, The American Jury 489, 496 (1966).

In contrast, jurors who must reach a unanimous verdict are more likely to engage in thorough deliberation. See Kassin & Wrightsman, supra, at 201. Thus, the analogy to the ideal jury also flows from the fact that it is both democratic (in that it is intended to represent a cross-section of the community and that it serves an educative and legitimating function by allowing direct participation in the administration of justice) and that it is deliberative. See Hayden J. Trubitt, Patchwork Verdicts, Different Jurors Verdicts, and American Jury Theory: Whether Verdicts Are Invalidated by Juror Disagreement on Issues, 36 Okla. L. Rev. 473, 474–75 (1983). See generally Muzafer Sherif & Carolyn Sherif, Groups In Harmony and Tension: An Integration of Studies on Intergroup Relations 284–85 (1973) (reporting results of classic study dividing boys into two competitive groups who grew to hate each other, yet, when boys in both groups had to struggle together to pull a truck that was stuck, the experience of personal cooperative contact reduced hostility). See also Daniel Goleman, New Way to Battle Bias: Fight Acts, Not Feelings, N.Y. Times, July 16, 1991, at C1 (citing a 1989 study of 3,200 students at five middle schools in Florida in which interracial learning teams produced least-prejudiced students). See also Robert Axelrod, The Evolution of Cooperation 20–21 (1984).

118. That is, pending bills of importance to minorities would be linked to pending bills of importance to the majority, and each legislator would have an aggregate number of votes to cast on the linked bills, although they would not be required to vote on each bill or to vote as a bloc.

119. The minority veto is simply another way of referring to the effect of supermajority requirements. As a form of supermajority voting, it is arguably comparable to weighted voting plans that have been used in some jurisdictions to give some representatives additional power to compensate for population inequalities. See generally Ronald E. Johnson, An Analysis of Weighted Voting As Used in Reapportionment of County Governments in New York State, 34 Alb. L. Rev. 1, 16–38 (1969) (describing the effects of weighted voting as applied in New York State). Instead of compensating for population inequalities, however, the minority veto would be used to reduce to a proportionate level the disproportionate power white voters or representatives currently enjoy. The minority veto, as a remedy, would not be much different from mathematical models used to equalize voting strength where majority blocs based on regional or political affiliation are disaggregated. See R. Alta Charo, Designing Mathematical Models to Describe One-Person One-Vote Compliance by Unique Governmental Structures: The Case of the N.Y.C. Board of Estimate, 53 Fordham L. Rev. 735, 776–84 (1985); Franklin Krause, 298 N.E. 2d 68(N.Y. 1973), appeal dismissed, 415 U.S. 904 (1974); Iannucci v. Bd. of Supervisors, 229 N.E. 2d 195 (N.Y. 1967).

120. Quoted in Robert Pear, Under the Voting Law, Citizens' Rights Get More Than Lip Service, N.Y. Times, July 21, 1991, at E4, col. 1.

121. The choice of decisional rule in such circumstances means the majority gets to exercise 100%, and the minority representative none, of the legislative power. Cf. Grofman, Alternatives to Single-Member Plurality Districts: Legal and Empirical Issues *in* Representation and Redistricting Issues 107, 128 (Bernard Grofman, Arend Lijphart, Robert McKay, and Howard A. Scarrow eds., 1982) at 128 (stating that if there is a three-member commission in which A and B each have two votes and C has one, the decisional rule determines C's power; that is, if four is the decisional rule, C's vote is never decisive—in game theory terms, C is the dummy—but if three is the decisional rule, C's voting strength equals that of A and B). In the case of racial bloc

voting, on a three-person commission it is as if the two white commissioners each had two votes to the black commissioner's one using a decisional rule of four.

122. Certainly, legitimate questions can be raised about the degree to which courts or the United States Department of Justice can or should micromanage legislative bodies. I do not advocate investigating the political consequences for minorities every time, for example, committee assignments are reshuffled and a black, who had been appointed to chair an important committee, is reassigned in the normal course of legislative business. On the other hand, one could argue that the decision of who gets to attend an informal meeting is a decision that affects voting power and should be covered under section 5, where the challenged decision reflects a clear departure from past practice. For example, if the traditional practice of a particular committee to caucus informally were to be changed suddenly following the admission of a black committee member, section 5 might cover that decision, especially if the decision changes the membership base for informal gatherings to include all but the new black member. Perhaps the answer is to trigger preclearance review by the filing of a nonfrivolous complaint, thus placing the burden on anyone who opposes a particular exclusionary change to point to some plausible, potential detriment to minorities, at which point, if coverage were established, the burden would shift to the locality to rebut the allegation of detriment. Cf. Daniel H. Lowenstein, Political Bribery and the Intermediate Theory of Politics, 32 UCLA L. Rev. 784, 827–28 (1985) (arguing that a legislator's decision on who gets access to him or her is an "official action" for purposes of bribery statute).

123. Indeed, given the unwritten rule of circumvention nothing may ultimately make a difference. One could also argue convincingly that blacks will never achieve political equality until they first achieve social and economic equality. In addition, the political status quo factors that defeat the traditional black electoral success model will predictably dilute any concerted effort to improve legislative performance on behalf of black interests. As Professor Bell suggests with his interest-convergence hypothesis, any alternatives with real potential for effectiveness will attract fierce—and, ultimately, successful—opposition. See Bell, Brown v. Board of Education and the Interest-Convergence Dilemma, 93 Harv. L. Rev. 518 (1980). But cf. Michael J. Klarman, The Puzzling Resistance to Political Process Theory, 77 Va. L. Rev. 747, 777 (1991) (arguing that access to the ballot, standing alone, is sufficient to produce legislative benefits for blacks).

124. Cynthia V. Ward, The Limits of "Liberal Republicanism": Why Group-Based Remedies and Republican Citizenship Don't Mix, 91 Colum. L. Rev. 581, 593 (1991).

125. Lipset, supra note 89, at 80–81.

126. Of course, this is a problem primarily where the threshold for representation is extremely low. For example, in Israel the threshold for representation is apparently 1%. See C. Paul Bradley, Parliamentary Elections in Israel 21–22 (1985). By contrast, in my model, the threshold would be considerably higher. The threshold of exclusion would be jurisdiction-specific and possibly as high as 20% or 25%. In a proportionate interest representation scheme, the threshold of exclusion would be based on the number of votes necessary to ensure representation of the smallest politically cohesive minority that "deserved" representation. This number is concededly arbitrary, but no more so than existing preferences for dividing power based on arbitrarily limiting the number of seats within the legislative body.

127. Miller, supra note 99, at 743.

128. Cook, supra note 23, at 412; see also C. Edwin Baker, Neutrality, Process, and Rationality: Flawed Interpretations of Equal Protection, 58 Tex. L. Rev. 1029, 1044–45, 1053 (1980) (arguing that decisions to continue subordination of minorities can occur even if political process considers their interests); Laurence H. Tribe, The Puzzling Persistence of Process-Based Constitutional Theories, 89 Yale L.J. 1063, 1077 (1980) (arguing that protecting minorities requires theory of substantive rights).

129. See, e.g., Iris Young, Polity and Group Difference: A Critique of the Ideal of Universal Citizenship, 99 Ethics 250, 262–67 (1989). Indeed, from the minority perspective, the myth of the general perspective simply hides the ways that racial minorities have been specifically disadvantaged. The myth of the general perspective alienates because it does not include or recognize the validity of a distinct viewpoint of members of statutorily protected groups but simply ratifies their "distinctive group status" as "outside" or marginalized.

130. As Professor James Liebman has written:

> I realize that some people—perhaps, mostly white people—will disagree with these premises. For them, the pre- and post-desegregation situation more accurately would be encapsulated by a statement such as the following: "A year ago, we all were getting along fine. Then . . . [a]ll of a sudden, the whole community was disrupted, its citizens aroused and angry."

Liebman, Desegregating Politics: "All-Out" School Desegregation Explained, 90 Colum. L. Rev. 1463, 1618–19. Such statements manifest ongoing "racially selective sympathy and indifference" concerning minority victims. *Id.*

131. For example, exposing prejudice affirms the marginalized group's experience, even where such exposure by itself does nothing to change the behavior of prejudiced individuals.

132. Nevertheless, it may be that interest representation is based on a flawed empirical understanding. For example, there are certain configurations of preferences in which blacks may suffer under a proportionality principle. If fanatical racists or ultra-right wing extremists are equally numerous to blacks, disaggregating the majority may empower these groups as well. Also, a system that recognizes intensity of preferences may lead to stalemate, although stalemate is by no means inevitable in such a system. These are factual questions that I hope to answer eventually with the help of greater quantitative expertise. For the moment, however, I do not think that acknowledging these possibilities means they are probabilities. In any event, if either possibility materialized and resulted in racist legislation, constitutional prohibitions such as the right to equal protection of the laws would still be available as a basis for legal challenge. Moreover, where interest modifications have been implemented, they have apparently reinforced cooperative approaches to conflict resolution. See, e.g., Pamela Karlan, Maps and Misreadings, 24 Harv. C.R.-C.L. L. Rev. 173, at 246–47 (1989) (concluding that supermajority requirement "has distinctly improved political interaction between whites and blacks in Mobile").

133. Of course, increasing the accountability of minority representatives to their constituents requires more than mere structural reforms at either the electoral or legislative phases of the political process. Accountable representation, in my opinion, will not

be achieved without an insurgent model of citizen participation and monitoring throughout the extended political process. Indeed, political organizations and third political parties would be crucial to any model that anticipates an informed, mobilized electorate. In order to encourage the development of such organizations, the winner-take-all feature of majority rule must be eliminated. That is what this chapter urges.

134. The concept of proportional interest representation and the concept of proportional interest satisfaction, however, are not coterminous and objections to the interest satisfaction approach do not necessarily vitiate the value of interest representation.

135. Indeed, one might draw the lesson from my critique of black electoral success theory that no process-based reform, even one which attempts to enforce a substantive justice standard, may ultimately make a difference. One certainly could argue convincingly that blacks will never achieve political equality until they first achieve social and economic equality. As Professor Bell suggests with reference to the interest-convergence dilemma, see supra note 123, any alternative with real potential effectiveness will face fierce and politically powerful opposition. Others have also described this theme of pyrrhic victories. *See* Delgado, When a Story Is Just a Story: Does Voice Really Matter? 76 Va. L. Rev. 95, 196 (1990) (describing Law of Racial Thermodynamics in which "[r]acism is neither created nor destroyed" but merely has different guises, including "procedural" racism of seemingly neutral rules that predictably handicap blacks).

136. Hybrid forms of electoral representation, such as those I have advocated to satisfy proportionate interest representation, are better than exclusionary multimember election systems for all these groups. Depending on the particular facts, they are probably even preferable to single-member districts that waste votes within the district presumably controlled by the group and do not use efficiently group member votes in other majority-controlled districts. In any event, self-defining voluntary political constituencies including blacks will probably not come out worse under a hybrid form of representation and probably will come out much better, because they will be able to preserve both authenticity and reciprocity values. These distinctive self-defined groups will be able not only to elect candidates of choice but to become members of a coalition large enough to influence policy outcomes.

In addition, hybrid election reform "discards only the discriminatory part of the at-large system—the voting rule itself—and retains the part that is permissible—the underlying multimember district and the form of the elected body." Note, Alternative Voting Systems as Remedies for Unlawful At-Large Systems, 92 Yale L.J. 144, 158–59 (1982) (citation omitted).

137. See Still, Voluntary Constituencies: Limited Voting and Cumulative Voting as Remedies for Minority Vote Dilution in Judicial Elections, Yale L. & Pol. Rev. (1991). Of course, at the legislative level those cases will be hard to prove. Plaintiffs will have to put the local government on trial. This is problematic both as to a quantitative evidentiary analysis as well as the divisiveness with which any such inquiry is necessarily associated. A court might see fit to order a qualitative fairness remedy for legislative decisional rules only if plaintiffs prove high polarization thresholds and obviously discriminatory policy outputs over an extended period of time. This is also true if legislative remedies are implemented following proof of a violation at the electoral level.

138. The constitutional arguments against interest representation that will be treated elsewhere include the political question doctrine and legislative immunity.

139. 42 U.S.C. § 1973(a) (1988). Especially under section 5, which is a temporary measure supported by congressional findings justifying its extraordinary intrusion into the local affairs of covered jurisdictions, such judicial scrutiny is appropriate. Even under section 2, which is neither temporary nor jurisdiction-specific, providing judicial review of legislative voting rules is a necessary and proper exercise of congressional authority. Essentially, I would argue that the no-risk exclusion policy of the majority legislators, for whom single-member districts provide essential protection from defection as a result of their and their constituents' shared prejudice, justifies the need for greater scrutiny of internal legislative processes and a less deferential standard of review of certain legislative choices.

140. See, e.g., Oregon v. Mitchell, 400 U.S. 112 (1970); Katzenbach v. Morgan, 384 U.S. 641 (1966); South Carolina v. Katzenbach, 383 U.S. 301 (1966). These cases upheld Congress' broad remedial authority under the Constitution to enact measures to rectify the past discrimination in the provision of public services and to remove neutral devices that have the effect of perpetuating the intentional racial discrimination of the past.

141. Gingles v. Edmisten, 590 F. Supp. 345, 356–57 (E.D.N.C. 1984) (three-judge court) (footnotes omitted).

142. In this way, interest representation may constitute a "novel form of [self-]regulation" or "self-policing." Daniel Ortiz, Federalism, Reapportionment, and Incumbency: Leading the Legislature to Police Itself, 4 J.L. & Pol. 653, 658 (1988). Ortiz further notes that stringent remedial rules may dangle "carrots" of political preservation in front of incumbents by encouraging them to self-police the political process in order to avoid judicial scrutiny. Id.

143. As Samuel Issacharoff has written, interest representation should be "attractive to the courts as a proxy for the broader issue of the distributional consequences of political decisionmaking. . . . Polarized voting inquiry spares the court the need to review each item of legislative decisionmaking and, if need be, to strike it down as racially invidious." Issacharoff, supra note 101.

   Nevertheless, some argue that congressionally mandated judicial intervention to protect "group rights" inexorably leads to reverse discrimination. See Thernstrom, supra note 53, Ch. 3, at 242. But see Garza v. County of Los Angeles, 918 F.2d 763 (9th Cir. 1990) (rejecting counsel's claim that reverse discrimination results from the enforcement of the Voting Rights Act). Although it enforces a group right to representation, the interest representation approach seeks to answer the reverse discrimination argument by challenging the winner-take-all majority rule, which fixes political power mechanically and exogenously. Interest representation operates as a baseline against which to measure the unfairness of existing political arrangements even if it is not implemented exactly as I have proposed. Moreover, the interest representation remedial ideal, which incorporates a consensus, deliberative model of political process, is consistent with the dispersed power concept embedded in the American constitutional system of checks and balances.

144. See Reynolds v. Sims, 377 U.S. 533, 565 (1964); Wesberry v. Sanders, 376 U.S. 1, 8 (1964).

Chapter 5. *Groups, Representation, and Race Conscious Districting*

1. Robert G. Dixon, Jr., Democratic Representation: Reapportionment in Law and Politics 22 (1968) (emphasis added).

2. I use the term "race-conscious districting" to describe the practice of consolidating the number of minority group members in a single or a few winner-take-all subdistricts. Yet, in a racially polarized environment, the process of districting is inevitably race-conscious. *See* Lani Guinier, *The Representation of Minority Interests: The Question of Single-Member Districts,* 14 Cardozo L. Rev. 1135, 1135 n.2 (1993) (arguing that winner-take-all districts ultimately enable one group or another to dominate, meaning there is a racial consequence to the demographic constitution of all racially mixed districts if voting is racially polarized. *See also infra* notes 116–117 and accompanying text.

3. Jim Sleeper, *Rigging the Vote by Race,* Wall St., J., Aug. 4, 1992, at A14. Sleeper admits he has taken many of his ideas about the Voting Rights Act from Abigail M. Thernstrom, Whose Votes Count? (1987). *Id.*

4. *Id.*

5. *See ABC News Special: The '92 Vote* (ABC television broadcast, Nov. 3, 1992), *available in* LEXIS, CMPGN Library, ABCNEW File. It may be worth noting for the record that Ms. Roberts's mother, Lindey Boggs, was arguably "redistricted" out of a seat in Congress in response to a successful lawsuit under the Voting Rights Act. *See* Major v. Treen, 574 F. Supp. 325 (E.D. La. 1983).

6. *See* Shaw v. Reno, 113 S. Ct. 2816, 2828 (1993) ("For these reasons, we conclude that a plaintiff challenging a reapportionment statute under the Equal Protection Clause may state a claim by alleging that the legislation, though race-neutral on its face, rationally cannot be understood as anything other than an effort to separate voters into different jurisdictions on the basis of race, and that the separation lacks sufficient justification.").

7. I use the term "integrated" to describe a racial composition close to 50% black and 50% white.

8. *See* Jim Sleeper, The Closest of Strangers 159 (1990) ("Liberals and black civil rights activists thus shifted from demanding equality of individual opportunity which entails color-blind respect for a person's merits and rights beneath the skin, to demanding equality of condition, which submerges individual dignity beneath a color-based emphasis on the putative 'rights' of historically deprived ethnic groups.").

9. This is essentially the argument that there is a dominant "culture of whiteness" that is a unifying—even if unconscious—experience for some and an exclusionary experience for those who are not white. *See* Patricia J. Williams, Metro Broadcasting, Inc., v. FCC: *Regrouping in Singular Times,* 104 Harv. L. Rev. 525, 529–31 (1990).

10. By legitimacy I mean the perception that the process is fair, even from the perspective of adversely affected parties.

11. By this definition, the majority in *Shaw* misuses the term "gerrymandering" to describe a 54% black district which, as the majority concedes, was drawn to remedy a century of racial exclusion and which, as the majority also acknowledges, did not arbitrarily enhance or diminish the political power of any group. *See* Shaw v. Reno, 113 S. Ct. 2816, 2824, 2832 (1993) (mentioning North Carolina's checkered race-relation

past and noting that the plaintiffs did not claim that the redistricting would lead to the dilution of the European-American vote). Calling the district a racial gerrymander is simply inaccurate since it does not "arbitrarily allocate disproportionate political power" to any group. As the majority recognizes, all districting takes race into account. *Id.* at 2826. Thus this district, by its very terms, did nothing more than take race into account to create a racially competitive or racially integrated district. Its offense, to the extent the Court identifies the nature of the new constitutional injury, was that its "bizarre" shape was aesthetically unappealing to white voters and "stigmatizing" to black voters. *Id.* at 2824–25. Although Justice O'Connor thundered against "political apartheid," the claim that the district separated voters by race is not supported by the district's own racial composition, which is the most integrated district in the state.

In terms of the district's aesthetics, O'Connor is quite correct that drawn on a map, the shape of the district is "bizarre." But within a geography-is-a-proxy-for-interest paradigm, the relevant inquiry is not the district's shape but its feel: does it reflect an effort to connect voters who have a relevant community of interest? *Cf.* Dillard v. Baldwin County Bd. of Educ., 686 F. Supp. 1459 (M.D. Ala. 1988) (concluding that a district is sufficiently compact if it has a "sense of community"). The evidence in this and other North Carolina cases demonstrates that blacks in that state are politically cohesive. Thus, the evidence of persistent racial bloc voting and racial appeals in North Carolina means that it is not an assumption, but a fact, that blacks function as a racial as well as a political group. To call this fact a racial stereotype takes all meaning from the term, which is about prejudging, not observing.

12. A recent example is Chilton County, Alabama, where the first Republican and the first black were elected to the county commission when the county implemented a modified at-large system of election using cumulative voting. Jim Yardley, *1 Voter, 7 Votes? County Boosts Minority Clout,* ATLANTA J. & CONST., Oct. 23, 1992, at G5. Because the balance of power on the commission is now closely divided between white Republicans and white Democrats, even if voting is racially polarized the black Democrat may become an influential swing vote.

13. By representation of racial groups, I do not mean to suggest that only members of a group can represent its interests, that members of a group are necessarily racially similar, or that racial group members are necessarily homogeneous in thinking or interest. *See infra* note 53 and accompanying text.

14. In this sense I take issue with Judge Chapman's dissent in Collins v. City of Norfolk, 883 F.2d 1232, 1244–51 (4th Cir. 1989) (Chapman, J., dissenting), *cert. denied,* 498 U.S. 938 (1990). Judge Chapman suggests that vote dilution, which he defines exclusively in terms of electoral access, has nothing to do with the *ideas* of certain candidates. For him, "[r]epresentativeness in a Voting Rights context concerns access, and it does not create a right to the representation of certain ideologies." *Id.* at 1246. Chapman seems to suggest that ideological representation necessarily requires a "political litmus test" of minority-preferred candidates in which "there are 'proper' black political attitudes, and therefore under the Voting Rights Act some ideas are worth more than others." *Id.*

The one-vote, one-value standard does employ a political rather than a racial litmus test, but it allows the voters themselves to determine, at each election, what political attitudes they want represented.

15. For the liberal, "the ultimate unit is not class, estate, rank or interest, but the independent, rational man. . . . The people are a mass, an entity, and, ideally, act as one. Yet they achieve that unity of action by a series of individual acts of mind stimulated by common discussion." Samuel H. Beer, *The Representation of Interests in British Government: Historical Background,* 51 Am. Pol. Sci. Rev. 613, 634 (1957). But even those who argue that it is the individual who is being represented concede that the individual's vote is influenced by group affiliations. *See, e.g.,* V. P. Auerbach, *The Reapportionment Cases: One Person, One Vote–One Vote, One Value,* 1964, Sup. Rev. 55, 56.

    The right to vote also bears purely symbolic significance. *See* Judith N. Shklar, American Citizenship: The Quest for Inclusion 27 (1991) (arguing that civic significance comes from having the right to vote, not from actually casting a ballot).

16. The Court has described voting rights as "individual and personal in nature." *Reynolds,* 377 U.S. at 561. The Court continued, "Legislators represent people, not trees or acres. Legislators are elected by voters, not farms or cities or economic interests." *Id.* at 562.

17. John Low-Beer has distinguished the right to an equally weighted vote, which is implicated in reapportionment cases, from the right to an equally meaningful vote, which is implicated in gerrymandering cases. John R. Low-Beer, *The Constitutional Imperative of Proportional Representation,* 94 Yale L.J. 163, 164 n.3 (1984); *cf. Reynolds,* 377 U.S. at 579 (defining the "equal-population principle" as the standard for equal weighting); Terry v. Adams, 345 U.S. 461, 484 (1953) (finding that "an empty vote cast after the real decisions are made" did not provide a meaningful right to vote).

    The equal population principle is, however, an imperfect approximation of equally weighted voting because district size is based on population, rather than on voting age population or registered voters. *Cf.* Mahan v. Howell, 410 U.S. 315, 322 (1973) ("[P]opulation alone has been the sole criterion of constitutionality in congressional redistricting under Art. I, § 2."). If one-person, one-vote is satisfied by such population-based reapportionment, I would argue that this principle views representation as equal access to a representative, whether the voter voted for the representative or even voted at all. I have argued elsewhere that equally weighted voting really means an equal opportunity to influence the processes of government. *See* Guinier, *supra* Ch. 4. Under this view, the right to fair and effective representation subsumes both equally weighted voting and equally powerful voting.

18. *See id.* at 1633 (discussing the reapportionment cases' articulation of a political equality norm). Fair and effective representation envisions an equality norm—the right of all citizens to equal treatment as citizens in a democracy. In addition, the equality norm says that every *person* has an equal right to government services. An equal right to government services is not the same as a right to equal government services. In this sense, I am equating the right to services with a right of access to the benefits of government.

19. Kirkpatrick v. Preisler, 394 U.S. 526, 531 (1969).

20. The Supreme Court developed its one-person, one-vote jurisprudence in response to the disproportionate power exercised by a political minority. *See* Gray v. Sanders, 372 U.S. 368, 379 (1963) (expressing dissatisfaction with an electoral system that gives disproportionate weight to rural votes and to votes from less populous counties). The Court found a constitutional right to population-based apportionment on the theory

that the majority of the population should have a majority voice in the legislature. *Cf.* Reynolds v. Sims, 377 U.S. 533, 565 (1964) (noting that denying the majority the right to control the legislature would far surpass the dangers of any possible denial of minority rights). Of course, minority interests should also be represented. In fact, concern with representing group interests was a major theme of Justice Stewart's famous dissent in Lucas v. Forty-Fourth General Assembly, 377 U.S. 713, 744–65 (1964) (Stewart, J., dissenting). Stewart's group interests were determined by the state, not by the individual voter, in part because he perceived federalism concerns to be the missing element in the requirement of strict population equality. *Id.* at 744–45. Stewart's repeated references to the legitimacy of group interests as recognized by the state, *id.* at 748–49, 759, 765, reflect, however, an implicit faith in state government to provide a voice to minority interests.

Some argue, however, that the one-person, one-vote principle was designed primarily to restore a competing principle: majority rule or majority legislative power. *See* Gordon E. Baker, *The Unfinished Reapportionment Revolution, in* POLITICAL GERRYMANDERING AND THE COURTS 11, 14 (Bernard Grofman ed., 1990) (asserting that the outcome of an insistence on voter equality is "conditioned majoritarianism"). Yet majority rule need not mean that a simple majority inexorably prevails. Even if it does, there is a big difference between the majority winning legislative power and the majority controlling *all* the legislative power. I have argued elsewhere that winner-take-all majority rule is often fundamentally at odds with traditional notions of democracy. *See* Guinier, *supra* ch. 4. at 102ff (arguing that winner-take-all majority rule based on a prejudiced majority is itself illegitimate).

21. *See* Low-Beer, *supra* note 17, at 177. Low-Beer notes that individuals can be represented only insofar as they share certain interests:

> No meaningful voting right can be defined exclusively in individual terms. A legislator inevitably votes on behalf of the collective as well as the individual interests of her constituents. Only the provision of personal services or the sponsoring of a private bill involves purely personal representation.

Id.; see also MARTIN SHAPIRO, LAW AND POLITICS IN THE SUPREME COURT 249 (1964) (asserting that "one person, one vote" ignores "the group nature of politics" by assuming that each individual exercises her whole political power by voting); Alexander M. Bickel, *The Supreme Court and Reapportionment, in* REAPPORTIONMENT IN THE 1970s, 57, 59 (Nelson W. Polsby ed., 1971) ("We have, since Madison, realized that people tend to act politically not so much as individuals as in groups. . . ."). *See also* V. O. KEY, POLITICS, PARTIES, & PRESSURE GROUPS 589 (5th ed. 1969) (observing that because group affiliation is of special importance to political participation, persons with strong groups of organizational attachments are more likely to vote).

22. Davis v. Bandemer, 478 U.S. 109, 167 (1986) (Powell, J., concurring and dissenting).

23. Complaint at 16, Baker v. Carr, 175 F. Supp. 649 (M.D. Tenn. 1959) (Civ. A. No. 2724); Baker v. Carr, 369 U.S. 186, 272 (1962) (Frankfurter, J., dissenting). The dissenting opinions acknowledge the claim that the distribution of electoral strength among geographic units reflects a legislative judgment about the representation of interests. *See, e.g., id.* at 334 (Harlan, J., dissenting).

24. *See Davis,* 478 U.S. at 125 & n.9 (explaining that the racial gerrymandering cases established the objective of fair and adequate group representation). Justice O'Con-

nor's majority opinion in Shaw v. Reno, 113 S. Ct. 2816 (1993), however, may suggest that the Court will revisit this policy decision. As Justice Stevens suggests in dissent, the only group no longer entitled to fair representation may now be African-Americans. *See id.* at 2844–45 (Stevens, J., dissenting). If Justice Stevens's observation proves correct, such a "perverse" consequence would not eliminate the concept of group representation, which would still be available for "Polish Americans, or for Republicans." *Id.*

25. In asserting the prominence of group identity and the necessity of collective action to political organization and efficiency, I do not set out a theory of group rights. Nor do I yet define the parameters of group representation. Group status could mean a collection of people with identifiable characteristics. It could also mean a collection of people with common interests. In this chapter I simply pose the preliminary issue that the concept of representation necessarily applies to the representation of a group. Once I pass this threshold question, I will need to explore the next set of questions, one of which will certainly be: What is a group?

    There is in addition an important caveat to the claim here that the concept of representation necessarily applies to groups. I am not assigning value to groups over individuals. Individuals as the ultimate objects of concern do not disappear from view. Indeed, I attempt to recognize the individual by empowering each voter to choose her district, *i.e.*, her temporary group affiliation. Indeed, by advocating the benefits of modified-at-large elections, I seek to put in the hands of the voters the degree to which they want their race or other demographic characteristic to be represented, *i.e.*, the degree to which their group's status is salient or relevant.

26. Low-Beer, *supra* note 17, at 176 n. 63; *see also* DIXON, *supra* note 1, at 48–49 (contrasting proportional representation with districting based upon residency). Geographic districting necessarily advantages some groups and disadvantages others. In this sense, "all districting is 'gerrymandering.' " *Id.* at 462. The Supreme Court has recognized the impact that districting has on opposing groups:

    > It is not only obvious, but absolutely unavoidable, that the location and shape of districts may well determine the political complexion of the area. *District lines are rarely neutral phenomena.* They can well determine what district will be predominantly Democratic or predominantly Republican, or make a close race likely. Redistricting may put incumbents against one another or make very difficult the election of the most experienced legislator. *The reality is that districting inevitably has and is intended to have substantial political consequences.*

    Gaffney v. Cummings, 412 U.S. 735, 753 (1973) (emphasis added).

27. Lucas v. Forty-Fourth General Assembly, 377 U.S. 713, 750 (1964) (Stewart, J., dissenting); *see also* Reynolds v. Sims, 377 U.S. 533, 623–24 (1964) (Harlan, J., dissenting) (stating that constituents' interests often reflect their geographic location). Other commentators agree that geographic districts ensure interest representation. *See* Alexander M. Bickel, *Reapportionment & Liberal Myths*, 35 COMMENTARY 483, 489 (1963); Jo Desha Lucas, *Legislative Apportionment and Representative Government*, 61 MICH. L. REV. 711, 756–66 (1963); Phil C. Neal, Baker v. Carr: *Politics in Search of Law*, 1962 SUP. CT. REV. 252, 277–86; *see also* ALFRED DE GRAZIA, ESSAY ON APPORTIONMENT AND REPRESENTATIVE GOVERNMENT 28 (1963) (stating that "a legislature based solely on territorial apportionment will represent something of a community"). There

is very little actual individual representation, only community representation. "As it has developed historically, the territorial survey type of apportionment has granted emphasis to community representation and especially to local real property interests." *Id.*

28. ENID LAKEMAN, HOW DEMOCRACIES VOTE 29–30 (4th ed. 1974).

29. A. F. POLLARD, THE EVOLUTION OF PARLIAMENT 164 (2d ed. 1926). The English Parliament was originally an assembly of the "estates" of the clergy, the baronage, and the commons. *See generally* WILLIAM STUBBS, 2 THE CONSTITUTIONAL HISTORY OF ENGLAND 166–203 (1875) (recounting the history of the system of estates under Edward I). Members of medieval parliaments were selected by common consent in order to represent the unanimous mind of the county or borough that was being represented. JENNIFER HART, PROPORTIONAL REPRESENTATION: CRITICS OF THE BRITISH ELECTORAL SYSTEM 1820–1945, at 5 (1992). When this method of membership selection became unmanageable, a rule of the bare majority was established by which members of parliament were elected by relative majorities if a poll was held. *Id.* Enid Lakeman suggests that the system evolved to capture broadly the main trends of opinion rather than exact proportions of political interest. LAKEMAN, *supra* note 28, at 40.

30. PETER G.J. PULZER, POLITICAL REPRESENTATION AND ELECTIONS: PARTIES AND VOTING IN GREAT BRITAIN 32 (1967); *see* Beer, *supra* note 15, at 617 ("[The Old Whig theory, the dominant political theory of the eighteenth century,] conceived of representation as being not of individuals, but rather of corporate bodies, although not in the strict legal sense of the term."); *see also* PULZER, *supra*, at 14–15 ("In the eighteenth century, under the influence of Whig ideas, it was considered proper and desirable that representation should be by interest, even if these interests were no longer the corporations and estates of mediaeval society.").

31. Beer, *supra* note 15, at 618. In contrast to this Whig view, liberals assumed that representation was of individuals rather than of "corporate bodies" or interests and could best be realized by equal electoral districts. *Id.* at 629–30. . . . Liberals in America had a pronounced suspicion of interests although their fear was based primarily on the representation of special interests. *Id.* at 631. But as I argue, the liberal claim that rule by the majority would defeat special interests is in fact informed by Old Whig theories of virtual representation. *See infra* note 40 and accompanying text.

32. "It was not merely Parliament collectively, but the individual MP who was considered autonomous." PULZER, *supra* note 30, at 22. Likewise, in 1774, Edmund Burke asserted: "Parliament is not a *congress* of ambassadors from different and hostile interests; . . . but parliament is a *deliberate* assembly of *one* nation, with *one* interest, that of the whole. . . ." *Id.* (emphasis in original).

33. *See* Gerald E. Frug, *The City as a Legal Concept,* 93 HARV. L. REV. 1057, 1083 (1980) ("The medieval town was not an artificial entity separate from its inhabitants; it was a group of people seeking protection against outsiders for the interests of the group as a whole.").

34. *See* GORDON E. BAKER, THE REAPPORTIONMENT REVOLUTION: REPRESENTATION, POLITICAL POWER, AND THE SUPREME COURT 16 (1966) ("In view of this English background, it is not surprising that representation in colonial America was originally based on location.") This "representation by town" was illustrated in 1787 when the delegates gathered to create the United States Constitution and the smaller states were reluctant to yield their accustomed equality of status. *Id.* at 16–18; *see also* DE GRAZIA, *supra* note

27, at 26 ("Territorial representation, with equal representation to all men, was the ideal formula for a democratic rural society and was espoused as such . . . in America and elsewhere.")

Basing the franchise on the ownership of property also reflects this relationship. *Cf.* Minor v. Happersett, 88 U.S. (1 Wall.) 162, 172–73 (1874) (collecting state statutes that impose restrictions on the right to vote, some of which condition the franchise on property ownership); Beer, *supra* note 27, at 630 (discussing the importance of property in determining electoral participation in both Britain and the United States).

35. Frug, *supra* note 33, at 1098.

36. *See* Low-Beer, *supra* note 17, at 176 n. 63. *But cf.* Davis v. Bandemer, 478 U.S. 109, 173 n.13 (1986) (Powell, J., concurring and dissenting) (describing as "artificial communities" those district boundaries drawn with no rationality and finding that where district lines are irrational, they limit the opportunity of citizens "to become familiar with their voting districts, where they must focus their political activities" and "affect the ability of all voters to exercise their political influence").

37. Hierarchical relationships refer to associations or connections between people of unequal status and/or power. *See* Frug, *supra* note 33, at 1097 (describing the hierarchical relationships in early medieval towns); *cf.* Dunn v. Blumstein, 405 U.S. 330, 354–55 (1972) (striking down a durational residence requirement as an improper means of assuring that all residents share a local perspective); *see also infra* note 50 (describing the hierarchy of geography, which disadvantages those who live in poor neighborhoods).

38. *See Lucas,* 377 U.S. at 750 (Steward, J., dissenting) ("The Court today declines to give any recognition to these [local] considerations and countless others, tangible and intangible. . . .").

39. One difference between direct and indirect representation is the extent to which the voters' choice is considered paramount in defining the representational relationship. Direct representation is the representation by someone of the voters' choosing. Indirect representation, by contrast, is the representation of the voters' interests by someone for whom the voter did not vote. Another difference relates to the representative's role. Direct representation posits the representative as an agent or delegate who acts on behalf of, and at the direction of, those who selected her. Indirect representation, by contrast, incorporates a trustee concept of the representative. In a trustee relationship, the representative is public regarding and conscientious based on her own sense of the common good. For example, indirect representation assumes that the representative will act in the interests of political opponents to diffuse their opposition.

In sum, direct representation emphasizes the voters' participation and choice in initiating and terminating the relationship. Indirect representation focuses attention on the representative's capacity to negotiate consensus.

40. *See* Davis v. Bandemer, 478 U.S. 109, 132 (1986) ("[P]ower to influence the political process is not limited to winning elections."). *But see id.* at 170 (Powell, J., concurring and dissenting) ("[I]t defies political reality to suppose that members of a losing party have as much political influence over state government as do members of the victorious party. Even the most conscientious state legislators do not disregard opportunities to reward persons or groups who were active supporters in their election campaigns.").

41. *See supra* note 39 (identifying differences between direct and indirect representa-

tion). This critical view of direct representation of interests reflects a political judgment that interests, or factions, are the bane of democracy. Therefore, interests are suspect and expression of interests should be mutual or counterbalanced wherever possible. *See* HANNA F. PITKIN, THE CONCEPT OF REPRESENTATION 186–90 (1967). However, some commentators held the view that

> [t]he principle of representation is based on the assumed right on the part of the citizen to take part in the business of making the laws which are to govern him; as there are practical difficulties in the way of his doing so, he must appear by deputy—each man is entitled thus to appear by deputy. . . . [If votes are wasted in the election process] it as effectually disfranchises the citizen as though a positive law disqualified him from going to the polls; it gives him the semblance, but deprives him of the substance, of his right. Even the majorities that are represented are unfairly and improperly represented, as the voter is compelled to sink his individuality, and oftentimes his best political opinions, for the purpose of belonging to the represented class.

Simon Sterne, *The Representational Likeness,* in REPRESENTATION 73, 74–77 (Hanna F. Pitkin, ed., 1969).

42. Davis v. Bandemer, 478 U.S. 109, 132 (1986). *But see id.* at 169–70 n.7 (Powell, J., concurring and dissenting) (arguing that the plurality's finding that a "losing" voter will be adequately represented was a "leap" from the conclusion that a redistricting plan is not unconstitutional merely because it makes it harder for a group to elect its own candidate).

43. Theoretically, of course, it might be possible to draw random, competitive districts in which no "group" was assured of electoral control. In such districts, electoral control would presumably shift depending on issues, candidates, and local electoral events. But this possibility rests on a different premise from the traditional justification for districting—that districting presumes some group characteristics—and simply assumes that the groups can be fairly distributed without wasting their votes in the second sense of packing. This assumption, however, still allows wasting votes in the first sense in that some voters, albeit different voters each election, waste votes by voting for a political loser. The possibility of a "political fairness" approach—measuring fairness based on proportionate jurisdiction-wide influence—cannot be realized without an accurate measure of group voting strength. *Cf.* Davis v. Bandemer, 478 U.S., 109, 155 (O'Connor, J., concurring) (stating that allowing a "waste" of individual votes through a bipartisan gerrymander is contrary to the meaning of the Equal Protection Clause in that it confers more rights to politically powerful groups than to individuals).

44. People with low incomes are relegated to living in deteriorating neighborhoods; affluent and middle class residential areas are generally not accessible to them. *See, e.g., Housing and Urban Development Secretary Henry Cisneros' Remarks on "The Changing Federal Role in Urban Policy" at a Progressive Policy Institute Conference,* Reuter Transcript Rep., Apr. 19, 1993, *available in* LEXIS, Nexis Library, Wires File (noting that poverty is "geographically isolated, economically depressed, [and] racially segregated" and that cities "have become warehouses of our poorest").

45. *See, e.g.,* Davis v. Bandemer, 478 U.S. 109, 175 (1986) (Powell, J., dissenting) (warning that "[c]omputer technology now enables gerrymanderers to achieve their purpose while adhering perfectly to the requirements that districts be of equal population"); Whitcomb v. Chavis, 403 U.S. 124, 177–78 (1971) (Douglas, J., concur-

ring and dissenting) (explaining that despite achieving "substantial equality of population within each district," lines may nevertheless be drawn so as to favor a particular political party).

46. By group identity, I mean the tendency to self-identify as a group member and to perceive one's group membership as a salient feature in relationships with group and nongroup members. In another context, Professor Gerald Torres has suggested that this concept is captured by the question: Does your cultural grouping determine the narrative structure through which you organize your life? *See* Gerald Torres & Kathryn Milun, *Translating* Yonnondio *by Precedent and Evidence: The Mashpee Indian Case,* 1990 DUKE L.J. 625, 657–58.

47. Studies of black and female politicians do show that they have somewhat different agendas. *See* Rufus P. Browning et al., *Racial Politics in American Cities: Blacks and Hispanics in the U.S., in* POLITICAL MOBILIZATION, POWER AND PROSPECTS (1990); *see also* R. W. Apple, Jr., *Steady Local Gains by Women Fuel More Runs for High Office,* N.Y. TIMES, May 24, 1992, § 4, at 5 (reporting on a survey of approximately half of all state legislatures which found that "even when men and women shared the same party affiliation and ideology, women were much more likely to expend their energies on health care, children's and family questions and women's rights issues; survey also found that women public officials tend more than their male counterparts of the same party and ideology to involve private citizens in governmental process to focus on needs of the poor, and to conduct public business in the open rather than behind closed doors); Gwen Ifill, *Female Lawmakers Wrestle with New Public Attitude on 'Women's' Issues,* N.Y. TIMES, Nov. 18, 1991, at B7 (describing a study done by the Center for American Women and Politics at Rutgers University which found huge gaps between male and female legislators over issues involving women's rights, health care, and children).

48. PITKIN, *supra* note 41, at 89.

49. *See* Evelyn E. Shockley, Note, *Voting Rights Act Section 2: Racially Polarized Voting and the Minority Community's Representative of Choice,* 89 MICH. L. REV. 1038, 1061–62 (1991) (explaining that in determining the relevance of a candidate's race, the "best [judicial] approach relies on *sponsorship*: the minority community's 'representative of choice' can only be a candidate who was sponsored by that community," and that such an approach "will satisfy proponents of a focus on civil inclusion").

50. This use of geography as a proxy for "race" is not limited to voting rights. "Demographic red-lining" for marketing direct sales also relies on information about zip codes and housing tracts from census data. JEFFREY ROTHFEDER, PRIVACY FOR SALE 102–5 (1992) (describing how demographic redlining—based on detailed data information bases—has been correctly denounced as a form of racial discrimination). "Tell me someone's zip code, and I can predict what they . . . even think." *Id.* at 102–3.

51. *Cf.* James F. Blumstein, *Defining and Proving Race Discrimination Perspectives on the Purpose vs. Results Approach from the Voting Rights Act,* 69 VA. L. REV. 633, 636 (1983) (concluding that while minorities have the right to ballot access, there is no corresponding entitlement to racial group representation).

52. *Id.* at 712 n.378; *see also* Michel Rosenfeld, *Affirmative Action, Justice, and Equalities: A Philosophical and Constitutional Appraisal,* 46 OHIO ST. L.J. 845, 912 (1985) ("The right to vote is a paradigmatic individual right. Each individual has only one

vote, and absent any discrimination or unfair procedures, no group of voters has a right to complain that its candidate lost."); *cf.* Brian K. Landsberg, *Race and the Rehnquist Court,* 66 TUL. L. REV. 1267, 1305 (1992) (asserting that proponents of the individual-based model tend to oppose race-conscious affirmative action).

53. Of course, some commentators challenge race-conscious districting on grounds unrelated to group representation principles. To some of these critics, requirements to maximize minority representation are a quota system that awards benefits, *i.e.,* votes, through a racial entitlement. They view the arguments for minority representation in proportion to minority population ominously because the arguments rely on the implicit belief that maximizing minority representation means accepting the assumption that only minorities should represent minorities. Abigail Thernstrom, for example, is quoted as denouncing this assumption because it reflects the divisive notion that "this is a deeply divided society of separate nations." Ronald Brownstein, *Minority Quotas in Elections?* L.A. TIMES, Aug. 28, 1991, at A1, A14. Similarly, Judge Eisele asks, "Do we really believe in the idea of one political society or should this be a nation of separate racial, ethnic, and language political enclaves?" Jeffers v. Clinton, 730 F. Supp. 196, 227 (E.D. Ark, 1989) (Eisele, C.J., dissenting), *aff'd,* 498 U.S. 1019 (1991).

My response to this criticism is twofold. First, to some extent I agree that the current approach is divisive. Nevertheless, the right to vote is not a benefit but an essential element of our system's political legitimacy. Therefore, those who take issue with current approaches have a responsibility not just to criticize but to propose alternative solutions that protect the right of the minority to have its voice represented and heard in the legislative debate. Second, in light of recent events in Los Angeles, concerns about *unnecessarily* dividing society do not seem consistent with the divided society in which we already find ourselves. These concerns fail to acknowledge the prediction from twenty years ago of the Kerner Commission Report, that unfortunately we *are* becoming two nations, separate and unequal. *See* NAT'L ADVISORY COMM'N ON CIVIL DISORDERS, REPORT OF THE NAT'L ADVISORY COMM'N ON CIVIL DISORDERS 1 (1968); *see also* Samuel Issacharoff, *Polarized Voting and the Political Process: The Transformation of Voting Rights Jurisprudence,* 90 MICH. L. REV. 117 (1992) (documenting and analyzing the significance of racially polarized voting in contemporary political discourse). While concerns about balkanization are real, the solution to the problem of racial division is not to ignore the divisions but to attempt to heal them.

Other critics object to race-conscious districting on moral grounds. *See, e.g.,* T. Alexander Aleinikoff, *A Case for Race-Consciousness,* 91 COLUM. L. REV. 1060, 1063 (1991) ("[T]he race of a person tells us nothing about an individual's capabilities and certainly nothing about her moral worth. Race-consciousness, from this perspective, is disfavored because it assigns a value to what should be a meaningless variable. To categorize on the basis of race is to miss the individual."); Neil Gotanda, *A Critique of "Our Constitution is Color-Blind,"* 44 STAN. L. REV. 1, 16 (1991) (stating that opponents of race-conscious decisionmaking believe the approach is morally inferior to a technique which ignores race as a factor). My response to this objection rests, in part, on a claim that to a greater or lesser degree, all districting is gerrymandering. In other words, the criteria for drawing district lines are arbitrary and subject to the preferences of those drawing the districts.

54. *See, e.g.,* Shaw v. Reno, 113 S. Ct. 2816, 2827 (1993) (arguing that a "reapportionment plan that includes in one district individuals . . . who may have little in common

with one another but the color of their skin bears an uncomfortable resemblance to political apartheid"). The majority suggests that consciously drawing districts to represent black voters as a group is problematic, although in political terms, the districting plan is "fair." This is essentially a moral claim which the Court then constitutionalizes. *See supra* text accompanying note 6.

55. This particular concern is primarily hypothetical. Blacks are very unlikely to be elected from any majority white districts, and all majority black congressional districts now elect black officeholders. Bernard Grofman & Lisa Handley, *The Impact of the Voting Rights Act on Black Representation in Southern State Legislatures,* 16 Legis. Stud. Q. 111, 117 (1991).

56. This is not to suggest that arguments for group rights can be ignored. *See, e.g.,* Williams, *supra* note 9, at 545–46 (arguing that the Court should advance the rights of minority groups to achieve the socially desirable goals of diversity and multiculturalism); Melissa Williams, Memory, History and Membership: The Moral Claims of Marginalized Groups in American Political Representation, paper delivered at the Annual Meeting of the American Political Science Association, Chicago, Illinois (Sept. 3, 1992). I simply choose not to make such an argument here.

57. Unanimous constituencies are those in which all voters agree on a basic definition of their interests. A unanimous constituency lets the voters choose which interest is salient and should be promoted. In a divided constituency, it is the legislator whose choice is important as she attempts to strike a balance among her supporters. Unanimous constituencies focus on the role of the voter; divided constituencies adopt a trustee view of representation. The former is a bottom-up view of representation; the latter is top-down.

The bottom-up view of unanimous constituencies assumes that voters, not legislators, should be empowered to make legislative choices, at least initially, for several reasons. First, it adopts a delegate or agency view of representation that suggests legislators represent the parts in order to avoid viewpoint monopoly. By encouraging the active assertion of diverse perspectives, the legislative process is infused with more and different ideas. This discourages monolithic control of legislative agendas by assuring the active representation of unanimous, issue-oriented constituencies. The second assumption is that compromise should occur openly after an election as part of the deliberate process of legislative debate rather than behind closed doors, where office seekers pre-"position" themselves to camouflage mutually inconsistent or divergent philosophies. In this sense, it reflects a more participatory view of fairness as the balancing of perspectives rather than as the absence of a viewpoint.

Third, it assumes that issue-based, rather than candidate-based, constituencies will be mobilized to participate throughout the political process, not just on election day. In this way it responds to the increasing levels of alienation and passivity within the electorate. *Cf.* Burt Neuborne, *Of Sausage Factories and Syllogism Machines: Formalism, Realism, and Exclusionary Selection Techniques,* 67 N.Y.U. L. Rev. 419 (noting that allowing jurors to be excluded from juries because of their race leads the community to lose faith in the jury system).

58. Some suggest that state boundaries would not survive this approach. That question is beyond the scope of this chapter. Suffice it to say that retaining states as units of representation reflects deeply embedded constitutional and tradition-bound constraints.

59. Brownstein, *supra* note 53, at A1, A15.

60. The decision to live next to someone may suggest some connection, kinship, or community of interest, but only if the decision to move was the exercise of choice within a range of options. *Cf. supra* note 34 (discussing the historic link between geographic and political ties).

61. Pamela S. Karlan, *Maps and Misreadings: The Role of Geographic Compactness in Racial Vote Dilution Litigation*, 24 Harv. C.R.-C.L. L. Rev. 173, 177 (1989); *see also* Whitcomb v. Chavis, 403 U.S. 124, 131 n.8 (1971) (defining a ghetto as a residential area with a defined racial population of lower than average socioeconomic status *"whose residence in the area is often the result of social, legal, or economic restriction or custom"* (emphasis added)); Wright v. Rockefeller, 376 U.S. 52, 59 (1964) (Douglas, J., dissenting) ("Neighborhoods in our larger cities often contain members of only one race; and those who draw the lines of Congressional Districts cannot be expected to disregard neighborhoods in an effort to make each district a multiracial one.").

62. Karlan, *supra* note 61 at 177; *see also Whitcomb,* 403 U.S. at 135 (finding that ghetto residents have interests "diverging significantly from interests of nonresidents of the ghetto" (paraphrasing language of the lower court opinion that the Court overruled)).

63. Iris M. Young, Justice and the Politics of Difference 43–46 (1990) (arguing that "highly visible" groups—those who identify with a certain social status and have a common history produced by that status—are different from "mere 'combinations of people' "—such as voluntary clubs—which are defined by shared attributes).

64. A fractal is a set of jagged curves or surfaces that has "the same index of jaggedness when examined at any level of minuteness or abstraction." *See* Louise Weinberg, *The Federal-State Conflict of Laws: "Actual" Conflicts,* 70 Tex. L. Rev. 1743, 1777 n.120 (1992). Professor Pamela Karlan suggested the analogy to fractal geometry.

65. Alison Mitchell, *In Politics, There Is Only One Language,* N.Y. Times, July 19, 1992, at A29 (quoting David Santiago).

66. *Id.* (quoting Angelo Falcon, President of the Institute for Puerto Rican Policy).

67. Sam Roberts, *Does Politics of Fairness Mean Only Those From Minorities Should Apply?* N.Y. Times, July 27, 1992, at B4 (quoting Rep. Steven J. Solarz). Others suggest that politics, not principles of choice, motivated Solarz's decision. "When his polls showed he couldn't win against any incumbent," he ran in an open district created to enhance the power of Latino residents. *Id.* (quoting Fernando Ferrer, President of the Bronx Borough). Still others suggested that Solarz had an unfair advantage based not on his ethnic background but his financial foreground. "It's not a question of what background he is. It's the color of his money," said Herman Badillo, the city's first Latino congressman. *Id.*

68. *Id.*

69. The assumption is that race-conscious districting is necessary to remedy race-conscious exclusion. The exclusion is demonstrated by the unwillingness of the majority to include the minority in its governing coalition. Evidence of this premise is provided by patterns of racially polarized voting. *See* Guinier, *supra* ch. 4 (explaining that virtual representation assumes that "[t]he 51% will look out for the 49% minority as their proxy" because majority self-interest is consistent with the common good); yet, where a permanent and homogeneous majority consistently exercises all the power, that fixed majority loses the incentive to look out for or cooperate with the minority, since minority political support is unnecessary.

70. In the static view, representation is neither interactive nor engaging of the electorate. When the focus is on empowering voters by instantly emphasizing their opportunity to elect representatives of their choice, the result is that those choices are less important once the boundary lines of the district are set.

71. This virtual representation assumption is also reflected in psychological or filial terms used to describe a common cultural or ethnic heritage. Even where all members of the racial group did not actively support a racial group member, they each are nevertheless represented by someone who is a "role model," a source of pride, and a "sister or a brother."

72. Mary B. W. Tabor, *Loyalty and Labor*, N.Y. TIMES, Sept. 17, 1992, at B6.

73. *See* Lindsey Gruson, *For Solarz, A Career Ends in Grief and Relief*, N.Y. TIMES, Oct. 7, 1992, at B3 (attributing Ms. Velazquez's 1869-vote margin primarily to criticism of Solarz's decision to run in a "Hispanic district"); *New York: The Race for the House*, N.Y. TIMES, Sept. 16, 1992, at B8 (listing the final election returns from the Democratic primary for the 12th district). Incidentally, Ms. Velazquez was heavily outspent. Solarz spent $2 million in the race, about $220 for each of the 9138 votes he won. Alison Mitchell, *Rep. Solarz Loses in a New District*, N.Y. TIMES, Sept. 16, 1992, at A1 (noting that Solarz had a "campaign fund of $2 million, more than all the other candidates combined").

74. Under a cumulative voting mechanism, the shareholders of a corporation can multiply the number of votes they are entitled to cast by the number of directors on the ballot and then distribute these votes however they wish. For example, a shareholder could cast all of her votes for only one director in one race and forgo voting in the other elections. *See* REVISED MODEL BUSINESS CORP. ACT § 7.28 (1984). *See generally* Arthur T. Cole, Jr., *Legal and Mathematical Aspects of Cumulative Voting*, 2 S.C. L. Q. 225 (1949) (describing the cumulative voting process and analyzing a formula for calculating the maximum number of shares needed to elect a single or multiple director(s) under a cumulative voting arrangement); Amihai Glazer et al., *Cumulative Voting in Corporate Elections: Introducing Strategy into the Equation*, 35 S.C. L. REV. 295 (1984) (providing a modified formula for maximizing director representation where shareholders vote in blocs).

 In raising the idea of alternative remedies, I am not advocating a grand moral theory of representation. I introduce the idea of cumulative voting primarily as a means of broadening the debate about solutions to the continuing problem of racial discrimination and polarization in the political process. I do not believe that cumulative voting is a panacea. Nor do I suggest that it should be imposed on nonconsenting jurisdictions nationwide, or that it should be considered in the absence of evidence that existing electoral arrangements are operating unfairly.

75. The exclusion threshold is the minimum number of minority group members required to guarantee representation in a cumulative voting system.

76. The following formula determines the minimum number of voters needed to guarantee the election of one representative:

$$\frac{V}{R+1} + 1$$

See Cole, *supra* note 74, at 229. In this formula, V equals the total number of voters, and R equals the number of representatives to be elected. A minority group may assure itself of representation by having this number of voters plump their votes for a single candidate. In ch. 4 I suggested the following example of a jurisdiction that is to elect ten representatives:

> [I]n a jurisdiction with 1000 voters, 250 of whom are black, a modified at-large plan would use a threshold of exclusion of 1/11th based on the formula of one divided by one plus the number of open seats, plus one. This means that 1/11th of the voters could not be denied representation. The threshold exclusion would work out to be 91 voters (91 is 1/11th of 1000, plus 1). Here, there are 250 black voters. Blacks are more than 2/11th, but short of 3/11th, of the population.
>
>   If all voters had 10 votes and could plump them any way they wished, any candidate supported intensely (meaning receiving all 10 votes) by 92 voters would get elected.

Thus, by voting strategically and plumping their votes behind a single candidate, blacks in the scenario above could assure themselves of representation. If 182 black voters plumped their votes evenly behind two candidates, they could assure themselves of representation by two candidates.

77. An interest constituency need not be racially homogeneous from a physiological standpoint. In other words, interests may be racially identifiable in that members of a particular racial group are more likely to hold certain views. But not all members of the group are assumed to agree on all issues for the group to form an interest constituency. In addition, nongroup members may be part of the interest group to the extent they identify with the group's primary agenda. In this sense, an interest constituency is defined by racial identification, not by racial origin. Blacks in the United States are an obvious minority interest group, despite the presence of a range of ideologies and class status. Whites in South Africa are also a minority interest, although their choice to self-define is a function of their historical treatment of—not by—the numerically superior racial majority. *See generally* LEONARD THOMPSON & ANDREW PRIOR, SOUTH AFRICAN POLITICS 108–80 (1982).

78. Although some liberal theories of representation that focus on the importance of representing the individual sought fulfillment in the concept of the one-person, one-vote principle, systems of semiproportional representation represent groups and individuals better than nonproportional systems or winner-take-all equipopulous districts. In such districts, one-person, one-vote has been fulfilled, but it has not led to one-vote, one-value because the party winning 51% of the votes actually would capture 100% of the legislature seats. *See* SHAPIRO, *supra* note 21, at 222. In that scenario, 49% of the votes are wasted or lost. Votes then do not have equal values in plurality, single-member district systems, but they can have equal value in a proportional representation system where the seats awarded are directly proportional to the votes cast. PULZER, *supra* note 30, at 48, 49; *see also* DIXON, *supra* note 1, at 525 ("Pure proportional representation maximizes the number of votes that 'count' and minimizes the number of votes that are 'lost.' ").

   I should reiterate that my use of the term "proportional or semiproportional representation" is not an effort to reduce political equality to numerical head-counting or numerical shares, but describes instead the goal of political fairness or democratic fair play. I disavow the idea that political fairness is simply a function of numerical proportions or shares. Indeed, my project involves efforts to avoid binary win/lose terminology. In this sense, politics is not necessarily a zero-sum game, but a continuous process of negotiation, compromise, and consensus building toward positive-sum solutions.

79. Again, I do not argue that the 1982 amendments mandate this view. Especially in light of the Supreme Court's interpretation of the term "voting" in Presley v. Etowah County Comm'n, 112 S. Ct. 820 (1992), legislative action may be necessary in the context of § 5 to re-assert congressional intent about the scope of voting. At this point, I am simply suggesting an approach to curing political unfairness that borrows from the themes that have been the subject of the debate surrounding the 1965 Act and especially its 1982 amendments: How can we ensure political equality and meaningful opportunities to participate to a group that has historically been excluded from the franchise without reinforcing the polarization the Act is designed to remedy?

80. *See, e.g.,* McNeil v. Springfield, 851 F.2d 937, 939, 942–43 (7th Cir. 1988) (holding, as a threshold requirement, that a minority must "demonstrate that it is sufficiently large and geographically compact to constitute a majority in a single-member district" (quoting Thornburg v. Gingles, 478 U.S. 30, 50 (1986)), *cert. denied,* 490 U.S. 1031 (1989). See also McGhee v. Granville County, 860 F.2d 110 (4th Cir. 1988).

81. Bullet voting is a technique employed in at-large elections whereby a politically cohesive minority strategically concentrates its voting strength. By voluntarily abnegating the right to vote for a full slate of candidates and casting instead only one ballot for the "black" candidate, the minority bloc can increase the probability of electing their favored candidate. Bullet voting "forces a minority to limit its vote while the majority exercises control over the full slate." See Ch. 4.

82. Sail trimming refers to the phenomenon where blacks elected from majority-white multimember districts "defer to other blacks to introduce and promote controversial legislation that would affect black constituents." *Id.*

83. White voters in District 23 thus elected *all* the legislative representatives; without some white cross-over voting, the black candidate would not have received enough support, even with bullet voting by blacks.

84. This is true for conservative Republicans in Democratic communities or religious minorities within the larger white electorate.

85. For example, where local county governments, such as Chilton County, Alabama, have adopted a modified at-large election system, new interest constituencies have been recognized. For the first time this century, white Republicans and a black Democrat were elected to the county school board and county commission. But, the process of self-government has not broken down. In a county that is about one-sixth black, three white Republicans, three white Democrats and one black Democrat now sit on the school board and the commission. With the balance of power held so closely between Republican and Democratic commissioners, the black representative can be an influential swing vote.

86. David Myers, *America's Social Recession,* Chi. Trib., July 30, 1992, § 1, at 27.

87. Dixon, *supra* note 1, at 22 (emphasis added).

Chapter 6. Lines in the Sand

1. *See* Fried, Order and Law (NY, 1991), pp. 112–13. Hereinafter cited by page number only.
2. P. 90.

3. Pp. 225–26 n.51.
4. Pp. 118–19; 133.
5. "Lines in the sand" was a popular metaphor among Reagan Revolutionaries. Fried attributes it to Peggy Noonan, Ronald Reagan's speechwriter:

> She caught the cadences exactly right . . . [the] manly combativeness joined to an irresistibly winsome purity of heart. . . . [For example,] "show the flag," "stand up and be counted," . . . "go the extra mile," "draw a line in the sand" and my absolute favorite, "our judges up there have iron underpants."

Pp. 225–26 n.51.
The "lines in the sand" metaphor was also popular with the Bush Administration. *See* Michael Wines, *Bush Hits All Targets Except His Challenger,* N.Y. TIMES, Feb. 22, 1992, at 9 ("Mr. Bush invoked more of the Persian Gulf war oratory that he used in his State of the Union speech . . . , saying he is drawing 'a line in the sand' on tax increases.").

6. P. 14.
7. P. 14.
8. Erwin Griswold, *Review of C. Fried, Order and Law, in* 73 CONST. (Spring–Summer 1991). Fried quotes one of his career deputies for making just this point: "The Attorney General represents the administration. We represent the United States." P. 37. *See also* Michael W. McConnell, *The Rule of Law and the Role of the Solicitor General,* 21 LOY. L.A. L. REV. 1105, 1105–6 (1988) (describing the "independence" approach in which the Solicitor General makes substantively valid arguments without regard to interests of affected governmental clients, including the President); Eric Schnapper, *Becket at the Bar—The Conflicting Obligations of the Solicitor General,* 21 LOY. L.A. L. REV. 1187, 1269–71 (1988) (concluding that the Solicitor General's conflicting duties mandate semi-independent status); Burt Neuborne, *In Lukewarm Defense of Charles Fried,* 21 LOY. L.A. L. REV. 1069, 1069–71 (1988) (linking the prestige and influence of the Solicitor General to the office's traditional position as a "silent partner" or "friend" in the Supreme Court's jurisprudence and describing the traditional task of the Solicitor General as "provid[ing] the executive branch and the Supreme Court with technically excellent advice about the meaning and logical application of constitutional law as the Supreme Court had declared it to be"). *But cf.* John McGinnis, *Principle Versus Politics: The Solicitor General's Office in Constitutional and Bureaucratic Theory,* 44 STAN. L. REV. 799, 802–9 (1992) (rejecting the "dual obligation" theory, in which the Solicitor General owes conflicting duties to President and the Court, and proposing instead a single obligation theory of unvarnished loyalty to the President whose administration policies the Solicitor General is obliged to defend).
9. Stuart Taylor, Jr., *Solicitor General's Office: Tasting the Salty Air of Politics and Criticism,* N.Y. TIMES, July 18, 1986, at A8; *see also supra* note 8.
10. *See* Taylor, *supra* note 9. His career staff apparently complained that Fried, in forming views of a case before receiving a staff memo, missed the ideal of professional technique and service "apart from—maybe even above—politics." Pp. 36–37.
11. Erwin Griswold, for example, calls Fried's account of the Solicitor General's role "the most 'political' view of the Solicitor General's role that has yet appeared in print." ERWIN N. GRISWOLD, OULD FIELDS, NEW CORNE: THE PERSONAL MEMOIRS OF A TWENTIETH

CENTURY LAWYER 331 (1992). *See also* Neuborne, *supra* note 8, at 1070–71 (criticizing Fried's conception of the Solicitor General as "point man for the executive branch"). I use the term "political" to refer to ideological, not partisan, politics.

12. Stuart Taylor, *Court Voice of Reaganism: Charles Fried,* N.Y. TIMES, Oct. 24, 1985, at A9.

13. Taylor, *supra* note 9, at A8 (quoting Professor Burt Neuborne). *But cf.* John McGinnis, *supra* note 8, at 809–14 (criticizing Fried for failing to pursue relentlessly a single obligation theory in which the Solicitor General owes unvarnished loyalty to the President, and suggesting that Fried succumbed instead to the pull of the bureaucratic culture of career officials whose self-interest was to minimize intrusion in their "turf," to promote procedural traditions, and to gain respect of legal establishment).

14. Taylor, *supra* note 9.

15. Payne v. Tennesse, 111 S. Ct. 2597, 2619 (1991) (Marshall, J., dissenting).

16. Throughout this chapter I use the metaphor of geometry in service of two ideas. First, I argue that Fried attempts to persuade primarily through abstract thinking divorced from relevant empirical context. Second, geometric shapes help reveal, sometimes in elegant detail, Fried's particular preference for configuring hierarchies of power. For example, I suggest a correspondence between Fried's unitary executive separation of power thesis and two upright triangles forming the sides of pyramid, atop which sits the President rather than a sphinx. *See infra* note 59 and accompanying text.

17. Some would argue that the federal courts have always operated as simply another political institution. *See* GERALD N. ROSENBERG, THE HOLLOW HOPE 342 (1991) (noting that courts "must be treated as political institutions and studied as such").

18. *See* W.E.B. DU BOIS, THE SOULS OF BLACK FOLK 16–17 (1903), who describes, in a different context, the internalized struggle of warring identities:

> One ever feels his twoness,—an American, a Negro; two souls, two thoughts, two unreconciled strivings; two warring ideals in one dark body, whose dogged strength alone keeps it from being torn asunder.

See also infra note 50 (describing tension between sociological role and personal identity).

19. David Kaplan & Bob Cohn, *'Nine Scorpions in a Bottle,'* NEWSWEEK, July 13, 1992, at 20 (quoting Gary Bauer, a former Reagan domestic policy aide).

20. Indeed, because of what it reveals about just this dynamic, Planned Parenthood v. Casey, 112 S. Ct. 2791 (1992), which recently affirmed the central holding of Roe v. Wade, 410 U.S. 113 (1973), makes a thorough understanding of Fried's tenure especially timely. The *Casey* decision may simply identify the natural schisms within the conservative movement, as its cohesiveness erodes under the pressure of deciding rather than dissenting. Some of the internal contradictions involve so-called libertarian (emphasizing freedom from government regulation and intrusiveness), populist (reinforcing strong local institutions as a bulwark of democracy), and statist (valuing government authority) impulses. Or, the fierce political advocacy of the last two Administrations may have finally prompted at least three conservative Justices to reconsider issues of judicial power.

In its first paragraph, which Justice Souter read from the bench, the co-authored opinion takes special notice of the frequency with which the United States urged the Court to overrule its earlier precedent. *Casey,* 112 S. Ct. at 2803. The opinion expressed concern that overruling "under fire" an earlier decision would be seen as "a surrender to political pressure" that would exact a "terrible price" because the public would come to see judges as no different than politicians. *Id.* at 2814–15. "If the Court's legitimacy should be underminded, then, so would the country be in its very ability to see itself through its constitutional ideals. The Court's concern with legitimacy is not for the sake of the Court but for the sake of the Nation to which it is responsible." *Id.* at 2816. Despite the Solicitor General's unrelenting pressure, "the center held." Linda Greenhouse, *Slim Margin: Moderates on Court Defy Predictions,* N.Y. TIMES, July 5, 1992, § 4, at 1.

21. P. 15.
22. P. 16.
23. Pp. 16–17.
24. *See supra* note 16.
25. *See* p. 17 (describing the Solicitor General's role in reforming the courts).
26. P. 88.
27. Intellectual warriors, Fried reminds us, were crucial to legitimate the revolution that had been conceived and zealously proselytized by the hard-line "movement conservatives" and young advisors drawn from the ranks of the Federalist Society. *See* pp. 176, 183.
28. P. 70.
29. P. 19.
30. P. 176.
31. P. 41.
32. Fried generally went along with Reynolds's program despite his reservations—often aided by "a stiff drink and a long walk." *Id.*
33. Pp. 186–88. Ironically, Fried bristled early in his tenure at suggestions that briefs he filed were done in response to political "instructions." *See* Taylor, *supra* note 9, at A8 (reporting that Fried was bitter at the charge that his abortion brief was so contrary to his office's traditional deference to the Court that it apparently "was filed pursuant to instructions"). Here, he appears to confess to doing exactly that, as long as he perceived a legal argument could be made.
34. P. 41.
35. Fried provides texture to the man many loved to hate. Fried sympathizes with Reynolds, whom he saw as publicly and perhaps unfairly humiliated by those who opposed the policy positions for which he was the point person. Yet Reynolds's bitterness was also of his own making, a result of his willingness to be the bully:

> Brad's technique in opposition would be to say little in a meeting, but what he did say dripped scorn and was rich in spoken or implicit accusations of apostasy and unmanly cowardice. And along with the browbeating, he would threaten that, if he did not get his way, then "the AG" would hear about it. At first I found this a little terrifying. . . . the challenge was to avoid martyrdom while keeping my virtue.

Pp. 42–43.
36. Pp. 182–83.
37. In an earlier generation, Alexander Bickel made a similar observation. *See* ALEXANDER M. BICKEL, THE LEAST DANGEROUS BRANCH 64–65 (2d ed. 1986).
38. Pp. 186–87. Fried also ascribes some of his dislike of government to "being a Czech

Jew—driven out of a prosperous, bourgeois country first by one total vision of government and then by another." Pp. 13–14.

39. Reagan signed a "federalism Executive Order," which Fried construed as the equivalent of a direct order. P. 188.

40. For example, the loyalty issue arose for Fried in two cases involving government compensation for taking of property. Land regulations were challenged in California on the grounds that they had adversely impinged on the economic interests of private property owners. Although the challenge was successful, the regulators apparently could avoid compensating the landowner by simply rescinding the challenged regulation. Attorney General Meese wanted Fried to advocate an interim-damages thesis that required compensation to an ultimately successful landowner for losses throughout the time the landowner's economic interests were affected by the challenged regulation. P. 183.

Fried disagreed on the merits with the Attorney General's position. He disavowed aggressive libertarian forays into constitutionalizing every government imposition on private property. Fried claimed loyalty to a principled systemic vision of less government. Deregulation and tax cuts, not "ad hoc, sentimental redistributive adjudication," would control "the leveling tendencies of the welfare state." P. 185. But when forced to reassess by the political demands, Fried relented and filed a brief supporting compensation for the landowners in the two California cases. *See* First English Evangelical Lutheran Church of Glendale v. County of Los Angeles, 482 U.S. 304 (1987); MacDonald, Sommer & Frates v. County of Yolo, 477 U.S. 340 (1986).

Although Fried had reservations about the way an interim-damages thesis might be used by liberals to protect "the new property," he compromised with the Attorney General's position. He filed a brief advocating a halfway position in which the government officials, but not the government, would be liable where they had tied up the property owner in protracted procedures. Pp. 185–86. The Court ultimately adopted the Attorney General's original position and, in a Rehnquist opinion from which Brennan dissented, subsequently rejected attempts to use the interim-damages thesis on behalf of a welfare recipient. *See* Schweiker v. Chilicky, 487 U.S. 412 (1988).

41. Elsewhere, in discussing his geometric theorem of separation of powers, Fried rediscovers this distinction. Here, however, he frames the loyalty discussion within an appointment hierarchy of loyalty to a President who is both the head of a political movement and a government: "If decisiveness in command is a virtue in the chief, then it would seem that loyalty is the corresponding virtue of the subordinate officer." P. 173.

Yet neither option squares with the role claimed by Fried's predecessors who viewed themselves as lawyers to "the law" or the Court, but not directly to the President. *See supra* note 8. By contrast, for example, Erwin Griswold claims his client "was the United States," not the President of the United States. *See* Griswold, *supra* note 11, at 327; *see also* Archibald Cox, *The Government in the Supreme Court,* 44 Сні. В. Rec. 221, 222 (1963) (arguing that the Solicitor General must balance advocacy for the executive against obligations as an officer of the Court); Schnapper, *supra* note 8, at 1265 (noting that "[t]he statutory responsibility of the Solicitor General is to represent 'the interests of the United States'" and suggesting that those interests arguably invoke the Solicitor General's obligations to the judicial and legislative branches); Joshua I. Schwartz, *Two Perspectives on the Solicitor General's Indepen-*

dence, 21 Loy. L.A. L. Rev. 1119, 1152–64 (1988) (arguing that the Solicitor General should recognize an obligation to be faithful to the congressional interpretation of a statute to foster interbranch comity); McConnell, *supra* note 8, at 1105 (identifying three alternative models of the Solicitor General's responsibilities).

42. Fried expresses affinity for what he terms a Burkean view of a Solicitor General who "uses his own judgment and values to make the best and most coherent whole out of his administration's projects and tendencies." P. 173. He borrows from political science literature the delegate-trustee dichotomy used to describe political representatives. For Fried, the Solicitor General is a political appointee who should function as a trustee, not a delegate. Political appointees are "not just . . . embodied representatives of abstract programs," p. 205, but are charged to exercise their own interpretative judgment rather than to guess at what their "constituent," the President, might say about a particular, technical matter. *See* pp. 188–92. Where their judgment conflicts with that of a political superior, they should strive for an "independent concordance" or resign. Pp. 192–98.

   Fried claims that exercise of autonomous judgment by a political subordinate is consistent with a strong chief executive, who retains the power to fire or force a resignation. Yet Fried never satisfactorily reconciles this retrospective argument for executive branch independence with an argument he advances for a unitary, geometric theory of separation of powers in which all presidential power must be exercised subject to direct presidential control. He articulated this latter theory of the Presidency in cases before the Supreme Court.

43. Fried tries to show that the line exists because he did sometimes temper loyalty to the President. For example, when he first arrived, Fried confronted career attorneys who shared Griswold's belief that it was the Solicitor General's job to represent the United States and the Attorney General's role to represent the president. Fried disagreed, but not to the extent expected by his political colleagues in the administration. They had made clear their expectation that Fried's status as a Harvard professor would provide cover for a wholesale purge of the career attorneys in the Solicitor General's office. *See* p. 38. Fried, however, claims his effort to establish independence from the career lawyers was limited to hiring an outside deputy. While this move provoked three resignations, Fried avoided massive personnel change. But now he had to watch his political back. He turned his attention to protecting himself from the "Holy Office" of the hard-line movement outsiders. *See* p. 35. Fried mustered all the folksy "stuff" of a Harvard academic to provide the stature and compassion to repackage the devotees of extreme libertarianism from the federalism police of the coldly contemptuous Brad Reynolds to the careful, sophisticated advocacy of a philosopher-king. *See* pp. 66, 106.

   Fried also suggests the line exists because he submitted on the merits to political pressure only where a technical legal argument could be found. But his refusal to purge the career staff on the one hand and his reliance on technical legal points on the other seem to suggest instead that the principal distinction he makes is between personal chivalry and uncouth behavior. *See infra* notes 48–50 and accompanying text.

44. *See, e.g.,* pp. 105–6.

45. Griswold and others may have also struggled with loyalty dilemmas, but these would most likely have involved a different constituency. Even when Fried is being "principled," it is in ways abhorrent to Griswold's notion of loyalty to the Court or the Constitution. *See supra* notes 8, 11, 41 and accompanying text.

46. Regents of the University of California v. Bakke, 438 U.S. 265 (1978).
47. P. 201 (quoting JOSEPH CALIFANO, GOVERNING AMERICA) 237 (1981).
48. P. 201. "It is as if a guest in your home berated your cook for oversalting the soup." *Id.*
49. *See supra* note 40.
50. *See* Thomas L. Shaffer, *Christian Theories of Professional Responsibility,* 48 S. CAL. L. REV. 721, 731 (1975):

> If I close my eyes and imagine a lawyer, I expose myself to a *role.* If I close my eyes and see me, I expose myself to an *identity.* And if I close my eyes and see myself as a lawyer, I expose myself to the conflict between my role and my identity. The role concept is socio-logical—seen from the outside in; the identity concept is psychological—seen from the inside out. The conflict is existential, of course. . . .

> Fried could not be oblivious to the conflict between his traditional, conservative legal process instincts on the one hand and his revolutionary fervor for the Administration's jurisprudential agenda on the other. This conflict raises the question whether a legal revolutionary can ever be "principled" in the incrementalist, legal process sense and still remain revolutionary. A second, related question is whether the Solicitor General's office, which by instinct and membership is committed to a "bureaucratic culture" of professionalism and turf based on its special expertise, is an appropriate place for a revolutionary. *Cf.* McGinnis, *supra* note 8, at 809–12 (explaining that the bureau-cratic culture of the Solicitor General's office emphasized the office's autonomy and unique role, and thus limited Fried's ability to fully advance the President's jurispru-dence). *See also infra* note 53 and accompanying text.

51. *Cf.* Stuart Taylor, Jr., *Justice Dept. Aide Under Fire for Comment on High Court,* N.Y. TIMES, Mar. 28, 1987, at 1 (quoting Fried: "I take the obligation of civil and respectful discourse very seriously."). I do not intend to disparage the importance of civility as a means of establishing or maintaining human relationships, especially to bridge gaps in human understanding. Indeed, much of recent political culture appears preoccupied with identifying signs of disrespect. Especially in presidential election cycles, Demo-cratic nominees often become entangled in controversy based on questions of auton-omy and respect. Both Michael Dukakis and Bill Clinton found themselves criticized during the primary season for not showing Jesse Jackson "respect." One failed to no-tify Jackson in advance of his selection for Vice President; the other failed to consult Jackson about his intention at a Jackson-sponsored convention to condemn a rap sing-er's racial commentary. My point here is that respect, politeness, and civility are im-portant, but not enough.
52. The closest Fried comes is when he defends himself against career staff complaints that by forming views prior to reading their memos, Fried was politicizing the office. Fried's response is that the ideal of professional service "apart from—maybe even above—politics" simply ignores the encrustation of liberal ideology within the exist-ing bureaucratic ideal. *See* pp. 36–38.
53. *See infra* notes 84–105 and accompanying text (discussing the theory of the unitary executive); *see also supra* notes 8, 11, and 41 (discussing alternative views of the So-licitor General's duties). To some extent, Fried underwrites his one-dimensional ap-proach with his view that partisanship is a lawyer's primary professional responsibility. *See* Charles Fried, *The Lawyer as Friend: The Moral Foundations of the Lawyer-Client Relation,* 85 YALE L.J. 1060, 1066 (1976) (arguing that it is both legally and

morally right that a lawyer "adopt as his dominant purpose the furthering of his client's interests" because a lawyer should put a client's interests above "some idea, however valid, of the collective interest"). Fried characterizes a lawyer as a "limited purpose friend" who "adopts your interests as his own." *Id.* at 1071. This may explain why Fried seems to perceive no conflict in consulting his own conscience as a way of accessing his client's interests. *See supra* text accompanying note 50.

54. My point here is that Fried fails to persuade not because he is a poor logician or a politician. His effort to bring order fails because he fails fairly to consider alternative assumptions and competing models of reality. *See supra* notes 8, 11, and 41; *cf.* McGinnis, *supra* note 8 (offering both a more comprehensive and theoretical defense of the Solicitor General's role as a jurisprudential activist for his client, the President).

55. *Cf.* GRISWOLD, *supra* note 11, at 331 (stating that the Solicitor General's proper role "is much more complicated . . . than Mr. Fried indicates in his book").

56. *See supra* note 5.

57. P. 17.

58. *Cf.* Poach A. Lewis, *Selection of Conservative Judges Insures a President's Legacy*, N.Y. TIMES, July 1, 1992, at A13 (noting that President Bush built on President Reagan's record to remake the federal judiciary; 60% of sitting federal judges were selected by either Bush or Reagan, and their choices are generally white, wealthy, male, and relatively young; by putting in place an unusually youthful federal judiciary with its own distinct conservative philosophy, Bush and Reagan attempted to dominate the courts for decades).

59. Fried uses a geometric vision to resolve conflicts between the three branches. *See, e.g.,* pp. 141, 143, 165. He employs two triangles to express the tripartite architecture that cleanly separates the division of authority between the branches. In one, the president, as chief of an executive branch, straddles the obtuse angle at the apex; the acute angles are formed by the independent agencies and the cabinet departments. In the second, the president is again hoisted astride an upright triangle in which the lesser two angles are formed by the judicial and legislative branches.

60. P. 143.

61. Because Fried is skeptical of "permanent government," of a "headless 4th branch," pp. 157, 155, run by faceless government bureaucrats, he joined forces with the bureaucrats to solidify executive autonomy and control for a Republican President. *See* pp. 36–40, 133.

62. P. 168.

63. *See* p. 170.

64. *See infra* note 202.

65. P. 87.

66. P. 84 (emphasis added).

67. P. 58.

68. Pp. 61–65.

69. P. 59.

70. Pp. 60–61.

71. P. 70.

72. *See supra* note 59.

73. In this project, Fried follows in the footsteps of another Harvard law professor, Christopher Columbus Langdell. *See, e.g.,* Thomas C. Grey, *Langdell's Orthodoxy*, 45 U.

Pɪᴛᴛ. L. Rᴇv. 1, 16 (1983) (explaining that the classical legal science of Langdell likened the application of legal rules to the application of geometric theorems). For Langdellian legal scientists, the "fundamental principles of the common law were discerned by induction from cases; rules of law were then derived from principles conceptually; and finally, cases were decided, also conceptually, from rules." *Id.* at 19. The effort to portray law as science (or the belief that it is in fact a science) was popular as a late nineteenth-century claim. *See* Edwin W. Patterson, *The Case Method in American Legal Education: Its Origins and Objectives,* 4 J. Lᴇɢᴀʟ Eᴅᴜᴄ. 1, 4 (1951). The scientific analogy presumes law to be descriptive, akin to a laboratory specimen— either it has certain characteristics or it does not. In this understanding, a statement of what is the law is not normative, nor does it hold any prescriptive meaning. *Id.*

74. Not only must laws be fixed so individuals can tailor their actions accordingly; laws must also mean the same thing to all. According to Fried, "[l]anguage must have a public meaning if it is to order our common life." P. 64.

75. Because all government power is checked by the courts, "if we cannot know where we stand with them then our liberty is only as sure as the whims and politics of judges." P. 59.

76. P. 59.

77. "Though the laws restrict liberty, without rules liberty cannot exist." P. 60. Liberty, for Fried, essentially means the freedom to be left alone. *See infra* note 104.

78. P. 60. "We," of course, is the conservative administration and those who support it.

79. P. 65. He maintains that it is the public text of the Constitution that was put in force, and so the intents of the voters who passed it as well as the Framers who drafted it have no independent relevance. Pp. 64–65.

80. P. 65.

81. Pp. 170–71.

82. P. 171 (quoting Myers v. United States, 272 U.S. 52, 177 (1926) (Holmes J., dissenting)). To be fair, this quotation from Justice Holmes is one Fried uses against himself.

83. This is the legal realists' insight. *See* Daniel A. Farber, *The Inevitabilty of Practical Reason: Statutes, Formalism, and the Rule of Law,* 45 Vᴀɴᴅ. L. Rᴇv. 533, 536–37 (1992) (explaining that legal realists take an instrumental view of the law in which judges base decisions on their own experiences and conceptions of the social interests at stake).

84. Although I read Fried's discussion of separation of powers to endorse the "rigorous" view, it is also possible that Fried is recounting the prevailing view in the Administration without necessarily subscribing to it.

85. *See* p. 133. He rejects an explicitly political basis for presidential authority in which the President rules because "he has a project for the nation as the head of his political party." P. 148. He accepts instead "the prerogatives" of presidential power, finding executive authority in legal and moral space opened up by John Locke and the natural prestige of the office. *See* pp. 148–49.

86. P. 145.

87. P. 152.

88. Justice Scalia favors a bright-line analysis. Under this approach, each branch and its functions are hermetically sealed from the other branches. According to Scalia, the President must exercise all executive power, the legislature all legislative power, and

the judiciary all judicial power. Morrison v. Olson, 487 U.S. 654, 709 (1987) (Scalia, J., dissenting) ("It is not for us to determine . . . how much of the purely executive powers of government must be within the full control of the President. The Constitution prescribes that they *all* are."). Scalia's orthodoxy over separation of powers seems driven by a fear of government tyranny. According to Scalia, the Framers created three branches of government with separate powers to prevent the concentration of enforcement, lawmaking, and judicial powers in any one branch. *Id.* at 697–99. For Scalia, fear of governmental tyranny justifies absolute power for each branch in its respective function, even if such absolute power leads to abuse. *See* Daniel N. Reisman, *Deconstructing Justice Scalia's Separation of Powers Jurisprudence: the Preeminent Executive*, 53 Alb. L.J. 49, 49 (1988); M. David Gelfand & Keith Werhan, *Federalism and Separation of Powers on a Conservative Court: Currents and Cross-Currents from Justices O'Connor and Scalia*, 64 Tul. L. Rev. 1443, 1465 (1990).

89. Mistretta v. United States, 488 U.S. 361, 419 (1989) (Scalia, J., dissenting).

90. *See* Green v. Bock Laundry Mach., 490 U.S. 504, 528–30 (1989) (Scalia, J., concurring); Blanchard v. Bergeron, 489 U.S. 87, 98–99 (1989) (Scalia, J., concurring); Edwards v. Aguillard, 482 U.S. 578, 636–40 (1987) (Scalia, J., dissenting); Hirschey v. FERC, 777 F.2d 1, 7–8 (D.C. Cir. 1985) (Scalia, J., concurring). Scalia grounds his contempt for legislative history in his suspicion of its generating process. *See* Arthur Stock, Note, *Justice Scalia's Use of Sources in Statutory and Constitutional Interpretation: How Congress Always Loses*, 1990 Duke L.J. 160, 161. First, he contends that he "frankly doubt[s] that it is ever reasonable to assume that the details, as opposed to the broad outlines of purpose, set forth in a committee report come to the attention of, much less are approved by, the house which enacts that committee's bill." *Hirschey*, 777 F.2d at 7 (Scalia, J., concurring). Second, even if legislators are aware of the language in the legislative history, such statements may not embody the legislators' reasons for voting for particular legislation. *Green*, 490 U.S. at 528; *Edwards*, 482 U.S. at 637. Finally, even if the legislative history embodies the intent of the house passing legislation, since it is not reviewed by the other house or by the President upon signing the bill, it is not part of the law. Stock, *supra*, at 166. According to Scalia, the danger of legislative history is that committee staffers and special interests through such staffers, both of whom are unaccountable to the people, are given too great power. *See* Blanchard, 489 U.S. at 98–99.

91. Scalia's interpretation that the Constitution requires a rigid separation of powers in fact has been criticized for its tendency to exalt the power of the executive at the expense of the other branches of government. This result follows, not simply from Scalia's insistence that executive, legislative, and judicial power must be kept rigidly separate, but from a combination of his formalist approach with his conceptions of executive, legislative and judicial power. *See* Stock, *supra* note 90, at 160 (suggesting that "the most significant aspect of Justice Scalia's approach to the use of sources . . . is the *effect* it has on redistributing power among the three branches of government"); *see also* Reisman, *supra* note 88, at 50 ("Justice Scalia's vision of a powerful and largely unchecked executive power . . . is the transcendent guiding principle of his jurisprudence"). Reisman argues that Scalia's eagerness to expand executive power is accompanied by "little textual and historical support." *Id.* at 60.

92. For example, his refusal to defer to legislative history reduces legislative power and increases the room for the executive and judicial branches to pursue their own agen-

das. Likewise, his criticism of power sharing and his preference for absolute boundaries between the executive and the legislature attempt to limit congressional incursions into the executive domain. He writes that "a certain degree of discretion, and thus of lawmaking *inheres* in most executive or judicial action, and it is up to Congress, by the relative specificity or generality of its statutory commands, to determine—up to a point—how small or how large that degree shall be." Mistretta v. United States, 488 U.S. 361, 417 (1989) (Scalia, J., dissenting).

93. It has been suggested that Scalia's preference for an executive branch unfettered by congressional and judicial meddling may stem from his professional background and experience. Scalia occupied many high-level positions in the federal executive branch and may have experienced firsthand intrusions by Congress on executive prerogative. Gelfand & Werhan, *supra* note 88, at 1447 n.13, 1473–74. The more vulgar explanation, at least for the attractiveness of Scalia's views, is that in an era of conservative Republican presidents and more liberal Democratic Congresses, a tilt toward the Presidency has obvious meaning apart from where Republicans worked.

94. Morrison v. Olson, 487 U.S. 654 (1988).

95. Under the Independent Counsel law, Congress can pressure the Attorney General to submit a request to a panel of judges for the appointment of a special prosecutor to investigate administrative officers who refuse to enforce laws passed by Congress if a matter is referred by certain members of Congress. *See* 28 U.S.C. § 592(g) (1988). The issue was joined in a separation of powers context when the Independent Counsel law was challenged in connection with a congressionally initiated investigation of the Environmental Protection Agency. *Morrison,* 487 U.S. at 665–68. EPA Administrator Anne Burford claimed executive privilege on orders from the White House. Fried describes Buford's claim as a "declaration of war." P. 135. Office of Legal Counsel Chief Ted Olson had urged the White House to make the claim and simultaneously to ask a federal court to uphold the claim. Congressman Rodino invoked the Independent Counsel law to investigate Olson for criminally defying Congress. *Id.*

96. Brief for the United States as Amicus Curiae Supporting Appellees at 1–5, Morrison v. Olson, 487 U.S. 654 (1988) (No. 87-1279); pp. 139–40.

97. P. 153.

98. P. 152. The executive power must be comprehensible and accountable to the people. "The lines of responsibility should be stark and clear, so that the exercise of power can be comprehensible, transparent to the gaze of the citizen subject to it." P. 153. Fried rejects accountability through congressional oversight of the executive because that would "split loyalty." P. 152.

99. *See* p. 145; *cf.* ARTHUR M. SCHLESINGER, JR., THE IMPERIAL PRESIDENCY 14 (1973) (noting that an "executive perspective" emerged from operational compulsion, "a diffused feeling that the executive branch, with superior information, control of information, and direct responsibility, was the source of judgments to which Congress, without abdicating its separate powers, should customarily defer"). The executive is also, according to Fried, better able to cope with emergencies. P. 145; *see also* SCHLESINGER, *supra,* at 8 (arguing that the Founders took the notion of executive prerogative from Ch. 14, *Of Prerogative,* in JOHN LOCKE, SECOND TREATISE OF GOVERNMENT that executive prerogative was based on the exercise of the law of self-preservation, and that in an emergency, responsible rulers could resort to exceptional power).

100. By Fried's logic, the example of the monarch serves the President, who best embodies the authority of the nation as a whole. *See* p. 145; *see also* ROBERT MICHELS, PO-
LITICAL PARTIES 212–14 (Eden Paul & Cedar Paul trans., 1962). Michels describes
how a plebiscitary Presidency could be seen as the fulfillment of constitutional democracy; suggests the rational of "personal dictatorship conferred by the people in
accordance with constitutional principles"; and notes that "[o]nce elected, the chosen of the people can no longer be opposed in any way. *He personifies the majority
and all resistance to his will is antidemocratic.* . . . He is, moreover, infallible, for 'he
who is elected by six million votes, carries out the will of the people; he does not
betray them.'" *Id.* at 212–13 (emphasis added). The chief executive would be, as
Laboulaye said of Napoleon III, "democracy personified, the nation made man." *Id.*
at 213.

101. Pp. 151–54; *cf.* SCHLESINGER, *supra* note 99, at 253 (suggesting that proponents of a
strong executive believed Congress had no ordered means of setting national priorities or of controlling aggregate spending; Congress, which was fragmented, paro-
chial, selfish, cowardly, without dignity, discipline or purpose, could not be trusted
with secrets). "The Presidency had not stolen its power; rather congress had surren-
dered it out of fear of responsibility and recognition of incapacity." *Id.*
  In this view, democratic outcomes are more likely to find expression in the executive than the legislature because the executive is less likely to be captured by special
interests. This aspect of the first assumption borrows from Calvin Coolidge, who
observed: "It is because in their hours of timidity the Congress becomes subservient
to the importunities of organized minorities that the President comes more and more
to stand as the champion of the rights of the whole country." *Id.* at 404–5 (quoting
Calvin Coolidge, *The President Lives Under a Multitude of Eyes,* AM. MAG., Aug.
1929, at 146). By contrast, legislative enactments are perceived to offer a weak form
of participation and to reflect actions that are not necessarily voluntary and autonomous, meaning the product of deliberation and choice. *Cf. id.* at 405–6 ("[Congress]
was inherently incapable of conducting government and providing national leadership. Its fragmentation, its chronic fear of responsibility, its habitual dependence on
the executive for ideas, information and favors—this was life insurance for the Presidency.").

102. P. 157. Fried considered the informal network of experienced bureaucrats "one of
the biggest obstacles to the administration's programs." P. 155.

103. *See* p. 143.

104. *See* pp. 151–52 (arguing that liberty means freedom from arbitrary government authority).

105. P. 154.

106. As vanguard as Fried may be politically, in his approach to legal reasoning he displays
remarkable affinity for old-fashioned, conservative, legal process scholarship. In this
sense, Fried grafts legal arguments for the Reagan Revolution on traditional arguments that fit some of the Revolution's preferred outcomes, but not necessarily its
methods.

107. P. 170.

108. P. 160.

109. Fried tried to adopt the step-by-step approach of the "NAACP's brilliant campaign
against state-imposed segregation," but the indiscretions of others meant he was

unable to keep his grand design hidden from the Court. P. 159. In subsequent correspondence with this author, Fried explains his position as follows: "What I say at 159 is that of course the Court knows what the administration agenda is. . . . But public pronouncements by high officials force its hand by making it choose up sides sooner than they may wish." *See* letter to Lani Guinier from Charles Fried, Feb. 15, 1993.

By his comparison with the *Brown v. Board of Education* campaign, Fried seems to suggest the virtue of much more patience and less clarity (to the litigants and the public) regarding their ultimate goals. *Cf.* Richard Kluger, Simple Justice. On the other hand, the post-Fried Supreme Court Terms might seem to validate an aggressive, giant-step approach, where the composition of the Court itself is successfully revolutionized. *See infra* notes 206–8.

110. P. 160.
111. Taylor, *supra* note 12, at A9. I do not mean to claim that Fried's effort was necessarily either self-serving or hypocritical. Instead, I suggest it may be reflective of deep ambivalence about his role. *See supra* note 50.
112. *See supra* note 59.
113. *See* Michael Fitts, *Can Ignorance Be Bliss? Imperfect Information as a Positive Influence in Political Institutions*, 88 Mich. L. Rev. 917 (1990). Constitutional and statutory debates on the separation of powers and limits on the power of the executive branch have become politicized because of the long-running Democratic control of Congress and simultaneous Republican presidencies. *Id.* at 976. Since 1968, the Republican Party has tended to envision its political interests "as tied to the particular institution that [it] inhabit[s]." *Id.* at 974. In this way, the absolutist theory of the unitary executive is a new version of an old argument. President Nixon resurrected the notion of "a presidential mandate" to use the reserved powers of his office in an "imperial presidency." Schlesinger, *supra* note 99, at 255. Like Nixon, the Reagan Administration used the absolutist view of separation of powers to overcome its own chafing under its restraints:

> [T]he [Nixon] White House defined the presidential mandate as definitive and overriding and declared it the duty of Congress to support the President. . . . The mandate became the source of wider power than any President had ever claimed before. Whether a conscious or unconscious revolutionary, Nixon was carrying the imperial Presidency toward its ultimate form in the plebiscitary Presidency—with the President accountable only once every four years, shielded in the years between elections from congressional and public harassment, empowered by his mandate to make war or to make peace, to spend or to impound, to give out information or to hold it back, superseding congressional legislation by executive order, all in the name of a majority whose choice must prevail till it made another choice four years later—unless it wished to embark on the drastic and improbable course of impeachment.

Id.; see also Edwin S. Corwin, The President: Office and Powers, 1787–1984, 28 (1984) (quoting Henry J. Ford, The Rise and Growth of American Politics 293 (1898), describing "the presidency as an elective kingship"). Nixon modeled the presidency on imperial authorities such as Napoleon and de Gaulle. *See* Schlesinger, *supra* note 99, at 254 (asserting that Nixon's "model lay not in Britain but in France—in the France of Louis Napoleon and Charles de Gaulle"). Nixon was moving toward a plebiscitary Presidency. "A plebiscitary Presidency, unlike a parliamentary regime, would not require a new Constitution; presidential acts, confirmed by a Supreme Court of his own appointment, could put a new gloss on the old one." *Id.*

114. P. 133.

115. P. 136.

116. P. 121.

117. P. 121.

118. P. 120.

119. Pp. 89–90.

120. P. 17.

121. P. 133.

122. P. 112.

123. U.S. Const. art. II, § 3.

124. For example, Kevin Phillips in *The Emerging Republican Majority* wrote that "Congress's separate power is an obstacle to modern policymaking." That separate power was itself further separated among the multitude of congressional committees. The answer, Phillips argued, lay in "a fusion of powers tying Congress and the executive together, eliminating checks and balances and creating a new system." Kevin Phillips, *Our Obsolete System*, Newsweek, April 23, 1973, at 13. This has often been described as Justice White's view of governmental authority. *See infra* notes 138, 241, and 243 and accompanying text.

125. The Federalist No. 51, at 322 (James Madison) (Clinton Rossiter ed., 1961) ("[A]mbition must be made to counteract ambition. . . .").

126. Both Jefferson and Madison, as traditional advocates of the congressional role, "were generally zealous defenders of that free flow of information which served itself as a check on presidential adventurism as well as a means of rallying national opinion." Even Hamilton was a strong believer in "concurrent authority." Schlesinger, *supra* note 99, at 34; *see also id.* at 375 ("Wilson said long ago that the 'informing function' of Congress was even to be preferred to its legislative function." (quoting Woodrow Wilson, Congressional Government 303 (15th ed. 1901))).

127. Heidi M. Hurd, *Justifiably Punishing the Justified*, 90 Mich. L. Rev. 2203, 2264 (1992).

128. *See* Julian N. Eule, *Judicial Review of Direct Democracy*, 99 Yale L.J. 1503, 1526–27 (1990); *see also* Hurd, *supra* note 127, at 2264 ("Since each individual in a democratic legislature requires for her purposes the powers accorded to other individuals, each individual is constrained by others in her ability to act self-interestedly.").

129. The Founders feared despotism and believed that Presidents might abuse their power. They were therefore determined to provide the new republic with a way of removing any who did (impeachment power). *See* Schlesinger, *supra* note 99, at 10. The impeachment power was considered "the main spring of the great machine of government. It is the pivot on which it turns. . . . In this mode, the machine will be kept in motion by its own powers and on a proper balance." James Monroe, The People, The Sovereigns 15–16 (Samuel J. Gouverneur ed., 1987).

As Thomas Jefferson wrote to James Madison on March 15, 1789, six weeks before George Washington's first inauguration: "The tyranny of the legislature is the most formidable dread at present, and will be for long years. That of the executive will come in it's [sic] turn, but it will be at a remote period." Letter from Thomas Jefferson to James Madison (Mar. 15, 1789) *in* 14 THE PAPERS OF THOMAS JEFFERSON 659, 661 (Julian P. Boyd ed., 1958).

130. Arthur Schlesinger elaborated on the Founders' view of congressional and presidential powers:

> Given the clear priority the Founding Fathers assigned to commercial over political relations, it is significant that the Constitution vested control over this primary aspect of foreign policy in Congress, assigning it the definite and unqualified power "to regulate Commerce with foreign Nations." The Constitution also brought Congress into the treaty-making process, withholding from the President the exclusive authority enjoyed by European monarchs to make treaties. Where the British King, for example, could conclude treaties on his own, the American President was required to win the consent of two thirds of the Senate.

SCHLINGER, *supra* note 99, at 2.

Even Alexander Hamilton, the most consistent advocate of executive centralization, proposed in the Constitutional Convention that the Senate "have the sole power of declaring war" with the executive to "have the direction of war when authorized or begun." Speech of Alexander Hamilton on June 18, 1787, to the Constitutional Convention, *in* 1 THE RECORDS OF THE FEDERAL CONVENTION 282, 292 (Max Ferrand ed., 1937).

131. But their experience under the Articles of Confederation led the Framers "to favor more centralization of executive authority than they had known in the Confederation." SCHLESINGER, *supra* note 99, at 2. They recognized that the advantage of a single executive was the ability to fix accountability. *Id.* at 384. Under the Articles of Confederation, executive as well as legislative authority was given to Congress, "establishing in effect parliamentary government without a prime minister." *Id.* at 2.

Many probably agreed with Hamilton's statement in the 70th Federalist that "[e]nergy in the executive is a leading character in the definition of good government." THE FEDERALIST No. 70, at 423 (Alexander Hamilton) (Clinton Rossiter ed., 1961). A directorate "would serve to destroy, or would greatly diminish, the intended and unnecessary responsibility of the Chief Magistrate himself." *Id.* at 429.

Jefferson had favored a plural executive under the Articles of Confederation, but he later observed that if Washington's cabinet in which he served had been a directorate, "the opposing wills would have balanced each other and produced a state of absolute inaction." Letter of Thomas Jefferson to A.C.V.C. Destutt de Tracy (Jan. 26, 1811), *in* 11 THE WRITINGS OF THOMAS JEFFERSON 181, 184 (Paul Leicester Ford ed., 1905). Washington provided the "regulating power which would keep the machine in steady movement." *Id.* at 185.

132. Gordon S. Wood, *Classical Republicanism and the American Revolution,* 66 CHI.-KENT L. REV. 13, 14–15 (1990); *see also* Pamela Karlan, *Undoing the Right Thing: Single Member Offices and the Voting Rights Act,* 77 VA. L. REV. 1, 21 n.73 (1991) (noting that the public was concerned that the Senate would become "a fixed and unchangeable body of men and the president a king for life" (quoting GORDON S. WOOD, THE CREATION OF THE AMERICAN REPUBLIC, 1776–1787, at 521 (1969)). In a letter to his law partner, W.H. Herndon, President Lincoln wrote that the reason why the Constitution had given the war-making power to Congress was because kings had always been involving and impoverishing their people in wars. "This, our

[constitutional] convention understood to be the most oppressive of all Kingly oppressions; and they resolved to so frame the Constitution that *no one man* should hold the power of bringing this oppression upon us. But your view destroys the whole matter, and places our President where Kings have always stood." ABRAHAM LINCOLN: HIS SPEECHES AND WRITINGS 220–21 (1946).

133. *See* WOOD, *supra* note 132, at 87 (relating early public hostility toward leaders who "behaved as though they thought they had some sort of fee simple" in their positions).

134. *See* The Federalist No. 48, at 310–311 (James Madison) (Clinton Rossiter ed., 1961); *see also* A.H.M. JONES, ATHENIAN DEMOCRACY 106 (1969) (asserting that such concern has historically generated support for term limitations and rotation requirements). When James Wilson first moved in the Convention that the executive consist of a single person, there ensued, as Madison put it in his notes, "a considerable pause." 1 THE RECORDS OF THE FEDERAL CONVENTION OF 1787 at 65 (Max Ferrand ed., 1911). Finally, Benjamin Franklin observed that this was an important point and he would like to hear some discussion. Wilson said that a single magistrate would impart "most energy, dispatch and responsibility" to the office. *Id.* Edmund Randolph of Virginia then strenuously opposed the idea as "the foetus of monarchy," proposing instead a three-man magistracy. *Id.* at 66. A plural executive, according to Hamilton, is divided within itself, would lead the country into factionalism and anarchy and, if united, could lead it to tyranny. When power was placed in the hands of a group small enough to admit "of their interests and views being easily combined in a common enterprise, by an artful leader, it becomes more liable to abuse, and more dangerous when abused, than if it be lodged in the hands of one man, who, from the very circumstances of his being alone, will be more narrowly watched and more readily suspected. . . . From such a combination America would have more to fear, than from the ambition on any single individual." THE FEDERALIST No. 70, at 430 (Alexander Hamilton) (Clinton Rossiter ed., 1961).

135. THE FEDERALIST No. 75, at 452 (Alexander Hamilton) (Clinton Rossiter ed., 1961). Hamilton said, "The one can perform alone what the other can do only with the concurrence of a branch of the legislature." *Id.* No. 69, at 420. Article I, Section 8 of the Constitution showed that the Founders were determined to deny the American President what Blackstone had assigned to the British King—"the sole prerogative of making war and peace." *See* E.S. CORWIN, THE PRESIDENT: OFFICE AND POWERS 154 (1940) (quoting WILLIAM BLACKSTONE, COMMENTARIES °257). According to James Madison, there was "a partial mixture of powers" that was indispensable to the system, because unless the branches of government "be so far connected and blended as to give to each a constitutional control over the others, the degree of separation which the maxim requires, as essential to a free government, can never in practice be duly maintained." SCHLESINGER, *supra* note 99, at 7 (citing THE FEDERALIST No. 48, at 304, 308 (James Madison) (Clinton Rossiter ed., 1961)).

136. Karlan, *supra* note 132, at 19 (citing examples of local governments that divide executive power among various independently elected officials); *see also* Arend Lijphart, (unpublished manuscript) (citing Swiss example of executive council and rotating power).

137. *See, e.g.,* RICHARD J. VAN LOON & MICHAEL S. WHITTINGTON, THE CANADIAN POLITICAL SYSTEM: ENVIRONMENT, STRUCTURE, & PROCESS 174 (1971) (stating that the culturally distinct provinces, especially Québec, required the local autonomy of federalism to

preserve their unique heritage); MANGAL CHANDRA JAIN KUGZI, 1 THE CONSTITUTION OF INDIA 81–82 (1984) (suggesting that post-independence desire for local autonomy in linguistically and religiously diverse India made the separated powers of a federal system the only viable form of government); *cf.* JEAN-FRANÇOIS AUBERT, 1 TRAITÉ DE DROIT CONSTITUTIONNEL SUISSE 34–35 (1967) (pointing out that the Swiss constitution of 1848 left a politically significant portion of power to the cantons).

For the Founders, shared decisionmaking was the supreme governing principle. "The whole purpose of democracy is that we may hold counsel with one another, so as not to depend upon the understanding of one man, but to depend upon the counsel of all." WOODROW WILSON, THE NEW FREEDOM 50, 72 (1961). The supreme neutral principle, as vital in domestic policy as in foreign policy, was that all great decisions of the government must be shared decisions. SCHLESINGER, *supra* note 99, at 406; *see also id.* at 407 (maintaining that shared decisions are more likely to be wise).

138. P. 144.
139. Justice Blackmun apparently articulates this theory as well. *See* Mistretta v. United States 488 U.S. 361 (1989).
140. *See* p. 144 (giving Fried's view of Justice White's conception of Congress); *see generally* Paul M. Bator, *The Constitution as Architecture: Legislative and Administrative Courts Under Article III,* 65 IND. L.J. 233 (1990) (arguing that the necessary and proper clause gives Congress power over every branch of the federal government).
141. *See* Lucas v. Forty-Fourth Gen. Assembly of Colorado, 377 U.S. 713, 751 (1964) (Stewart, J., dissenting) (noting the "strongly felt American tradition that the public interest can better be expressed by a medley of component voices than by the majority's monolithic command"); THE FEDERALIST No. 10 (James Madison) (Clinton Rossiter ed., 1961) (proposing that the regulation of many different interests forms the principal task of modern government).
142. Many now question traditional notions of a competitive meritocracy in which "the cream rises to the top." The critics are not just poststructuralists who argue in academic journals for context, or postmodernist feminists who argue that hierarchical structures either reproduce themselves without regard to the potential contribution of outsiders who might enrich the debate or, like the Darwinian theory of reproduction, through mutation possibly develop the organism in more creative, sustaining ways. *Cf.* Joan Williams, *Dissolving the Sameness/Difference Debate: A Post-Modern Path Beyond Essentialism in Feminist and Critical Race Theory,* 1991 DUKE L.J. 296 (criticizing the analysis of race and gender differences for failure to focus on structural disadvantages and unfair "neutral" societal standards).

Now captains of industry also question performance evaluation under the old merit system. For example, branches of Eastman Kodak, General Motors, and AT&T are seeking more egalitarian approaches based on teamwork. Claudia Deutsch, *Less Is Becoming More at A.T.& T.,* N.Y. TIMES, June 3, 1990, at 25 (reporting that teamwork is becoming the norm for the 1990s employee); Andrea Gabor, *Take This Job and Love It,* N.Y. TIMES, Jan. 26, 1992, at 1 (reporting that some managers believe that the merit system nourishes short-term performance, rivalry and politics instead of long-term planning, teamwork, and the search for quality and solutions). Some companies now claim that rewarding a handful of winners may be consistent with the ingrained culture of American individualism, but it discourages cooperation and may damage morale. *Id.*

143. *See, e.g.,* Ch. 4.
144. *See, e.g.,* David Osborne & Ted Gaebler, Reinventing Government: How the Entrepreneurial Spirit is Transforming the Public Sector 250–71 (1992).
145. *See, e.g.,* Martha Minow, Making All the Difference 377, 381 (1990) (arguing that justice requires an appreciation of a multitude and variety of arguments rather than affirming the conclusiveness of a single solution; innovations initially designed to accommodate outsiders may actually yield benefits for others). Participation or self-determination values also suggest the advantages of plural power centers. "While a benevolent despot might better achieve decisions that are in the greatest interest of the community, such a governor thwarts self-determination, and thus renders it impossible for citizens to develop character traits that are crucial to their intellectual and moral development." Hurd *supra* note 127, at 94 (summarizing Carole Pateman's's argument that democracy is important because political participation fosters important personal qualities).
146. *See* 42 U.S.C. § 1971 (1988) (establishing the uniform right of all citizens to vote without distinction based on race, color, or previous condition).
147. *See id.* § 1973 (establishing the right of all citizens to "participate in the political process and to elect representatives of their choice").
148. Nicholas R. Miller, *Pluralism and Social Choice,* 77 Am. Pol. Sci. Rev. 734, 735 (1983) (quoting Earl Latham, *The Group Basis of Politics: Notes for a Theory,* 46 Am. Pol. Sci. Rev. 376, 390 (1952)).
149. Karlan, *supra* note 132, at 40.
150. *See* Butts v. City of New York, 779 F.2d 141, 148 (2d Cir. 1985) (concluding there is no such thing as a share of a single person or executive office); Anthony Gay, Congressional Term Limits: Good Government or Minority Vote Dilution, 141 U. Pa. L. Rev. 2311, 2336–41, 2368 (1993) (arguing that access to legislative representation is critical for minority political participation because minority interests are less likely to be represented where authority is centralized). *See also* Lucas v. 44th General Assembly, Colorado, 377 U.S. 713, 744–65 (1964) (Stewart, J., dissenting) (observing that diverse interests better expressed by a medley of component voices).
151. *Cf.* Michael Fitts, *Can Ignorance Be Bliss? Imperfect Information as a Positive Influence in Political Institutions,* 88 Mich. L. Rev. 917, 980 (1990) (noting that centralized executive authority in a single-party-dominated presidency "creates legitimate concerns of tyranny, one-party control of executive decisions, and substantially reduced public dialogue and public participation").
152. P. 171.
153. P. 101.
154. *See* Plessy v. Ferguson, 163 U.S. 537, 549 (1896) conceding that the reputation of belonging to the dominant white race is property.
155. P. 122 (citing Wards Cove Packing Co. v. Atonio, 490 U.S. 642, 644 n.4 (1989) (Stevens, J., dissenting)).
156. P. 122.
157. P. 122.
158. Michael W. McConnell, *Multiculturalism, Majoritarianism, and Educational Choice: What Does Our Constitutional Tradition Have to Say?* 1991 U. Chi. Legal F. 123, 124 (arguing that multiculturalism threatens to undermine common traditions, norms, and educational experience). Critics of multiculturalism warn that it

"fosters a sense of difference where there is already too much; it undermines rather than aids induction into a common 'civic culture.' " *Id.* at 128 (quoting Robert K. Fullinwider, *Multicultural Education,* 1991 U. Chi. Legal F. 75, 88).

159. *Id.* at 128.

160. *See* Neil Gotanda, *A Critique of "Our Constitution Is Color-Blind,"* 44 Stan. L. Rev. 1, 59–60 (1991) (likening the color-blind assimilationist vision to cultural genocide).

161. P. 105.

162. P. 105.

163. P. 106. Here Fried embraces the liberal view of individual rights and rejects the collectivist vision that he elsewhere associates with "liberalism." He applauds Justice Powell's opinion in *Wygant,* saying Powell came closer to getting it right than he had. P. 113. "The Constitution does not allocate constitutional rights to be distributed like bloc grants within discrete racial groups." Wygant v. Jackson Bd. of Educ., 476 U.S. 267, 282, (1986). Powell rejected victim-specificity, a policy Fried felt obligated to argue although he says his heart was not in it. P. 106.

164. Johnson v. Transportation Agency, 480 U.S. 616 (1987) (holding that taking sex into account as one factor in determining whether a person should be promoted is consistent with Title VII of the Civil Rights Act of 1964); United States v. Paradise, 480 U.S. 149 (1987) (holding that a 50 percent promotion requirement for black state troopers is permissible under the Equal Protection Clause of the Fourteenth Amendment); Local 28, Sheet Metal Workers v. EEOC, 478 U.S. 421 (1986) (holding that a court-imposed quota plan for nonwhite membership goals was proper and did not violate Title VII of the Civil Rights Act of 1964 or the Constitution).

165. P. 119.

166. P. 112.

167. Fried, for example, would allow stricter rules for governments than private parties seeking to employ racial preferences. P. 130. What offends Fried are the efforts by local governments to implement loose antidiscrimination ordinances that are simply "crude political gestures." P. 128. Fried tolerates government injunctions against discrimination, but not government action to promote nondiscrimination, diversity, or other morally just policies. P. 130. While recognizing the attractiveness of Scalia's push for clear rules mandating color-blindness everywhere, in this area Fried believes that kind of definiteness is unattainable. Fried is willing to pursue "humbler, more local truths." P. 131.

168. P. 90.

169. P. 90.

170. P. 100.

171. *Id.*

172. P. 112.

173. P. 119.

174. Pp. 99–101.

175. 478 U.S. 30 (1986). The reader is entitled to know I was a trial counsel and counsel of record in the Supreme Court for the appellees.

176. City of Mobile v. Bolden, 446 U.S. 55 (1980) (plurality opinion).

177. 42 U.S.C. § 1973 (b) (1988).

178. *See* S. Rep. No. 417, 97th Cong., 2d Sess. 68 (1982).

179. 42 U.S.C. § 1973 (c) (1988).

180. Beer v. United States, 425 U.S. 130, 141 (1976).
181. Brief for the United States as Amicus Curiae Supporting Appellants at 6, Thornburg v. Gingles, 478 U.S. 30 (1986) (No. 83-1968).
182. *Id.* at 8 n.12.
183. *Id.* at n.12.
184. Motion for Leave to File and Brief of Senator Dennis DeConcini, Robert J. Dole, et al. as Amicus Curiae in Support of Appellees, Thornburg v. Gingles, 478 U.S. 30 (1986) (No. 83–1968). In his book, although not his brief, Fried describes the Administration's legislative position in opposition to the extension of the Act as one of two "spectacularly misconceived projects." P. 102. (The other was its position in the Bob Jones case.) In the book, Fried describes his effort as a "sensible construction" of "incomprehensible" language. Pp. 104–5.

The brief, however, attempts to relitigate claims the Administration had lost in Congress, urging the Court to defer to President Reagan's construction of the statute, suggesting that his "support" "ensured its passage." Brief for the United States, *supra* note 181, at 8 n.6, 12; *see also* Schnapper, *supra* note 8, at 1266. The Court rejected the Solicitor General's position. *See Gingles,* 478 U.S. at 43 n.7.

The fact that members of Congress retained separate counsel to represent their interests in the case is one result feared by those who criticize Fried's conception of his role as exclusively representing the President's and not the Congress' wishes. *See, e.g.,* Schwartz, *supra* note 41, at 1157–61.

185. Brief for the United States, *supra* note 181, at 21–22. His brief suggested that the provision, which was "enacted after an intense legislative struggle," represents a consensus ceiling on minority political aspirations. *Id.* at 6. The statutory standard guarantees only "equal access" to the electoral process: this means each minority citizen should enjoy an "equal opportunity to participate" not "guarantee[d] continued minority electoral success." *Id.* at 6–7.
186. Gingles v. Edmisten, 590 F. Supp. 364 (E.D.N.C. 1984) (three-judge court).
187. Howard Kurtz, *10 Lawmakers Join Voting-Rights Case; Dole Group Calls Justice Dept. 'Misguided,'* WASH. POST, Aug. 31, 1985, at A1. The Court's view acknowledged the unfortunate reality demonstrated by the evidence in the case: on average 81.7% of whites refused to vote for a black candidate even in instances in which the only other choice was to vote for no one.
188. *See Gingles,* 478 U.S. at 80 (concluding that in light of the evidence presented, blacks' ability to participate in the electoral process and elect the candidate of their choice was impaired).
189. Gingles v. Edmisten, 590 F. Supp. 345, 364–75 (E.D.N.C. 1984) (citing the extent to which blacks had been elected to public office in each of the challenged districts).
190. Presley v. Etowah County Comm'n, 112 S. Ct. 820 (1992).
191. *Id.* at 832 (interpreting 42 U.S.C. § 1973 (c) (1988)).
192. *Id.* (noting that "the Voting Rights Act is not an all-purpose antidiscrimination statute," although the conduct at issue may be "actionable under a different remedial scheme").
193. The Justice Department filed a brief supporting the black voters. Brief for the United States as Amicus Curiae supporting Appellants, Presley v. Etowah County Comm'n, 112 S. Ct. 820 (1992). In ruling against the black voters' claim, the Court ignored its

prior precedents, its tradition of deference to the Attorney General's special expertise, and the judgment of Congress.

194. *Presley,* 112 S. Ct. at 835 (Stevens, J., dissenting) (quoting McCain v. Lybrand, 465
U.S. 236, 243 (1984) (quoting South Carolina v. Katzenbach, 383 U.S. 301, 309
(1966))).

195. *Id.* at 832–33 (Stevens, J., dissenting). Whatever its meaning or its standing, formal
equality does not resolve the more profound claim for justice: "that *differently situated* people be treated *fairly.*" Gerald Torres, *Critical Race Theory: The Decline of
the Universalist Ideal and the Hope of Plural Justice—Some Observations and Questions of an Emerging Phenomenon,* 75 MINN. L. REV. 993, 994 (1991) (emphasis
added).

196. *See* George F. Will, *A Step Backward on Voting Rights, or the Right Step? In His
First Real Test, Thomas Stood on the Side of the Law,* PHILA. INQUIRER, Feb. 2, 1992,
available in DIALOG, PHILINQ File (praising the court's "courage [in] let[ting]
the injustice stand rather than resort[ing] to judicial overreaching").

197. It thus reflects his willingness to construct an abstract argument independent of empirical evidence or based on one lone exception that is supportive of his preferred
outcome. *Cf.* Schnapper, *supra* note 8, at 1225 (concluding that the Solicitor General's role may require the use of innovative or novel arguments).

198. Gingles v. Edmisten, 590 F. Supp. 345, 374 (E.D.N.C. 1984) (finding that black
political participation was adversely affected by the use of racial appeals still prevalent in political campaigning, the existence of persistent and severe racial bloc voting,
and the lingering effect of a history of disenfranchisement), *aff'd in part, rev'd in
part sub nom.* Thornburg v. Gingles, 478 U.S. 30 (1986).

199. *See* p. 18.

200. *See* Sheldon Goldman, *The Bush Imprint on the Judiciary: Carrying on a Tradition,*
74 JUDICATURE 294, 298–303 (1991) (reporting that only 8.3% of President Reagan's
district court appointments went to women, compared to 14.4% of President Carter's, and that 5.1% of Reagan's circuit court appointees were women, compared to
19.6% of Carter's).

201. While the story may be apocryphal, Senator Warner allegedly told the former Republican dean of a Virginia law school that he was ineligible for a federal judgeship
because, by current administration standards, at the age of 50, he was too old.

202. *See* Linda Greenhouse, *Lightening Scales of Justice: High Court Trims Its Docket,*
N.Y. TIMES, Mar. 7, 1992, at 1, 12 (asserting that Solicitors General have been steadily
filing fewer appeals as the government loses fewer cases, because 11 years of Republican appointments have homogenized federal courts in a manner consistent with
the philosophy of the current Supreme Court majority).

203. P. 159.

204. P. 128.

205. During his tenure, a pragmatic Court often found Fried's attempts at principled
reasoning no more intrinsically appealing than alternative approaches to problem
solving. Fried's political platform as legal text was not compelling. Indeed, consistent
with his openly political agenda, Fried's reasoning was often dismissed as an after-
the-fact rationalization of the Administration's policy choices. *See* LINCOLN CAPLAN,
THE TENTH JUSTICE 235–54 (1987) (detailing the ways in which Fried overstated his
victories and understated his losses, and concluding that the Supreme Court rejected

more of Fried's arguments than of any other Solicitor General in history). The Court seemed more persuaded by its tradition of deference toward Congress and the restraining force of its own precedents. This may no longer be true. *See, e.g.,* Presley v. Etowah County Comm'n, 112 S. Ct. 820, 832 (1992) (construing a previous decision referring to congressional concern for the protection of voting rights as inapplicable to a case in which power was stripped from elected positions after the election); Rust v. Sullivan, 111 S. Ct. 1759, 1767–68 (1991) (refusing to find a clear congressional intent, and instead deferring to the expertise of the agency charged with administering the status in question).

206. Linda Greenhouse, *supra* note 202, at 12 ("By the end of 1991, Presidents Reagan and Bush had appointed 64 percent of all Federal appellate judges. . . .").

207. *See* Acel Moore, *Thomas Has Left Little Doubt Now: Put Him on the Right with Scalia,* PHILA. INQUIRER, Feb. 27, 1992, *available in* DIALOG, PHILINQ File; . . . *see also* Linda Greenhouse, *Judicious Activism: Justice Thomas Hits the Ground Running,* N.Y. TIMES, Mar. 1, 1992, at E1, ("Justice Thomas has joined the Court's dominant conservative bloc, . . . cast[ing] his lot with the brand of conservative activism exemplified by Justice Antonin Scalia. . . .").

208. P. 160.

209. P. 18.

210. David Kairys, *Conservative Legal Thought Revisited,* 91 COLUM. L. REV. 1847, 1858 (1991) (reviewing Fried's book).

211. P. 118.

212. The Reagan-Bush agenda of deregulating government in this case became deregulating the Supreme Court, minimizing its role in protecting individual freedoms against government intrusion, while maximizing its retreat from monitoring executive authority. *See supra* notes 199–207.

213. P. 160 (referring specifically to the Court's hesitancy to subject independent agencies to the control of the executive).

214. In this Part I propose a preliminary and tentative sketch of an argument that I expect to elaborate upon in a future article.

215. GERALD N. ROSENBERG, THE HOLLOW HOPE: CAN COURTS BRING ABOUT SOCIAL CHANGE? (1991).

216. Legal victories lead social reformers to celebrate the "illusion of change." *Id.* at 340. But the very success of the Reagan Revolution in the courts, despite a recalcitrant Congress, tends to undermine this claim.

217. *Id.* at 343.

218. *Id.* at 341. ("[C]ourts act as 'fly-paper' for social reformers who succumb to the 'lure of litigation.' ").

219. *Id.* at 343 ("Social reformers, with limited resources, forgo other options when they elect to litigate. Those options are mainly political and involve mobilizing citizens to participate more effectively."); *see also* JACK W. PELTASON, FIFTY-EIGHT LONELY MEN 103 (1961) (arguing that litigation is an ineffective foundation on which to build a mass movement).

220. STUART A. SCHEINGOLD, THE POLITICS OF RIGHTS: LAWYERS, PUBLIC POLICY, AND POLITICAL CHANGE 145 (1974).

221. Rosenberg, *supra* note 215, at 343.

222. *Id.* at 341.

223. *Id.* at 340.

224. *Id.* at 341 (noting that "data suggest that court decisions may mobilize opponents").

225. *Id.* at 342 (observing that pro-choice forces appeared reinvigorated following the Supreme Court's 1989 *Webster* decision and that this anomalous finding suggests that one result of litigation is to strengthen the opponents of judicially inspired reform).

226. By focusing on the triumph of winners over losers, the losers may not share a commitment to meaningful implementation. In such a case, litigation victories may also be ultimately emptied of importance. This theme of Pyrrhic victories has been termed the "interest-convergence dilemma" or the "Law of Racial Thermodynamics." *See* Derrick A. Bell, Jr. *Brown v. Board of Education and the Interest-Convergence Dilemma,* 93 HARV. L. REV. 518 (1980); Richard Delgado, *When a Story Is Just a Story: Does Voice Really Matter?* 76 VA. L. REV. 95, 106 (1990). Certainly this informs Derrick Bell's "interest-convergence" principle. Bell's insight is that blacks only achieve significant reform when whites perceive it to be in their own interest. Indeed, the history of civil rights litigation has been a series of successful court decisions, whose incremental value is quickly eroded as the locus of discrimination shifts.

227. *See, e.g.,* John E. Jackson & Maris A. Vinovskis, *Public Opinion, Elections, and the 'Single-Issue' Issue, in* THE ABORTION DISPUTE AND THE AMERICAN SYSTEM 64, 73 (Gilbert Steiner ed. 1983) (describing how the political organization of the pro-choice groups dissipated after *Roe v. Wade*). "Everyone assumed that when the Supreme Court made its decision in 1973 that we'd got what we wanted and the battle was over. The movement afterwards lost steam." After the decisions, "state-level pro-choice groups disbanded, victory seemedly achieved." *Id; see also* EVA R. RUBIN, ABORTION, POLITICS AND THE COURTS 169 (1982) (noting that by winning a court case without the organization needed to cope with a powerful opposition, pro-choice forces vastly overestimated the power and influence of the Court).

228. Of course, this model exaggerates reality in that the civil rights struggle proceeded for years in court, accompanied by sustained political struggle. Moreover, in cases in which poor people have lost, such as San Antonio Indep. Sch. Dist. v. Rodriguez, 411 U.S. 1 (1973) (holding that the disparity in wealth among Texas public school districts does not violate the Equal Protection Clause of the Fourteenth Amendment), they did not subsequently mobilize politically. One might attempt to explain the latter phenomenon in contrasting ways. First, poor people's litigation is really paternalism on the part of the lawyers who are the real parties in interest. *See* Derrick A. Bell, Jr., *Serving Two Masters: Integration Ideals and Client Interests in School Desegregation Litigation,* 85 YALE L.J. 470, 512 (1976) (observing that attorneys in school desegregation cases often take the attitude that they know what is best for their clients). Second, even where the lawyers are truly serving genuine clients, they may have failed to proceed incrementally and with an adequate grass-roots base of support. *See id.* at 491 (arguing that civil-rights attorneys have failed to generate a consensus within the black community on appropriate school desegregation goals because they have lost touch with the beliefs and goals of a majority of the community). Third, much of the poverty law battle goes on, but in the *state* courts. Lawyers learn to live with lesser goals, more patience, state judges, and arguably some success. *See* Alan W. Houseman, *The Vitality of* Goldberg v. Kelly *to Welfare Advocacy*

in the 1990's, 56 BROOK. L. REV. 831, 837 (1990) (observing that there has been a trend toward greater use of state courts in poverty-law litigation since the mid-1970s). Finally, all of Rosenberg's arguments are also true of legislative "battles" as well since the limits of zero-sum solutions apply to multiple fora.

229. Brown v. Board of Educ., 349 U.S. 924 (1954).

230. Some might argue that this is simply sour grapes. Indeed, the *Brown* campaign could itself be attacked as a politically expedient, ideological campaign. For this reason, I think it worth pointing out a few differences. First, the litigants in *Brown* were not also in control of the judicial appointment process; indeed, it was their very isolation from the political process that some have argued justified judicial intervention. *See* Rodney A. Smolla, *Integration Maintenance: The Unconstitutionality of Benign Programs That Discourage Black Entry to Prevent White Flight,* 1981 DUKE L.J. 891, 917 (explaining that a core protection of *Brown* was the insulation of "minorities without political power from the machinations of the political process"). Second, the litigants in *Brown* did not enjoy a special relationship with the Supreme Court, a relationship on which some would say the Court can no longer rely. Nevertheless, the criticism cannot be discounted, which may be another argument for deemphasizing litigation as a forum for resolving ideological disputes.

231. Indeed, concern about the Court's legitimacy seems to have stirred at least three members to resist politicization by legal pamphleteering. *See supra* notes 19 and 20 and accompanying text. *See* CAPLAN, *supra* note 205, at 107 (quoting Solicitor General Rex Lee for the phrase "pamphleteer general").

232. *See supra* note 20 (discussing the eroding cohesiveness of the conservative movement, and describing libertarian, statist and populist fissions).

233. *See, e.g.,* Jane Gross, *Court's Ruling on Terms Gives Boost to Backers,* N.Y. TIMES, Mar. 10, 1992, at A14 (observing that Supreme Court's action leaving California term limits intact gives a booster shot to the movement in other states). In the wake of the Hill-Thomas hearings, a recent letter to the editor in the *Philadelphia Inquirer* suggested term limits for federal judges, or at least an initial probationary status. *See, e.g.,* Stephen Carter, *Why the Confirmation Process Can't Be Fixed,* 1993 UNIV. OF ILLINOIS L. REV. 1, 15 (proposing limited terms as a heuristic).

234. *Cf.* McGinnis, *supra* note 8 (arguing that "political office, like any other economic commodity, provides a psychic income stream during incumbency and the promise of either higher office, or a greater monetary gain upon graceful resignation or retirement"); A. Leon Higginbotham, *The Case of the Missing Black Judges,* N.Y. TIMES, July 29, 1992, at A21 (quoting Judge Stephen Reinhardt of the U.S. Court of Appeals for the Ninth Circuit, who called the Courts of Appeal "a symbol of white power").

235. *See, e.g.,* Lucie E. White, *Mobilization on the Margins of the Lawsuit: Making Space for Clients to Speak,* 16 N.Y.U. REV. L. & SOC. CHANGE 457, 533 (1989); Susan P. Sturm, *A Normative Theory of Public Law Remedies,* 79 GEO. L.J. 1355, 1391 (1991) (describing the view of process critics that full party participation in legal proceedings is necessary for a legitimate judicial process); Kathryn Abrams, *Hearing the Call of Stories,* 79 Calif. L. Rev. 971 (1991). These scholars argue that lawyers should not rely solely on their mastery of legal jargon or technical arguments that remove the discourse from the grasp of most lay people. Where lawyers define the issues in terms of developing legal doctrine and establishing legal precedent, their clients become

important, but secondary, players in a formal arena that requires lawyers to translate lay claims into technical speech. The lawyers then disembody the plaintiffs' claims in judicially manageable or judicially enforceable terms, which may nevertheless be unenforceable without more lawyers.

236. The claim is that a focus on appellate cases too often distorts the real stories told at the trial level. In this understanding, storytelling is important to integrate the experience of outsiders into the legal text. *See* Richard Delgado, *Storytelling for Oppositionists and Others: A Plea for Narrative,* 87 MICH. L. REV. 2411, 2412–13, 2436, 2439 (1989) (arguing that stories by outsiders and majority group members help construct a means of psychic self-preservation, lessen outsider subordination, and may enrich the reality of majority group members); Richard Delgado, *When a Story Is Just a Story: Does Voice Really Matter?* 76 VA. L. REV. 95, 109 (1990) ("Heeding new voices can stir our imaginations and let us begin to see life through the eyes of an outsider."); Mari J. Matsuda, *Public Response to Racist Speech: Considering the Victim's Story,* 87 MICH. L. REV. 2320 (1989) (explaining that the methodology of outsider jurisprudence focuses on the particulars of the social reality and experiences of groups outside the mainstream of society). As Professor Charles Lawrence says, stories make minorities and women the subject, not merely the object, of legal dialogue. Charles Lawrence, Remarks at the Critical Race Theory Conference, University of Wisconsin Law School (Nov. 1990).

Others suggest that storytelling helps confront the current crises of confidence in judicial legitimacy through affirmative action, but as Patricia Williams points out, "not just . . . programs like affirmative action but affirmative action as a socially and professionally pervasive concept." Patricia Williams, *The Obliging Shell: An Informal Essay on Formal Equal Opportunity,* 87 MICH. L. REV. 2128, 2142 (1989). By this Professor Williams means affirmative action as affirmation: the affirmative act of *hearing,* "an act of verification and of vision." *Id.* at 2142–43.

237. The term "opposition narrative" is taken from the title of Richard Delgado's article, *Storytelling for Oppositionists and Others: A Plea for Narrative, supra* note 236.

238. As Adeno Addis, a law professor at Boston University, writes, "narratives of subordinated groups represent the struggle 'of [their] memory against [the] forced forgetting' imposed by official abstraction." Kathryn Abrams, *Hearing the Call of Stories,* 79 CAL. L. REV. 971, 1051 (1991) (quoting Adeno Addis, The Communications Process and Minorities (unpublished manuscript) (citing PAUL CONNERTON, HOW SOCIETIES REMEMBER 15 (1989))).

239. *See* Richard Delgado, *Norms and Normal Science: Toward a Critique of Normativity in Legal Thought,* 139 U. PA. L. REV. 933, 933, n.3 (1991) (asserting that naming is a necessary conceptual first step in dealing with new inquiries).

240. Litigation as storytelling seeks to incorporate alternative viewpoints by involving the participants themselves in telling and resolving their disputes, maximizing opportunities for input. *See, e.g.,* Susan P. Sturm, *A Normative Theory of Public Law Remedies,* 79 GEO. L.J. 1355, 1410 (1991) (identifying participation as an essential quality of effective remedial processes). For litigators, storytelling becomes a platform into people's living rooms; litigation becomes guerrilla theater within which to work through theoretical issues in a local, participatory context. Guerrilla theater includes dramatic stagings in contemporary and accessible settings. *See, e.g.,* Lani Guinier, *Celebrating Marshall as a Jurist But Especially as an Advocate,* PHILA. INQUIRER,

Mar. 7, 1993, at H3 (book review of two biographies of Justice Thurgood Marshall that demonstrate how, as NAACP LDF attorney, Marshall saw the potential of litigation to tell the stories of oppression).

241. *See, e.g.,* Jerry L. Mashaw, *The Economics of Politics and the Understanding of Public Law,* 65 CHI.-KENT L. REV. 123, 130 (1989) ("Politics is . . . the transformation of private interests into public interests through discussions and persuasion."). Some civic republicans seem to focus more on the Supreme Court rather than political institutions generally. *Compare* Frank I. Michelman, *The Supreme Court, 1985 Term—Foreword: Traces of Self-Government,* 100 HARV. L. REV. 4, 256 (1986) (arguing that "law is best understood as a form of politics") *with* Frank Michelman, *Law's Republic,* 97 YALE L.J. 1493 (1988) (arguing that political liberty can be achieved only when legislative politics and constitutional adjudication protect individual rights).

242. *See* Cass R. Sunstein, *Beyond the Republican Revival,* 99 YALE L.J. 1539, 1544–45 (1988) ("Politics . . . is the only avenue by which public values . . . might possibly be determinable and accessible."); Frank Michelman, *Bringing the Law to Life: A Plea for Disenchantment,* 74 CORNELL L. REV. 256–57 (1989); Michelman, *Law's Republic, supra* note 241, at 1501–3.

243. *See* INS v. Chadha, 462 U.S. 919, 967 (1983) (White, J., dissenting) (arguing that the legislature should retain power to implement legislative veto); Michael A. Fitts, *Look Before You Leap: Some Cautionary Notes on Civic Republicanism,* 97 YALE L.J. 1651, 1651 (1988) ("[M]odern civic republicans articulate . . . a model of policymaking in which decisions are made in the legislative process through principled deliberation and reasoned dialogue.")

244. *See* Robin West, *The Supreme Court—Foreword: Taking Freedom Seriously,* 104 HARV. L. REV. 43, 62–63 (1990) (collecting sources). West cites an unpublished manuscript of Cass Sunstein. Sunstein writes:

> [I]t is important to recognize that the Supreme Court is not the only institution in government charged with fidelity to the Constitution. Crabbed understandings from the Court are nothing to be pleased about; but there will be advantages if other officials are willing to pick up the slack. In any case, legislators, executive officials, and even citizens are under a responsibility to vindicate constitutional principles. If the Court, for institutional or other reasons, interprets the Constitution too narrowly, this responsibility becomes all the more insistent.

Cass R. Sunstein, Constitutional Politics and the Conservative Court, Am. Prospect, Spring 1990 at 51, 61 (quoted in unpublished form by West, *supra,* at 62).

245. West, *supra* note 244, at 66 (citing VACLAV HAVEL, LETTERS TO OLGA 268 (Paul Wilson translation, 1988).

246. West, *supra* note 244, at 106.

247. VACLEV HAVEL, LIVING IN TRUTH at 55.

248. West, *supra* note 244, at 66.

249. Living in truth is what Fried claims he was doing when he sought to articulate an alternative vision to that of the hard-line movement conservatives to whom he was politically responsible. But living in truth is not what Fried describes when he consistently defends his decisions to submit to higher political authorities as long as there was a legal claim to be made. Here, Fried relies on a higher legal, not moral, authority to support his choices. Alternatively, he defends a more linear, respectful process of

decisionmaking that would reach the same outcomes but at less personal cost. This is a very different take on democratic accountability than offered by Havel.

250. *See, e.g.,* Richard Delgado, *Pep Talks for the Poor: A Reply and Remonstrance on the Evils of Scapegoating,* 71 B.U. L. Rev. 525, 526 (1991) (arguing that West's proposal that progressives should direct their energies to the people and their legislatures rather than rely on the courts "ignores history and misdiagnoses society's needs").

251. *See* Ch. 4. The problem with a winner-take-all model is that it "create[s] winners who take all rather than winners who share in power, thus making politics into a battle for total victory rather than a method of governing open to all significant groups." *Id.* (quoting Edward Still, *Alternatives to Single-Member Districts, in* Minority Vote Dilution 249, 264 (Chandler Davidson ed., 1984). Because they do not necessarily recognize the salience of minority interests, or the intensity by which minority groups value their interests, winner-take-all majoritarian systems do not necessarily give minority groups a reason to support the ultimate bargain or to believe the outcome is public-regarding or legitimate.

Winner-take-all collective decisionmaking, which presents an efficient opportunity for determining the public good, is not necessarily constrained by the need to bargain with minority interests. Other than the promise of becoming a majority, the minority lacks any present mechanism for holding the majority to account or even to listen. Nor does simple, 51% majority rule that simply leads to ratification of majority preferences necessarily promote deliberation or consensus. Moreover, where there are universal losers but some people win 100% of the power, the political system is less likely to be legitimate.

The fundamentally important question of political stability is how "to induce losers to continue to play the political game, to continue to work within the system rather than to try to overthrow it." *Id.* at 1478 n.230 (quoting Nicholas R. Miller, *Pluralism and Social Choice,* 77 Am. Pol. Sci. Rev. 734, 742 (1983)). The potential for instability exists where any significant group of people ends up as permanent losers. Where the minority experiences the alienation of complete defeat, they lack incentive to respect laws passed by the majority over their opposition. This is especially problematic to defeated groups that do not possess means to bargain over proposals and acts that directly affect them or that they value intensely.

Concern over majority tyranny has typically focused on the need to monitor and constrain the substantive outputs of the decisionmaking process. But insistence on political rather than judicial solutions suggests the need to look even more closely at aspects of institutional legitimacy and accountability.

Acknowledgments

The "poet" who is not in trouble with the king is in trouble with her work. I thank Cheryl Harris for bringing to my attention this observation of West African novelist Chinua Achebe. Certainly I know what it is like to be in trouble with the king. I leave it to the readers to judge whether I am also in trouble with my work.

I do not claim direct lineage from Achebe's poet. I have tried simply to be a voice of conscience. To the extent I have succeeded, it is because of the many "poets" who shared with me the fruits of their own toil. I especially thank Alex Aleinikopf, Derrick Bell, James Blacksher, Stephen Carter, Dayna Cunningham, Harlon Dalton, Colin Diver, Frank Goodman, Bernie Grofman, Penda Hair, Sam Issacharoff, Pamela Karlan, Randy Kennedy, Charles Lawrence, Mari Matsuda, Frank Michelman, Richard Pildes, Susan Sturm, Gerald Torres, and Patricia Williams, all of whom shared their ideas and their criticisms of my ideas, and showed me by their own example that ideas matter. Some went even further to remind me that genuine friendship is the basis of a noble collaboration. I thank my mother, Genii Guinier, for pushing me to be more clear so that she could understand in writing what I was saying to her in conversation.

I thank Barbara Arnwine, Barbara Beck, Jim Coleman, William T. Coleman, Jr., Phoebe Haddon, Wade Henderson, Elaine Jones, The Honorable Damon J. Keith, Patricia King, Charisse Lillie, Aretha Marshall, Gwen McKinney, Linda Wright Moore, Debbie Stachel, Roger Wilkins, and Barbara Bennett Woodhouse for their many, many acts of selflessness and caring during my nomination ordeal, acts that I do not deserve to expect even from devoted friends. To Carolyn Osolinik and Eddie Correia, I extend a very, very, very special thanks. Good thing it was not Bosnia; even better, you were there.

I also thank the many litigants, lawyers, judges, students, and activists whose energy and courage continue to inspire my work. Some are too numerous to list, such as those affiliated with the NAACP Legal Defense Fund, Inc. as staff, cooperating attorneys and clients. Others would be slighted simply by listing their names without recalling their specific, invaluable contributions. I thank Bruce Nichols, my editor, for calling me in the fall of 1992 and inviting me to write a book about democracy. I thank Mary Frances Berry for her sage advice, including directing me to Charlotte Sheedy whose contacts made this book possible.

I thank Kirsten Barton, age 11, and her sixth grade teacher for suggesting, albeit indirectly, that my speech upon the withdrawal of my nomination be included as the epilog to this collection of essays. That the interest in my ideas extends to a succeeding generation is an endearing reminder that concerns about fairness and justice are deeply held American values. For introducing me to those values I credit my father, Ewart Guinier, who died in 1990. It was at his knees that I first heard stories about unfairness and injustice. It was accompanied by his enduring spirit that I stood fast during the Spring and Summer of 1993.

Finally I dedicate this book to Nolan and Nikolas, my husband and my son. Nolan gave me my first computer and then even more generously gave me the time to use it. Nikolas reminds me daily that in the realm of participatory democracy the philosophy of my century will become the common sense of his.

List of Cases

Subject Index

Abrams, Kathy, 66, 232nn186–187, 233n188, 233n190

Accountability
in decision to accept majority rule, 77–78
of incumbents with interest representation, 100
in proportionality principle, 92, 104

Acton, John (Lord), 173

Affirmative action
argument of electoral, 36
proposed repeal, 23

Alienation from voting, 218n99, 225n139, 236n210, 247n51, 248n53, 253n87, 254nn88–89, 255n90

Allies
need for 61, 63, 64, 228n160, 230n172, 231nn176–77
See also Cross-racial coalitions

Alston, Chuck, ix

Apportionment, automatic, self-defined, 140

Arnold, Richard, 12

Artificial district, 129–30, 136–37, 247n49

At-large elections
bullet voting, 279n81
challenge to, 150–51

effect of, 7, 49–50, 212n59
modified, 95

At-large voting systems, modified
by cumulative voting, 95
effect of, 250n68
function of, 95, 137, 141, 153
mechanism creating, 150–51
recommendation for use of, 149
See also Cumulative voting

Authentic black representation, 55–58

Authenticity
of black electoral success theory, 53
criticism of, 12–13, 58, 62–63, 83
cultural and psychological, 13, 56–58
definition of, 12–13, 55–56
as empowerment tool, 58, 67
political, 56
reflecting voter choice, 13, 47–48, 52, 263n136
reinforced by subdistricts, 96

Authentic representatives
as candidates of community's choice, 47–48, 52, 263n136
defined, 13, 52
effectiveness of, 62–64

313

318 *Subject Index*

Influence (*cont.*)
districts with electoral, 86–89
effect of single-member districts
on, 81–82, 91
See also electoral influence; swing
voters
Influence districts, minority
defined, 84, 86, 90
electoral influence of, 246n45
strong influence claim, 89
weak influence claim, 87–88
Interest proportionality principle,
105–6
Interest representation
constitutionality of, 114–17
in context of federalism and separation of powers, 114–16
in context of one person/one vote
principle, 116
criticism of, 109–10
desegregation goal of, 105
distinguishes between voters,
249–50n65
examines procedural rules, 104
function of, 94–99, 117–18
proportionate, 113–14
provision for nonvoters, 155
relies on voluntary constituencies,
253n83
requirements for, 98–99
response to criticism, 110
stabilizing effect of, 111–13
See also Winner-take-only-some
voting system
Interest representation model,
94–95
Interests
of blacks in virtual representation
theory, 37
defined, 97–98
differentiation between whites
and blacks on issues, 52,
252n82

effect of proportionality principle
on, 104
racial interest constituencies, 149
self-identified, 94
See also Choices; Preferences

Jackson, Jesse, 30–31, 33
Johnson, Lyndon B., 40
Judicial interpretation
to achieve political fairness, 122
of at-large elections, 150–51
decision in *Presley*, 179–80
decision in *Thornburg v. Gingles*,
177–79
interpretation of Voting Rights
Act, 49–50, 115, 211n55
interpretation of Voting Rights
Act, Section 2, 26–27
reapportionment decisions,
212n61, 259n115
of voting, 125
Jury deliberation
as model for legislative decisionmaking, 107–8
Justice Department, Civil Rights
Division
administration of Section 5, 27
criticism of Reagan Administration, 24–30
enforcement responsibility, 25,
29–30
recommendations for, 38–39

Karlan, Pamela, 66, 141
Katzenbach, Nicholas, 38
Kennedy, Randall, 6, 18–19
Kennedy Administration, 44,
205n17
King, Martin Luther, Jr., 9, 48

Leadership Conference on Civil
Rights (LCCR) report, 26
Leahy, Patrick, xi

in conjunction with geography,
142
in definition of authenticity,
55–56
differences recognized in Voting
Rights Act, 52
differentiation of groups by,
141–42
as political proxy, 137–38
as proxy for interests, 138
Race-conscious districting
attempted provisions of, 135
critics of, 120–21, 139, 140–41,
274n53
effect of interest representation
on, 100
function of, 139, 142
questions raised by, 143–49
response to critics of, 274n53
strategies for, 142
as winner-take-all districting,
156
Racial bloc voting
analyses of, 213n68
effect of, 139
evidence for, 51
evidence of, 67
existence and effect of, 60
litigation focus on, 50–54
minority vote dilution with,
248n55
with winner-take-all majority rule,
102
See also Black voters; Polarization, racial; White voters
Racial-group identity. *See* Group
identity
Racial justice model, 52–53
Racism
effect in political process, 66
effect of, 103
legislative, 80–81, 242–43n29
ways to remedy for, 19

Reagan Administration
criticism of enforcement rights
policies, 25–26, 194n5
determinants of civil rights policy,
23–24
effect of civil rights legacy, 22
interpretation and enforcement of
Voting Rights Act, 25–29
judicial legacy, 23–24
redirection of courts, 159
Reagan Revolution
effect of, 183
hidden agenda of, 166
Reciprocity
for acceptance of majority decision, 77
in collaborative efforts, 64
Golden Rule, 4, 147
in proportionality principle, 92,
104
Remedial intervention
in collective decisionmaking,
107–8
conditions for, 73
fashioning of, 115
focus of, 91
in interest representation, 99–
101, 107–14
Representation
bottom-up view, 125, 127, 139,
275n57
defined in black electoral success
theory, 54–69
direct and indirect, 271n39, 271–
72n41
group-based nature of, 124–37,
140
one-vote, one-value concept in
transformation of, 152
right to vote in minority, 35–36
by semiproportional representation systems, 278n78
Thernstrom's theory of, 217n97

Representation (*cont.*)
  top-down view, 126, 131, 145–46,
    275n57
  See also Authentic black repre-
    sentation; Black representation;
    Group representation; Interest
    representation; Proportional
    representation; Virtual repre-
    sentation
Representation threshold, 105, 258–
  59n113, 261n126
Responsive policies as incentive for
  participation, 239n7, 248n58
Responsiveness assumption, 66–69
  See also Unresponsiveness
Reverse discrimination, 23, 193n4
Reynolds, William Bradford, 162
  Fried's interpretation (Guinier),
    162–64
  Justice Department policy of,
    25–28
Right to vote
  as individual right, 124, 126
  minority political participation in,
    36
  with one-person, one-vote inter-
    pretation, 124–27
  recognition of black, 64
  source of, 35–36
Robledo, Milagros, 12
Rosenberg, Gerald, 183–84, 185

Safe districting, 154
Sail trimming, 151, 279n82
Scalia, Antonin, 170
Semiproportional voting systems
  criticism of, 153
  effect of, 149
  function of, 137, 155
  See also Cumulative voting
Shields, Mark, xi
Shklar, Judith, xiii, xiv
Simpson, Alan, ix

Single-member districts
  in black electoral success theory,
    53–54
  effect of remedial focus on, 91
  effect on black political influence,
    81–82
  judicial perception of, 151
  limitations of, 83–86
  potential influence of, 91
  power of blacks elected from, 65
  proportional legislative power in,
    79
  representatives from majority
    black, 75–76
  See also Subdistricts; Winner-
    take-all districts
Social choice theory, 240–41n22,
  242n26
Solarz, Stephen, 143, 146
Spokesmodels, 42, 67, 217n96
Stability
  in decision to accept majority
    rule, 77
  in proportionality principle, 104
Stevens, John Paul, 180
Stewart, Potter, 20, 127, 130
Still, Ed, 102–3
Stoner, Kenneth, 10
Subdistricts
  in black electoral success theory,
    53
  as empowerment enforcement
    mechanism, 74
  function of, 96
  goals of representatives in, 81
  in one-vote, one-value voting sys-
    tem, 154–55
  power of legislative votes in, 79
Supermajority voting
  function of, 16, 17
  in legislative decisionmaking, 108
  minority veto as outcome of, 17,
    116–17, 260n119